EDUCATIONAL PSYCHOLOGY READER

WITHDRAWN

WITHDRAWN

DON HAMACHEK
MICHIGAN STATE UNIVERSITY

EDUCATIONAL PSYCHOLOGY READER

Toward the Improvement of Schooling

MACMILLAN PUBLISHING COMPANY   NEW YORK

Editor: Robert Miller
Production Supervision: P. M. Gordon Associates
Text Design: Kate Nichols
Cover Design: Jane Edelstein
Cover Illustration: Miriam Recio

This book was set in Times Roman by Digitype, Inc.,
and printed and bound by Viking Press.
The cover was printed by Phoenix Color Corp.

Copyright © 1990 by Macmillan Publishing Company,
a division of Macmillan, Inc.

Printed in the United States of America

All rights reserved. No part of this book may be reproduced or
transmitted in any form or by any means, electronic or mechanical,
including photocopying, recording, or any information storage and
retrieval system, without permission in writing from the Publisher.

Macmillan Publishing Company
866 Third Avenue, New York, New York 10022

Collier Macmillan Canada, Inc.

Library of Congress Cataloging-in-Publication Data

Educational psychology reader : toward the improvement of schooling /
   Don Hamachek.
      p.   cm.
   ISBN 0-02-349336-4
   1. Educational psychology—United States.   2. Learning, Psychology
of.   3. Child development—United States.   4. School improvement
programs—United States.   I. Hamachek, Don E.
LB1051.E37   1990   89-36849
370.15—dc20   CIP

Printing: 1 2 3 4 5 6 7   Year: 0 1 2 3 4 5 6

Photo Credits: *Page 1:* Alan Carey/The Image Works; *page 37:* J. Berndt/The Picture Cube; *page 75:* Elizabeth Crews/Stock, Boston; *page 101:* Elizabeth Crews/Stock, Boston; *page 161:* Paul Conklin/Monkmeyer Press Photo Service; *page 227:* Jean-Claude Lejeune/Stock, Boston.

Preface

This book represents an effort to pull together a coherent collection of contemporary ideas and research advances within the field of educational psychology that may help us understand the complex interplay among teachers, learners, schooling processes, and educational outcomes. The idea that schooling involves a continual interplay among many complex factors served as a kind of guiding objective as I assembled and organized the contents of this volume. Thus, this book focuses on different views about the nature of schooling and how it should be conducted; it also focuses on developmental process and growth outcomes, with an eye to how these are influenced by genetics and environment. It surveys what research is teaching us about how the brain grows and functions, along with an examination of new ways for understanding and conceptualizing cognitive and intellectual functioning; it overviews various approaches to enhancing learning, and suggests strategies for helping us figure out ways to promote it. In addition, it examines how information processing is linked not only to how we learn, but also to how we retain what we learn.

Further, there are discussions about what it means to be a good teacher and how to practice effective teaching behaviors and positive classroom management skills. There are also clarifying analyses related to measurement issues and common research methodologies.

This volume also focuses on students, including those who do well in school and are eager to learn, those we call "exceptional students," those who have trouble in school and drop out, and those with exceptional disabilities, on the one hand, or exceptional capabilities, on the other. Suggestions are offered for how to identify these students and for how to make their schooling as positive as possible.

All in all, the forty-three articles in this volume range over twenty-one different journals and magazines and one book. Each article was selected with three criteria in mind: (1) readability, (2) relevancy, and (3) authoritativeness. Readability was especially important because I realize that in order for ideas to be usable they must first be understandable. With this as a guide, I made an effort to avoid highly technical articles and those full of jargon—typically found in specialized professional journals in which psychologists and researchers communicate essentially to one another. Rather, I made an effort to choose articles that are largely interpretive and explanatory, intended primarily for readers interested either in applying new knowledge in their professional work or learning about new information as a matter of personal interest. Thus, the selections in this book are not reports of singular research efforts, but they tend to be interpretive discussions that examine more broadly the results of many research findings variously related to helping us understand the dynamics involved in growth, teaching, and learning.

I have organized this volume into six major parts and fifteen chapters. Each of the parts represents a broad category of issues and concerns, which are treated more specifically in the associated chapters. There is a certain amount of overlap among the different parts and chapters because of their relationships to one another. For example, it is difficult to talk about teaching without also considering learning, difficult to discuss schooling in the broader context without also considering teaching and learning, and so on. With these overlapping tendencies in mind, I made an effort to highlight the particular thrust of each article by placing it within that chapter heading most appropriate to its content emphasis.

Implicit in the undercurrent of this volume is the idea that there are many ways to go about the business of being a good teacher or, for that matter, a good learner. There are many ways to be effective at these activities, or ineffective, as the case may be. It depends on many things—the person, the mix of teacher and students, the combination of learner and subject matter, and of course the interfacing of such variables as intelligence, motivation, and developmental history.

Hence, a major objective I had in mind as I assembled this volume was to bring together a collection of readings that reflects not only the enormous complexity involved in various growth processes and in teaching and learning but that also reflects the important gains we have made in understanding these processes so we can make schooling more effective and more meaningful for more students.

That the book begins with three different views about "what is important in education" is no accident. Different views stimulate discussion; discussion provokes questions; questions lead to research; and research sometimes helps us find new ways, and if not that, at least better ways to make schooling a positive experience for all students.

Thus, this volume will expose you to a wide range of views about the nature of schooling, growth, learning, and teaching. No book can possibly include all there is to know about a particular discipline, and this volume is surely no exception. I have, however, tried hard to include a broad sampling of some of the major issues, ideas, and research advances associated with our knowledge of human development and contemporary schooling practices.

At the end of each major part of the book you will find a series of study and discussion questions, which are presented for discussion purposes, to assist you in identifying major ideas, and also to help you organize your thinking about some of the central themes and issues associated with each chapter.

The creative and intellectual efforts of many people go into a volume of this sort, and I want to extend a hearty thank you to those authors whose articles appear in this anthology. Special thanks to professors Richard Hamilton, University of Houston; William R. Jenson, University of Utah; Michael S. Meloth, University of Colorado at Boulder; and Richard J. Mueller, Northern Illinois University, for their critical reviews of the original proposal for this volume and helpful suggestions for its improvement.

D.H.

Brief Contents

PART ONE
Schooling: Approaches and Outcomes

CHAPTER ONE   Three Viewpoints About What Is Important in Education   4

1. The Shame of American Education   *B. F. Skinner*   4
2. The Key to Improving Schools: An Interview with William Glasser   *Pauline B. Gough*   10
3. Humanistic Education: Too Tender for a Tough World?   *Arthur W. Combs*   17

CHAPTER TWO   Effective Schools: What They Are and How They Make a Positive Difference   23

4. Schools Make a Difference: Evidence, Criticisms, and New Directions   *Thomas L. Good and Rhona S. Weinstein*   23
5. New Evidence of Effective Elementary Schools   *Peter Mortimore and Pam Sammons*   29

PART TWO
Growth, Development, and Behavior

CHAPTER THREE   Developmental Dynamics and Growth Outcomes   39

6. Children in a Changing Society   *Joe L. Frost*   39
7. Those Gangly Years   *Anne C. Petersen*   45
8. Resilient Children   *Emmy E. Werner*   50
9. Males and Females and What You May Not Know About Them   *Changing Times*   55

CHAPTER FOUR   The Great Behavioral Shapers: Genetics and Environment   60

10. The Eerie World of Reunited Twins   *Clare Mead Rosen*   60
11. Societal Influences on Children   *Joan Isenberg*   66

PART THREE
Brain Development and Intellectual Expressions

CHAPTER FIVE How the Brain Develops and Functions — 78
12. Making of a Mind *Kathleen McAuliffe* — 78
13. Right Brain, Left Brain: Fact and Fiction *Jerre Levy* — 83
14. New Evidence Points to Growth of Brain Even Late in Life *Daniel Goleman* — 86

CHAPTER SIX Contemporary Views About the Nature of Intelligence — 89
15. Developing the Spectrum of Human Intelligences *Howard Gardner* — 89
16. Three Heads Are Better Than One *Robert J. Trotter* — 93

PART FOUR
Learning: Process and Strategies

CHAPTER SEVEN Strategies for Promoting Learning — 104
17. Rediscovering Discovery Learning *Ray T. Wilcox* — 104
18. Bloom's Mastery Learning: A Legacy of Effectiveness *Thomas R. Guskey* — 108
19. Cooperative Learning and Student Achievement *Robert E. Slavin* — 112
20. Courseware: A Practical Revolution *M. D. Roblyer* — 115
21. Putting Learning Strategies to Work *Sharon J. Derry* — 118

CHAPTER EIGHT Understandings About Metacognition, Critical Thinking, and Information-Processing — 125
22. From the Mystery Spot to the Thoughtful Spot: The Instruction of Metacognitive Strategies *Annemarie Sullivan Palincsar and Kathryn Ransom* — 125
23. Critical Thinking—What Can It Be? *Matthew Lipman* — 129
24. Research on Memory: Major Discoveries, Major Educational Challenges *Robert Sylwester* — 135

CHAPTER NINE The Effects of Grouping, Class Size, and Retention on Learning — 142
25. Synthesis of Research on Grouping in Elementary and Secondary Schools *Robert E. Slavin* — 142
26. The Effect of Class Size on What Happens in Classrooms *Mary Lee Smith and Gene V. Glass* — 151
27. Grade Retention and Social Promotion Practices *Gary Cooke and John Stammer* — 153

PART FIVE
An Overview of What It Takes to Be a Good Teacher

CHAPTER TEN   The Many Faces of Good Teaching — 164

28. Research on Teacher Effects: Uses and Abuses   *Jere Brophy* — 164
29. Teaching Students to Examine Their Lives   *Carolyn J. Sweers* — 172
30. Psychodynamics of Teachers' Expectations   *Don Hamachek* — 174
31. In Praise of Teachers   *Mark Medoff* — 180

CHAPTER ELEVEN   Motivational Strategies for Encouraging Student Achievement — 183

32. Synthesis of Research on Strategies for Motivating Students to Learn   *Jere Brophy* — 183
33. "If at First . . .": Attribution Theory in the Classroom   *Madeline Hunter and George Barker* — 191
34. How to Reach the Underachiever   *Sylvia B. Rimm* — 195

CHAPTER TWELVE   Strategies Useful for the Practice of Positive Classroom Discipline — 198

35. A Primer on Classroom Discipline: Principles Old and New   *Thomas R. McDaniel* — 198
36. Classroom Management as Instruction: Socializing Self-Guidance in Students   *Jere Brophy* — 203

CHAPTER THIRTEEN   Basic Understandings About Testing and Educational Research — 210

37. Norm-Referenced vs. Criterion-Referenced Tests   *Lorrie Shepard* — 210
38. Taking the Terror Out of Research   *Robert Gable and Vincent Rogers* — 216

PART SIX
Exceptional Students: Problems and Challenges

CHAPTER FOURTEEN   Toward Understanding Students Who Have Trouble Learning — 230

39. Learning: Abilities and Disabilities   *Melvin Levine* — 230
40. Deciphering Dyslexia   *John Langone* — 233
41. Reaching Out to America's Dropouts: What to Do?   *Andrew Hahn* — 236

CHAPTER FIFTEEN   Toward Identifying and Reaching Exceptionally Able Students — 246

42. The Nature of Giftedness and Talent   *A. Harry Passow* — 246
43. Curriculum-Based Programs for the Gifted   *Byron L. Barrington* — 252

Index — 257

Detailed Contents

PART ONE
Schooling: Approaches and Outcomes

CHAPTER ONE   Three Viewpoints About What Is Important in Education   4

1. **The Shame of American Education**   *B. F. Skinner,* American Psychologist, *September 1984*   4

   Skinner maintains that most of our educational problems could be solved with programmed instructional materials, so designed that students are often right and learn at once that they are. The shame, he claims, is that we have the technology to improve education but don't use it.

2. **The Key to Improving Schools: An Interview with William Glasser**   *Pauline B. Gough,* Phi Delta Kappan, *May 1987*   10

   Glasser argues that for an educational system to be successful, students must have a sense of their own personal power. He argues further that a stimulus-response system of education, such as that advocated by Skinner, puts too much emphasis on events that are external to students, thus reinforcing feelings of powerlessness. Glasser suggests specific ideas for involving students in shaping their education as opposed to their simply being shaped by it.

3. **Humanistic Education: Too Tender for a Tough World?**   *Arthur W. Combs,* Phi Delta Kappan, *February 1981*   17

   The author points out that a successful educational experience is one that takes into account student self-concepts, values, personal needs, perceptions of challenge and threat, and the learner's feeling of belonging or identification. He maintains that humanistic education is no flash in the pan, but an established point of view trying to put into practice what is known about human behavior.

CHAPTER TWO   Effective Schools: What They Are and How They Make a Positive Difference   23

4. **Schools Make a Difference: Evidence, Criticisms, and New Directions**   *Thomas L. Good and Rhona S. Weinstein,* American Psychologist, *October 1986*   23

   Research indicates that the school a student attends can make a big difference in the education received; schools are not interchange-

xii *Detailed Contents*

able. Far more is known about effective classroom teaching than about effective school-level learning processes for students. The authors suggest that teachers develop a greater sense of community so that knowledge and expectations are expanded beyond individual classrooms.

5. New Evidence of Effective Elementary Schools *Peter Mortimore and Pam Sammons,* Educational Leadership, *September 1987*   29

The authors discuss results of a four-year study conducted in London that identified twelve factors—most under control of the principal and teachers—that distinguish effective schools from less-effective ones. Whether or not a school is effective is very much affected by the policies and processes of the principal and teachers.

Part One Study and Discussion Questions   34

PART TWO
Growth, Development, and Behavior

CHAPTER THREE   Developmental Dynamics and Growth Outcomes   39

6. Children in a Changing Society *Joe L. Frost,* Childhood Education, *March/April 1986*   39

Many societal changes are occurring in the lives of today's children. There are more single-parent families, more youthful television viewing, wider use of drugs and alcohol, growing numbers of abused children, and increasing numbers of teen pregnancies. The author maintains that we must make children *number one* in the lives of families if we are to have a positive impact on their growth.

7. Those Gangly Years *Anne C. Petersen,* Psychology Today, *September 1987*   45

Although early adolescence is clearly a difficult transition in development because of the number of changes young people experience, the impact of those changes is quite varied. The outcome seems to depend on prior strengths and vulnerabilities.

8. Resilient Children *Emmy E. Werner,* Young Children, *November 1984*   50

In spite of coming from terrible home conditions or suffering physical handicaps, some children seem to develop stable, healthy personalities and display a remarkable degree of resilience. The author points to protective factors within the child, within the family, and outside the family that help explain how this happens.

9. Males and Females and What You May Not Know About Them   Changing Times, *September 1981*   55

The differences between men and women emerge in the realms of education, child rearing, sports, the military, and the workplace. This article highlights those differences and discusses the implications for intellectual and social development.

CHAPTER FOUR The Great Behavioral Shapers: Genetics and Environment — 60

10. The Eerie World of Reunited Twins *Clare Mead Rosen,* Discover, *September 1987* — 60

A longitudinal study of a large group of reunited twins that began in 1979 at the University of Minnesota is providing answers to questions about the relative effects of environment on such aspects of behavior as intelligence, temperament, homosexual tendencies, and physical characteristics.

11. Societal Influences on Children *Joan Isenberg,* Childhood Education, *June 1987* — 66

Pressured by such socializing agents as family, school, peers, and television, today's children are experiencing shortened childhoods. Too often, children are forced to be grown-ups before they are through being children. The author suggests remedies for this situation.

Part Two Study and Discussion Questions — 73

PART THREE
Brain Development and Intellectual Expressions

CHAPTER FIVE How the Brain Develops and Functions — 78

12. Making of a Mind *Kathleen McAuliffe,* Omni, *October 1985* — 78

Brain research is showing that the mind, in the very first years—perhaps even months—of life, is the crucible in which many of children's deepest values are formed. Brain development continues deep into life. Although the adult brain does not generate new brain cells, it can generate new nerve connections.

13. Right Brain, Left Brain: Fact and Fiction *Jerre Levy,* Psychology Today, *May 1985* — 83

It is largely a myth to say that each hemisphere of our brain is so specialized that it functions as an independent half-brain. The author points to research showing that normal people have one gloriously differentiated brain, with each hemisphere contributing its specialized abilities.

14. New Evidence Points to Growth of Brain Even Late in Life *Daniel Goleman,* The New York Times, *July 30, 1985* — 86

Although environment's influence on the brain is particularly strong during fetal development, early infancy, and early childhood, the author points to recent research showing that even in old age, brain cells respond to a stimulating environment by forging new connections with other cells.

CHAPTER SIX Contemporary Views About the Nature of Intelligence — 89

15. Developing the Spectrum of Human Intelligences *Howard Gardner,* Harvard Educational Review, *Spring 1988* — 89

The author claims that current conceptions of intelligence are too narrow. He offers his theory of multiple intelligences, delineating

xiv *Detailed Contents*

seven different "intelligences" that have been identified from his research.

16. Three Heads Are Better Than One *Robert J. Trotter,* Psychology Today, *August 1986* **93**

The author discusses Robert Sternberg's triarchic theory, which suggests that there are three basic kinds of intelligence: componential, experiential, and contextual. Abilities associated with each are explained in this article.

Part Three Study and Discussion Questions **99**

PART FOUR
Learning: Process and Strategies

CHAPTER SEVEN Strategies for Promoting Learning 104

17. Rediscovering Discovery Learning *Ray T. Wilcox,* The Clearing House, *October 1987* **104**

Discovery learning methods can be nicely combined with expository approaches to enhance students' learning. The author discusses ten discovery methods that he has found to be the most helpful supplements.

18. Bloom's Mastery Learning: A Legacy of Effectiveness *Thomas R. Guskey,* Educational Horizons, *Winter 1986* **108**

Within a mastery learning framework, instruction is organized into smaller, sequentially ordered units, and students receive regular and specific feedback on their progress, which is designed to help them remedy their learning errors and reach a high standard of learning before moving on to the next unit. The author discusses how this approach has enhanced school learning.

19. Cooperative Learning and Student Achievement *Robert E. Slavin,* Educational Leadership, *October 1988* **112**

Cooperative learning has been proposed as a solution to a broad array of problems. Although it has had large success, the author points to research showing that achievement gains are most likely to occur when these methods include *both* a group goal and individual accountability.

20. Courseware: A Practical Revolution *M. D. Roblyer,* Educational Technology, *February 1986* **115**

The author outlines five primary uses of computer products that evolved as a direct result of common instructional needs. He discusses how computer coursework can be used to help teachers promote student learning.

21. Putting Learning Strategies to Work *Sharon J. Derry,* Educational Leadership, *December 1988/January 1989* **118**

The author suggests that we can increase students' repertoires for learning by using certain principles derived from cognitive psychology. New knowledge is likely to be used only if it is understood when learned and only if it is stored within well-structured networks of meaningfully related ideas.

CHAPTER EIGHT   Understandings About Metacognition, Critical Thinking, and Information-Processing   125

22. From the Mystery Spot to the Thoughtful Spot: The Instruction of Metacognitive Strategies   *Annemarie Sullivan Palincsar and Kathryn Ransom,* The Reading Teacher, *April 1988*   125

   The authors argue that it is important for teachers to find out about students' strategies for learning—their metacognitions—and then, based on this knowledge, instruct them in the use of more effective metacognitive approaches to classroom learning. Suggestions for how to do this are presented.

23. Critical Thinking—What Can It Be?   *Matthew Lipman,* Educational Leadership, *September 1988*   129

   A contrast is made between critical thinking, which is well-founded, structured, reinforced thinking, and uncritical thinking, which is amorphous, haphazard, and unstructured. The author points to three criteria for judging whether or not thinking is of the critical variety and suggests ways to encourage critical thinking.

24. Research on Memory: Major Discoveries, Major Educational Challenges   *Robert Sylwester,* Educational Leadership, *April 1985*   135

   The processing of information involves a complex series of stages in which new data are processed in our limited-capacity sensory and short-term memory systems. If not used, it is quickly forgotten; if used it may pass into long-term memory. The author discusses how this happens, along with implications for helping students develop their capacities for long-term memory storage.

CHAPTER NINE   The Effects of Grouping, Class Size, and Retention on Learning   142

25. Synthesis of Research on Grouping in Elementary and Secondary Schools   *Robert E. Slavin,* Educational Leadership, *September 1988*   142

   This article summarizes what is known about the effects of grouping on students' achievement. There is an endless array of grouping possibilities within classes and between classes, and not all are helpful to students. The author points to the advantages and disadvantages of various kinds of grouping.

26. The Effect of Class Size on What Happens in Classrooms   *Mary Lee Smith and Gene V. Glass,* The Education Digest, *March 1980*   151

   In this meta-analysis of research, the authors report that the effect of class size is positive, no matter how that effect is measured. Smaller classes are particularly beneficial for children twelve years and under but appear to make less difference for those eighteen and older.

27. Grade Retention and Social Promotion Practices   *Gary Cooke and John Stammer,* Childhood Education, *Vol. 61, 1985*   153

   The authors address themselves to the question of whether or not grade retention is helpful to students who do poorly. They conclude that neither grade retention nor "social" promotion necessarily solves the problem of low-achieving students. Alternatives to retention and social promotion are presented.

Part Four Study and Discussion Questions   **157**

PART FIVE
An Overview of What It Takes to Be a Good Teacher

CHAPTER TEN   The Many Faces of Good Teaching   **164**

28. **Research on Teacher Effects: Uses and Abuses** *Jere Brophy,* The Elementary School Journal, *September 1988*   **164**

    The author shows persuasively that the adage "Those who can, do, and those who can't, teach" is patently untrue. Rather, teaching is a highly complex task, one that demands a high degree of knowledge and skill.

29. **Teaching Students to Examine Their Lives** *Carolyn J. Sweers,* Educational Leadership, *May 1988*   **172**

    Genuine Socratic teaching does more than question students about their understanding of books; it challenges them to think critically about their behavior and beliefs by encouraging them to question their own lives and beliefs.

30. **Psychodynamics of Teachers' Expectations** *Don Hamachek,* Encounters with the Self, *3rd ed., Holt, Rinehart & Winston, 1987*   **174**

    Teachers have a powerful impact on students' self-perceptions of their ability to do school work. They communicate their expectations for students' performance both covertly and overtly. How this happens, along with what teachers can do to communicate positive expectations, is discussed.

31. **In Praise of Teachers** *Mark Medoff,* The New York Times Magazine, *November 9, 1986*   **180**

    Mr. Medoff, winner of the 1980 Tony Award for his play *Children of a Lesser God,* and himself a college professor and teacher, remembers the teachers he had as a growing boy and young man. This praise of teachers may deepen your knowledge about what it is that makes good teachers good in the first place.

CHAPTER ELEVEN   Motivational Strategies for Encouraging Student Achievement   **183**

32. **Synthesis of Research on Strategies for Motivating Students to Learn** *Jere Brophy,* Educational Leadership, *October 1987*   **183**

    The author encapsulates thirty-two conclusions drawn from his review of the literature on motivation conducted to identify principles suitable for use by teachers, especially principles for motivating students to do better in their academic work.

33. "If at First . . .": Attribution Theory in the Classroom
Madeline Hunter and George Barker, Educational Leadership, *October 1987*   **191**

Attribution theory is concerned with our constant search for the causes of our successes and failures. The authors argue that students are better learners if they believe that their success depends more on effort than on luck or ability. Suggestions are made to help teachers assist students to see that effort is the key to successful learning.

34. How to Reach the Underachiever *Sylvia B. Rimm,* Instructor, *September 1985*   **195**

The author paints a picture of the underachiever and colors it with vivid descriptions of the behaviors most commonly seen in students who do less than their best. Suggestions are offered for ways to help underachievers.

CHAPTER TWELVE Strategies Useful for the Practice of Positive Classroom Discipline   **198**

35. A Primer on Classroom Discipline: Principles Old and New *Thomas R. McDaniel,* Phi Delta Kappan, *September 1986*   **198**

The author offers ten principles—an eclectic combination of traditional and modern, practical and theoretical, pedagogical and psychological—to serve as general guidelines to help teachers discipline in positive ways.

36. Classroom Management as Instruction: Socializing Self-Guidance in Students *Jere Brophy,* Theory into Practice, *Autumn 1985*   **203**

The author suggests that classroom management may be thought of as a form of instruction instead of as a form of discipline or control. Suggestions are made for how to develop self-guidance in students.

CHAPTER THIRTEEN Basic Understandings About Testing and Educational Research   **210**

37. Norm-Referenced vs. Criterion-Referenced Tests
Lorrie Shepard, Educational Horizons, *Fall 1979*   **210**

Distinctions are made between criterion-referenced and norm-referenced testing, along with a discussion about when it is appropriate to use each kind. For day-to-day decisions about student achievement, criterion-referenced tests are recommended.

38. Taking the Terror Out of Research *Robert Gable and Vincent Rogers,* Phi Delta Kappan, *May 1987*   **216**

Clearly and succinctly, the authors spell out the basic differences between quantitative and qualitative research and discuss the basic research methods associated with each. Suggestions are made to teachers for how to use these methods in their own classrooms. Gathering research data is not so terrifying as it may seem.

Part Five Study and Discussion Questions   **223**

Detailed Contents

PART SIX
Exceptional Students: Problems and Challenges

CHAPTER FOURTEEN Toward Understanding Students Who Have Trouble Learning 230

39. Learning: Abilities and Disabilities *Melvin Levine,* Harvard Medical School Health Letter, *September 1984* 230

   The meaning and definition of a learning disability are discussed. The author also describes some of the common symptoms associated with learning disabilities along with suggesting ways to identify and treat these disabilities.

40. Deciphering Dyslexia *John Langone,* Discover, *August 1983* 233

   Dyslexia is a learning disorder that sorely hampers a person's ability to read, write, spell, and even speak correctly. The author discusses the scope of what is known about this learning disability and points to evidence suggesting that the cause of the problem may be a malfunction deep in the brain.

41. Reaching Out to America's Dropouts: What to Do? *Andrew Hahn,* Phi Delta Kappan, *December 1987* 236

   High dropout rates not only represent a terrible waste of young lives but also threaten the nation's productivity. The author outlines the causes and consequences of dropping out of school and looks at what we have learned from programs that identify and assist dropouts.

CHAPTER FIFTEEN Toward Identifying and Reaching Exceptionally Able Students 246

42. The Nature of Giftedness and Talent *A. Harry Passow,* Gifted Child Quarterly, *Winter 1981* 246

   Behaviors and characteristics associated with gifted and talented students are identified. The author discusses the many ways that giftedness and talent can be manifested.

43. Curriculum-Based Programs for the Gifted *Byron L. Barrington,* The Educational Digest, *January 1987* 252

   The author argues that many gifted education programs are ineffective and suggests an outline for a curriculum-based model that relies heavily on those teaching subject areas. Advantages to this approach, along with frequently raised objections, are discussed.

Part Six Study and Discussion Questions 255

Index 257

EDUCATIONAL PSYCHOLOGY READER

PART ONE

Schooling: Approaches and Outcomes

The two chapters and five articles in this section will expose you to a range of views about what constitutes positive school experiences and to considerations about what makes effective schools effective in the first place.

The first chapter begins with the unique views of three prominent psychologists, each of whom has had a significant impact on the course and direction of educational practices. In Reading 1, B. F. Skinner discusses why he believes that problems associated with motivation and learning could be solved with the proper use of programmed materials designed such "that students are very often right and learn at once that they are." He is convinced that we have the technology to set up this kind of success system if we choose to do so.

In Reading 2, William Glasser discusses how what he calls "control theory" can be a means by which schools can motivate students. Whereas the major premise of stimulus/response theory is that all behavior is caused by external events, the primary tenet of control theory is that all human behavior is generated by what goes on *inside* a person. Glasser thus advocates an approach to schooling that helps students develop a sense of power by encouraging more involvement in decision making and more emphasis on cooperative learning.

In Reading 3, Arthur W. Combs presents a case for humanistic/perceptual psychology as another approach to schooling, one that views learning as a "deeply human, personal, affective experience." Basically, it is an approach to education from the inside out, in the sense that it emphasizes the importance of perceptions and the discovery of personal meaning. From Combs's point of view, this is simply the recognition of the primacy of human values and human needs when it comes to perceiving what is or is not meaningful. Thus, from a humanistic/perceptual point of view, if schooling is to be more effective, we need to spend less time figuring out ways to manipulate students from the outside in, and more time motivating them from the inside out.

Whereas Chapter One offers us the opportunity to compare three different approaches to schooling, Chapter Two opens the door to our examination of how schooling makes a difference for better or worse. Thomas L. Good and Rhona S. Weinstein's review of research in Reading 4 indicates that schools do make a difference, but that the differences in achievement outcomes varies greatly among schools, even those serving similar populations. They build a strong case for building new and expanded models of effective schooling to make education more equitable.

In an effort to answer the question about what it is that makes some schools better than others, Peter Mortimore and Pam Sammons present the results of a four-year study of fifty different elementary schools in which they identify twelve key factors characteristic of effective educational practices. Not all schools are effective. You will learn why in this selection.

Part One is the backdrop: It sets the stage and raises important issues and questions for what is ahead. What part should reinforcement schedules play in schooling? Is the idea of giving students more control over their educational destinies a realistic one? How much stock should we place in the argument that school can be successful only if students find personal meaning in it? Given the great diversity among schools and approaches to education, what can be done to make school more equitable for more students? What, exactly, goes into making an effective school effective in the first place?

CHAPTER ONE

Three Viewpoints About What Is Important in Education

READING 1 B. F. SKINNER
The Shame of American Education

On a morning in October 1957, Americans were awakened by the beeping of a satellite. It was a Russian satellite, Sputnik. Why was it not American? Was something wrong with American education? Evidently so, and money was quickly voted to improve American schools. Now we are being awakened by the beepings of Japanese cars, Japanese radios, phonographs, and television sets, and Japanese wristwatch alarms, and again questions are being asked about American education, especially in science and mathematics.

Something does seem to be wrong. According to a recent report of the National Commission on Excellence in Education (1983), for example, the average achievement of our high-school students on standardized tests is now lower than it was a quarter of a century ago, and students in American schools compare poorly with those in other nations in many fields. As the commission put it, America is threatened by "a rising tide of mediocrity."

The first wave of reform is usually rhetorical. To improve education we are said to need "imaginative innovations," a "broad national effort" leading to a "deep and lasting change," and a "commitment to excellence." More specific suggestions have been made, however. To get better teachers we should pay them more, possibly according to merit. They should be certified to teach the subjects they teach. To get better students, scholarship standards should be raised. The school day should be extended from 6 to 7 hours, more time should be spent on homework, and the school year should be lengthened from 180 to 200, or even 220, days. We should change what we are teaching. Social studies are all very well, but they should not take time away from basics, especially mathematics.

As many of us have learned to expect, there is a curious omission in that list: It contains no suggestion that teaching be improved. There is a conspiracy of silence about teaching as a skill. The *New York Times* publishes a quarterly survey of education. Three recent issues (Fisk, 1982, 1983a, 1983b) contained 18 articles about the kinds of things being taught in schools; 11 articles about the financial problems of students and schools; 10 articles about the needs of special students, from the gifted to the disadvantaged; and smaller numbers of articles about the selection of students, professional problems of teachers, and sports and other extracurricular activities. Of about 70 articles, only 2 had anything to do with how students are taught or how they could be taught better. Pedagogy is a dirty word.

In January 1981, Frederick Mosteller, president of the American Association for the Advancement of Science, gave an address called "Innovation and Evaluation" (Mosteller, 1981). He began with an example of the time which can pass between a scientific discovery and its practical use. The fact that lemon juice cures scurvy was discovered in 1601, but more than 190 years passed before the British navy began to use citrus juice on a regular basis and another 70 before scurvy was wiped out in the mercantile marine — a lag of 264 years.

From B. F. Skinner, "The Shame of American Education," *American Psychologist* (September 1984):947–954. Copyright 1984 by the American Psychological Association. Adapted by permission of the publisher and author.

Lags have grown shorter but, as Mosteller pointed out, are often still too long. Perhaps unwittingly he gave another example. He called for initiatives in science and engineering education and said that a major theme of the 1982 meeting of the association would be a "national commitment to educational excellence in science and engineering for all Americans" (p. 886).

When Mosteller's address was published in *Science,* I wrote a letter to the editor (Skinner, 1981) calling attention to an experiment in teaching algebra in a school in Roanoke, Virginia (Rushton, 1965). In this experiment an eighth-grade class using simple teaching machines and hastily composed instructional programs went through *all* of ninth-grade algebra in *half* a year. Their grades met ninth-grade norms, and when tested a year later the students remembered rather more than usual. Had American educators decided that that was the way to teach algebra? They had not. The experiment was done in 1960, but education had not yet made any use of it. The lag was already 21 years long.

A month or so later I ran into Mosteller. "Did you see my letter in *Science* about teaching machines?" I asked. "Teaching machines?" he said, puzzled. "Oh, you mean *computers*—teaching machines to *you.*" And, of course, he was right. Computer is the current word. But is it the right one? Computers are now badly misnamed. They were designed to compute, but they are not computing when they are processing words, or displaying Pac-Man, or aiding instruction (unless the instruction is in computing). "Computer" has all the respectability of the white-collar executive, whereas "machine" is definitely blue-collar, but let us call things by their right names. Instruction may be "computer aided," and all good instruction must be "interactive," but machines that teach are teaching machines.

I liked the Roanoke experiment because it confirmed something I had said a few years earlier to the effect that with teaching machines and programmed instruction one could teach what is now taught in American schools in half the time with half the effort. I shall not review other evidence that that is true. Instead I shall demonstrate my faith in a technology of teaching by going out on a limb. I claim that the school system of any large American city could be so redesigned, at little or no additional cost, that students would come to school and apply themselves to their work with a minimum of punitive coercion and, with very rare exceptions, learn to read with reasonable ease, express themselves well in speech and writing, and solve a fair range of mathematical problems. I want to talk about why this has not been done.

The teaching machines of 25 years ago were crude, of course, but this is scarcely an explanation. The calculating machines were crude, too, yet they were used until they could be replaced by something better. The hardware problem has not been solved, but resistance to a technology of teaching survives. The rank commercialism which quickly engulfed the field of teaching machines is another possible explanation. Too many people rushed in to write bad programs and make promises that could not be kept. But that should not have concealed the value of programmed instruction for so many years. There is more than that to be said for the marketplace in the selection of a better mousetrap.

PSYCHOLOGICAL ROADBLOCKS

I shall argue that educators have not seized this chance to solve their problems because the solution conflicts with deeply entrenched views of human behavior, and that these views are too strongly supported by current psychology. Humanistic psychologists, for example, tend to feel threatened by any kind of scientific analysis of human behavior, particularly if it leads to a "technology" that can be used to intervene in people's lives. A technology of teaching is especially threatening. Carl Rogers has said that teaching is vastly overrated, and Ivan Illich has called for the de-schooling of society. I dealt with the problem in *Beyond Freedom and Dignity* (Skinner, 1971). To give a single example, we do not like to be told something we already know, for we can then no longer claim credit for having known it.

To solve that problem, Plato tried to show that students already possess knowledge and have only to be shown that they possess it. But the famous scene in Plato's *Meno* in which Socrates shows that the slaveboy already knows Pythagoras's theorem for doubling the square is one of the great intellectual hoaxes of all time. The slaveboy agrees with everything Socrates says, but there is no evidence whatsoever that he could then go through the proof by himself. Indeed, Socrates says that the boy would need to be taken through it many times before he could do so.

Cognitive psychology is causing much more trouble, but in a different way. It is hard to be precise because the field is usually presented in what we may call a cognitive style. For example, a pamphlet of the National Institute of Education (1980) quotes with approval the contention that "at the present time, modern cognitive psychology is the dominant theoretical force in psychological science as opposed to the first half of the century when behavioristic, anti-mentalistic stimulus-response theories of learning were in the ascendance" (p. 391). (The writer means "ascendant.") The pamphlet tells us that cognitive science studies learning, but not in quite those words. Instead, cognitive science is said to be "characterized by a concern with understanding the mechanisms by which human beings carry out complex intellectual activities including learning" (p. 391). The pamphlet also says that cognitive science can help construct tests that will tell us more about what a student has learned and hence how to teach better, but here is the way it says this: "Attention will be placed on two specific topics: Applications of cognitive models of the knowledge structure of various subject matters and of learning and problem solving to construction of tests that identify processes underlying test answers, analyze errors, and provide information about what students know and don't know, and strategies for integrating testing information with instructional decisions" (p. 393). Notice especially the cognitive style in the last phrase —the question is not "whether test results can suggest better ways of teaching" but "whether there are strategies for integrating testing information with instructional decisions."

The Commission on Behavioral and Social Sciences and Education of the National Research Council (1984) provides a more recent example in its announcement of a biennial program plan covering the period 1 May 1983 to 30 April 1985. The commission will take advantage of "significant advances . . . in the cognitive sciences" (p. 41). Will it study learning? Well, not exactly. The members will "direct their attention to studies of fundamental processes underlying the nature and development of learning" (p. 41). Why do cognitive psychologists not tell us frankly what they are up to? Is it possible that they themselves do not really know?

Cognitive psychology is certainly in the ascendant. The word *cognitive* is sprinkled through the psychological literature like salt—and, like salt, not so much for any flavor of its own but to bring out the flavor of other things, things which a quarter of a century ago would have been called by other names. The heading of an article in a recent issue of the APA *Monitor* (Turkington, 1983) tells us that "cognitive deficits" are important in understanding alcoholism. In the text we learn simply that alcoholics show losses in perception and motor skills. Perception and motor skills used to be fields of psychology; now they are fields of cognitive science. Nothing has been changed except the name, and the change has been made for suspicious reasons. There is a sense of profundity about "cognitive deficits," but it does not take us any deeper into the subject.

Much of the vogue of cognitive science is due to advances in computer technology. The computer offers an appealing simplification of some old psychological problems. Sensation and perception are reduced to input; learning and memory to the processing, storage, and retrieval of information; and action to output. It is very much like the old stimulus-response formula patched up with intervening variables. To say that students process information is to use a doubtful metaphor, and how they process information is still the old question of how they learn.

Cognitive psychology also gains prestige from its alignment with brain research. Interesting things are certainly being discovered about the biochemistry and circuitry of the brain, but we are still a long way from knowing what is happening in the brain as behavior is shaped and maintained by contingencies of reinforcement, and that means that we are a long way from help in designing useful instructional practices.

Cognitive science is also said to be supported by modern linguistics, a topic to which I am particularly sensitive. Programmed instruction emerged from my analysis of verbal behavior (Skinner, 1957), which linguists, particularly generative grammarians, have, of course, attacked. So far as I know they have offered no equally effective practices. One might expect them to have improved the teaching of languages, but almost all language laboratories still work in particularly outmoded ways, and language instruction is one of the principal failures of precollege education.

Psycholinguistics moves in essentially the same direction in its hopeless commitment to development. Behavior is said to change in ways determined by its structure. The change may be a function of age, but age is not a variable that one can manipulate. The extent to which developmentalism has encouraged a neglect of more useful ways of changing behavior is shown by a recent report (Siegler, 1983) in which the number of studies concerned with the development of behavior in children was found to have skyrocketed, whereas the number concerned with how children learn has dropped to a point at which the researcher could scarcely find any examples at all.

There are many fine cognitive psychologists who are doing fine research, but they are not the cognitive psychologists who for 25 years have been promising great advances in education. A short paper published in *Science* last April (Resnick, 1983) asserts that "recent findings in cognitive science suggest new approaches to teaching in science and mathematics" (p. 477), but the examples given, when expressed in noncognitive style, are simply these: (a) Students learn about the world in "naive" ways before they study science; (b) naive theories interfere with learning scientific theories; (c) we should therefore teach science as early as possible; (d) many problems are not solved exclusively with mathematics; qualitative experience is important; (e) students learn more than isolated facts; they learn how facts are related to each other; and (f) students relate what they are learning to what they already know. If these are *recent* findings, where has cognitive science been?

Cognitive psychology is frequently presented as a revolt against behaviorism, but it is not a revolt; it is a retreat. Everyday English is full of terms derived from ancient explanations of human behavior. We spoke that language when we were young. When we went out into the world and became psychologists, we learned to speak in other ways but made mistakes for which we were punished. But now we can relax. Cognitive psychology is Old Home Week. We are back among friends speaking the language we spoke when we were growing up. We can talk about love and will and ideas and memories and feelings and states of mind, and no one will ask us what we mean; no one will raise an eyebrow.

SCHOOLS OF EDUCATION

Psychological theories come into the hands of teachers through schools of education and teachers' colleges, and it is there, I think, that we must lay the major blame for what is happening in American education. In a recent article in the *New York Times* (Botstein, 1983), President Leon Botstein of Bard College proposed that schools of education, teachers' colleges, and departments of education simply be disbanded. But he gave a different reason. He said that schools of that sort "placed too great an emphasis on pedagogical techniques and psychological studies" (p. 64), when they should be teaching the subjects the teachers will eventually teach. But disbanding such schools is certainly a move in the wrong direction. It has long been said that college teaching is the only profession for which there is no professional training. Would-be doctors go to medical schools, would-be lawyers go to law schools, and would-be engineers go to institutes of technology, but would-be college teachers just start teaching. Fortunately it is recognized that grade- and high-school teachers need to learn to teach. The trouble is, they are not being taught in effective ways. The commitment to humanistic and cognitive psychology is only part of the problem.

Equally damaging is the assumption that teaching can be adequately discussed in everyday English. The appeal to laymanship is attractive. At the "Convocation of Science and Mathematics in the Schools" called by the National Academies of Sciences and Engineering, one member said that "what we need are bright, energetic, dedicated young people, trained in mathematics . . . science . . . or technology, mixing it up with 6- to 13-year-old kids in the classroom" (Raizen, 1983, p. 19). The problem is too grave to be solved in any such way. The first page of the report notes with approval that "if there is one American enterprise that is local in its design and control it is education" (p. 1). That is held to be a virtue. But certainly the commission would not approve similar statements about medicine, law, or science and technology. Why should the community decide how children are to be taught? The commission is actually pointing to one explanation of why education is failing.

We must beware of the fallacy of the good teacher and the good student. There are many good teachers who have not needed to learn to teach. They would be good at almost anything they tried. There are many good students who scarcely need to be taught. Put a good teacher and a good student together and you have what seems to be an ideal instructional setting. But it is disastrous to take it as a model to be followed in our schools, where hundreds of thousands of teachers must teach millions of students. Teachers must learn how to teach, and they must be taught by schools of education. They need only to be taught more effective ways of teaching.

A SOLUTION

We could solve our major problems in education if students learned more during each day in school. That does not mean a longer day or year or more homework. It simply means using time more efficiently. Such a solution is not considered in any of the reports I have mentioned—whether from the National Institute of Education, the American Association for the Advancement of Science, the National Research Council, or the National Academies of Sciences and Engineering. Nevertheless, it is within easy reach. Here is all that needs to be done.

1. Be clear about what is to be taught. When I once explained to a group of grade-school teachers how I would teach children to spell words, one of them said, "Yes, but can you teach spelling?" For him, students spelled words correctly not because they had learned to do so but because they had acquired a special ability. When I told a physicist colleague about the Roanoke experiment in teaching algebra, he said, "Yes, but did they learn algebra?" For him, algebra was more than solving certain kinds of problems; it was a mental faculty. No doubt the more words you learn to spell the easier it is to spell new words, and the more problems you solve in algebra the easier it is to solve new problems. What eventually emerges is often called *intuition*. We do not know what it is, but we can certainly say that no teacher has ever taught it directly, nor has any student ever displayed it without first learning to do the kinds of things it supposedly replaces.

2. Teach first things first. It is tempting to move too quickly to

final products. I once asked a leader of the "new math" what he wanted students to be able to do. He was rather puzzled and then said, "I suppose I just want them to be able to follow a logical line of reasoning." That does not tell a teacher where to start or, indeed, how to proceed at any point. I once asked a colleague what he wanted his students to do as a result of having taken his introductory course in physics. "Well," he said, "I guess I've never thought about it that way." I'm afraid he spoke for most of the profession.

Among the ultimate but useless goals of education is "excellence." A candidate for president recently said that he would let local communities decide what that meant. "I am not going to try to define excellence for them," he said, and wisely so. Another useless ultimate goal is "creativity." It is said that students should do more than what they have been taught to do. They should be creative. But does it help to say that they must acquire creativity? More than 300 years ago. Molière wrote a famous line: "I am asked by the learned doctors for the cause and reason why opium puts one to sleep, to which I reply that there is in it a soporific virtue, the nature of which is to lull the senses." Two or three years ago an article in *Science* pointed out that 90% of scientific innovations were accomplished by fewer than 10% of scientists. The explanation, it was said, was that only a few scientists possess creativity. Molière's audiences laughed. Eventually some students behave in creative ways, but they must have something to be creative with and that must be taught first. Then they can be taught to multiply the variations which give rise to new and interesting forms of behavior. (Creativity, incidentally, is often said to be beyond a science of behavior, and it would be if that science were a matter of stimulus and response. By emphasizing the selection action of consequences, however, the experimental analysis of behavior deals with the creation of behavior precisely as Darwin dealt with the creation of species.)

3. Stop making all students advance at essentially the same rate. The phalanx was a great military invention, but it has long been out of date, and it should be out of date in American schools. Students are still expected to move from kindergarten through high school in 12 years, and we all know what is wrong: Those who could move faster are held back, and those who need more time fall farther and farther behind. We could double the efficiency of education with one change alone—by letting each student move at his or her own pace. (I wish I could blame this costly mistake on developmental psychology, because it is such a beautiful example of its major principle, but the timing is out of joint.)

No teacher can teach a class of 30 to 40 students and allow each to progress at an optimal speed. Tracking is too feeble a remedy. We must turn to individual instruments for part of the school curriculum. The report of the convocation held by the National Academies of Sciences and Engineering refers to "new technologies" which "can be used to extend the educational process, to supplement the teacher's role in new and imaginative ways" (Raizen, 1983, p. 15), but no great enthusiasm is shown. Thirty years ago educational television was promising, but the promise has not been kept. The report alludes to "computer-aided instruction" but calls it the latest "rage of education" and insists that "the primary use of the computer is for drill" (p. 15). (Properly programmed instruction is *never* drill if that means gong over material again and again until it is learned.) The report also contains a timid allusion to "low-cost teaching stations that can be controlled by the learner" (p. 15), but evidently these stations are merely to give the student access to video material rather than to programs.

4. Program the subject matter. The heart of the teaching machine, call it what you will, is the programming of instruction—an advance not mentioned in any of the reports I have cited. Standard texts are designed to be read by the students, who will then discuss what they say with a teacher or take a test to see how much has been learned. Material prepared for individual study is different. It first induces students to say or do the things they are to learn to say or do. Their behavior is thus "primed" in the sense of being brought out for the first time. Until the behavior has acquired more strength, it may need to be prompted. Primes and prompts must then be carefully "vanished" until the behavior occurs without help. At that point the reinforcing consequences of being right are most effective in building and sustaining an enduring repertoire.

Working through a program is really a process of discovery, but not in the sense in which that word is currently used in education. We discover many things in the world around us, and that is usually better than being told about them, but as individuals we can discover only a very small part of the world. Mathematics has been discovered very slowly and painfully over thousands of years. Students discover it as they go through a program, but not in the sense of doing something for the first time in history. Trying to teach mathematics or science as if the students themselves were discovering things for the first time is not an efficient way of teaching the very skills with which, in the long run, a student may, with luck, actually make a genuine discovery.

When students move through well-constructed programs at their own pace, the so-called problem of motivation is automatically solved. For thousands of years students have studied to avoid the consequences of not studying. Punitive sanctions still survive, disguised in various ways, but the world is changing, and they are no longer easily imposed. The great mistake of progressive education was to try to replace them with natural curiosity. Teachers were to bring the real world into the classroom to arouse the students' interest. The inevitable result was a neglect of subjects in which children were seldom naturally interested—in particular, the so-called basics. One solution is to make some of the natural reinforcers—goods or privileges—artificially contingent upon basic behavior, as in a token economy. Such contingencies can be justified if they correct a lethargic or disordered classroom, but there should be no lethargy or disorder. It is characteristic of the human species that successful action is automatically reinforced. The fascination of video games is adequate proof. What would industrialists not give to see their workers as absorbed in their work as young people in a video arcade? What would teachers not give to see their students applying themselves with the same eagerness? (For that matter, what would any of us not give to see ourselves as much in love with our work?) But there is no mystery; it is all a matter of the scheduling of reinforcements.

A good program of instruction guarantees a great deal of successful action. Students do not need to have a natural interest in what they are doing, and subject matters do not need to be dressed up to attract attention. No one really cares whether Pac-Man gobbles up all those little spots on the screen. Indeed, as soon as the screen is cleared, the player covers it again with little spots to be gobbled up. What is reinforcing is successful play, and in a well-designed instructional program students gobble up their assignments. I saw them doing that when I visited the project in Roanoke with its director, Allen Calvin. We entered a room in which 30 to 40 eighth-grade students were at their desks working on rather crude teaching machines. When I said I was surprised that they paid no attention to us, Calvin proposed a better demonstration. He asked me to keep my eye on the students and then went up on the teacher's platform. He jumped in the air and came down with a loud bang. Not a single student looked up. Students do not have to be made to study. Abundant reinforcement is enough, and good programming provides it. . . .

REFERENCES

Botstein, L. (1983, June 5). Nine Proposals to Improve Our Schools. *New York Times Magazine*, p. 59.
Fisk, E. B. (Ed.). (1982, November 14). Fall Survey of Education [Supplement]. *New York Times*.
Fisk, E. B. (Ed.). (1983a, January 9). Winter Survey of Education [Supplement]. *New York Times*.
Fisk, E. B. (Ed.). (1983b, April 24). Spring Survey of Education [Supplement]. *New York Times*.
Goodlad, J. L. (1983). *A Place Called School*. New York: McGraw-Hill.
Mosteller, F. (1981). Innovation and Evaluation. *Science, 211,* 881–886.
National Commission on Excellence in Education. (1983, April). *A Nation at Risk: The Imperative for Educational Reform*. Washington, DC: U.S. Department of Education.
National Institute of Education. (1980). Science and Technology and Education. In *The Five-Year Outlook: Problems, Opportunities and Constraints in Science and Technology* (Vol. 2, 391–399). Washington, DC: National Science Foundation.
National Research Council, Commission on Behaviorial and Social Sciences and Education. (1984). Biennial program plan, May 1, 1983–April 30, 1985. Washington, DC: National Academy Press.
Raizen, S. (1983). *Science and Mathematics in the Schools: Report of a Convocation*. Washington, DC: National Academy Press.
Resnick, L. B. (1983). Mathematics and Science Learning: A New Conception. *Science, 220,* 477–478.
Rushton, E. W. (1965). *The Roanoke Experiment*. Chicago: Encyclopedia Britannica Press.
Siegler, R. S. (1983). Five Generalizations About Cognitive Development. *American Psychologist, 38,* 263–277.
Skinner, B. F. (1957). *Verbal Behavior*. New York: Appleton-Century-Crofts.
Skinner, B. F. (1971). *Beyond Freedom and Dignity*. New York: Alfred A. Knopf.
Skinner, B. F. (1981). Innovation in Science Teaching. *Science, 212,* 283.
Turkington, C. (1983, June). Cognitive Deficits Hold Promise for Prediction of Alcoholism. APA *Monitor*, p. 16.

READING 2   PAULINE B. GOUGH
The Key to Improving Schools: An Interview with William Glasser

William Glasser, M.D., is a board-certified psychiatrist who has won international recognition for his work on reality therapy. He is the founder and president of the Institute for Reality Therapy, located in Canoga Park, California, and the author of *Reality Therapy* (Harper & Row, 1965).

When Dr. Glasser applied to education the concepts of reality therapy and the insights he had gained from extensive work in the schools of Sacramento, Palo Alto, and Los Angeles, the result was a widely read book, *Schools Without Failure* (Harper & Row, 1969), which still influences practice throughout North America.

In the mid-1970s Dr. Glasser began to add the new and powerful concepts of control theory to his approach to education. In this interview he summarizes many of the ideas contained in his latest book, *Control Theory in the Classroom* (Harper & Row, 1986), another significant and highly readable work that promises to influence practice appreciably. Educators who wish to explore Dr. Glasser's ideas more fully should read not only his most recent book, but also *Control Theory* (Harper & Row, 1985).

Kappan: You are no fan of the National Commission on Excellence in Education and of its recommendations, in *A Nation at Risk,* that U.S. high schools increase coursework requirements and raise academic standards. Why is that?

Glasser: I think that the commission missed the problem. The problem is that at least half of all students are making little or no effort to learn, because they don't believe that school satisfies their needs. To make school harder — to increase the length of the school year or the school day, to assign more homework, to require more courses in science and mathematics — is not going to reach those students. It's only going to increase the separation between the half who are already working and the half who are not.

The commission tried to solve the problem traditionally, by stimulating teachers and students in the hope that they would work harder — regardless of whether what is being asked of them is satisfying or not. Stimulus/response psychology has never worked in the past, and it won't work now. We can't do anything *to* people, or really even *for* people, to get them to produce more. We have to change the school itself, so that students look at it and say, "In this school and with these teachers I can satisfy my needs, if I work hard." The commission did not address itself to this basic psychological issue, and thus its report will have no impact on the huge number of students who refuse to work hard in schools that do not satisfy their needs.

Kappan: In your new book, *Control Theory in the Classroom*, you have suggested specific means by which secondary schools can deal more effectively with unmotivated students. Before we examine the changes you propose, would you explain the theory undergirding those changes?

Glasser: Nothing will change for the better until educators and others understand that stimulus/response theory — under which everyone (including the commission) currently operates — is wrong. According to stimulus/response theory, human behavior is caused by external events. For example, a person stops at a traffic light because it turns red.

By contrast, the major premise of control theory is that all human behavior is generated by what goes on *inside* the behaving person. Therefore, a person stops at a traffic light *not* because the light turns red, but because that person says, "I want to stay alive." In other words, all that we get from the outside world is information. We then choose to act on that information in the way we believe is best for us.

Kappan: Could you give us an example in a school setting?

Glasser: What students get from school — from their English class, for example — is information. They then ask, "Will this information satisfy my needs, and should I work hard to get more of it?" As a society, we're failing to understand that students will not work in classes that do not satisfy their needs. It doesn't help to say to these students, "You should appreciate the fact that what we do is for your benefit. Look at how many students are working. You should work hard, too."

It's not that students aren't working in schools; as many as half *do* work in good schools, because they see schoolwork as satisfying. My point is, if half of all students are *not* working because they perceive that school will not satisfy their needs, we have to attend to the fact that a major institution in our

From Patricia B. Gough, "The Key to Improving Schools: An Interview with William Glasser," *Phi Delta Kappan* (May 1987):656–662. © 1987, Phi Delta Kappan, Inc. Reprinted by permission.

society — perhaps the one on which we spend the most money — follows a theory that does not address itself to the needs of more than half of its clients. The old theory, "We can make 'em work; all we have to do is get tough," has never produced intellectual effort in the history of the world, and it certainly won't work in this situation.

Kappan: What are the needs of students that the schools are failing to address?

Glasser: The needs of students are the same as those of everyone else. As I mentioned with regard to the traffic light, we all need to survive. But survival is not the major concern of most American students. They believe that they are going to survive, and they don't see school as related to that survival — even though we adults often warn them, "If you don't get a good education, you won't make it."

Except for those who live in deepest poverty, the psychological needs — love, power, freedom, and fun — take precedence over the survival needs, which most of us are able to satisfy. All our lives, we search for ways to satisfy our needs for love, belonging, caring, sharing, and cooperation. If a student feels no sense of belonging in school, no sense of being involved in caring and concern, that child will pay little attention to academic subjects. Instead, he or she will engage in a desperate search for friendship, for acceptance. The child may become a behavioral problem, in the hope of attracting attention.

As important as belonging is, that need is much easier for most of us — especially students — to satisfy than another basic need, the need for *power*. Each of us wants to be able to say, "Someone listens to me; someone thinks that what I have to say is important; someone is willing to do what I say." But in the classroom, this need is largely ignored, especially at the secondary level.

I've interviewed students across the U.S. When I've asked high schoolers whether they have friends in school, virtually every one of them has responded affirmatively. But when I've asked them whether they are important in school, most of them have looked at me as though I had asked, "Are you horseradish in school? Are you applesauce in school?" At first, I thought that they didn't understand the meaning of the word *important*. But when I prodded, I discovered that they understood the word; they just didn't see how it relates to what they do in school.

I believe that the need for power is the core — the absolute core — of almost all school problems. Even the good students don't feel all that important in school, and the students who receive poor grades certainly can't feel important from the standpoint of academic performance. So they say to themselves, "I won't work in a place in which I have no sense of personal importance, in which I have no power, in which no one listens to me." Literally no one in the world who isn't struggling for bare survival will do intellectual work, unless he or she has a sense of personal importance.

There is also a need for freedom, but I don't think this need is severely frustrated. Students accept the fact that they can have only a limited amount of freedom in school, but they would work harder if they had a little more freedom regarding what to do and what to say.

As to the need for fun, there's plenty of fun in schools — much of it informal — but a little more fun in the classroom would help. As I said, though, the need for power is the core of the problem. No one even wants to talk about the need for power, much less do something about it. Until we confront this issue, we will not persuade more than half of the students to work hard, even in the best public secondary schools.

Kappan: How did you arrive at control theory?

Glasser: In 1976 I wrote a book, *Positive Addiction*, which dealt with how a person could become addicted to a positive activity such as running. And at the same time I started to wonder what causes people to become addicted to an activity of that nature. So I began to try to find out how the human brain actually functions. (Although I'm a physician, I'd never been taught anything about how the brain works, beyond some structure and some chemistry.)

In the course of my research, I came across a book, *Behavior: The Control of Perception*, written by William Powers and published by Aldine Press in 1973. I found the book obscure and difficult to understand, but Powers was one of the first to give the concepts of control theory (which, at that time, were engineering concepts) a biological application. Working a little bit with Powers and a great deal on my own, I refined those ideas and applied them to human behavior. The refining took place in the course of writing three books on the subject, the major one being *Control Theory* (which was published in 1985, one year before *Control Theory in the Classroom*).

Control theory is based on the fact that we're internally motivated and driven by needs that are built into our biological structure, just as our arms and legs are built into our biological structure. From birth we *must* struggle — we have no choice — to try to survive and to try to find some love, some power, some fun, and some freedom. To the extent that we can satisfy these needs on a regular basis, we gain effective control of our lives.

Kappan: How does control theory deal with the problem of discipline in the schools?

Glasser: Understanding control theory is crucial both to understanding and to solving the problem of discipline in the schools. There are a plethora of discipline programs on the market these days, but

> **U**nderstanding control theory is crucial both to understanding and to solving the problem of discipline in the schools.

all of them are based on stimulus/response psychology—on doing something *to* the student (a scare technique, a small punishment, writing the student's name on the chalkboard, or some other consequence). For students who want to behave, these small stimuli serve as reminders that they are out of order, but for students whose needs are not being satisfied, they are useless. Our jails are filled with people who have been disciplined up to their ears—and, because most of them are lonely and powerless, they continue to commit crimes.

According to control theory, discipline problems do not occur in classrooms in which students' needs are satisfied. An administrator who is concerned about the discipline problems in his or her school has only to mentally review the behaviors of the teaching staff to discover that six or seven teachers *never* complain of discipline problems. And the administrator has only to observe in the classrooms of those six or seven teachers to discover that they run their classes according to the concepts of control theory. Their students not only like them but also have a sense of importance, because they take part in class meetings and discussions that allow them to feel accepted and significant in the *academic* environment. Since discipline problems do not exist in the classrooms of such teachers, good discipline is clearly a matter of running the schools so that students say, "This school makes sense to me. I won't break the rules of a place in which I can get what I need."

Take a close look at any school function where the students are in good order, and you'll find satisfied students. Does the band teacher, the chorus teacher, the drama teacher, or the football coach have problems with students not working, not paying attention, not behaving? Rarely. That's because, in these situations (and you'll notice that I've picked out, for the most part, group situations), the students are satisfied.

Kappan: Would you describe the restructured secondary school, as you envision it?

Glasser: In the beginning, the teachers, the administrators, the school board, and as many parents as can be lured to the school would be enrolled in a course or a series of discussion groups led by someone who understands control theory. This would help them begin to understand the difference between control theory (which says that motivation comes from within and that we all have to figure out satisfying ways to live our lives) and stimulus/response theory (which got schools into all this difficulty in the first place). It would also help the participants begin to use control theory in their own lives. This is the key to restructuring the schools.

Kappan: That all sounds very theoretical.

Glasser: I know it does, but it's really not. If we attempt to put together a control-theory school in which people neither understand nor believe in control theory, it just won't happen. So widespread understanding and use of the theory is the first step. I'm working on some films and other materials, which I hope will be ready [soon] to help schools get started.

Kappan: And the next step?

Glasser: The next step is to ask ourselves, "Where in schools do things work well now?" I've already mentioned some of those areas: the band and the orchestra, the drama program, athletics, the school newspaper and the yearbook. In each of these situations, students are working together in some sort of a group that I prefer to call a learning team, though this kind of endeavor has also been accurately labeled "cooperative learning." I like "learning team" better, because I think it's easier for the average student and teacher to understand.

At any rate, the idea of having students function as a group to produce some results has been carefully studied, and it works. It brings into the classroom the same approach that schools use so successfully in extracurricular activities.

In today's typical classroom, each student works alone. He or she is told, "Keep your eyes on your own work; don't share; don't compare; don't talk; don't help." This approach is totally contrary to the basic human need to belong. It also ignores the need for personal importance. How can you feel important if you're working by yourself? Who recognizes you? Who talks to you? Who pays attention to you? Some of the great individual performers—John McEnroe, for example, or Pablo Casals—can feel important by themselves. They know how good they are at what they do. But most of us feel important only as members of a team. David Johnson and Roger Johnson at the University of Minnesota, Robert Slavin at Johns Hopkins, and others have done considerable research and writing on the effective use of small learning teams.

Learning in teams is totally different—I've seen it in my work with the teachers at Calabasas High School (which I mention in my book). Students begin to realize, "I'm a member of a learning team. I can contribute; I can talk to the others; we cooperate; we can earn a grade for what we do together." Students are also able to earn grades *individually*; there's nothing rigid

> The idea of having students function as a group to produce some result has been carefully studied, and it works.

about the learning-team approach. But students work in teams often enough to find school a satisfying place.

Kappan: What role does the teacher play, in dealing with learning teams?

Glasser: The teacher acts as a consultant, a facilitator—someone who lectures once in a while, who teaches traditionally at times, but who also teaches nontraditionally, moving (as a good manager) from team to team to give leadership, support, and encouragement to the students (who are the workers). *Control Theory in the Classroom* contains an important chapter on the teacher as a manager—because, if teachers see themselves as workers, they will try to stimulate the students, and, in doing so, they will treat the students more as objects and less as human beings. This new role for the teacher is another facet of my vision of a control-theory school.

In a control-theory school, as I have said, students would spend more time working together in classes, and—since they, too, would be taught control theory—they would understand why they do so. As I have already noted, teachers in such a school would stop seeing themselves as workers who must try to sand, polish, and paint students into educated "objects." Instead, teachers would say to themselves, "The students are the workers. How can we, as good managers, persuade these workers that it is to their benefit to work harder and to produce more—not for *our* benefit, but for *theirs*?" Ultimately, in a control-theory school, students get the vital idea that knowledge really is power.

Kappan: When you speak in your new book of restructuring the schools, why do you focus primarily on secondary schools?

Glasser: I've asked students across the nation to describe "a good student"—and I've found that even poor students can do this well. They say that a good student works hard, pays attention, and "has the right attitude." Then I've asked them to describe a poor student, and they say, "Well, a poor student has the wrong attitude; a poor student doesn't see that school is valuable; a poor student doesn't work; a poor student doesn't like to be in school; a poor student is thinking about drugs and disruptions and how to get attention or feel good."

Next I ask these students, who are probably eighth- or ninth-graders (I prefer to talk to that age group, because its members have just lived through the major crisis of their school lives: transferring from the elementary school to the junior high) to tell me how many students are working in school. Youngsters attending an inner-city school in Detroit told me that 25% of their peers are working and 75% are not. Students living in affluent locales tend to say that 50% of their peers are working in school, but the figure never goes higher than that.

Then I've asked these youngsters, "Did some students who aren't working now work in elementary school?" And they've responded, "Yes, they did. Sometimes in fourth, fifth, and even sixth grade they were working." So I've prodded, "Then why aren't they working now?" And the youngsters have told me, "Well, it all changed when we went to junior high. The teachers in junior high have less time for students; their attitude is, 'Do it, and don't ask questions.'" These youngsters are really saying that junior high school is much less satisfying than elementary school, because in the junior high they feel so unimportant.

The ideas I present in *Control Theory in the Classroom* are not exclusively for secondary schools; elementary schools could certainly profit from them, as well. But I really believe that the secondary schools will never improve their performance unless they put these ideas to use. Following stimulus/response theory is like using a manual typewriter: no matter what you do or how hard you hit it, you can only do so much. And that's where our secondary schools are today. No matter how many external stimuli we apply, the situation will not change. If we could begin to restructure secondary schools in the ways I've suggested, elementary educators would see the advantages of bringing these ideas into their classrooms, and change would follow in the elementary schools, as well.

But if I say to the secondary people, "The fault's in the elementary schools," then the secondary schools will never change, because secondary educators believe that the students sent to them are ill-prepared. For this reason, I think we have to focus particularly on the junior high school or middle school, and then move these ideas up as well as down.

Kappan: In your book, you draw a parallel between athletic teams and learning teams, and you've alluded to the similarity between the two here. Would you explain in greater detail . . . just why the two kinds of teams are similar?

Glasser: They're very similar; in both instances, progress depends on what the team members do together. One basketball player may average 30 points per game and another player may average only two points per game, but the first player is not necessarily considered better than the second. The player who scores only two points may feed the ball to the player who scores 30 points; without his or her accurate passes, the high scorer would be helpless. The coach doesn't give the high scorer a better grade than the low scorer. Since the team's grade is the final score, which members of the team earn together, the coach tries to teach them to cooperate, to talk to each other on the floor, to pass the ball off, to make each game as much a team effort as possible.

Most classrooms today are exactly the opposite, but they don't have to be. There's tradition, but there's no law saying that students must work alone, never sharing what they do.

Kappan: Could you be more specific about ways to use this team approach in the classroom?

Glasser: Why shouldn't students put their heads together and produce a team effort in mathematics, in history, in English? They could write a skit together, discuss a book together, write a paper together, do some research together. That's the way they're going to work in the world outside of school. The pattern for team effort is already in place in band and orchestra, on the school newspaper, and in athletics. The only place that teams are missing is in the classroom.

Recently, as I mentioned in my book, I visited a class that was ending its first learning-team assignment with some skits. When I arrived, the teacher told me that one of his good students would probably not be present for the activity. When I asked why not, he told me that she was a member of the soccer team and had been excused from her last-period class to go to a game. But when the students came in, she was there—and she played a major role in one of the skits.

She had to dash off after class, but the next day her teacher asked her, "Why didn't you go to the soccer game instead of coming to English class?" She responded that her team had worked hard in preparing its skit, and she didn't want to let the other members of the group down. So she'd arranged to get to the game by herself, instead of leaving early with the team.

If she had been working alone, she wouldn't have given a thought to being late for the game just to work by herself in class. She stayed because she was a member of the team. Clearly, when learning teams work well, comparing them to athletic teams is apt.

Kappan: Can you offer any advice to teachers on setting up learning teams?

Glasser: As a general rule, teachers should *select* the members of learning teams. A four-member team, for example, might include one top-notch student, one low-achieving student, and a couple of average students. But teachers will find that youngsters work harder on teams, and teachers won't always be able to tell which team member was formerly the poor student and which team member was formerly the good student. When the so-called poor student says, "I feel important here; they depend on me; they encourage me; they want me to produce—and I'm *going* to produce, because I don't want to let anyone down," he or she is no longer a poor student.

As I said earlier, only individuals who are very exceptional can obtain a sense of power by themselves. The rest of us have to obtain a sense of power through membership in some sort of team: a family, a group at work, an athletic team, whatever. Note that the Nobel Prize is as often given to a group of people who worked together on a project as to an individual. The people who win Nobel Prizes are stars—but even they work together.

Kappan: How will schoolpeople have to change, in order to use learning teams effectively?

Glasser: Teachers will have to change the way they look at themselves. And to make that possible, administrators will have to change the way they look at teachers.

Too often, today's administrators view teachers as workers who can be stimulated into greater productivity. In schools that operate under the stimulus/response theory, teachers are expected to do what they're told and produce educated students. This view of teachers as workers permeates our whole society.

But a student is not an inert object to be worked on; a student is a human being with needs. And school systems must recognize that everyone will benefit, if the schools satisfy students' needs in ways that encourage students to learn those things that society considers essential. Teachers who simply say to their students, "This is the essential knowledge; learn it," are not effective. That approach works only with those students who agree with this point of view—up to 50% in the best schools and a lot less in most schools.

Kappan: Then what is the teacher's role?

Glasser: The teacher's job is to facilitate. I don't like to use the word *motivate,* because it's an "external" word. Like the rest of us, students have plenty of motivation. The question is, Will they be motivated to learn what we believe they should learn? We can't force "our" knowledge down students' throats —though that's what the public

> **T**eachers can't make students learn, but they can certainly set things up so that students want to learn.

is asking teachers to do, in a sense, when it tells teachers to raise Scholastic Aptitude Test scores. *Teachers* can't raise SAT scores. Teachers can only teach in a way that makes students *want* to learn. When students learn, they do well on the SAT.

The teacher's role is to set up a workplace that persuades students to say, "Aha! I see that, if I work in this place, it's going to satisfy me. I see, in this place, that knowledge is power." Teachers can't *make* students learn, but they can certainly set things up so that students *want* to learn.

As I note in my book, you can lead a horse to water, but you can't make him drink. However, Madeline Hunter (a good friend of mine and an outstanding educator) points out that you can't make him drink, but you *can* put some salt in his oats. And she's 100% correct. The teacher who's a good manager will figure out how to put some salt in the oats. That's what *Control Theory in the Classroom* is all about.

Kappan: In addition to changing their role rather radically, in the ways that you've just described, what other problems will teachers face as they try to implement learning teams? And how can they cope with those problems?

Glasser: The first thing that teachers will be concerned about is losing power, losing control. They'll ask themselves, "Can I trust students to work together? Will the good students do all the work, while the poor students just hitchhike along? Will students go home and complain, 'Oh, the teacher is making me work in a group, and it's slowing me down'? If they do, how will I handle that problem?"

There are going to be *plenty* of problems. The old way has been in place for centuries. Socrates complained about students being lazy and not paying attention. What I'm trying to do, in a quiet way, is to create a different approach to working with people — be it in the classroom, in the clinic, in the hospital, or in the family. As I point out in my book, control theory applies to all aspects of our lives. But the transition to control theory is going to be difficult.

Kappan: Why do you say that?

Glasser: During the last 50 or 75 years, we've tried all kinds of innovative approaches in education — but almost all of them have been based on stimulus/response psychology. We are now moving further and further into what I call the "identity society" — an affluent society in which most people are less concerned about bare survival and more concerned about their feelings of importance and their sense of belonging. At the same time, we are continuing to use stimulus/response psychology, which is antagonistic to those concerns.

The outcomes are easy to predict: fewer and fewer students will be actively involved in education, and alcohol and drug use (which gives the illusion of satisfaction) will increase. Unaware of control theory, people in power continue to say, "Push them harder; our concern is not what satisfies them, but what satisfies us." Control theory provides an alternative to this outmoded approach.

Kappan: What advice would you give educators who wish to implement control theory in their schools?

Glasser: I propose a three-pronged implementation program: 1) teach control theory to teachers, 2) implement learning teams and other control-theory approaches in the classroom, and 3) teach students control theory, starting in kindergarten. Teach students that they have needs, that they're always trying to satisfy those needs, and that, when they behave well or badly in the classroom, those are *choices* that they are making in an attempt to satisfy their needs.

I'm currently producing a drug education program for schools that will teach students about control theory, so that they know they have choices. Telling students to "just say no" is not enough. Students have to know what the choices are so that, when they say no, they can also say yes to something better. In my experience, students can learn control theory, and they get very excited about it. If the teaching begins in kindergarten or first grade, students can actually begin to use control theory in their own lives well before they enter junior high school.

Kappan: That's an interesting point. Meanwhile, what kinds of assignments would a teacher who uses learning teams have to devise? And would those assignments differ radically from what teachers are doing in classrooms today?

Glasser: Yes, I think that they would. There's no point in assembling a team of students and then telling that team to answer the questions at the end of the chapter. Students can complete an assignment of that sort individually. If a teacher gave a learning team such an assignment, a couple of students would answer the questions, and the others would hitchhike along without really becoming involved. It's as if the basketball coach, knowing John to be a crack shot, didn't bother to set up plays to get the ball to John.

By way of analogy, a teacher might say to a team of four students, "Here are four 50-pound sacks of cement. Will you, as a team, move them outside?" Let's assume that the team includes one big, strong boy. So the others say to him, "You're big and strong. You move the sacks outside." And he's a nice person, so he moves them, while the other members of the team just sit there.

What is needed instead is a *team* assignment, one that can't be completed unless the team works together. A team assignment would require the team to move a 200-pound sack of cement. One student couldn't budge it alone. To move the sack outside, the team would have to work together.

There are a variety of ways to set up good team assignments. My book provides several examples of such assignments—academic tasks that cannot be accomplished adequately by an individual student. A good team assignment also causes students to *want* to work together, because they perceive that together they can do a great job, but independently they can do very little.

Kappan: If a teacher is interested in trying the learning team approach, how should he or she get started?

Glasser: Teachers can start on their own, reading about learning teams and maybe observing a teacher who is experienced in the use of such teams. Later on, some formal training would probably be helpful—and such training is widely available.

A teacher could start independently, but that teacher would find it easier and more fun to work with a group of colleagues who want to try learning teams in their classrooms. Learning with others is not only in the spirit of the model; it *is* the model. A learning team of teachers could start by discussing control theory and trying to understand how it applies to them and to their students. Later on, the teachers could work together to plan good team assignments, and they could actually begin to use learning teams in their classrooms. As other teachers in the building see the new model at work, many of them will also begin to use learning teams.

Kappan: Do learning teams change the way teachers relate to their students?

Glasser: Of course. I've asked a lot of teachers who don't use learning teams, "How many students are actively involved with you in the learning process?" They tend to respond: "Six," "Eight," "10." The number doesn't matter. On their own, these students have formed their own little team. They may still function as individuals, but they get involved in discussions, and they ask the questions. Some of the other students are involved in learning, as well—but about half of the students in every class are not. The teacher doesn't get to know those students, and they feel unimportant.

When the teacher puts the uninvolved students on learning teams, things change, however. As the teacher moves from team to team, spending several minutes with each, the teacher gets to know those students. The teacher sits with them—at their level—and talks directly to them about academic matters. That gives the students a sense of belonging and a sense of importance.

Kappan: Is there any place in a learning-team classroom for large-group instruction?

Glasser: Oh, certainly. Lectures are fine, but teachers can't lecture 180 days a year. That's excessive. There are many creative ways to integrate lectures with learning teams, too. For example, in a 15- or 20-minute lecture, a teacher might supply the basic information about a project or a topic. Then that teacher might ask the students to sit down in learning teams to talk over the information and to raise questions.

I don't think that traditional teaching is 100% bad. Anything that works for 50% of the students in good schools can't be 100% bad. In good schools, though, lecturing is rarely the only approach that teachers use.

Kappan: You've talked a lot about cooperative learning and cooperative team assignments. What place does competition have in a classroom that uses the model of cooperative learning teams?

Glasser: Individual competition is intimidating, and most people shun it unless they believe they have a good chance to win. But human beings often compete as members of teams, and, even when they lose, it's not as devastating. Moreover, individual competition is usually not fair. Some people are more gifted or more determined than others, and they're going to win every time. Teams make competition fairer, and, if one team wins too often, the teacher can redistribute its members.

Robert Slavin uses a lot of competition, especially with elementary students who are learning basic skills. Slavin encourages learning teams to compete with one another, and the students are highly motivated by such activities. They name their teams, form leagues, keep score—but Slavin makes sure that all teams have a chance to win.

Kappan: So you would recommend that teachers incorporate some competition at the team level?

Glasser: I think it's fun to compete, but much competition in this world is unfair. When horses race, the officials put more weight on the fastest horses to even the odds. In school, we tend to do the opposite; using poor grades as a handicap, we put more weight on the poor students and give more opportunities to the good ones. Naturally, the good students always win. Learning teams, by contrast, give students a way to compete that is usually fair.

Kappan: If you had to distill the message of your new book, *Control Theory in the Classroom,* into just a few sentences, what would those sentences be?

Glasser: There is no doubt that knowledge is power, but U.S. schools aren't getting that message across. Most students do not see their schools as places that make them feel important—although that will happen in control-theory schools, as I have explained. In control-theory schools, discipline problems will disappear, the number of teenage pregnancies will drop, drug use will diminish—because all of these are self-destructive ways for young people to gain the sense of power and importance that they aren't finding today in their classrooms.

Kappan: Will implementing control theory in the classroom be costly?

Glasser: No, not at all. Schools are currently spending a disproportionate amount of money on what is, too often, a futile attempt to educate those students who choose not to work in school. Special programs have proliferated—especially programs for the "learning disabled," a group of students whose major disability is that they do not see school or education as need-satisfying.

In a control-theory school, this group would be substantially reduced. The resultant savings would be far larger than the small amount of money it would take to implement the program that I have suggested here. To get started, administrators need only begin to treat teachers as managers. That costs nothing and would benefit the educational system greatly, whether or not the rest of the program were ever put into place. Keep in mind, though, that students whose needs are satisfied learn more and cost less.

READING 3 ARTHUR W. COMBS
Humanistic Education: Too Tender for a Tough World?

Many people regard the humanist movement in education as a fad perpetrated by fuzzy-minded, soft-headed people sadly out of touch with the *real* values of education. Others believe that humanistic education is usurping the prerogatives of home and church. A few even refer to it as "secular humanism" and so regard it as ungodly or antireligious. Still others believe that humanism is a nice idea but much too soft to prepare youth for the tough world of reality. All of these misconceptions only confuse the issues and delay what is an absolute necessity for American education.

What is humanistic education? The Working Group on Humanistic Education of the Association for Supervision and Curriculum Development (ASCD) defined it as follows: Humanistic education is a commitment to educational practice in which all facets of the teaching/learning process give major emphasis to the freedom, value, worth, dignity, and integrity of persons.* More specifically, humanistic education:

1. accepts the learner's needs and purposes and develops experiences and programs around the unique potential of the learner;
2. facilitates self-actualization and strives to develop in all persons a sense of personal adequacy;
3. fosters acquisition of basic skills necessary for living in a multicultured society, including academic, personal, interpersonal, communicative, and economic proficiency.
4. personalizes educational decisions and practices (to this end it includes students in the processes of their own education via democratic involvement at all levels of implementation);
5. recognizes the primacy of human feelings and uses personal values and perceptions as integral factors in educational processes;
6. develops a learning climate that nurtures learning environments perceived by involved individuals as challenging, understanding, supportive, exciting, and free from threat; and
7. develops in learners genuine

From Arthur W. Combs, "Humanistic Education: Too Tender for a Tough World?" *Phi Delta Kappan* (February 1981):446–449. © 1981, Phi Delta Kappan, Inc. Reprinted by permission.

*Arthur W. Combs, ed., *Humanistic Education: Objectives and Assessment* (Alexandria, Va.: ASCD, 1979). This publication also contains a checklist for humanistic schools.

concern and respect for the worth of others and skill in conflict resolution.

The humanist movement is no fad, destined to come into being for a short time and quickly fade away. Quite the contrary, it is part of a worldwide movement in human thinking. It does not exist only in education. There are humanist movements in psychology, sociology, anthropology, political science, theology, philosophy, and medicine. The humanist movement in education is simply another expression of these larger events. If it did not exist, we would have to invent it. There are three major reasons why this is so.

I. CHANGE IN THE NATURE OF HUMANITY'S MOST PRESSING PROBLEMS

A great revolution has been creeping up on us for nearly a hundred years, but especially so in the last 30. Since the first appearance of human beings on earth, the major problem of humankind has been control of the environment. For at least a million years people were engaged in a continuous struggle to wrest from their environment food, clothing, shelter, and personal or collective power for the safety and welfare of themselves and those they cared for. For a million years that goal was the paramount problem facing humanity. With the coming of science and industry all of that has changed. The fantastic discoveries of science have provided the know-how to feed, clothe, and house the entire world. At the same time, engineering and industry have provided the techniques to put that knowledge into practice, so that we stand today with the know-how and the technology to solve the age-old problem of humankind. If we do not feed, clothe, and house the entire world, it is no longer because we don't know how. If we don't do it, it is because we cannot get ourselves and other human beings to work together to reach that goal.

We have solved our ancient problem only to find ourselves faced with a new one, the people problem. The coming of science and industry has made our society, of necessity, the most interdependent, cooperative one the world has known since the dawn of history. Each of us is totally dependent on other people for even the simplest things of life. Few of us could live more than a few days completely cut off from others. Thousands of people whom we have never seen or heard of are required to provide so simple a requirement as a quart of milk. We are totally dependent upon other people's "doing what they're supposed to."

Moreover, we have created a world in which the power of each individual for good or evil has been enormously increased. The more interdependent a society, the greater the possibilities for individuals to disrupt the system. Today, anyone can buy a gun from a mail-order house. Poisons are available in any seed store. Each of us travels our highways encased in a ton of steel capable at any moment of becoming an engine of death and destruction for dozens of other people. It is this utter interdependence that has made it possible for terrorists to threaten multitudes. A few people in the right place at the right time can create international havoc by holding a few hostages, killing a John Kennedy or a Martin Luther King, and so throwing the rest of us into turmoil.

All of this interdependence has made *human* problems the most pressing ones we face. And that pressure is bound to become ever greater. With each new technological discovery we become more utterly dependent upon each other. We have left the era of the physical sciences and entered the era of the social sciences.

To live successfully in an increasingly interdependent world requires, at the very least, intelligent citizens who understand themselves and the dynamics of human interaction and who can be counted on to pull their own weight, to be concerned for other people, and to behave as responsible, problem-solving human beings.

Intelligent problem solvers are absolutely essential in an increasingly complex world. Education in the past could be content with providing youth with the basic skills to deal with "things." That is no longer enough for the world into which we are moving. The future already upon us calls for education that prepares young people to understand themselves and human interaction. Our society can get along very well with a bad reader; a bigot is a danger to everyone. We have done a great deal about reading, very little about bigotry.

A glance around shows the truth of my assertion that our gravest problems are human ones. Problems of population, pollution, ecology, energy, poverty, war, peace, civil rights, starvation, physical and mental health, and terrorism are all essentially human problems. Even the atom bomb is a human rather than a technical problem. It is not the bombs we need fear but the persons who might use them. And the futurists tell us that this is only the beginning. The one characteristic of the future they predict with absolute certainty is that problems of personal growth and human interaction will become increasingly critical.

This great revolution in human thought has evolved so gradually that few people are even aware of its existence. Our public schools, charged with the responsibility of training youths for the future, ought to be among the first institutions to be aware of and to adapt to new data about the world into which we are moving. Unfortunately, most educators are unaware of this revolution, and few schools have made significant adjustments in curricula or practice to meet these new demands. It is fascinating, for example, that the social sciences of psychology, sociology, anthropology, and political science—specifically constructed to deal with human problems—are each more than a hundred years old. Yet in most places they have not yet been admitted to the curricula of our public schools except, occasionally, as an elective course for high school seniors—and then only as a "reward" for good grades in traditional courses.

The standard curriculum is no longer enough to prepare today's youths for the world they will enter; adherents of humanistic education believe that our public schools must pay far greater attention to the human condition. A new focus on the *person in the process* is needed. The healthy growth of students as persons—with clear understanding of the dynamics of human interaction and in possession of personal skills for living effectively with other people—must find an important place among the primary objectives for today's, and tomorrow's, schools.

II. CONCERN FOR THE INNER LIFE OF STUDENTS

The majority of today's teachers and administrators were schooled in some form of behavioristic psychology as the theoretical base for their professional thinking. Such views concentrate attention primarily upon behavior and the external conditions that produce it. Stimulus-response psychology, for example, concentrates attention on manipulation of the stimulus to produce desired behaviors. More recently, behavior modification concentrates attention on the consequents of behavior to achieve behavior change. Such frames of reference regard the student as object—to be made, molded, formed in some preconceived image—while motivation becomes a problem of manipulating stimuli or consequents in such a fashion as to produce behavior desired by the teacher. Such conceptions are often used in producing precisely defined behaviors such as fundamental skills of reading or mathematics. They are also useful for managing people when desired behaviors can be precisely defined in advance and the means of control are available to the teacher.

Lately, however, perceptual/humanistic psychology has provided us with another view of persons extending beyond behaviorism to provide new possibilities for human growth and development. This new view holds that behavior is only a symptom. The *causes* of behavior are deemed a more adequate basis for professional decisions. Few of us, after all, would be very happy going to a physician who dealt only with our symptoms. Perceptual/humanistic psychologists point out that people do not behave according to the facts. When people misbehave, it is rarely because they do not know what they "ought" to do. The causes of behavior lie, rather, in people's beliefs, feelings, attitudes, likes, dislikes, hopes, fears, aspirations, and goals. These are the primary determinants of behavior. They are also the characteristics that make us human and the reason for the label "humanistic education." Humanistic educators believe that, in order to produce the healthy, responsible, effective persons the future demands, educational processes must deal not only with student behavior but also with the inner life of students, especially with student self-concepts, values, and feelings.

Perhaps the most important single contribution of humanistic psychology over the past 30 years has been recognition of the crucial importance of the self-concept to every aspect of human growth and behavior. A person's image or beliefs of self are a vital part of his or her every activity. People behave in terms of what they believe about themselves. People who believe they can, do; people who believe they cannot, avoid the confrontation. Exhaustive research has shown us that the self-concept is a vital factor in a person's success or failure in school, on the job, or in social interaction. It is also a vital factor in determining psychological health or adjustment. Healthy people see themselves in positive ways as liked, wanted, acceptable, able persons of dignity and integrity. The opposites of such self-perceptions are characteristic of delinquents, criminals, and the mentally ill. Since the self-concept is learned from experience, it cannot be ignored as an important factor in education. Student self-concepts control what students learn. They are also subject to change for better or worse by student experiences in school.

The future requires responsible citizens skilled in social interaction and capable of effective problem solving *on the spot*. To live successfully in a world of ever-increasing choices calls for persons with clear conceptions of what is good, right, and desirable. People's values determine their choices. *An effective school system cannot ignore so vital a factor in the preparation of youth.* Since people behave in terms of their values, value exploration must be an important objective in the curriculum. This does not mean schools must "teach" values in the sense of deciding what values students should hold and then indoctrinating them. Values are personal, private, internal characteristics derived from personal experience, exploration, and discovery. This calls for schools that, on the one hand, demonstrate positive values in every aspect of their organization and practice and, on the other, encourage and facilitate student exploration of values throughout the system.

Since human feelings, attitudes, and beliefs are basic to behavior, they must rank high on any list of public school objectives. Controlling behavior is dealing only with symptoms. Changes in feelings, attitudes, and beliefs can make behavior control unnecessary. The behavior of a black child picking on a white one can be controlled by a teacher's using methods of behavior modification so that the black child learns not to pick on the white one —at least in that teacher's class or when that teacher is in the neighborhood. If the same child, however, can be helped to see his white classmate as "a kid just like me," as someone with similar problems, as someone who likes many of the same things, then the aggressive behavior may disappear of itself, not just temporarily while the teacher is around but for all time.

It is indeed strange that so many people, inside and outside professional education, have come to believe that schools should only be objective. Several years ago I reviewed the objectives for public education, from the early schools in Massachusetts right down to the latest White House conference. I was impressed with the fact that the objectives America has asked of its schools over and over again can be neatly encompassed in the famous Seven Cardinal Principles. In addition to the acquisition of basic skills in reading, writing, and arithmetic, we have *always* called for education for worthy home membership, for civic responsibility, for physical and mental health, for vocational preparation, for beneficial use of leisure time, and for moral and ethical conduct. Such objectives cannot be attained by treating students as objects. Nor can they be accomplished by complete objectivity or by dealing solely with facts. Most of the items on that list can only be achieved as a function of student values, feelings, beliefs, and attitudes. Advocates of humanistic education believe that our educational system can only hope to meet its long-standing goals for youths through recognition of the central importance of the internal life of students. Acceptance of the characteristics that make us human must be a prime factor in all aspects of organization and practice.

II. LEARNING IS A PERSONAL, HUMANISTIC, AFFECTIVE PROCESS

In the behavioral view of learning, teaching is regarded as a management problem having to do with the manipulation of stimuli or consequents to produce clearly defined behavioral outcomes. Such a view can provide important guidelines for teaching when goals can be precisely stated in behavioral terms and when the control of stimuli and consequents are readily available to teachers. These conditions are often present in the early grades. They are less and less in evidence as we climb the educational ladder to increasingly complex content. Process goals such as problem solving, intelligent behavior, and effective interaction also do not lend themselves to precise behavioral definition. For such conditions a more adequate concept of learning is needed.

Fortunately, humanistic thinking has provided us with a second view of learning that is capable of providing more adequate guidelines for teaching complex subject matter or facilitating the learning of process goals. Perceptual/humanistic psychologists point out that learning always has two parts: exposure to new information or experience, on the one hand, and the personal discovery of meaning on the other. Most educators know very well how to deal with the first of those two facets. We are experts at giving people information. We have been doing it for years. It is the thing we know how to do best. Helping students discover the personal meaning of information is a very different matter and the source of most of our failures. The dropout, for example, is not a dropout because we didn't *tell* him or her. We did that, over and over. The student dropped out because he or she never discovered the personal meaning of what we had to offer.

Learning, from a perceptual orientation, is understood as the personal discovery of meaning. Its basic principle might be stated thus: Any information will affect a person's behavior only insofar as he or she has discovered the personal meaning of that information. As an example, let us suppose that I turn on my car radio while driving to work and hear the latest hog market quotations. Since I have no hogs, this information drifts through my consciousness, in one ear and out the other with no effect on my behavior. Next I hear a report of an auto accident this morning in the neighborhood of my university. I hear that Mrs. Joe Brown has been seriously injured and taken to the hospital. This information has a little more meaning to me. I do not know Mrs. Brown, but I am riding in a car, so I think to myself, "That's a terrible thing. Another accident. Something ought to be done about it!" And I slow down for a block or two. Now suppose I recognize that Mrs. Joe Brown is the wife of one of my colleagues. Suddenly this same information has more meaning to me and affects my behavior accordingly. I think about it all the way to the office. I talk to my secretary and other colleagues on the faculty. It becomes a matter for conversation and concern. Let's go one step further: If Mrs. Brown happens to be the name of my married daughter, my behavior may be violently affected as I drop everything and race to the hospital. The more important the personal meaning, the greater the effect on behavior. This explains in large part why so much of what we learn in school has so little effect. We never discovered its personal meaning.

Effective learning is also *affective.* We experience feelings or emotion when events are important to us. For example, a young woman with a lover overseas hears that he will be home in six months. That is not much to be excited about. Then she hears he will be home next month, then next week. He's on his way. He's back in the country. It's time to go to the airport. Here comes his plane! There he is! The closer an event is perceived to the self, the greater the degree of emotion experienced.

Affect or feeling is an indicator of the degree of personal meaning. In light of that fact, if education is not affective, it is probable that little of significance has occurred. The hysterical opposition to affective education that has become manifest in some quarters is also downright destructive. Significant learning is always accompanied by emotion or feeling, and classrooms that rule it out simultaneously reduce their effectiveness.

Learning is a deeply human, personal, affective experience. Humanists point out that it is also profoundly influenced by student self-concepts, values, personal need, experience of challenge and threat, and the learner's feelings of belonging or identification:

Self-concept—People behave according to their beliefs. As I mentioned earlier, students who believe they can, will. Students who do not will find ingenious ways to avoid involvement. People learn best when they see themselves in positive ways.

Values—Values provide the criteria by which we make our choices. People seek what they value and avoid what they do not. Students who value what they are being taught are eager learners. Schools that ignore the values of students are ignoring important determinants of the very education they are charged with producing.

Personal need—If there is one thing psychologists know about learning, it is that people learn best when they have a need to know. People work hard for things they need. They ignore or avoid what seems irrelevant or destructive to their personal fulfillment. For generations schools have been trying to teach pupils "what they will need to know some day," while students are preoccupied by what they need in the here-and-now.

Challenge or threat—The discovery of personal meaning is deeply affected by student experience of challenge or threat. People are challenged by goals that interest them and that they believe they can achieve. People are threatened by events with which they feel inadequate to cope. It follows, then, that schools must find ways of challenging students without threatening them.

Feeling of belonging, identification—Effective learning is also deeply influenced by student feelings of belonging or being cared for. One need but compare the words we use to describe our feelings of belonging and those we use to describe our feelings of alienation. For most people the experience of belonging is accompanied by feelings of excitement, interest, desire to be involved, and the like. Feelings of alienation, on the other hand, are often accompanied by desire to avoid embarrassment or humiliation and by feelings of dejection, apathy, disappointment, anger, or hostility. Which of these sets of feelings is more likely to result in effective learning? The answer is self-evident.

If learning is personal and affective, conditions that induce feelings of belonging should be apparent in the classroom. If learning is deeply affected by student self-concepts, values, needs, and feelings of challenge and belonging, those facts must find expression in educational thinking and practice. Humanistic teachers and administrators are trying to do just that in the philosophy they espouse and the practices they employ.

To recapitulate, humanistic education is an absolute necessity for three reasons: 1) Everything we know about the world into which we are moving demands responsible citizens capable of understanding and dealing with human problems with which they will inevitably be faced. 2) Since the causes of behavior lie in the qualities that make us human—our feelings, attitudes, beliefs, values, understandings, hopes, and aspirations—an effective educational system must deal with such matters to fulfill its obligations to youth and our society. 3) Humanistic education is essential because learning itself is a deeply human, personal, affective process.

Humanistic education is no fad, no flash in the pan. It is firmly rooted in new conceptions of the nature of the human organism, the causation of behavior, and the processes of learning. These are facts of life. They will not go away, and they cannot be ignored because they are inconvenient. To do so is as silly as saying, "I know my car needs a carburetor, but I'm going to run mine without one!"

We educators are great faddists. We keep hoping some gadget, gimmick, method, organization, or legislative or administrative mandate is going to save us. Over the years we have seen them come and go by the dozens—radio, television, audiovisual, teaching machines, new math, new science, languages in the early grades, paraprofessionals, open schools and open classrooms, phonics, programmed instruction, and, most recently, behavioral objectives, competency-based instruction, and back-to-basics. Some people believe that humanistic education is destined to run a similar course and quietly fade away.

Such a notion is a serious mistake. Humanistic education is not a gadget, not a gimmick, not even a method, technique, or way of organizing. It is an understanding about the human condition, what people are like, how they behave and learn, and what problems they face. Methods, techniques, and ways of organizing may come and go. Basic changes in thinking about people and learning can last for generations.

The humanist movement is here to stay. When I began teaching in 1935 there were very few humanistic teachers around. Today there are thousands and the number keeps growing. They do not fly banners or advertise their allegiances. They are only beginning to develop formal organizations to advance their interests. Many would be surprised to hear themselves described as humanistic teachers. They understand humanist thinking and apply it in their teaching but have never adopted the humanist label. I have even seen humanistic teachers operating successfully in schools and systems under the direction of autocratic, dictatorial administrators.

That students and teachers are happier in humanistic schools and classrooms is not a sign of weakness. Neither does humanistic education require the surrender of traditional goals and objectives. I am not a humanist simply because I want to go around being nice to people. I am a humanist because I *know* that when I apply humanist thinking to problems in teaching, students learn *anything* better. They will be better writers, readers, mathematicians, farmers, physicians, truck drivers—whatever.

Humanism is no fragile flower, too tender for a tough world. Quite the contrary. It is a systematic, conscious attempt to put into practice the best we know about the nature of human beings and how they learn. That is the scientific approach advocated by educators for generations. Putting humanist thinking to work is not misguided. Ignoring its message is a far greater error. Humanistic education maintains that what students experience about themselves and their world is far too important for education to overlook. Instead, such human considerations must be included in every aspect of educational thinking and practice.

CHAPTER TWO

Effective Schools: What They Are and How They Make a Positive Difference

READING 4 — THOMAS L. GOOD AND RHONA S. WEINSTEIN

Schools Make a Difference: Evidence, Criticisms, and New Directions

Research shows that the school a student attends can make a substantial difference in the education received; schools are not interchangeable. Student progress clearly varies from school to school, but the most important issue is whether variation in achievement among schools is affected by school processes or whether this variation can be explained entirely by differences in students' entering characteristics (e.g., aptitude). If there is meaningful variation among schools in student performance, then it should be possible to improve student performance in many schools.

Until recently, it was generally believed that resources invested in schools, as well as schooling in general, were not related to school performance. Following the publication of the well-known Coleman et

From Thomas L. Good and Rhona S. Weinstein, "Schools Make a Difference: Evidence, Criticisms, and New Directions," *American Psychologist* (October 1986):1090–1097. Copyright 1986 by the American Psychological Association. Adapted by permission of the publisher and authors.

al. (1966) report, many researchers attempted to relate school inputs (e.g., number of books in the library) to school outputs (student achievement). However, this research ignored what took place in schools (e.g., Do teachers take advantage of libraries by allowing students to use them?). Extensive reviews of the input–output literature (e.g., Averch, Carroll, Donaldson, Kiesling, & Pincus, 1974) suggest that these studies fail to provide any consistent evidence for a relationship between school resources and outcomes such as achievement. However, this early research did help clarify a largely overlooked issue—that the utilization of resources was far more important than the level of resources available.

In this article we discuss recent school effectiveness research that includes measures of school processes and addresses how variation in school processes affects student achievement. However, as we argue later in the article, the term *effective*

schools is highly misleading. As critical as this documented variation among schools is, it is important to emphasize that the literature does not provide information about schools that are effective over a broad range of outcomes. Rather, studies primarily inform us about factors associated with students' performance on standardized achievement tests. By now, school effects on student achievement have been thoroughly documented. Continued focus on this question to the neglect of other more compelling questions appears less productive.

We begin by presenting evidence that schools differentially affect student achievement as measured by standardized achievement tests. Then we critique the methodology and conceptions of schools that characterize the research. We examine applications of these findings to the improvement of schools and explore recent conceptions of schooling. Finally, we offer new directions for school research.

SCHOOL EFFECTIVENESS RESEARCH

It should be emphasized that despite the methodological weaknesses that characterize research on effective schools (which will be discussed later), the *consistency of findings* documented across studies provides compelling evidence that differences among schools are associated with different levels of student performance beyond what could be predicted by entering student characteristics. The power of the findings is not in the quality of any one study, but in the fact that investigators from different academic disciplines, using various methodologies, assumptions, and theories, have reached surprisingly similar conclusions about what school factors are associated with higher student scores on standardized achievement tests.

Outlier Case Studies

Outlier studies statistically identify unusually effective and ineffective schools and then examine behavior in those schools to determine what accounts for the differences. We examine two such studies in detail (Brookover, Beady, Flood, Schweitzer, & Wisenbaker, 1979; Rutter, Maughan, Mortimore, Ouston, & Smith, 1979) because they are relatively comprehensive and describe effective schools at the secondary and elementary levels.

A Secondary-school Example
In a sample of 12 secondary schools in London, Rutter et al. (1979) found that despite large differences in student characteristics (e.g., some schools admitted as few as 7% of boys with behavior or reading problems, whereas others took as many as 48% to 50% with such problems), after statistically equating pupil input, substantial and statistically significant differences between schools remained.

The school processes examined were derived from seven broad conceptual areas: academic emphasis, teacher actions in lessons, rewards and punishments, conditions of learning for pupils, pupils' responsibilities and participation in school, stability of teaching, and friendship-group organization. Data on processes were derived from interviews with teachers, pupils' questionnaire responses, and classroom observation (consisting of one week's observation in each school in middle-ability, third-year classes).

The investigators reported large differences in attendance rates across schools, even after differences in student characteristics were controlled. Pupil behavior such as tardiness or being off task or disruptive varied considerably across schools, as did achievement. For example, after adjusting for student characteristics, students in the bottom 25% of verbal ability in the most successful school obtained on the average as many exam passes as did pupils in the top 25% of verbal ability in the least successful school.

Rutter (1983) came to the following conclusions: (a) Secondary schools in inner London differed markedly in the behavior and achievement students showed (after intake differences in students were considered). (b) Individual schools performed fairly similarly on all outcome measures. That is, schools in which students had better-than-average behavior also had students with better achievement and less delinquency. There were some exceptions to this pattern, but the trends were substantial. (c) The differences among schools in outcomes were systematically related not to physical factors such as the size of the school but to school characteristics (e.g., identifiable factors such as academic emphasis and teacher behavior). (d) The association between the combined measure of overall school process and each of the outcome measures was much stronger than was the relationship between any single process variable and outcome measure. This suggests that these various social factors may combine to create a school ethos, or set of values, attitudes, and behaviors that characterize a school.

This important study helps to illustrate the difference between old input–output studies and recent studies of school effects. Rutter et al. (1979) found that physical factors and school resources did not predict student success; however, differences in classroom processes (e.g., academic emphasis) were associated with variation in student achievement. This study collected more and better process data than did previous school-effects studies. Still, the sample of teachers observed in each school and the range of process variables studied provide only a limited view of school life at one grade level. Although generalizing data collected in London to American schooling is an issue, it is clear that American researchers have reached similar conclusions (see Purkey & Smith, 1983).

An Elementary-school Example
Brookover et al. (1979) studied 68 schools drawn from a state pool that represented a random sample of Michigan fourth- and fifth-grade students. Data were obtained from (a) the Michigan School Assessment reports, (b) questionnaires administered to fourth- and fifth-grade students, as well as (c) questionnaires administered to teachers and school principals. Important school variables assessed were (a) social composition of the student body, (b) school social structure, and (c) school climate. Major outcome variables studied were (a) student achievement (average percentage of students who mastered each of the 40 objectives in the Michigan School Assessment Test), (b) self-concept of academic ability, and (c) self-reliance.

Brookover et al. (1979) found that much of the variation in outcomes was explained by complex school social-system characteristics. Brookover et al. (1979) supplemented their statistical analyses with classroom observations and interviews with participants in four low socioeconomic status schools (two high- and two low-achieving schools). They found that teachers in the higher achieving schools spent more time on instruction and that teachers and students had more academic interactions in these schools than in the low-achieving schools.

This study illustrates that student characteristics do not predict student outcomes independent of school processes. Climate variables (although highly correlated with input variables) explained as much variation in achievement as did input variables. Although the data collected in this study do not yield definitive statements about processes in more and less effective schools, they do suggest that schools with comparable resources can have very different climates. The data provide a base on which future studies using a fuller range of dependent measures and more comprehensive observational measures can build.

We have discussed two examples of the numerous diverse studies that have attempted to relate school processes to student outcomes (for an extended review, see Purkey & Smith, 1983). Relatively few of these studies, however, include detailed observational information about school processes (how principals interact with teachers, teacher–teacher communication, teacher–student communication). Hence, many of the claims about effective schooling are based on information from interviews and questionnaires. Having stated this caveat, we now turn to a synthesis of findings from this literature.

Integrative Reviews of School-Effectiveness Research

Not only have there been many attempts to define and study effective schools, there are also reviews that order and integrate studies that have been conducted. Until his untimely death in 1983, Ronald Edmonds had been one of the key figures in the school effectiveness movement. His work was a major, integrative attempt to demonstrate that schools, particularly urban schools serving large minority populations, are not interchangeable and that some schools obtain much better student achievement than others that have similar resources and serve similar populations.

His most salient contribution was a model characterizing effective schools that has stimulated much of the school improvement research now being implemented in many American schools. Edmonds (1983) contended that the characteristics of effective schools are (a) leadership of the principal reflected by substantial attention to the quality of instruction; (b) a pervasive and broadly understood instructional focus; (c) an orderly, safe climate conducive to teaching and learning; (d) teacher behaviors that convey the expectation that all students are to obtain at least minimum mastery; and (e) the use of measures of pupil achievement as the basis for program evaluation.

Purkey and Smith's (1983) review examined various types of school effectiveness research including outlier studies, case studies, surveys, and evaluations, as well as studies of program implementation and theories of organization in schools and other institutions. They found the following variables to be important process measures of school effectiveness: (a) School-site management—a number of studies indicate that the leadership and staff of a school need considerable autonomy in determining how they address problems. (b) Instructional leadership—although Purkey and Smith were suspicious of the "great principal" theory, it seems clear that leadership is necessary to initiate and maintain school improvement (although it does not necessarily have to come from the principal). (c) Staff stability—once a school experiences success, training the staff seems to maintain effectiveness and to promote further success. (d) Curriculum articulation and organization—at the secondary level, a planned, purposeful program of courses seems to be academically more beneficial than an approach that offers many electives and few requirements. (e) Schoolwide staff development—essential change involves altering people's attitudes and behavior as well as providing them with new skills and techniques. (f) Parental involvement and support—although the evidence on this issue is mixed, it is reasonable to assume that parents need to be informed of school goals and school responsibilities. (g) Schoolwide recognition of academic success—a school's culture is partially reflected in its ceremonies, its symbols, and the accomplishments it officially recognizes. (h) Maximized learning time—if schools emphasize academics, then a greater proportion of the school day will be devoted to academic subjects. (i) District support—fundamental change, building-level management, and staff stability all depend on support from the district office.

Purkey and Smith (1983) argued that although the evidence is not quite as strong, other process variables must be present as well: (a) collaborative planning and collegial relationships, (b) a sense of community, (c) clear goals and high expectations, and (d) order and discipline.

There have also been attempts to go beyond lists of characteristics in order to generate explanations of why effective schools work. For example, Cohen (1983) suggested three characteristics of effective schools that can be used to organize existing research. First, school effectiveness is clearly dependent on effective classroom teaching. Second, school effectiveness requires the careful coordination and management of the instructional program at the building level. Finally, effective schools generate a sense of shared values and culture among both students and staff. This integration underlies the necessity to tie together classroom- and school-level variables. . . .

RECENT, COMPREHENSIVE STUDIES OF SCHOOLS AND SCHOOLING

Researchers have begun to study school effects more comprehensively, including the experiences of individuals in schools. There have also been many recent policy reports on schooling—for example, *A Nation At Risk: The Imperative for Educational Reform* (National Commission on Excellence in Education, 1983); *Becoming a Nation of Readers* (National Academy of Education's Commission on Education and Public Policy, 1985); and Boyer's 1983 report—that include important statements about both the deficiencies and potential of schools. In addition, research on schooling has benefited from qualitative studies of selected exemplary schools drawn from diverse populations (private schools, low-income public schools, rich suburban schools, etc., see, e.g., "America's Schools: Portraits and Perspectives," 1981). In this section we review two examples of the new literature that illustrate the diversity of the work and the different levels of reform that are called for.

Goodlad (1984)

One significant recent study of schools is Goodlad's (1984) work *A Place Called School: Prospects for the Future*. In contrast to earlier focused but limited examinations of schooling, Goodlad's effort is strikingly bold and comprehensive. The study sample included 38 elementary and secondary schools serving diverse populations in various communities. Despite some variation found between schools, Goodlad stressed that the general form of schooling is everywhere very much the same. That is, teachers rarely abandon lectures, workbooks, and written exercises in favor of observation of things outside school, examination of primary documents, and collaboration with colleagues. Goodlad pointed out that rewards in most schools are for individual student achievement, and he argued that the division of schooling into subjects and periods encourages a segmented rather than an integrated view of knowledge.

Goodlad (1984) argued that it is important to improve the skills of individual teachers and to provide instructional leadership and positive school expectations (as do other school effectiveness researchers). However, he also pointed out the need to alter the form of schooling itself (e.g., teacher-dominated instruction, little group work). Goodlad's primary concern was reorganizing large schools into smaller units that correspond more closely to the developmental needs of students at various age levels. He emphasized that schools must present major academic knowledge but must also pay more attention to the personal problems and needs of individual students. Reorganization may enable schools to accomplish these tasks better.

Sizer (1984)

Sizer's (1984) *Horace's Compromise: The Dilemma of the American High School* examines teachers, students, and the curriculum in over 100 schools. Sizer contended that any effort to improve American high schools must consider these three factors simultaneously. As did Goodlad, Sizer emphasized the similarity in the structure and purposes of schools. He contended that the framework that includes grades, schedules, calendars, and general rituals is highly uniform in rural, urban, and suburban high schools.

Sizer argued that a basic problem of the high school is mediocrity—that students are not encouraged to be thoughtful. He contended that there are five imperatives for better schools: (a) Give room to teachers and students to work and learn in their own, appropriate ways; (b) insist that students clearly exhibit mastery of schoolwork; (c) use appropriate incentives for students and teachers; (d) focus schoolwork on the *use* of students' minds; and (e) keep the structure of schools simple and thus flexible.

New Definitions of Schooling

Most recent examinations of schooling and policy reports accept the growing consensus that teachers and schools make a difference in student achievement (on conventional measures); however, there is also increasing insistence that schools can and should do more. Thus, although recent studies such as Goodlad's and Sizer's offer new definitions of what schools can and should become, they have not developed methods for assessing those definitions rigorously, that is, for examining classroom and school variables simultaneously. We believe that what is needed at this point, however, is both a new vision of schooling as well as a methodology that is appropriate for understanding how multiple levels of schooling interact to affect educational outcomes. In the section that follows, we go beyond extant information and begin to outline steps necessary for conducting research that will help us both to understand and to design schools for tomorrow.

NEW DIRECTIONS IN SCHOOL EFFECTIVENESS RESEARCH

Considering the wide-reaching findings of this literature, the national climate of school reform, and the enthusiasm of the educational community at large for implementing the qualities identified as characteristics of effective schools, it becomes critical to clearly frame future research efforts in this area. Research must broaden its focus to include student outcomes other than performance on standardized achievement tests. Research must also examine for whom, and for how many, schools are effective. Finally, studies must address variability and coordination of practice within schools and attempt to identify how classroom and school processes combine to create an effective learning environment.

Alternative Outcomes for Schooling

It is beyond the scope of this article to argue that schools should be held accountable for goals other than achievement on standardized tests. Yet research on effectiveness cannot be limited simply by what is currently taught in the majority of the nation's schools. Considering that in the future, computers will rapidly simplify our access to information, the schools' major role will likely shift from providing students with information (a factual approach) toward helping students develop analytical skills for critically evaluating information. In addition to interpretive knowledge, schools need to broaden and diversify what they teach students in the various content areas. For example, many process studies of mathematics show that mathematics is taught as a means of producing exact answers. Relatively little time is spent on mathematical problem solving or on using mathematics for estimation and for dealing with uncertainties, despite the fact that much of our society's application of mathematics involves such activities.

Several recent examinations of schooling also conclude that schools spend too much time developing isolated skills for which students have little enthusiasm and that, over time, students become passive players in the schooling process, simply doing what is required and little else. By expanding the range and diversity of student learning, we increase the opportunities for a variety of students to succeed in school.

The competence at stake concerns not only intellectual gains but also the development of emotional, social, and moral capacities. School is a place where children develop or fail to develop a variety of competencies that come to define self and ability, where friendships with peers are nurtured, and where the role of community member is played out, all during a highly formative period of development. Thus, the building of self-esteem, interpersonal competence, social problem-solving skills, responsibility, and leadership becomes important both in its own right and as a critical underpinning of success in academic learning.

Clearly, future research must identify what goals schools can reasonably be expected to address effectively. Studies must also examine the extent to which these student outcomes are consonant or conflict with each other.

Effective for All Students

A fundamental defining criterion of American schools is their obligation to serve a large number of diverse students in the same place (Cusick, 1983). This obligation reflects what Sarason and Klaber (1985) described as the three major revolutions in our nation's educational policy—compulsory education, desegregation, and mainstreaming. This obligation alters the social context of schooling and raises the questions of how schools are effective, in what ways, for whom, and for how many. Thus, we must consider both *quality* as well as *equality* of opportunity to learn. It is critical that future research on school effectiveness examine how diverse groups of children fare within a school.

A general finding across all the studies that distinguish effective from ineffective schools is the belief on the part of teachers in effective schools that all children can learn and that the school is responsible for that learning. Subsequent studies must systematically explore the conditions under which schools and teachers hold high expectations for the performance of various types of students and how such expectations are perceived by students (Weinstein, 1985).

High expectations for the teachability of all students are hindered by beliefs in a single intelligence that falls in a normal distribution and by a heavy reliance on standardized achievement tests. Instructional practices such as ability-based reading groups and tracking, plus accompanying lock-step curricular differentiation, further reduce the opportunities to examine the range and levels of a child's capacities and to develop high but more differentiated expectations about needed pedagogical interventions.

Rutter (1983) noted that it is unlikely that changes in schooling similar to those in the effective-schools model will reduce the range of individual differences among students. One could argue that it is critical for future studies to examine the consistency of the individual differences obtained. Given a broader model of effective schooling that includes more than demonstrated mastery of basic skills by most students, might not individual differences become less predictable, less related to group membership (such as minority or social class status), and less consistent across subject areas? That is, with changes in the processes of schooling, will more children succeed and will we see a flowering of diverse talent? And can we track these patterns in future research?

Interrelationships Between Classroom and School Processes

Part of the necessary work ahead as we try to conceptualize what makes a school effective is to study the varied levels of schooling and to acknowledge that piecemeal tinkerings will not work—a theme of Sarason's (1982) critique of misguiding and asocial attempts to improve schools. The theoretical model needed to examine these interrelationships is not a simple one because of the nested aspect of relationships; that is, the classroom is a subsystem embedded in a school, a community, and a culture. Ecological models of schooling provide a particularly appropriate paradigm from which to examine interrelationships between kinds of effectiveness, types of students, and conditions of schooling (Bronfenbrenner, 1977; Hamilton, 1983).

Researchers need to examine school and classroom processes simultaneously, identifying interrelationships that facilitate or hinder goals at each level. Research efforts need to focus on instruction at both levels as well as on the conditions that lead to high-quality instruction. What are the learning opportunities for students—the opportunities for practice, display, and reward of learning accomplishments? Far more is known about effective classroom teaching than about effective school-level learning processes for students (e.g., participation in school newspapers and journals, and school-wide assemblies). How consistent are effective practices across classrooms and grade levels? To what extent can school processes overcome weak classroom teaching and to what extent does strong classroom teaching depend on school support? How are these class and school activities planned, coordinated, and managed? By whom and in what form?

What processes facilitate effective instruction in the classroom and in the school at large? Differences in teaching styles are not only inevitable but in many circumstances have positive effects on students. Thus, there is no need for teachers in the same building or the same school system to utilize similar styles and practices. The idea of working with peers is to exchange ideas and to improve instruction; the goal is not to match or to model someone else's behavior. However, if schools themselves are to significantly affect student outcomes, teachers must be cognizant of how other teachers in the same school teach, including teachers at other grade levels.

What we are discussing here is broader than teachers simply sharing information. We refer to a sense of community among teachers who attempt to develop appropriate, positive expectations for all students and to challenge and stimulate students by use of information obtained in carefully planned and coordinated discussions with other teachers.

CONCLUSION

In this article we argue that schools make a difference. Variation in achievement among schools serving similar populations is often substantial and has significant implications for social policy. We believe that teaching-effects and school-effects research provides needed and long-awaited evidence that variation in teaching and schooling is associated with important differences in student achievement. We agree with Resnick (1984) that "we must now make it possible for everyone to meet standards of educational performance that once were expected of a much smaller segment of the population" (p. 36).

We stress the need for future research to move beyond narrow schooling outcomes and beyond extant school processes. Researchers now need to examine in more detail why variation among schools occurs and whether most schools can educate students in areas where few schools presently achieve success. We believe that schools can jointly address issues of equality and excellence, and we have described some dimensions with which researchers can study these issues. Careful, systematic research must test theories concerning how the factors that characterize effective schools interact in various contexts.

Although reports like *A Nation At Risk* (National Commission on Excellence in Education, 1983) and *Becoming a Nation of Readers* (National Academy of Education's Commission on Education and Public Policy, 1985) have spurred general interest in schooling, it is now time for the development of expanded models of effective schools—models built on and tested by new types of research. Increased funding will be necessary for conducting this research. Further, we hope that in the future, research by a wider range of social scientists will complement the efforts of the relatively small number of scholars who currently explore school environments. If public education is to be understood and improved, it must be studied using diverse theoretical frameworks. We need studies that examine extant practice, but we also need researchers who build new models of what schools can be and who are willing to help implement these strategies in the complex social settings in which school-effects research—its strengths and weaknesses—and our suggestions for future research will stimulate social scientists to study schooling.

REFERENCES

America's schools: Portraits and perspectives [Special issue]. (1981, Fall). *Daedalus*.

Averch, H. A., Carroll, S. J., Donaldson, T. S., Kiesling, H. J., & Pincus, J.

(1974). *How effective is schooling? A critical review of research.* Santa Monica, CA: Rand Corporation.
Boyer, E. L. (1983). *High school: A report on secondary education in America.* New York: Harper & Row.
Bronfenbrenner, U. (1977). Toward an experimental ecology of human development. *American Psychologist, 32,* 513–531.
Brookover, W. B., Beady, C., Flood, P., Schweitzer, J., & Wisenbaker, J. (1979). *School social systems and student achievement: Schools can make a difference.* New York: Praeger.
Cohen, M. (1983). Instructional, management and social conditions in effective schools. In A. Webb & L. Webb (Eds.), *School finance and school improvement: Linkages in the 1980's.* Cambridge, MA: Ballinger.
Coleman, J., Campbell, E., Hobson, C., McPartland, J., Mood, A., Weinfield, F., & York, R. (1966). *Equality of educational opportunity.* Washington, DC: U.S. Government Printing Office.
Cusick, P. A. (1983). *The egalitarian ideal and the American high school: Studies of three schools.* New York: Longman.
Edmonds, R. R. (1983). *Search for effective schools: The identification and analysis of city schools that are instructionally effective for poor children* (Final report). East Lansing: Michigan State University.
Goodlad, J. I. (1984). *A place called school: Prospects for the future.* New York: McGraw-Hill.
Hamilton, S. F. (1983). The social side of schooling: Ecological studies of classrooms and schools. *Elementary School Journal, 83,* 313–334.
National Academy of Education's Commission on Education and Public Policy. (1985). *Becoming a nation of readers* (Report of the Commission on Reading). Washington, DC: National Institute of Education.
National Commission on Excellence in Education. (1983). *A nation at risk: The imperative for educational reform.* Washington, DC: National Institute of Education.
Purkey, S. C., & Smith, M. S. (1983). Effective schools: A review. *Elementary School Journal, 83*(4), 427–452.
Resnick, L. B. (1984). *Cognitive science as educational research: Why we need it now.* Washington, DC: National Academy of Education.
Rutter, M. (1983). School effects on pupil progress: Research findings and policy implications. In L. Shulman & G. Sykes (Eds.), *Handbook of teaching and policy* (pp. 3–41). New York: Longman.
Rutter, M., Maughan, B., Mortimore, P., Ouston, J., & Smith, A. (1979). *Fifteen thousand hours: Secondary schools and their effects on children.* Cambridge, MA: Harvard University Press.
Sarason, S. B. (1982). *The culture of the school and the problem of change* (2nd ed.). Boston: Allyn & Bacon.
Sarason, S. B., & Klaber, M. (1985). The school as a social situation. *Annual Review of Psychology, 36,* 115–140.
Sizer, T. (1984). *Horace's compromise: The dilemma of the American high school.* Boston: Houghton Mifflin.
Snow, R. E. (1986). Individual differences and the design of educational programs. *American Psychologist, 41,* 1029–1039.
Tittle, C. K. (1986). Gender research and education. *American Psychologist, 41,* 1161–1168.
Weinstein, R. S. (1985). Student mediation of classroom expectancy effects. In J. B. Dusek (Ed.), *Teacher expectancies* (pp. 329–350). Hillsdale, NJ: Erlbaum.

READING 5   PETER MORTIMORE AND PAM SAMMONS
New Evidence of Effective Elementary Schools

Teachers and researchers have long debated what makes some schools better than others. To investigate this question, the Inner London Education Authority conducted a four-year study of the effectiveness of elementary education. If some schools are more effective in promoting students' learning and development, what factors contribute to the positive effects?

From Peter Mortimore and Pam Sammons, "New Evidence of Effective Elementary Schools," *Educational Leadership* (September 1987):4–8. Reprinted with permission of the Association for Supervision and Curriculum Development. Copyright © 1987 by ASCD. All rights reserved.

From detailed examination of our data, we found that much of the variation between schools can be accounted for by differences in school policies and practices within control of the principal and teachers. From this, we were able to identify 12 key factors that combine to form a picture of what constitutes effective elementary education.

BACKGROUND FOR THE STUDY

Coleman and colleagues (1966) and later Jencks and colleagues (1972) argue that differences among schools have relatively little impact on student achievement. Both classroom practitioners and research at the elementary school level (Weber 1971, Brookover et al. 1976, Edmonds et al. 1979) have challenged this conclusion. Similarly, Summers and Wolfe (1977) and Goodlad (1979) have disputed the claim that high schools have little influence and suggest that some have powerful effects upon their students.

In the United Kingdom most research on school effects has been conducted in secondary schools (see

Madaus et al. 1979 and Rutter et al. 1979), and results have pointed to substantial differences among schools. In both the United States and the United Kingdom theoretical and methodological issues have been extensively debated. Some studies failed to control fully for the different backgrounds of students entering the schools. Most focused only on reading and mathematics. Though valuable, such studies have frequently suffered from conceptual and methodological weaknesses, as the reviews by Purkey and Smith (1983) noted.

We began our study in September 1980, when nearly 2,000 seven-year-olds entered school, and concluded it four years later when the students transferred to high schools.[1] Our randomly selected sample of 50 elementary school, from a total of 636 within our jurisdiction, proved to be representative of both schools and students in the area served by the Inner London Education Authority.

Our study attempted to answer three questions.

1. Are some schools more effective than others in promoting students' learning and development, when account is taken of variations in the students' backgrounds?
2. Are some schools more effective than others for particular groups of children (for girls or boys, for those of different social class origins or different racial backgrounds)?
3. If some schools are more effective than others, what factors contribute to such positive effects?

Our colleagues comprised an interdisciplinary group of researchers and experienced elementary teachers. We worked together as a team for four years. In our view it was crucial that teachers were involved both in designing the study and in working directly as field officers with the schools in the sample.

INFORMATION ABOUT STUDENTS, SCHOOLS, AND TEACHERS

In order to answer the questions we had set ourselves, we collected information on three topics: students' characteristics, students' learning and development, and school characteristics.

For each child in the 50 schools, we obtained detailed information about social, ethnic, language, and family background; kindergarten experiences; and initial attainments at entry to elementary school. We needed these data to establish the impact of background factors on students' attainments, progress, and development; to take into account differences among school populations; to quantify the relative importance of school experience compared with background as influences; and to explore the effectiveness of schooling for different groups.

The second set of information we gathered related to students' learning and development, and our interest went beyond their attainment in basic skills. So, in addition to reading and written math, we examined students' practical math skills. To assess creative writing, we used measures which included the quality of language and ideas, as well as more technical aspects. To broaden our assessment of language, we also studied students' speaking skills. Our assessments of speech focused on the ability to communicate effectively, and children were not penalized for using nonstandard English.

We were equally interested in the social outcomes of education, which previous studies of school differences have tended to neglect. We sought information, therefore, about students' attendance, their behavior in school, their attitude toward school and various school activities, and their self-concepts, including perceptions of themselves as learners.

The third set of information we collected related to the schools' characteristics, their organization, and the learning environment experienced by students. Field officers also made detailed observations and kept extensive field notes about teachers and students in the classroom.

MEASURING SCHOOL EFFECTS

Our intention was to determine the impact of schools on students' progress and development, once account had been taken of attainment at entry to elementary school and of the influences of age, sex, and other background factors. Therefore, each student's initial attainment at entry was the baseline against which we measured his or her progress during later years.

We found strong relationships between background factors (especially age, social class, sex, and race) and students' attainment and development and, to a lesser extent, relationships between these factors and their progress during the elementary years. Full account, therefore, had to be taken of these relationships before we could examine schools' effects on their students.

SCHOOL DIFFERENCES

Even after controlling for characteristics on entry to school, however, our data show, in answer to our first question, that the school contributed substantially to students' progress and development. In fact, for many of the educational outcomes —especially progress in cognitive areas—the school is much more important than background factors

---

[1] British elementary school is for four years.

in accounting for variations among individuals.

In our measurement of reading progress, we found the school to be about six times more important than background. For written math and writing, the difference is tenfold. The analyses of speech and of the social outcomes also confirm the overriding importance of school.

We calculated the size of the effects of each school on each of our measures of educational outcomes and found striking differences between the least and the most effective schools. If we take reading as one example, the most effective school improved a student's attainment by an average of 15 points above that predicted by each child's attainment at entry to elementary school, taking into account personal background. But in the least effective school, each child's attainment was on average 10 points lower than predicted. This outcome compares with an overall average reading score for all students of 54 points, with a maximum possible of 100.

Of the 50 schools, 14 had positive effects on students' progress and development in most of the cognitive and noncognitive outcomes. These can be seen as the generally effective schools. In contrast, five schools were rather ineffective in most areas.

EFFECTS ON DIFFERENT GROUPS

To answer our second question, we compared the schools' effects on the progress of different groups of students. Generally, however, we found that schools which are effective in promoting the progress of one group are also effective for other groups, and those that are less effective for one group are also less effective for others. An effective school tends to "jack" up the performance of all students irrespective

> Even after controlling for characteristics on entry to school, our data show that the school contributed substantially to students' progress and development.

of their sex, social class origins, or race. Moreover, the evidence indicates that although overall differences in attainment were not removed, on average a student from a blue-collar worker's family attending an effective school achieved more highly than one from a white-collar family background attending one of the least effective schools.

UNDERSTANDING SCHOOL EFFECTIVENESS

In order to answer our third question, we needed to establish what factors and processes are related to positive school effects. In other words, how do the more effective schools differ from those which are less effective?

We found that much of the variation among schools in their effects on students' progress and development is accounted for by differences in school policies and practices. Furthermore, a number of the significant variables are themselves associated. Through a detailed examination of the ways in which classroom and school processes are interrelated, we gained a greater understanding of the important mechanisms by which effective education is promoted.

From these analyses, we identified a number of factors that might account for the differential effectiveness of schools. These factors are not purely statistical constructs obtained solely through quantitative analysis. Rather, they are derived from a combination of careful examination and discussion of the statistical findings and an interpretation of the research results by an interdisciplinary team of researchers and teachers.

We found that although some schools are more advantaged in terms of their size, status, environment, and stability of teaching staff, these favorable characteristics do not, by themselves, ensure effectiveness. They provide a supporting framework within which the principal and teachers can work to promote student progress and development. However, it is the policies and processes within the control of the principal and teachers that are crucial. These factors can be changed and improved.

Our work identified 12 key factors of effectiveness.

1. *Purposeful leadership of the staff by the principal.* "Purposeful leadership" occurs where the principal understands the needs of the school and is actively involved in the school's work, without exerting total control over the staff. In effective schools, principals are involved in curriculum discussions and influence the content of guidelines. They also influence teachers' strategies, but only selectively, where they judge it necessary. These leaders also believe in monitoring students' progress through the years.

2. *Involvement of the assistant principal.* Assistant principals can play a major role in the effectiveness of elementary schools. Our findings indicate that where the assistant principal is absent frequently or for a prolonged period, students' progress and development suffer. Also important are the responsibilities undertaken by assistant principals. Where the principal involves

the assistant in policy decisions, students benefit. This is particularly true in terms of allocating teachers to classes.

3. *Involvement of teachers.* In successful schools, teachers are involved in curriculum planning and participate in developing their own curriculum guidelines. As with the assistant principal, teacher involvement in decisions concerning which classes they are to teach is important. Similarly, discussion with teachers about decisions on resource spending is important. Schools in which teachers are consulted on policy issues as well as issues affecting them directly appear to be more successful.

4. *Consistency among teachers.* Students benefit not only from continuity of staffing but also from consistency in teacher approach. For example, in schools where all teachers follow guidelines in the same way (whether closely or selectively), the impact on students' progress is positive. Variation among teachers in their use of guidelines has a negative effect.

5. *Structured sessions.* Students benefit when their school day has sufficient structure. In effective schools, teachers organize the work and ensure that students always have plenty to do. In general, teachers who organize a framework within which students can work, yet allow them some freedom within this structure, are most successful.

6. *Intellectually challenging teaching.* Unsurprisingly, progress is greater in classes where students are stimulated and challenged. The content of teachers' communications is vitally important. Positive effects occur where teachers communicate interest and enthusiasm to the children and use higher-order questions and statements that encourage them to use creative imagination and powers of problem solving. On the other hand, teachers who more frequently direct students' work without discussing it or explaining its purpose have a negative impact.

Creating a challenge for students suggests that the teacher believes they are capable of responding to it. That effective teachers have high expectations is further seen in their encouraging students to take responsibility for managing individual pieces of work.

7. *Work-centered environment.* A high level of industry in the classroom characterizes a work-centered environment. Students appear to enjoy their work and are eager to commence new tasks. The noise level is also low, although this is not to say that there is silence in the classroom. Furthermore, movement around the classroom is not excessive and is generally work-related.

In schools where teachers spend more of their time discussing the content of work and less time on routine matters and the maintenance of work activity, the impact is positive. Students also seem to benefit when teachers take the time to give them feedback about their work.

8. *Limited focus within sessions.* Learning appears to be facilitated when teachers devote their energies to work in one particular curriculum area within a session, although at times, work can be undertaken in two areas and also produce positive effects. However, where sessions are organized such that three or more curriculum areas are concurrent, students' progress is marred. A focus upon one curriculum area does not imply that all students are doing exactly the same work. Variation exists both in terms of choice of topic and level of difficulty. Positive effects occur where the teacher gears the level of work to individual needs.

9. *Maximum communication between teachers and students.* Students gain from having frequent communication with the teacher, either individually or with the whole class. Because most teachers in our study devoted the majority of their attention to speaking with individuals, each child could expect to receive only a few individual contacts each day (on average only 11). By speaking to the whole class, teachers can increase the overall number of contacts with children and, in particular, those of a higher order. Furthermore, where children work in a single curriculum area within sessions (even if they are engaged in individual or group tasks), it is easier for teachers to raise an intellectually challenging point with all students.

10. *Record keeping.* The value of record keeping has already been noted in relation to the purposeful leadership of the principal; however, it is also an important aspect of teachers' planning and assessment. Where teachers report keeping written records of individuals' work and using them to monitor progress, the impact is positive.

11. *Parental involvement.* Our research found parental involvement to be a positive influence upon students' progress and development. Parental involvement includes helping in classrooms and on educational visits and meeting with school staff to discuss their children's progress. The principal's accessibility to parents is also important; schools with an informal "open-door" policy are more effective. Parental involvement in students' educational development within the home is also beneficial. Parents who read to their children, listen to them read, and provide them with access to books at home affect their children's learning in a positive way.

12. *Positive climate.* Our study confirms that an effective school has a positive ethos. Both around the school and within the classroom, results are favorable when there is less emphasis on punishment and critical control and greater attention to praising and re-

> For many of the educational outcomes— especially progress in cognitive areas—the school is much more important than background factors in accounting for variations among individuals.

warding students. Teachers contribute to children's progress and development by encouraging self-control, not stressing the negative aspects of their behavior. What appears to be important is firm but fair classroom management.

Teachers who obviously enjoy teaching and communicate this to their students contribute to a favorable climate. They aid their children's progress by taking a personal interest in them and by devoting time to nonschool discussion or "small talk." Outside the classroom, teachers create a positive atmosphere by organizing lunchtime and after-school clubs, eating lunch at the same tables with the children, organizing trips and visits, and using the local environment as a learning resource.

The climate created by teachers for students *and* by the principal for teachers is an important aspect of a school's effectiveness. Where teachers have preparation time, the impact on student progress and development is noticeable. Furthermore, positive climate appears to be reflected in effective schools by happy, well-behaved students who are friendly toward each other and outsiders and by the absence of graffiti around the school.

EFFECTIVE ELEMENTARY SCHOOLS

From our detailed examination of the factors and processes related to schools' effects, a picture evolves of what constitutes effective elementary education. We have described only briefly the 12 key factors, and these factors depend on specific behaviors and strategies employed by the principal and staff. The school and the classroom are in many ways interlocked: what the teacher can or cannot do often depends on what is happening in the school as a whole.

Thus, while the 12 factors do not constitute a "recipe" for effective elementary schooling, we feel that they provide a framework within which the various partners in the life of the school—principal and staff, parents and students, and the community—can operate. Each partner has the capacity to foster the success of the school. When each participant plays a positive role, the result is an effective school.

REFERENCES

Brookover, W. B., et al. *Elementary School Climate and School Achievement.* East Lansing: Michigan State University, College of Urban Development, 1976.

Coleman, J. S., et al. *Equality of Educational Opportunity.* Washington, D.C.: National Center for Educational Statistics, 1966.

Edmonds, R. R., et al. "Effective Schools for the Urban Poor." *Educational Leadership* 37 (October 1979):15–27.

Goodlad, J. I., et al. *A Study of Schooling.* Bloomington, Ind.: Phi Delta Kappa Inc., 1979.

Jencks, C. S., et al. *Inequality: A Reassessment of the Effect of Family and Schooling in America.* New York: Basic Books, 1972.

Madaus, G. F., et al. "The Sensitivity of Measures of School Effectiveness." *Harvard Educational Review* 49 (1979):207–230.

Purkey, S. C., and M. S. Smith. "Effective Schools: A Review." *Elementary School Journal* 83, 4 (1983):427–452.

Rutter, M., et al. *Fifteen Thousand Hours.* London: Open Books, 1979.

Summers, A. A., and B. L. Wolfe. "Do Schools Make a Difference?" *American Economic Review* 64 (1977):639–652.

Weber, G. *Inner City Children Can Be Taught to Read: Four Successful Schools.* Washington, D.C.: Council for Basic Education, 1971.

PART ONE
Study and Discussion Questions

CHAPTER ONE Three Viewpoints About What Is Important in Education

Reading 1 *The Shame of American Education*

1. Basically, what is it about American education that Skinner finds "shameful"?
2. Skinner sees cognitive psychology as constituting a roadblock to improving educational practices. What is his reasoning for this assertion?
3. How would you explain the essence of Skinner's "solution" to the ills of American schooling? How would you feel about sending your own children through Skinner's system?

Reading 2 *The Key to Improving Schools: An Interview with William Glasser*

1. When Glasser says that half of all students are not working because they perceive schools as not satisfying their needs, what does he mean?
2. If asked to describe the central ideas behind Glasser's approach to improving schools, how would you respond?
3. What basic differences do you see between Skinner's and Glasser's suggestions for improving schooling? To which do you feel closer? Why?

Reading 3 *Humanistic Education: Too Tender for a Tough World?*

1. How would you explain humanistic education to someone who didn't know what it is?
2. When Combs makes a statement like ". . . people do not behave according to the facts," what is his reasoning? Do you agree?
3. Explain the following statement: "Effective education is also affective."
4. What similarities and differences do you see among the positions about schooling by Skinner, Glasser, and Combs?

CHAPTER TWO Effective Schools: What They Are and How They Make a Positive Difference

Reading 4 Schools Make a Difference: Evidence, Criticisms, and New Directions

1. Based on this Reading, how would you describe effective schools?

2. What particular teacher behaviors contribute to making effective schools effective?

3. If you were to make policy recommendations to a school board about how to make schooling more successful for more students, what recommendations would you make?

Reading 5 New Evidence of Effective Elementary Schools

1. The authors note that much of the variation among schools in their effects on students' achievement is accounted for by differences in school policies and practices. What policies and practices are they referring to?

2. Is the following statement true or false? "Schools that are effective in promoting the progress of one group are also effective for other groups." Explain your answer.

PART TWO

Growth, Development, and Behavior

Growth processes and maturational differences are developmental undercurrents that affect all aspects of schooling. The purpose of Part Two is to provide an overview of the research and ideas related to various aspects of development from childhood through adolescence.

Chapter Three concentrates on developmental issues and behavioral outcomes that are particularly important to our understanding of the psychology of children and adolescents. In Reading 6, Joe L. Frost maps out the major changes that are occurring with greater frequency these days in the lives of growing children, such as drug use, teen pregnancy, and child abuse, to name a few.

Anne C. Petersen, in Reading 7, examines the "gangly years" of adolescence in an effort to help us both understand and anticipate the marked shifts in mood and behavior so often experienced by youngsters at that time.

In spite of experiencing harsh emotional conditions in their early years, many children end up being strong, healthy, "resilient" childen who face life's vicissitudes with strength and a positive attitude. Emmy E. Werner analyzes how this happens in Reading 8 and also suggests steps we can take to make these outcomes more possible for more children.

We have always known that males and females are different, but the specifics about how they are different have become clearer in recent years. Reading 9 will give you a broad overview of the major ways that males and females differ in physical and intellectual development, along with some interesting facts about sex differences in learning.

Chapter Four is an overview of the great behavioral shapers: genetics and environment. Data are beginning to emerge from a massive long-term study of twins at the University of Minnesota, and in Reading 10, Clare Mead Rosen tours us through some of the fascinating findings that have surfaced so far. Surprising results are beginning to emerge about the relative effects on behavior of environment and heredity. Genetics may play a more important role in shaping behavior than we thought.

The effects of environment on development are powerful and persistent. In Reading 11, Joan Isenberg discusses how social pressures emanating from family, schools, peers, and television can have adverse effects on children's development and makes recommendations for countering those effects.

What are the greatest dangers faced by children growing up in today's society? How does puberty affect mood and behavior? What are the reasons behind the fact that some children remain emotionally healthy in childhood and others do not? How can we account for the intellectual and physical differences that are evident between males and females? Do environment and genetics have equal power in determining behavior, or is one dominant?

These are the kinds of questions that will be explored in Part Two.

CHAPTER THREE

Developmental Dynamics and Growth Outcomes

READING 6   JOE L. FROST
Children in a Changing Society

We can borrow from the Socratic era and say that these are troubled times in the care and education of children. This assembly of classroom teachers and others concerned with education is aware that children and youth are rebelling against traditional norms of social behavior; they are becoming increasingly alienated from their parents and teachers; they are experiencing more difficulties in the family and in school. Society at large has taken a hard look at these phenomena, claiming to have identified their major roots. If the conclusions of several recent national task-force reports can be believed, teachers and teachers of teachers are at fault; the schools are failing our young. Parents doubt our commitment; governors and legislators question our competence; popular media depict us as absent-minded, bungling, comical and incompetent.

From Joe L. Frost, "Children in a Changing Society," *Childhood Education* (March/April 1986): 242–249. Reprinted with permission of Joe L. Frost and the Association for Childhood Education International, 11141 Georgia Avenue, Suite 200, Wheaton, MD. Copyright © 1986 by the Association.

Despite these indictments, I would like to propose that teachers are fully as competent in *their* roles as legislators, lawyers, business people and psychiatrists are in theirs— perhaps even more honest and hard-working. If society really wants to know why children are falling apart at the seams, there are other places than schools, other people than teachers, other circumstances than classroom instruction to be examined. Consider Susan.

It is 4:30 in the year 1985. Five-year-old Susan is dropped off at her home by the day care bus. As she enters the courtyard leading to the apartment she shares with her father, Juan and Maria invite her to come in and see the space game they received for Christmas. Their baby sitter tells them their mother will be home from work in an hour and leaves to travel to her evening job. Because her father has warned her not to stop off on the way from school, Susan goes home, takes a new coke from the refrigerator and settles down to watch "Marvel Woman" on TV.

A child of the 1980s, Susan lives with a single parent, attends day care part-time but spends a great deal of time alone watching television. Her mother has remarried and lives in another city with Susan's 3-year-old brother and her new husband. Susan's father is a salesman. His working hours sometimes extend into the evening. He usually calls when he will be home after 6:00 so she can go to a neighbor's house until he arrives. Ever since her mother left two years ago, Susan cries nearly every day, hates going to day care, argues with her father a lot and wets the bed.

Almost all of the adults in Susan's apartment complex are single and all have children, so she has playmates and friends of all ages. Some of the preschool-age children go to day care but others can't afford it. Some go to Head Start but there isn't room for everyone. Some go to both Head Start and day care. Many join the children being looked after by a parent between regular jobs or by one of the teenagers who have dropped out of school. Susan and her friends are warned to avoid talking to strangers and to keep their doors locked because of "child-snatchers," men hired by their absent parents to snatch them away and take them to live in a strange place. Several of the children in the neighborhood have had friends who disappeared. Some never returned.

Susan hears familiar sounds outside and moves to the window to watch the elementary school children arriving home, while keeping her attention directed to "Marvel Woman." A few of the children linger in the courtyard but are told to go home by the caretaker who fears they will trample the new plants he has been tending. The phone rings and Susan learns that her father is going to happy hour with Gail, his girlfriend, and will not be home until late. Susan is to go to Joan's house. Joan is a friend of her father's. She has a teenage daughter, Sonja, whom Susan dislikes. Joan is working late but Sonja and her boyfriend Mike invite Susan to come in and make sandwiches and watch TV with Sonja's 2-year-old son and her two elementary school–age sisters. Shortly, several of Sonja and Mike's friends arrive with beer and wine and funny-smelling cigarettes that they sometimes let them try. The younger children are shuttled off to a bedroom so Sonja and her friends can use the living room for dancing. Sonja's younger sister, Tammy, begins to cry because the last time her mother came home to find a party in progress she became very angry. When Sonja storms out with her friends she shouts, screams and beats Tammy with her boyfriend's belt.

This scenario of the 1985 American family is not drawn from outlandish, atypical situations *unlikely* to occur in "good" families but from data and trends established in the 1970s and continued in the 1980s. Without recourse to speculation but merely projecting the trends of the past decade, the portrait that unfolds by the year 1990 follows:

The typical (over 50 percent) American child in the year 1990 will experience a major family disruption due to divorce. Consequently, the child will live in a one-parent home with a parent who holds regular employment outside the home. He/she will enter several substitute child care arrangements and spend a great deal of time alone. By school age, the child's time will be occupied in terms of duration by television, school and family in that order, with family a poor third. TV programs watched will grow rapidly from *PG* to *R* to *X rated*, with all forms available in most homes. During the teen years, the child will use one or more illicit drugs plus alcohol and tobacco, and will father or mother a child or have an abortion. The child will be subjected to abuse by a parent or friend of the family and some of his/her friends and acquaintances will attempt suicide.

The data to support these trends are far too extensive for complete documentation here but a selective overview will illustrate their scope.

The Child Will Experience the Divorce of His/Her Parents

Children under 18 years who were involved in divorces during 1979 are estimated at 1,181,000. This figure is more than triple the number in 1957, having increased steadily with only two interruptions (1960 and 1970) from 6.4 per 1000 children in 1957 to 18.9 per 1000 children in 1979 (U.S. Bureau of the Census). The National Center for Health Statistics estimates the number of divorces for 1980 at 1,182,000 or three times the figure recorded 20 years ago. This boils down to one divorce for every two marriages.

There is perhaps no greater tragedy in the life of a child than the loss of a parent — not through death, for death is natural and can be comprehended and overcome, but through divorce. Divorce is an injury that may never heal. The guilt and frustration felt by a child when a parent chooses to absent him/herself may continue into adulthood. Judith Wallerstein reported to the American Academy of Child Psychiatry on a ten-year study of California couples. She concluded that divorce can be so traumatic for young children that they become adults who are psychologically incapable of leading happy lives. Like paper towels, we now have throwaway marriages. A recent cartoon depicted a bride and groom sitting sadly on a bed in their honeymoon suite with the bride saying, "I'm sorry, Sam, I just met my dream man in the reception line."

The Child Will Live with a Single Parent

In March 1980, 14.6 percent of 8,530,000 families were maintained by female householders. This figure has doubled in the past 20 years. Ninety-six percent of all children under 18 years of age live with one or both parents. The number living with one parent more than doubled from 9 percent in 1960 to 19 percent in 1978 and soared to 25 percent in 1985 (Stengel, 1985). Sixty percent will live with one parent before age 18. Two out of three children who reside with one parent live with a divorced or separated parent. The child loses the financial as well as the emotional support of the absent parent. Only one-fourth receive all their support payments, one-fourth receive some and one-half receive none (U.S. Bureau of the Census).

An analysis of 12,000 American teenagers by Stanford University's Center for the Study of Youth Development (1985) indicates that children in single-parent families headed by a mother have higher arrest rates, more disciplinary problems in school, and a greater tendency to smoke and to run away from home than do their peers who live with both natural parents — no matter what their income, race or ethnic background.

Related conclusions from a study by the National Center for Education Information (Feistritzer, 1985) show that a student's home life determines how well the child does in school—no matter what is taught in the classroom. Students who live with both parents tend to score higher on achievement tests than students who live with one parent.

The Child's Mother Will Work Outside the Home

Participation in the labor force has increased more rapidly for married women with children of preschool age. The numbers tripled from 12 percent to 42 percent between 1950 and 1978. Currently, 60 percent of married women with children of preschool age are in the work force. The number will increase to 80 percent by 1990 and 50 percent, or over 10,000,000 children, will have to be cared for in formal child care facilities. Three of every four divorced women are in the labor force compared to 60 percent of married women (U.S. Bureau of the Census, 1985).

NBC'S White Paper (1985) painted a troublesome future for family stability. As women enter the work force, men are not assuming their share of home chores. The working mother performs two major roles, professional woman and homemaker—either of which could be considered full-time roles. The addition of a baby adds complexity as the mother assumes a third major role—infant care. Since it appears clear that few indeed can effectively manage all three roles, something must break. All too frequently it is the marriage. Many mothers are now putting in 16-hour days, competing with men at work—men who don't have dual and triple roles. Family relationships become strained as one or both parents become exhausted. There is not enough talk, not enough romance, and strained sex lives. Husbands feel deserted, wanting wives to focus more on home and family. The typical American work place does not accommodate dual roles. Pregnancy can damage chances of promotion and job security. Increasingly, the goal of achieving the chic businesswoman image portrayed by the media drives women to emulate the slick, driving, competitive, demanding male entrepreneur, whose qualities they so recently disdained.

The Child's Major Activity Will Be Watching Television

Between the ages of 6 and 18, children view 15 to 16,000 hours of television compared to 13,000 spent in school and have been exposed to 350,000 commercials are 18,000 murders. According to the Neilsen Report on Television for 1980, children watch 30 to 31 hours of TV weekly—more time than is spent in any other activity except sleep. By graduation day, the average high school student has seen 18,000 murders in 22,000 hours of television viewing (*U.S. News and World Report,* 1985).

Over 2,500 studies of children and television support "overwhelmingly" one conclusion: violence on TV breeds aggression and violent behavior in children (Pearl, 1982). A California study of a half million public school students in the 6th through 12th grades concluded that the more a student watches television the worse he/she does in school (*Austin American Statesman,* 1980). This finding held across I.Q. and socioeconomic levels. Furthermore, a recent study by Dietz and Gertmaker (1985) shows that watching TV makes kids fat. TV contributes to obesity by promoting extended resting metabolic rates, by reducing energy-expensive activities, and by promoting consumption of caloric dense or junk food through advertisements.

Sedentary lifestyles and junk food, coupled with increased emphasis upon academics and reduced emphasis on physical education, play and physical work, have led to a nation of flabby, short-winded kids with elevated cholesterol and blood-pressure levels and declining strength and heart-lung endurance (Winston, 1984).

The violent, sexual, fairy-tale world of TV is increasingly replacing parents as role models. Seventy-five percent of a sample of 850 American high school students in four states said they would replace their parents if they could (*Austin American Statesman,* 1979). Their top choices were Cheryl Ladd and Burt Reynolds. In a poll by *U.S. News and World Report* (1985), young adults named Clint Eastwood and Eddie Murphy as heroes more frequently then they named President Reagan, Pope John Paul II and Mother Teresa. When 4- to 6-year-olds were asked in a two-year study, "Which do you like better, TV or Daddy?" almost half said they preferred TV (*Austin American Statesman,* 1975). And the feeling seems to be mutual. When Ann Landers asked her readers, "If you had it all to do over again, would you have children?" 70 percent of the 10,000 respondents said "No" (*Austin American Statesman,* 1976).

The Female Will Become Pregnant During the Teen Years or Before

The rate of American teenage pregnancy is the highest among developed nations—at 96 per 1000 for 15- to 19-year-olds and over five per 1000 for 14-year-olds (*Education Week,* 1985). If the present trend continues, four of 10 or 40 percent of today's 14-year-olds will become pregnant during their teen years. Nearly one-third of the 175,588 abortions *reported* in 1978 were performed on teenagers. It is widely acknowledged that most abortions go unreported. Nationally, the illegitimacy rate leaped between 1960 and 1982 to 20 percent of all births.

In New York City in 1984, the rate was 37 percent; in central Harlem the rate was 80 percent (Children's Defense Fund, 1985a, 1985b).

The Child Will Use Illicit Drugs, Alcohol and Tobacco

In a study of high school seniors by Johnson and O'Malley (1985), 65 percent reported having used illicit drugs (hallucinogens, cocaine, heroin or other opiates, stimulants, sedatives or tranquilizers not prescribed by a doctor, with marijuana as the most prevalent drug). About 40 percent had used illicit drugs other than marijuana. Ninety-three percent had used alcohol, 71 percent during the past month. Seventy-one percent had used cigarettes, 72 percent during the past month. In 1985 a report from the House Select Committee on Narcotics Abuse and Control stated that the U.S. is becoming a nation of junkies—with over 20 million Americans using marijuana regularly, 8 to 20 million using cocaine regularly, a half million using heroin, one million using hallucinogens and 6 million abusing prescription drugs. Marijuana, at $14 billion annually, is the nation's leading cash crop; children of 10 to 12 are joining public officials, bankers, police, sports figures and TV stars in peddling heroin and cocaine on the streets of inner cities.

An Increasing Number of Children Will Commit Suicide

The number-two national killer of young people from 15 to 24 years of age is suicide and the statistics do not reflect apparent accidents that may have been suicides. In a major city suburb in 1984, six teenagers committed suicide in six weeks. About 5,000 teenagers committed suicide in 1984 and 500,000 tried (*U.S.A. Today*, 1985). Both the suicide rate and the homicide rate for white males ages 15 to 19 have more than doubled in the past 15 years.

The Child Will Be Abused or Kidnapped

The 1980s will be identified by historians as the period in which child abuse was recognized as a national problem. In early 1985, the Secretary of Health and Human Services issued a report (*Parade Magazine*, 1985) revealing that one in every four or five girls and one in every nine or ten boys are sexually abused before they reach 18. In almost 90 percent of the cases, close relatives, family friends or neighbors are implicated. Over three-fourths of the abusers are parents.

Child abuse has reached such proportions that children are warned not to speak to adults in their own neighborhood. The new awareness is creating a climate of fear. The National Hotline on Child Abuse received twice as many calls in 1985 as in 1984. Some complain about seeing an adult in a day care center holding a child in the lap. In some centers, adults no longer change a diaper without a witness present. Lawyers advise teachers, "Don't be caught alone with children unless they are your own." Males are beginning to leave the child care profession and insurance rates are increasing to the point of putting some day care centers out of business. The fears of parents, teachers and children are intensified by the disappearance of one and one-half million children annually.

CHANGING ATTITUDES OF CHILDREN

A very provocative report by Zimiles (1982) addressed the questions: Just how are today's children affected by such factors as divorce, working mothers, disruption of families, changing sexual mores and technological advances when compared to children 25 to 30 years ago? One hundred seventy kindergarten, elementary and secondary teachers from both rural and urban areas, each with over 20 years' teaching experience, were interviewed about their perceptions of middle-class children.

Today's children know more, are freer and grow up more rapidly. They are street wise and more worldly, more mobile, travel more widely, have more money, and from watching television have headline knowledge of a wide range of phenomena. Whatever the criterion—social poise, physical appearance, puberty, investment in the peer group, sexual interest—children are reaching developmental landmarks earlier.

Television, toys and travel have formed a barrage of information input but for many schools these are not suitable devices for extending what children already know. The knowledge they bring to school is sketchy and incomplete, lacking in substance and integration. On the one hand, the teacher is dealing with more knowledgeable persons; on the other, she/he is dealing with more confused persons, who are accustomed to being confused and see little need to sort out and clarify their experiences.

There are fewer instances in which the child wishes or needs to delay gratification or in which the adult tries to impose delays in gratification. Children have little tolerance for delays and insist on immediate payoff; the instability of their lives inspires little confidence in a stable, predictable future. Accustomed to functioning in the visual world of television, children are less tuned in auditorially; activities that require attention to detail, memorization or story construction are easily stymied. The rules and organization of the classroom are no match for slick, Hollywood-style television productions. Reading and writing, indeed the school itself, are no longer seen as major windows to success in the world as television is. Children are too filled with anxiety stimulation to confront school experiences in any meaningful way.

For some, school can be regarded as a period of recovery from TV.

Family upheavals, poverty, emotional and physical handicaps lead children to become autonomous at an early age, less dependent upon parents, teachers, schools and churches, but more dependent upon their peer groups. As divorce rates rise and adults admit defeat and exhibit disarray in their lives, they have less guidance to offer the next generation. Children are drawn to peers because they cannot count on adults whose energies are exhausted working out family and work-place conflicts, finishing their education, striving to preserve their own youth, securing the materialistic symbols of wealth and status.

Children have more possessions but have less guidance from adults; many drive cars their borderline poverty-ridden teachers can't afford. Indeed, teachers themselves are seen as failures by those measuring success by abundance of goods, vacations abroad, and size and location of residence.

Today's children have few heroes but aspire to be cool, self-sufficient, wise-cracking individuals and turn to TV and sports for models to emulate. Their dramatic play is dominated by TV models of violence and sexual promiscuity depicted in programs like "The A Team" and "Three's Company." Petty thievery and cheating on tests seem trivial and unimportant in light of the flow of horrors children live with and ignore. Early initiation to sex, indeed pregnancy, is becoming a status symbol to junior high and high school students as some girls seek to have babies so they will "have someone to love and someone to love them." For the middle and upper classes, abortion is an easy way out for a "troublesome problem."

In the past, education was seen as a privilege and teachers were valued members of the community. Now teachers are viewed as a link in a network of child-caring services along with baby sitters, tutors, day care givers and coaches. Indeed, children of working parents are increasingly passed through a staggering array of service people throughout the day—before-school care; half day at a kindergarten; half day at a child care center; baby sitters in the evening; relatives on the weekend; and in the summer a new group of service providers, camp directors, child care centers and special tutors. Travelers on commercial airlines now see more and more "suitcase children" with identification tags pinned to their clothing, traveling alone for thousands of miles during holidays and summer vacations to visit parents and grandparents. Others, less fortunate, are "kidnapped" by their parents and spend months or years in fear and frustration.

HISTORICAL BASES

Considering that as recently as the 1950s and 1960s, child development professionals and educators were speaking in glowing terms of achieving "the golden age of childhood," how did we arrive at such a fragile state of childrearing?

Children were regarded as little adults until about the turn of the century. Child abuse, infanticide, abandonment and severe physical punishment were characteristic of centuries-long eras extending through recorded history. Childrearing in colonial America was tied to harsh practices of the Old World and to conditions of economic necessity. Children frequently were put to work at an early age and the biblical admonition "Spare the rod and spoil the child" was applied literally by fathers and schoolmasters alike. Yet, by the turn of the present century, diversity in childrearing was established.

During the early 1900s, as the child-centered views of European romanticists like Froebel and Pestallozi were embraced and elaborated by American child developmentalists, child study became a topic of intense inquiry and scientific interest. National organizations such as the Association for Childhood Education International (established 1892) were formed and the first White House Conference on Children was held in 1907.

Despite a global war, semi-primitive medical care and transportation, and the lack of sophisticated mass communication during the period of the 1930s and 1940s, the 1950s appear to have brought us about as close to "the golden age of childhood" as we are likely to get in this century. The 1930s and 1940s were reaping benefits of two decades of child study. Industrialization was simplifying work roles and freeing time for leisure. Medicine was healing diseases and extending life spans. Childhood was gradually being acknowledged and valued for its own sake and, except for the requirements of war, families were remaining intact and children were being nurtured by fathers, mothers, grandparents and other relatives. Ironically, the seeming disadvantages of primitive transportation and media—horse-drawn wagons and vintage automobiles instead of today's jet airplanes and sports cars, occasional newspapers and radio broadcasts instead of today's high-tech media bombardment—may have been blessings in disguise. Families were intrigued by these new developments and they put them to good use, yet they were not bombarded with stimuli, and technology had not begun to supplant traditional family practices.

We saw in the baby-boom generation of the 1960s radical new pressures of generation size—enlargement of schools and accompanying shifts from traditional modes of authority, direct and personal to legal and contractual. Education in this era was a story of experiments and reforms, a struggle between the values of traditionalism—merit, competition, self-restraint, self-discipline, family stability, moral universals—and those of modernism—sensual gratification, self-expression, deviant family forms and ethical relativism.

For the first time, the moral virtues of parents were beginning to be held up to examination by children. They were seeing adults whose demands reflected the virtues of traditionalism while their actions increasingly modeled the vices of modernism. In this context, homework and family activities increasingly gave way to TV and its obsession with the sexual, the violent and the bizarre. Currently, primary grade children arrive at school either bleary-eyed from late-night viewing of Playboy, adult comedies and violent movies with their parents or in a state of mental anguish over the impending loss of a parent through desertion or divorce.

A central, largely overlooked point must be made in the context of contemporary criticism of teachers: receptivity, motivation and parental support of children have declined dramatically over the past 15 to 20 years while the quality of instruction and personal commitment by teachers has probably improved. To put it bluntly, teachers have become the doormat for society's frustrations and excesses. The upshot of all this is that the modernistic ethic has now permeated both the school and the family. Teachers are in a Catch-22 situation if they attempt to teach values contradictory to those of their children's parents. Since it is difficult—perhaps impossible—to teach in an ethically/morally neutral dialogue, the teacher unwittingly contributes to children's frustrations by failure to model consistent or clear values.

I cannot offer a sure-fire formula for reversing the trends toward damaged families and increased failure rates in school. But I am convinced that the fault does not rest with schools alone, that it is a global, societal problem, and that we must make children *number one* in the lives of families. They cannot be subordinated to parents' desire for success in the marketplace, for personal fulfillment in career and travel, for the pleasure of a new mate.

MAKING CHILDREN NUMBER ONE

- Children need parents with clear ideas of right and wrong. No other social institution is so well quipped to transmit values to the young as the family.
- Children need rules and regulations in their lives. Recent British studies show that simple rules and sanctions in the home by adults present to enforce them (TV-viewing, homework, curfews) dramatically affect children's behavior and success in school.
- Teachers need to insist that parents assume responsibility for their children's behavior in school. Teachers are in schools primarily to teach. They should call parents to school, even from their work places, to help handle their children's serious discipline problems—thus helping them to understand that their children's problems are also their problems.
- Children need parents with a deep commitment to their families. "Incompatibility" and "irreconcilable differences" in marriage too often mean that one or both partners are hooked on booze, sleeping around, seeking "personal fulfillment," or unwilling to accept the responsibilities of maintaining a family.
- Parents and teachers need the support of society in childrearing and education. While parental rearing of children must remain the norm, it's time to recognize that caring for children is everybody's business. Increasing numbers of mothers are forced by economic necessity to work outside the home and fathers are not assuming their fair share of child care. Some parents are not around to care for their children, some are too sick and a few don't know how. Employers, community agencies and governments must assume greater responsibility in child care. This must be done in ways that allow close, regular contacts between parents and children and promote a clear commitment to fundamental values of civilized societies.
- Legislators must explore beyond surface issues in their efforts at "school reform." The currently popular efforts—competency testing, career ladders, essential elements, extension of school time, no pass – no play—have precious little support in research or philosophy. As a group, these solutions are punitive, shallow and unimaginative, focusing on reward-punishment motivation and narrow curriculum emphases. Research has demonstrated repeatedly that quality counts more than quantity in the education of children.
- Society must reexamine itself to reestablish the common value that says NO to drug abuse. The parent who abuses his/her own body and that of the unborn child through misuse of alcohol, tobacco, prescription or illegal drugs is a living model for such behavior in children.
- Society must reexamine its values and, consequently, its institutions to assist parents and teachers in shaping children's values. It's time to declare that most television is garbage—distorting children's values, influencing bizarre behaviors, misshaping attitudes, eliminating quality time with parents, prompting violence and reducing school achievement. Our social institutions must help parents with this problem, and

parents must commit themselves to regulating their children's television-viewing and to making time for constructive family activities.

If we are to recapture children's hearts and minds, society must recommit itself to the fundamental values of civilized people everywhere and rebuild the moral fiber of its families and institutions. Unless this is done, we will continue to be unhappy with our schools and the achievement of our young. Teachers cannot do the job alone; we must now seek the same responsible conduct from parents and others that they expect from us. This is the challenge and, I believe, a central challenge of our profession—and of society.

REFERENCES

Austin American Statesman. "Survey Shows Viewing Tube Graded an F" (Nov. 8, 1980).
———. "Parents Say Kids Not Worth It" (Feb. 27, 1976).
———. "Teenagers Would Replace Their Parents" (Aug. 17, 1979).
———. "TV Rivals Dad in Survey" (Dec. 1, 1975).
Childen's Defense Fund. *Preventing Children Having Children.* Clearinghouse Paper Number 1. Washington, DC: Author, 1985b.
———. *The Data Book: A Summary. Adolescent Pregnancy Prevention.* Washington, DC: Author, 1985a.
Dietz, William H., and Steven L. Gertmaker. "Do We Fatten Our Children at the Television Set? Obesity and Television Viewing in Children and Adolescents." *Pediatrics* 75 (May 1985): 807–12.
Education Commission of the States. "Reconnecting Youth: The Next Stage of Reform." Denver: Author, 1985.
Education Week. "U.S. Leads Developed Nations in Rate of Teen-Age Pregnancy." Report of a study by the Alan Guttmacher Institute (Mar. 20, 1985): 1, 13.
Feistritzer, Emily. *Cheating Our Children: Why We Need Reform.* Washington, DC: National Center for Education Information, 1985.
House Select Committee on Narcotics Abuse and Control. "Report on Narcotics Use." Washington, DC: Author, 1985.
Johnston, Lloyd, and Patrick O'Malley. Reported in the *Daily Texan* (Sept. 19, 1985):3.
Parade Magazine. "Preventing Sexual Abuse of Children" (May 26, 1985): 16.
Pearl, David. "Television and Behavior: 10 Years of Scientific Progress and Implications for the Eighties." Washington, DC: Government Printing Office, 1982.
Schroeder, Donald, "Sex Without Marriage." *The Plain Truth* (Apr. 1985): 11–14, 37–38.
Stanford University's Center for the Study of Youth Development. "Analysis of U.S. Department of Health and Human Services National Health Examination Survey." *Chronicle of Higher Learning* (Apr. 10, 1985).
Stengel, Richard. "Snapshot of a Changing America." *Time* (Sept. 2, 1985): 16–18.
U.S.A. Today (May 15, 1985): 9A.
U.S. News and World Report. "What Entertainers Are Doing to Your Kids." (Oct. 28, 1985): 46–49.
Winston, Pamela. "Despite Fitness Boom, the Young Remain Unfit." *Education Week* (Oct. 31, 1984): 9.
Zimiles, Herbert. "The Changing American Child: The Perspective of Educators." A Report to the National Commission on Excellence in Education, Oct. 1982.

See also:

Quisenberry, James D., ed. *Changing Family Lifestyles: Their Effect on Children.* Wheaton, MD: ACEI, 1982.
Umansky, Warren. *On Families and the Re-valuing of Childhood.* ACEI Position Paper. Wheaton, MD: ACEI, 1983.

READING 7   ANNE C. PETERSEN
Those Gangly Years

"How can you stand studying adolescents? My daughter has just become one and she's impossible to live with. Her hormones may be raging, but so am I!" A colleague at a cocktail party was echoing the widespread view that the biological events of puberty necessarily change nice kids into moody, rebellious adolescents. The view has gained such a foothold that some parents with well-behaved teenagers worry that their kids aren't developing properly.

They needn't worry. My research, and that of many others, suggests that although the early teen years can be quite a challenge for normal youngsters and their families, they're usually not half as bad as they are reputed to be. And even though the biological changes of puberty do affect adolescents' behavior, attitudes and feelings in many important ways, other, often controllable, social and environmental forces are equally important.

One 14-year-old, for example, who tried to excuse his latest under-par report card by saying, "My problem is testosterone, not tests," only looked at part of the picture. He ignored, as many do, the fact that, because of a move and the

---

From Anne C. Petersen, "Those Gangly Years," *Psychology Today* (September 1987):28–34. Reprinted with permission from *Psychology Today* magazine. Copyright © 1987 (PT Partners, L.P.).

shift to junior high school, he had been in three schools in as many years.

My colleagues and I at Pennsylvania State University looked at a three-year span in the lives of young adolescents to find out how a variety of biological and social factors affected their behavior and their feelings about themselves. A total of 335 young adolescents were randomly selected from two suburban school districts, primarily white and middle- to upper-middle-class. Two successive waves of these kids were monitored as they moved from the sixth through the eighth grade. Twice a year we interviewed them individually and gave them psychological tests in groups. When the youngsters were in the sixth and eighth grades, we also interviewed and assessed their parents. Just recently we again interviewed and assessed these young people and their parents during the adolescents' last year of high school.

We followed the children's pubertal development by asking them to judge themselves every six months on such indicators as height, public hair and acne in both boys and girls; breast development and menstruation in girls; and voice change and facial-hair growth in boys. We also estimated the timing of puberty by finding out when each youngster's adolescent growth spurt in height peaked, so we could study the effects of early, on-time or late maturing.

Although we have not yet analyzed all the data, it's clear that puberty alone does not have the overwhelming psychological impact that earlier clinicians and researchers assumed it did (see "The Puzzle of Adolescence," this article). But it does have many effects on body image, moods and relationships with parents and members of the opposite sex.

Being an early or late maturer (one year earlier or later than average), for example, affected adolescents' satisfaction with their appear-

> I didn't like being early. But by eighth grade, everyone wore a bra and had their period. I was normal.

ance and their body image—but only among seventh- and eighth-graders, not sixth-graders. We found that among students in the higher two grades, girls who were physically more mature were generally less satisfied with their weight and appearance than their less mature classmates.

A seventh-grade girl, pleased with being still childlike, said, "You can do more things—you don't have as much weight to carry around." A girl in the eighth grade, also glad to be a late maturer, commented, "If girls get fat, they have to worry about it." In contrast, an early-maturing girl subsequently commented, "I didn't like being early. A lot of my friends didn't understand." Another girl, as a high school senior, described the pain of maturing extremely early: "I tried to hide it. I was embarrassed and ashamed." However, her discomfort ended in the eighth grade, she said, because "by then everyone wore a bra and had their period. I was normal."

We found the reverse pattern among boys: Those who were physically more mature tended to be more satisfied with their weight and their overall appearance than their less mature peers. One already gangling seventh-grade boy, for example, said he liked being "a little taller and having more muscle development than other kids so you can beat them in races." He conceded that developing more slowly might help "if you're a jockey" but added, "Really, I can't think of why [developing] later would be an advantage." In reflecting back from the 12th grade, a boy who had matured early noted that at the time the experience "made me feel superior."

For seventh- and eighth-grade boys, physical maturity was related to mood. Boys who had reached puberty reported positive moods more often than their prepubertal male classmates did. Pubertal status was less clearly and consistently related to mood among girls, but puberty did affect how girls got along with their parents. As physical development advanced among sixth-grade girls, their relationships with their parents declined; girls who were developmentally advanced talked less to their parents and had less positive feelings about family relationships than did less developed girls. We found a similar pattern among eighth-grade girls, but it was less clear in the seventh grade, perhaps because of the many other changes occurring at that time, such as the change from elementary to secondary school format and its related effects on friendship and school achievement.

The timing of puberty affected both school achievement and moods. Early maturers tended to get higher grades than later maturers in the same class. We suspect that this may stem from the often documented tendency of teachers to give more positive ratings to larger pupils. Although early maturers had an edge academically, those who matured later were more likely to report positive moods.

As we have noted, among relatively physically mature adolescents, boys and girls had opposite feelings about their appearance: The boys were pleased, but the girls were not. We believe that, more generally, pubertal change is usually a positive experience for boys but a negative one for girls. While advancing maturity has some advantages for girls, including gaining some of the rights and privileges granted to maturing boys, it also brings increased limitations and restrictions related to their emerging womanhood. One sixth-grade girl stated emphatically, "I don't like the idea of getting older or any of that. If I had my choice, I'd rather stay 10." Or, as one seventh-grade boy graphically explained the gender differences, "Parents let them [boys] go out later than girls because they don't have to worry about getting raped or anything like that."

Differences in the timing of puberty also affect interactions with members of the opposite sex. But it takes two to tango, and in the sixth grade, although many girls have reached puberty and are ready to socialize with boys, most boys have not yet made that transition. Thus, as one girl plaintively summed up the sixth-grade social scene, "Girls think about boys more than boys think about girls."

In the seventh and eighth grades, the physically more mature boys and girls are likely to be pioneers in exploring social relations with members of the opposite sex, including talking with them on the phone, dating, having a boyfriend or girlfriend and "making out." We had the sense that once these young people began looking like teenagers, they wanted to act like them as well.

But puberty affects the social and sexual activity of individual young adolescents both directly and indirectly; the pubertal status of some students can have consequences for the entire peer group of boys and girls. Although dating and other boy-girl interactions are linked to pubertal status, and girls usually reach puberty before boys do, we found no sex differences in the rates of dating throughout the early-adolescent period. When the early-maturing kids began socializing with members of the opposite sex, the pattern quickly spread throughout the entire peer group. Even prepubertal girls were susceptible to

Shifting schools exposes teens to new extracurricular activities—licit and illicit.

thinking and talking about boys if all their girlfriends were "boy crazy."

The physical changes brought on by puberty have far-reaching effects, but so do many other changes in the lives of adolescents. One we found to be particularly influential is the change in school structure between the sixth and eighth grades. Most young adolescents in our country shift from a relatively small neighborhood elementary school, in which most classes are taught by one teacher, to a much larger, more impersonal middle school or junior high school (usually farther from the child's home), in which students move from class to class and teacher to teacher for every subject. This shift in schools has many ramifications, including disrupting the old peer-group structure, exposing adolescents to different achievement expectations by teachers and providing opportunities for new extracurricular activities—licit and illicit.

Both the timing and number of school transitions are very important. In our study, for example, students who changed schools earlier than most of their peers, as well as those who changed schools twice (both experiences due to modifications of the school system), suffered an academic slump that continued through eighth grade. Therefore, early or double school transition seemed stressful, beyond the usual effects of moving to a junior high school.

Puberty and school change, which appear to be the primary and most pervasive changes occurring during early adolescence, are often linked to other important changes, such as altered family relations. Psychologist Laurence Steinberg of the University of Wisconsin has found that family relationships shift as boys and girls move through puberty. During mid puberty, he says, conflict in family discussions increases; when the conflict is resolved, boys usually become more dominant in conversations with their mothers. (Psychologist John Hill of Virginia Commonwealth University has found that family conflict increases only for boys.) Other research, however, suggests that adolescents wind up playing a more equal role relative to both parents.

In our study, the parents of early-maturing girls and late-maturing boys reported less positive feelings about their children in the sixth and eighth grades than did parents of boys and girls with other patterns of pubertal timing. (These effects were always stronger for fathers than for mothers.) The adolescents, however, reported that their feelings about their parents were unrelated to pubertal timing.

The feelings of affection and support that adolescents and their parents reported about one another usually declined from the sixth to the eighth grades, with the biggest decline in feelings between girls and their mothers. But importantly, the decline was from very positive to less positive—but still not negative—feelings.

Early adolescence is clearly an unusual transition in development because of the number of changes young people experience. But the impact of those changes is quite varied; changes that may challenge and stimulate some young people can become overwhelming and stressful to others. The outcome seems to depend on prior strengths and vulnerabilities—both of the in-

The Puzzle of Adolescence

At the turn of the century, psychologist G. Stanley Hall dignified adolescence with his "storm and stress" theory, and Anna Freud subsequently argued influentially that such storm and stress is a normal part of adolescence. Ever since, clinicians and researchers have been trying—with only limited success—to develop a coherent theory of what makes adolescents tick.

Psychoanalytic theorist Peter Blos added in the late 1960s and 1970s that adolescents' uncontrolled sexual and aggressive impulses affect relationships with their parents. He suggested that both adolescents and their parents may need more distant relationships because of the unacceptable feelings stimulated by the adolescents' sexuality.

Research conducted in the 1960s showed that not all adolescents experience the storm and stress psychoanalytic theory predicts they should. Many studies, including those of Roy Grinker; Joseph Adelson and Elizabeth Douvan; Daniel Offer; and Albert Bandura, demonstrated that a significant proportion of adolescents make it through this period without appreciable turmoil. These findings suggest that pubertal change per se cannot account for the rocky time some adolescents experience.

Other theories of adolescent development have also been linked to pubertal change. For example, in his theory of how children's cognitive capacities develop, Swiss psychologist Jean Piaget attributed the emergence of "formal operational thought," that is, the capacity to think abstractly, to the interaction of pubertal and environmental changes that occur during the same developmental period.

Some researchers have linked the biological events of puberty to possible changes in brain growth or functioning. Deborah Waber, a psychologist at Boston Children's Hospital, has shown that the timing of pubertal change is related to performance differences between the right- and left-brain hemispheres on certain tasks and to the typical adult pattern of gender-related cognitive abilities: Later maturers, including most men, have relatively better spatial abilities, and earlier maturers, including most women, have relatively better verbal abilities.

It has also been suggested that pubertal change affects adolescent behavior through the social consequences of altered appearance. Once young adolescents look like adults, they are more likely to be treated as adults and to see themselves that way, too.

Coming also from a social psychological perspective, psychologist John Hill of Virginia Commonwealth University, together with former Cornell University doctoral student Mary Ellen Lynch, has proposed that pubertal change leads parents and peers to expect more traditional gender-role behavior from adolescents than from younger children; they suggest that both boys and girls become more aware of these gender stereotypes in early adolescence and exaggerate their gender-related behavior at this age.

Despite all these theories, most studies that look at how puberty affects adolescent development are finding that puberty per se is not as important as we once thought. Puberty does specifically affect such things as body image and social and sexual behavior, but it does not affect all adolescent behavior, and it affects some adolescents more strongly than others. In fact, many studies, like ours, are revealing that other changes in early adolescence, particularly social and environmental ones, are at least as important as biological ones.

---

dividual adolescents and their families—as well as on the pattern, timing and intensity of changes.

Youngsters in our study who changed schools within six months of peak pubertal change reported more depression and anxiety than those whose school and biological transitions were more separated in time. Students who experienced an unusual and negative change at home—such as the death of a parent or divorce of parents—reported even greater difficulties, a finding that supports other research. Sociologists Roberta Simmons and Dale Blyth have found that the negative effects of junior high school transitions, especially in combination with other life changes, continue on into high school, particularly for girls.

Many of the negative effects of transitions and changes seen in our study were tempered when adolescents had particularly positive and supportive relationships with their peers and family. The effects of all these early-adolescent changes were even stronger by the 12th grade than in 8th grade.

Overall, we found that the usual pattern of development in early adolescence is quite positive. More than half of those in the study seemed to be almost trouble-free, and approximately 30 percent of the total group had only intermittent problems during their early teen years. Fifteen percent of the kids, however, did appear to be caught in a downward spiral of trouble and turmoil.

> The vast majority of early teens we studied were trouble-free or had only intermittent problems. Only 15 percent were plagued by trouble and turmoil.

Gender played an important role in how young adolescents expressed and dealt with this turmoil. Boys generally showed their poor adjustment through external behavior, such as being rebellious and disobedient, whereas girls were more likely to show internal behavior, such as having depressed moods. But since many poorly adjusted boys also showed many signs of depression, the rates of such symptoms did not differ between the sexes in early adolescence.

By the 12th grade, however, the girls were significantly more likely than the boys to have depressive symptoms, a sex difference also found among adults. Boys who had such symptoms in the 12th grade usually had had them in the sixth grade as well; girls who had depressive symptoms as high school seniors usually had developed them by the 8th grade.

For youngsters who fell in the troubled group, the stage was already set—and the pathways distinguishable—at the very beginning of adolescence. There is an overall tendency for academic decline in the seventh and eighth grades (apparently because seventh- and eighth-grade teachers adopt tougher grading standards than elementary school teachers do). But the grades of boys with school behavior problems or depressive symptoms in early adolescence subsequently declined far more than those of boys who did not report such problems. Thus, for youngsters whose lives are already troubled, the changes that come with early adolescence add further burdens—and their problems are likely to persist through the senior year of high school.

One 12th-grade boy who followed this pathway described the experience: "My worst time was seventh to ninth grade. I had a lot of growing up to do and I still have a lot more to do. High school was not the 'sweet 16' time everyone said it would be. What would have helped me is more emotional support in grades seven through nine." In explaining that particularly difficult early-adolescent period he said, "Different teachers, colder environment, changing classes and detention all caused chaos in the seventh to ninth grades."

We did not find the same relationship between academic failure and signs of emotional turmoil in girls as in boys. For example, those seventh-grade girls particularly likely to report poor self-image or depressive symptoms were those who were academically successful. Furthermore, when these girls lowered their academic achievement by eighth grade, their depression and their self-image tended to improve. These effects occurred in many areas of girls' coursework but were particularly strong in stereotypically "masculine" courses such as mathematics and science. Like the pattern of problems for boys, the girls' pattern of trading grades to be popular and feel good about themselves persisted into the 12th grade. (Some girls, of course, performed well academically and felt good about themselves both in junior high school and high school.)

We think that for certain girls, high achievement, especially in "masculine" subjects, comes with social costs—speculation supported by the higher priority these particular girls give to popularity. They seem to sacrifice the longer-term benefits of high achievement for the more immediate social benefits of "fitting in." Other studies have revealed a peak in social conformity at this age, especially among girls, and have shown that many adolescents reap immediate, but short-term, social benefits from many types of behavior that adults find irrational or risky.

Our most recent research is focused on exploring further whether the developmental patterns established during early adolescence continue to the end of high school. We are also trying to integrate our observations into a coherent theory of adolescent development and testing that theory by seeing whether we can predict the psychological

> Parents let boys go out later than girls because they don't have to worry about them getting raped.

READING 8   EMMY E. WERNER
Resilient Children

Research has identified numerous risk factors that increase the probability of developmental problems in infants and young children. Among them are biological risks, such as pre- and perinatal complications, congenital defects, and low birth weight; as well as intense stress in the caregiving environment, such as chronic poverty, family discord, or parental mental illness (Honig 1984).

In a 1979 review of the literature of children's responses to such stress and risks, British child psychiatrist Michael Rutter wrote:

> There is a regrettable tendency to focus gloomily on the ills of mankind and on all that can and does go wrong. . . . The potential for prevention surely lies in increasing our knowledge and understanding of the reasons why some children are *not* damaged by deprivation. . . . (p. 49)

For even in the most terrible homes, and beset with physical handicaps, some children appear to develop stable, healthy personalities and to display a remarkable degree of resilience, i.e., the ability to recover from or adjust easily to misfortune or sustained life stress. Such children have recently become the focus of attention of a few researchers who have asked *What is right with these children?* and, by implication, *How can we help others to become less vulnerable in the face of life's adversities?*

THE SEARCH FOR PROTECTIVE FACTORS

As in any detective story, a number of overlapping sets of observations have begun to yield clues to the roots of resiliency in children. Significant findings have come from the few longitudinal studies which have followed the same groups of children from infancy or the preschool years through adolescence (Block and Block 1980; Block 1981; Murphy and Moriarty 1976; Werner and Smith 1982). Some researchers have studied the lives of minority children who did well in school in spite of chronic poverty and discrimination (Clark 1983; Gandara 1982; Garmezy 1981, 1983; Kellam et al. 1975; Shipman 1976). A few psychiatrists and psychologists have focused their attention on the resilient offspring of psychotic patients (Anthony 1974; Bleuler 1978; Garmezy 1974; Kauffman et al. 1979; Watt et al. 1984; Werner and Smith 1982) and on the coping patterns of children of divorce (Wallerstein and Kelly 1980). Others have uncovered hidden sources of strength and gentleness among the uprooted children of contemporary wars in El Salvador, Ireland, Israel, Lebanon, and Southeast Asia (Ayala-Canales 1984; Fraser 1974; Heskin 1980; Rosenblatt 1983). Perhaps some of the most moving testimonials to the resiliency of children are the life stories of the child survivors of the Holocaust (Moskovitz 1983).

All of these children have demonstrated unusual psychological strengths despite a history of severe and/or prolonged psychological stress. Their personal competencies and some unexpected sources of support in their caregiving environment either compensated for, challenged, or protected them against the adverse effects of stressful life events (Garmezy, Masten, and Tel-

From Emmy E. Werner, "Resilient Children," Young Children (November 1984):68–72. Copyright © 1984 by the National Association for the Education of Young Children, 1834 Connecticut Ave. N.W., Washington, D.C. 20009. Reprinted with permission.

legren 1984). Some researchers have called these children *invulnerable* (Anthony 1974); others consider them to be *stress resistant* (Garmezy and Tellegren 1984); still others refer to them as *superkids* (Kauffman et al. 1979). In our own longitudinal study on the Hawaiian island of Kauai, we have found them to be *vulnerable, but invincible* (Werner and Smith, 1982).

These were children like Michael for whom the odds, on paper, did not seem very promising. The son of teen-age parents, Michael was born prematurely and spent his first three weeks of life in the hospital, separated from his mother. Immediately after his birth, his father was sent with the Army to Southeast Asia for almost two years. By the time Michael was eight, he had three younger siblings and his parents were divorced. His mother left the area and had no further contact with the children.

And there was Mary, born to an overweight, nervous, and erratic mother who had experienced several miscarriages, and a father who was an unskilled farm laborer with only four years of education. Between Mary's fifth and tenth birthdays, her mother had several hospitalizations for repeated bouts with mental illness, after having inflicted both physical and emotional abuse on her daughter.

Yet both Michael and Mary, by age 18, were individuals with high self-esteem and sound values, caring for others and liked by their peers, successful in school, and looking forward to their adult futures.

We have learned that such resilient children have four central characteristics in common:

- an active, evocative approach toward solving life's problems, enabling them to negotiate successfully an abundance of emotionally hazardous experiences;
- a tendency to perceive their experiences constructively, even if they caused pain or suffering;
- the ability, from infancy on, to gain other people's positive attention;
- a strong ability to use faith in order to maintain a positive vision of a meaningful life (O'Connell-Higgins 1983).

PROTECTIVE FACTORS WITHIN THE CHILD

Resilient children like Mary and Michael tend to have temperamental characteristics that elicit positive responses from family members as well as strangers (Garmezy 1983; Rutter 1978). They both suffered from birth complications and grew up in homes marred by poverty, family discord, or parental mental illness, but even as babies they were described as active, affectionate, cuddly, good natured, and easy to deal with. These same children already met the world on their own terms by the time they were toddlers (Werner and Smith 1982).

> Resilient children tend to have temperamental characteristics that elicit positive responses from family members as well as strangers.

Several investigators have noted *both* a pronounced autonomy and a strong social orientation in resilient preschool children (Block 1981; Murphy and Moriarty 1976). They tend to play vigorously, seek out novel experiences, lack fear, and are quite self-reliant. But they are able to ask for help from adults or peers when they need it.

Sociability coupled with a remarkable sense of independence are characteristics also found among the resilient school-age children of psychotic parents. Anthony (1974) describes his meeting with a nine-year-old girl, whose father was an alcoholic and abused her and whose mother was chronically depressed. The girl suffered from a congenital dislocation of the hip which had produced a permanent limp, yet he was struck by her friendliness and the way she approached him in a comfortable, trustful way.

The same researcher tells of another nine-year-old, the son of a schizophrenic father and an emotionally disturbed mother, who found a refuge from his parents' outbursts in a basement room he had stocked with books, records, and food. There the boy had created an oasis of normalcy in a chaotic household.

Resilient children often find a refuge and a source of self-esteem in hobbies and creative interests. Kauffman et al. (1979) describes the pasttimes of two children who were the offspring of a schizophrenic mother and a depressed father:

> When David (age 8) comes home from school, he and his best friend often go up to the attic to play. This area . . . is filled with model towns, railroads, airports and castles. . . . He knows the detailed history of most of his models, particularly the airplanes. . . . David's older sister, now 15, is extraordinarily well-read. Her other interests include swimming, her boyfriend, computers and space exploration. She is currently working on a computer program to predict planetary orbits. (pp. 138, 139)

The resilient children on the island of Kauai, whom we studied for nearly two decades, were not unusually talented, but they displayed a healthy androgyny in their interests and engaged in hobbies that were not narrowly sex-typed. Such activities, whether it was fishing, swimming, horseback riding, or hula dancing, gave them a reason to feel proud. Their hobbies, and their lively sense of humor, became a solace when things fell apart in their lives (Masten 1982; Werner and Smith 1982).

In middle childhood and adolescence, resilient children are often engaged in acts of "required helpfulness" (Garmezy, in press). On Kauai, many adolescents took care of their younger siblings. Some managed the household when a parent was ill or hospitalized; others worked part-time after school to support their family. Such acts of caring have also been noted by Anthony (1974) and Bleuler (1978) in their studies of the resilient offspring of psychotic parents, and by Ayala-Canales (1984) and Moskovitz (1983) among the resilient orphans of wars and concentration camps.

PROTECTIVE FACTORS WITHIN THE FAMILY

Despite chronic poverty, family discord, or parental mental illness, most resilient children have had the opportunity to establish a close bond with at least one caregiver from whom they received lots of attention during the first year of life. The stress-resistant children in the Kauai Longitudinal Study as well as the resilient offspring of psychotic parents studied by Anthony (1974) had enough good nurturing to establish a basic sense of trust.

Some of this nurturing came from substitute caregivers within the family, such as older siblings, grandparents, aunts, and uncles. Such alternate caregivers play an important role as positive models of identification in the lives of resilient

> **M**ost resilient children establish a close bond with at least one caregiver from whom they received lots of attention during the first year of life.

children, whether they are reared in poverty (Kellam et al. 1975), or in a family where a parent is mentally ill (Kauffman et al. 1979), or coping with the aftermath of divorce (Wallerstein and Kelly 1980).

Resilient children seem to be especially adept at actively recruiting surrogate parents. The latter can come from the ranks of babysitters, nannies, or student roomers (Kauffman et al. 1979); they can be parents of friends (Werner and Smith 1982), or even a housemother in an orphanage (Ayala-Canales 1984; Moskovitz 1983).

The example of a mother who is gainfully and steadily employed appears to be an especially powerful model of identification for resilient girls reared in poverty, whether they are Black (Clark 1983), Chicana (Gandara 1982), or Asian-American (Werner and Smith 1982). Maternal employment and the need for sibling caregiving seems to contribute to the pronounced autonomy and sense of responsibility noted among these girls, especially in households where the father is permanently absent.

Structure and rules in the household and assigned chores enabled many resilient children to cope well in spite of poverty and discrimination, whether they lived on the rural island of Kauai, or in the inner cities of the American Midwest, or in a London borough (Clark 1983; Garmezy 1983; Rutter 1979).

Resilient children seem to be especially adept at actively recruiting surrogate parents. The latter can come from the ranks of babysitters, nannies, or student roomers (Kauffman et al. 1979); they can be and that God helps those who help themselves (Murphy and Moriarty 1976). This sense of meaning persists among resilient children, even if they are uprooted by wars or scattered as refugees to the four corners of the earth. It enables them to love despite hate, and to maintain the ability to behave compassionately toward other people (Ayala-Canales 1984; Moskovitz 1983).

PROTECTIVE FACTORS OUTSIDE THE FAMILY

Resilient children find a great deal of emotional support outside of their immediate family. They tend to be well-liked by their classmates and have at least one, and usually several, close friends and confidants (Garmezy 1983; Kauffman et al. 1979; Wallerstein and Kelly 1980; Werner and Smith 1982). In addition, they tend to rely on informal networks of neighbors, peers, and elders for counsel and advice in times of crisis and life transitions.

Resilient children are apt to like school and to do well in school, not exclusively in academics, but also in sports, drama, or music. Even if they are not unusually talented,

> **R**esilient children find a great deal of emotional support outside of their immediate family.

they put whatever abilities they have to good use. Often they make school a home away from home, a refuge from a disordered household. A favorite teacher can become an important model of identification for a resilient child whose own home is beset by family conflict or dissolution (Wallerstein and Kelly 1980).

In their studies of London schools, Rutter and his colleagues (1979) found that good experiences in the classroom could mitigate the effects of considerable stress at home. Among the qualities that characterized the more successful schools were the setting of appropriately high standards, effective feedback by the teacher to the students with ample use of praise, the setting of good models of behavior by teachers, and giving students positions of trust and responsibility. Children who attended such schools developed few if any emotional or behavioral problems despite considerable deprivation and discord at home (Pines 1984).

Early childhood programs and a favorite teacher can act as an important buffer against adversity in the lives of resilient young children. Moskovitz (1983), in her follow-up study in adulthood of the childhood survivors of concentration camps, noted the pervasive influence of such a warm, caring teacher.

Participation in extracurricular activities or clubs can be another important informal source of support for resilient children. Many youngsters on Kauai were poor by material standards, but they participated in activities that allowed them to be part of a cooperative enterprise, whether being cheerleader for the home team or raising an animal in the 4-H Club. Some resilient older youth were members of the Big Brothers and Big Sisters Associations which enabled them to help other children less fortunate than themselves. For still others emotional support came from a church group, a youth leader in the YMCA or YWCA, or from a favorite minister, priest, or rabbi.

THE SHIFTING BALANCE BETWEEN VULNERABILITY AND RESILIENCY

For some children some stress appears to have a steeling rather than a scarring effect (Anthony 1974). But we need to keep in mind that there is a shifting balance between stressful life events which heighten children's vulnerability and the protective factors in their lives which enhance their resiliency. This balance can change with each stage of the life cycle and also with the sex of the child. Most studies in the United States and in Europe, for example, have shown that boys appear to be more vulnerable than girls when exposed to chronic and intense family discord in childhood, but this trend appears to be reversed by the end of adolescence.

As long as the balance between stressful life events and protective factors is manageable for children they can cope. But when the stressful life events outweigh the protective factors, even the most resilient children can develop problems. Those who care for children, whether their own or others, can help restore this balance, either by *decreasing* the child's exposure to intense or chronic life stresses, or by *increasing* the number of protective factors, i.e., competencies and sources of support.

IMPLICATIONS

What then are some of the implications of the still tentative findings from studies of resilient children? Most of all, they provide a more hopeful perspective than can be derived from reading the extensive literature on problem children which predominates in clinical psychology, child psychiatry, special education, and social work. Research on resilient children provides us with a focus on the self-righting tendencies that appear to move some children toward normal development under all but the most persistent adverse circumstances.

Those of us who care for young children, who work with or on behalf of them, can help tilt the balance from vulnerability to resiliency if we

- accept children's temperamental idiosyncracies and allow them some experiences that challenge, but do not overwhelm, their coping abilities;

> **T**here is a shifting balance between stressful life events which heighten children's vulnerability and the protective factors in their lives which enhance their resiliency.

> **F**aith that things will work out can be sustained if children encounter people who give meaning to their lives and a reason for commitment and caring.

- convey to children a sense of responsibility and caring, and, in turn, reward them for helpfulness and cooperation;
- encourage a child to develop a special interest, hobby, or activity that can serve as a source of gratification and self-esteem;
- model, by example, a conviction that life makes sense despite the inevitable adversities that each of us encounters;
- encourage children to reach out beyond their nuclear family to a beloved relative or friend.

Research on resilient children has taught us a lot about the special importance of surrogate parents in the lives of children exposed to chronic or intense distress. A comprehensive assessment of the impact of siblings, grandparents, foster parents, nannies, and babysitters on the development of high risk children is elaborated upon in Werner (1984).

Outside the family circle there are other powerful role models that give emotional support to a vulnerable child. The three most frequently encountered in studies of resilient children are: a favorite teacher, a good neighbor, or a member of the clergy.

There is a special need to strengthen such informal support for those children and their families in our communities which appear most vulnerable because they lack —temporarily or permanently— some of the essential social bonds that appear to buffer stress: working mothers of young children with no provisions for stable child care; single, divorced, or teen-age parents; hospitalized and handicapped children in need of special care who are separated from their families for extended periods of time; and migrant or refugee children without permanent roots in a community.

Two other findings from the studies of resilient children have implications for the well-being of all children and for those who care for them.

(1) At some point in their young lives, resilient children were required to carry out a socially desirable task to prevent others in their family, neighborhood, or community from experiencing distress or discomfort. Such acts of *required helpfulness* led to enduring and positive changes in the young helpers.

(2) The central component in the lives of the resilient children that contributed to their effective coping appeared to be a feeling of confidence or faith that things *will work out* as well as can be reasonably expected, and that the odds *can* be surmounted.

The stories of resilient children teach us that such a faith can develop and be sustained, even under adverse circumstances, if children encounter people who give meaning to their lives and a reason for commitment and caring. Each of us can impart this gift to a child—in the classroom, on the playground, in the neighborhood, in the family—*if* we care enough.

BIBLIOGRAPHY

Anthony, E. J. "The Syndrome of the Psychological Invulnerable Child." In *The Child in His Family 3: Children at Psychiatric Risk*, ed. E. J. Anthony and C. Koupernik. New York: Wiley, 1974.

Antonovsky, A. *Health, Stress and Coping: New Perspectives on Mental and Physical Well-being.* San Francisco: Jossey-Bass, 1979.

Ayala-Canales, C. E. "The Impact of El Salvador's Civil War on Orphan and Refugee Children." M.S. Thesis in Child Development, University of California at Davis, 1984.

Bleuler, M. *The Schizophrenic Disorders: Long-term Patient and Family Studies.* New Haven: Yale University Press, 1978.

Block, J. H. and Block, J. "The Role of Ego-Control and Ego-Resiliency in the Organization of Behavior." In *The Minnesota Symposia on Child Psychology 13: Development of Cognition, Affect and Social Relations*, ed. W. A. Collins. Hillsdale, N.J.: Erlbaum, 1980.

Block, J. "Growing Up Vulnerable and Growing Up Resistant: Preschool Personality, Pre-Adolescent Personality and Intervening Family Stresses." In *Adolescence and Stress*, ed. C. D. Moore. Washington, D.C.: U.S. Government Printing Office, 1981.

Clark, R. M. *Family Life and School Achievement: Why Poor Black Children Succeed or Fail.* Chicago: University of Chicago Press, 1983.

Fraser, M. *Children in Conflict.* Harmondsworth, England: Penguin Books, 1974.

Gandara, P. "Passing Through the Eye of the Needle: High Achieving Chicanas." *Hispanic Journal of Behavioral Sciences* 4, no. 2 (1982): 167–180.

Garmezy, N. "The Study of Competence in Children at Risk for Severe Psychopathology." In *The Child in His Family 3: Children at Psychiatric Risk*, ed. E. J. Anthony and C. Koupernik. New York: Wiley, 1974.

Garmezy, N. "Children Under Stress: Perspectives on Antecedents and Correlates of Vulnerability and Resistance to Psychopathology." In *Further Explorations in Personality*, ed. A. I. Rabin, J. Aronoff, A. M. Barclay, and R. A. Zucker. New York: Wiley, 1981.

Garmezy, N. "Stressors of Childhood." In *Stress, Coping and Development*, ed. N. Garmezy and M. Rutter. New York: McGraw-Hill, 1983.

Garmezy, N. "Stress Resistant Children: The Search for Protective Factors." In *Aspects of Current Child Psychiatry Research*, ed. J. E. Stevenson. *Journal of Child Psychology and Psychiatry*, Book Supplement 4. Oxford, England: Pergamon, in press.

Garmezy, N.; Masten, A. S.; and Tellegren, A. "The Study of Stress and Competence in Children: Building Blocks for Developmental Psychopathology." *Child Development* 55, no. 1 (1984): 97–111.

Garmezy, N. and Tellegren, A. "Studies of Stress-Resistant Children: Methods, Variables and Preliminary Findings." In *Advances in Applied Developmental Psychology*, ed. F. Morrison, C. Lord, and D. Keating. New York: Academic Press, 1984.

Heskin, K. *Northern Ireland: A Psychological Analysis.* New York: Columbia University Press, 1980.

Honig, A. "Research in Review: Risk Factors in Infants and Young Children." *Young Children* 38, no. 4 (May 1984): 60–73.

Kauffman, C.; Grunebaum, H.; Cohler, B.; and Gamer, E. "Superkids: Competent Children of Psychotic Mothers." *American Journal of Psychiatry* 136, no. 11 (1979): 1398–1402.

Kellam, S. G.; Branch, J. D.; Agrawa, K. C.; and Ensminger, M. E. *Mental Health and Going to School.* Chicago: University of Chicago Press, 1975.

Masten, A. "Humor and Creative Thinking in Stress-Resistant Children." Unpublished Ph.D. dissertation, University of Minnesota, 1982.

Moskovitz, S. *Love Despite Hate: Child Survivors of the Holocaust and Their Adult Lives.* New York: Schocken Books, 1983.

Murphy, L. and Moriarty, A. *Vulnerability, Coping and Growth from Infancy to Adolescence.* New Haven: Yale University Press, 1976.

O'Connell-Higgins, R. "Psychological Resilience and the Capacity for Intimacy." Qualifying paper, Harvard Graduate School of Education, 1983.

Pines, M. "PT Conversation: Michael Rutter: Resilient Children." *Psychology Today* 18, no. 3 (March 1984): 60, 62, 64–65.

Rosenblatt, R. *Children of War.* Garden City, N.Y.: Anchor Press, 1983.

Rutter, M. "Early Sources of Security and Competence." In *Human Growth and Development,* ed. J. Bruner and A. Garton. New York: Oxford University Press, 1978.

Rutter, M. "Protective Factors in Children's Responses to Stress and Disadvantage." In *Primary Prevention of Psychopathology 3: Social Competence in Children,* ed. M. W. Kent and J. E. Rolf. Hanover, N.H.: University Press of New England, 1979.

Rutter, M.; Maughan, B.; Mortimore, P.; and Ouston, J; with Smith, A. *Fifteen Thousand Hours: Secondary Schools and Their Effects on Children.* Cambridge, Mass.: Harvard University Press, 1979.

Shipman, V. C. *Notable Early Characteristics of High and Low Achieving Low SES Children.* Princeton, N.J.: Educational Testing Service, 1976.

Wallerstein, J. S. and Kelly, J. B. *Surviving the Breakup: How Children and Parents Cope with Divorce.* New York: Basic Books, 1980.

Watt, N. S.; Anthony, E. J.; Wynne, L. C.; and Rolf, J. E., eds. *Children at Risk for Schizophrenia: A Longitudinal Perspective.* London and New York: Cambridge University Press, 1984.

Werner, E. E. *Child Care: Kith, Kin and Hired Hands.* Baltimore: University Park Press, 1984.

Werner, E. E. and Smith, R. S. *Vulnerable, but Invincible: A Longitudinal Study of Resilient Children and Youth.* New York: McGraw-Hill, 1982.

READING 9
Males and Females and What You May Not Know About Them

The potential difference between men and women begins with the assembly of a new set of chromosomes at conception, when one pair is coded either XX for females or XY for males. The difference a Y chromosome makes becomes physiologically explicit about six to seven weeks later. What else chromosome and hormone patterns do to set males and females apart—in behavior as well as body—is more problematic.

Most scientists believe both nature and nurture are responsible for sex differences. Some stress the striking degree of similarity between the sexes and the way this resemblance has grown through the ages.

Yet men and women *are* different, and these differences emerge in the realms of education, child rearing, sports, the military, the marketplace and the workplace, triggering some of the hottest social controversies of our day.

How, exactly, are they unalike? Here's what scientists know—and would like to know—about this engrossing topic.

BIGGER BOYS, MORE MATURE GIRLS

At birth, boys are on average half an inch longer and five ounces or so heavier than girls. They remain slightly larger throughout most of childhood. Newborn girls are about four to six weeks more advanced than boys in skeletal development, according to a leading expert on growth, Dr. J.M. Tanner of the University of London. Certain other organ systems are also more mature in female infants. Girls continue to mature more rapidly; according to some researchers they generally walk, talk and become toilet trained sooner than boys. Girls get their permanent teeth earlier and reach puberty about two years before boys do. They also have their adolescent growth spurt earlier, making them temporarily taller than boys.

But men end up longer-legged and about five inches taller. The average American woman between age 35 and 44 is 5 feet 4 inches tall and weighs 152 pounds; the average

Reprinted with permission from *Changing Times* Magazine, © 1981 Kiplinger Washington Editors, Inc., September 1981. This reprint is not to be altered in any way, except with permission from *Changing Times.*

man in the same age group is 5 feet 9 inches and weighs 179.

After puberty, males and females differ significantly in heart, lungs, blood, bone, muscle and fat. Boys develop larger hearts and lungs, more red blood cells and more hemoglobin. Their skeletons broaden at the shoulders; they put on muscle and develop a greater capacity than females for neutralizing the chemical by-products of muscular exercises.

The female skeleton at puberty broadens at the hips, and the female body builds up an energy reserve of fat—both changes in preparation for possible childbearing. Young adult males average about 50% muscle and 16% fat, females about 40% muscle and 25% fat.

More muscle is one reason why men tend to be better adapted for heavy physical work than women. Male and female muscle fibers are not very different in strength; however, men have more of them relative to their size.

The other key to physical performance is aerobic power, the maximum amount of oxygen an individual can get into the body and to the cells. Boys and girls start out about equal in this respect, but a Swedish study showed that after puberty women's aerobic maximums averaged about 80% to 85% of men's on the basis of weight. Under conditioning programs, however, women can narrow the gap in aerobic power and muscular strength. For example, sedentary college men in one study had 22% more aerobic power than sedentary college women before both went through an eight-week training program; men had only 8% more after.

Men and women differ most in muscular strength of the upper body, and they are most nearly equal in strength of legs and abdominal muscles. After seven weeks of Army basic training, women demonstrated, pound for pound, 84% as much strength as men in the abdominal muscles and 79% in the legs but only 70% in the upper body. Army physical training standards reflect the recognition of sex differences in strength. Young women must do at least 16 push-ups, for instance, but young men must do at least 40.

Both men and women athletes enjoy advantages related to their gender. Women gain balance and agility from their lower center of gravity. Men, with more muscle mass, more aerobic capacity, greater upper body strength and longer bones, can in general throw harder, jump farther and run faster.

The running and swimming speed gaps, however, have been narrowing in recent decades—men are only about 10% faster in current world records. In long-distance swims a woman's narrower shoulders, lighter body and insulating, buoyant body fat are a plus. The English Channel swimming record is held by a woman.

THE VULNERABLE MALE

In life as in sports, the physiological advantage of women is most apparent over the long haul. On average, American women live nearly eight years longer than men. Some researchers say that three-quarters of this sex difference can be explained by learned behavior that has been encouraged or condoned more for men than for women, especially smoking and the excessive competitiveness, aggressiveness, hostility and impatience often lumped together as "coronary prone" behavior.

Other investigators emphasize biological and genetic explanations for the male's greater vulnerability, which begins, in fact, at conception. Although at least 120 boys are conceived for every 100 girls, male rates of spontaneous abortions and stillbirths are so much higher that at birth the ratio is 105 to 100.

More males than female babies are born malformed; more die at childbirth, in the first week and year of life, and in every year thereafter. Men suffer from higher rates of chronic conditions that are leading causes of death. By the time the male and female survivors are old enough to have children, their numbers are about equal. By age 65 there are seven surviving men for every ten women.

Why should males be more fragile than females? Physiological maturity may be a factor. Girls, after all, are more mature in the womb and are born with a four- to six-week head start to help them weather the risks of infancy.

The endocrine system may hold a clue, too. Dr. Estelle Ramey and her colleagues at Georgetown University theorize that the male hormone testosterone has a gradually damaging system.

Another source of vulnerability is the difference in the sex chromosome pattern: XX for females, XY for males. The genes that govern the presence or absence of dozens of genetic diseases and disorders are carried on X chromosomes. Females with a defective gene on one X chromosome are likely to have a protective, healthy, matching gene on the other X. Males don't have a second X, so chances are that with one bad gene they will manifest— not just carry—such X-linked disorders as hemophilia and some kinds of muscular dystrophy.

The genetic shield of women doesn't end there. According to Dr. David T. Purtilo and Dr. John L. Sullivan of the University of Massachusetts Medical School, research indicates women have extra disease-fighting genes, twice as many as men carry on their sex chromosomes. Not surprisingly, the recovery rate of women from most diseases is better than that of men.

THE VULNERABLE FEMALE

The immunological advantage of females is a double-edged sword, Purtilo and Sullivan point out. It's good for fighting disease, but it also predisposes women to form antibodies against their own system, as in lupus erythematosus, a connective tissue disorder that strikes nine females for every male.

Women appear to be sick more frequently than men, and no one is certain of all the reasons. Data analyzed by University of Michigan demographer Dr. Lois M. Verbrugge shows women have more episodes of acute respiratory and gastrointestinal problems and higher rates of chronic conditions, such as arthritis, anemia, diabetes, hypertension and some forms of heart disease. They are also more poorly nourished and have poorer vision. On the other hand, females tend to have better teeth and better hearing than men.

In terms of absence from work, the two health profiles almost balance out: an average of 4.9 workdays a year lost by men, 5.7 lost by women.

THE WAY WE ACT

Mental illness strikes the sexes rather evenhandedly, with two exceptions. Men are more subject to personality disorders, including antisocial behavior and drug or alcohol abuse. Women seem more vulnerable to anxiety and depression—not just the everyday blues but also clinical depression, a mood disturbance severe enough to impair functioning.

In the case of depression, researchers are following tangled clues, biological as well as psychological and social. One difference they have uncovered is that marriage protects men from mental illness but increases the risk for women.

Research on sex differences in social behavior, learning, motivation and perception is extensive. Yet after scrutinizing hundreds of studies, Dr. Eleanor Maccoby and Dr. Carol Jacklin, Stanford University psychologists, found the evidence insufficient or too ambiguous to answer a number of key questions. For instance, they couldn't say with confidence whether females are more fearful, timid and anxious than males; whether males are more competitive; whether females are really more disposed to be nurturant or motherly.

What Maccoby and Jacklin could report in 1974 in *The Psychology of Sex Differences* (published by Stanford University Press) was that on most psychological measures males and females are more alike than different. They uncovered no proof that girls are more interested in social, boys in nonsocial stimulation. Studies indicated that the sexes persist on tasks to a similar degree, follow a similar course in the development of moral reasoning, and are about equally helpful and altruistic. Nevertheless, the researchers noted ways in which development varies.

- Boys tend to obey their parents less than girls do.
- Up to about age 18 months the incidence of angry outbursts triggered by frustration is similar in boys and girls. After that, such outbursts decrease quickly for girls but not for boys. One study found nursery school boys and girls crying with equal frequency but usually for different reasons: the girls because of physical injury, the boys because an object or adult wouldn't do what they wished.
- From as early as age 2 to 2½, males are more aggressive—readier to fight and more willing to hurt another person physically or verbally. This difference in aggression is the most solidly established sex difference in social behavior. Maccoby and Jacklin believe that although aggression is learned, there is a biological basis for boys' greater ease, on average, in absorbing the lesson.
- Neither sex appears to be more oriented toward people, but girls tend to stick together in pairs or small groups and to like their playmates. Boys congregate in larger groups, and liking or not liking each other seems secondary to the activity at hand.
- Maccoby and Jacklin found little reliable evidence that boys are consistently more active than girls, but beginning in the preschool years "boys appear to be especially stimulated to bursts of high activity by the presence of other boys." Boys also make many more attempts to dominate each other than girls do in their groups, possibly because large groups may need a pecking order more than small ones do. Boys tend to overestimate their status in their peer group more often than girls do.
- Girls generally get better grades than boys throughout their school years yet tend to underestimate their intellectual abilities more than boys. By the time they reach college, young women have less confidence in their ability to perform assigned tasks well.

Although they found no sex difference in overall intelligence, Maccoby and Jacklin found "fairly well established" evidence of some differences related to learning. On average, girls from age 11 on do better on tests of verbal skills, from spelling to understanding difficult passages and writing creatively. (Recent findings from the National Assessment of Educational Progress confirm this conclusion, with girls scoring three to four percentage points higher than male peers on reading tasks, as much as ten to 20 points higher on writing skills.)

Girls are also less vulnerable to language disturbances: Three to four times more boys than girls stutter; three to ten times more boys suffer reading disabilities.

From adolescence on, males outperform females on visual-spatial tasks—visualizing shapes and mentally moving or

Sex and the Teaching of Math

On the average, the sexes are intellectual specialists. Females tend to outperform men in verbal skills; males in general are better at math.

Lately, the mathematics gap has become a hot topic. According to Dr. Elizabeth Fennema of the University of Wisconsin, it should be. Lack of verbal skills doesn't seem to stand in the way of men's success, she says, but lack of math skills keeps women from doing a number of things, particularly from qualifying for well-paid jobs in science, engineering and technology.

Actually, the lack of language skills undoubtedly does hold some men back. But serious language deficiencies show up early in the school years, and the need to do something about them has been well accepted. As measured by the Scholastic Aptitude Test (SAT) verbal scores of high school seniors, college-bound boys eventually catch up to the girls. Since 1972 boys have even outperformed girls slightly.

The math disparity, on the other hand, doesn't show up until adolescence and has no similar tradition of remediation. Recent research has defined the discrepancy more precisely. In a national sample of 13-year-olds and of 12th-graders the younger girls did as well as their male counterparts on algebra and word problems and did better by five percentage points on computation. By senior year, boys and girls who had taken the same math courses achieved about the same in algebra and computation, but the boys outperformed the girls by six to 12 percentage points on word problems.

On the math section of the SAT, young men averaged 491 out of 800 possible points in 1980; young women averaged 443. Women are not absent from the higher-scoring SAT takers, just outnumbered — 10% of the females and 20% of the males score 600 or above.

Could there be some innate factor that primes men for superior math performance? If so, its identity is still unknown. Some researchers, thinking spatial visualization might be the key, have been searching for evidence of inborn spatial superiority. But that theory seems less convincing than it once did. In any event, no sex difference has been found in some recent tests of spatial visualization.

Another group of researchers used to believe that girls scored lower simply because they took fewer math courses. That argument, too, seems less persuasive these days. Fennema believes a more promising clue lies in the specific kind of math problem that tends to trouble girls more than boys. This stumbling block is the nonroutine problem that calls for putting math knowledge together on your own in a fresh way.

Why the difference? "Somewhere along the way we are not allowing girls to develop independence of thought in learning," Fennema warns. Yet the difference isn't inevitable. Some junior high classes do a good job of developing mathematical skills among both sexes. The University of Wisconsin researcher is trying to find out why.

Dr. Patricia Casserly of the Educational Testing Service has also been looking closely at individual math classrooms to see what elicits high performance. Out of about 100 high school advanced calculus classes in which boys and girls performed equally well and both achieved above the national average on standardized tests, she chose 20 classes with varied and modest family backgrounds. The key to the students' success turned out to be good instruction from teachers who had a degree in mathematics, science or engineering rather than in education. These teachers treated both boys and girls as "partners in a quest." They got across the idea that "all mathematicians have problems if they go far enough; it's O.K. to struggle," a particularly encouraging message for bright girls who are used to doing everything easily and well and face their first real challenge in math class.

---

rotating them. (However, a number of recent research studies, including two with a national sample, have not found this sex difference.)

- On average, boys do better than girls in math beginning about age 12 or 13.

ARE BRAINS ALIKE?

Now an intriguing new question arouses controversy. Do men and women act differently because their brains are different?

Primarily on the basis of work with lower animals, some respected researchers speculate that prenatal sex hormones program pathways in the brain and central nervous system, laying down predispositions for certain kinds of behavior.

As Dr. John Money, director of the Psychohormonal Research Unit at the Johns Hopkins Medical Institution, explains it, "... the irreducible difference between the sexes is that men impregnate, and women menstruate, gestate and lactate." Other than these biological functions, the sexes share all behaviors; only the prevalence of the behavior "or the ease with which it is elicited can be labeled masculine or feminine," Money writes. Parental care is a case in point: "... regardless of species, males or females can be parental, but the threshold for the release of parental care when the helpless young demand it is different, the mother being more immediately responsive."

A number of investigators are trying to relate left and right hemisphere brain organization to female verbal ability and male math and spatial ability. This research builds on the assumption that in most right-handed individuals, the left brain dominates verbal and sequential thought, and the right brain is more critical for the performance of spatial and other nonverbal tasks. Some studies suggest that women are more likely to use both sides of the brain for language, whereas men have a tendency to process it exclusively on the left, theoretically leaving the right hemisphere unimpeded for solving spatial problems.

However, Stanford psychologist Dr. Diane McGuinness and neuroscientist Dr. Karl Pribram point out a flaw in the theory: Some right hemisphere specialties, such as recognizing faces, are tasks in which women excel. They theorize that priming by prenatal hormones produces greater visual acuity in males and greater sensitivity to loudness and speech sounds in females. They also think it's possible that the difference in muscular competence (men do better with their large muscles and women excel in fine muscle and finger dexterity) reinforces the difference in sensory biases and leads to major differences in behavior and personality. McGuinness and Pribram point to the "manipulative" male who enjoys "the challenge of coming to grips with the physical environment" and the "communicative" female with "a strong interest in people and social situations."

BIOLOGY AND CULTURE

Even the most biologically oriented researchers warn that the human product is unpredictable because human beings, individually and in groups, are more susceptible than any other animal to learning and to being influenced by the impact of the social environment. Male and female Eskimos score the same on spatial tests. British boys often score better than girls on verbal tests. Is it their cultures that make the difference?

Then, too, a culture may assign roles with or without regard for innate qualifications. Although men in general are clearly better adapted than women for strenuous physical labor, there are societies in which women carry all the heavy burdens.

What is the most useful knowledge to be gleaned from all the research thus far? It may be this: As individuals, we are not predestined, bound or limited by the fact of gender. The only inevitable differences between the sexes are the few irreducible distinctions—the ones you knew about all along.

Can You Solve This Problem?

When the National Assessment of Educational Progress gave the following problem to a sample of 2,200 17-year-olds, 46% of the boys but only 39% of the girls were able to answer correctly in the 88 seconds allotted. Problems of this sort require not only basic computation but also use of various reasoning skills; some researchers attributed the different success rates to failure of the schools to encourage such skills in girls to the extent that they are encouraged in boys.

Juan's mother has three five-dollar rolls of dimes and two ten-dollar rolls of quarters to use for Juan's school lunch.

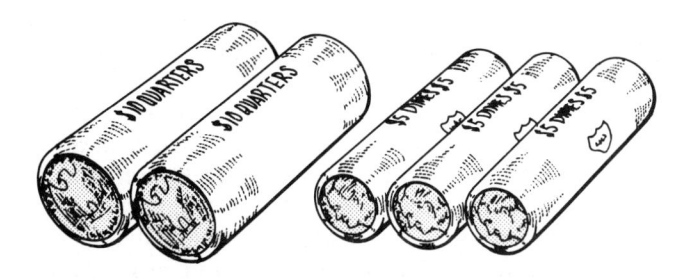

If Juan takes exactly 45 cents to school every day for his lunch, which of the following statements is true?

    A. He uses all of the quarters before all of the dimes.
    B. He uses all of the dimes before all of the quarters.
    C. He spends all of both coins at the same time.
    D. I don't know.

ANSWER: B

CHAPTER FOUR
The Great Behavioral Shapers: Genetics and Environment

READING 10   CLARE MEAD ROSEN
The Eerie World of Reunited Twins

Jerry Levey was uncomfortable. The New Jersey volunteer fire captain was ending a weekend at a local firefighters' convention and had stopped into a pub for a beer and a sandwich. From across the room, however, a conventioneer he had never met was staring at him curiously. Uneasy, Levey looked away. But each time he looked back, the stranger continued to gaze. Finally the man approached him. "He told me his name was Jim Tedesco," Levey recalls, "and then he asked me if I had a twin brother." Levey assured him he did not, but Tedesco persisted. There was a man in Paramus, he explained—another fire captain it so happened—who, except for a few extra pounds, could be Levey's double. Levey laughed it off. If he had a twin he'd certainly know it.

Tedesco wasn't swayed. Later he phoned Levey with more information: his Paramus friend was born on April 15, 1954. Was there anything special about that date? "I

From Clare Mead Rosen, "The Eerie World of Reunited Twins," *Discover* (September 1987):36–46. Clare Mead Rosen/© 1987, Discover Publications, Inc. Reprinted with permission.

nearly dropped the phone," Levey recalls. "That's my birthday."

Tedesco arranged for the two men to meet. When his mysterious friend entered Levey's firehouse, Levey went silent with wonder. "Lop off the extra pounds and I was looking in the mirror," he says. "We had the same mustache, same sideburns, even the same glasses." For a long moment the Paramus twin stared skeptically back at him. Suddenly the fire chiefs whooped in concert.

Later, sharing beers in a local bar, Levey and his brother—Mark Newman was the twin's name—began to assemble the jigsaw of their past. Each man already knew his biological parents had put him up for adoption, but neither had ever suspected that a sibling had been given up at the same time. As they talked and drank, the brothers discovered that they had more than looks and work in common. Both men drank only Budweiser; both held the bottle with the little finger stretched awkwardly beneath the bottom. Both were bachelors, both compulsive flirts, both raucously good-humored. "We kept making

the same remarks at the same time and using the same gestures," says Jerry. "It was spooky."

In the months following the reunion the spookiness began to fade, but the behavioral parallels continued to emerge. Though Mark and Jerry saw their strange history, and their even stranger similarities, as nothing more than wondrous curiosities, the scientific community sees things very differently. For behavioral researchers grappling with the old and stubborn question of whether it is our homes or our chromosomes that make us what we are, Jerry Levey and Mark Newman, and a tiny population of siblings like them, have always represented a rare research treasure: identical twins with perfectly matching genetic hardware but perfectly different lifetime programming.

Tantalizing though such subjects are, few researchers have ever attempted the painstaking job of tracking them down and bringing them in for a look. For close to half a century, only three studies—one in 1937 and two in the 1960s—tried to explore the mystery of twins reared apart. And even those surveys were, at best, cursory: the largest of the three tested 44 pairs of identical twins; the smallest investigated only 12 pairs.

But in 1979 all that began to change. That year Thomas Bouchard, Jr., a psychologist working at the University of Minnesota, Minneapolis, read an article about a pair of separated twins who had been reunited. Almost casually, he decided to contact them for study. After working with the pair, however, Bouchard grew hooked, and his goal gradually changed: he would study more reared-apart twins—not just a dozen sets, or even a *dozen* dozen—but all he could find. Twins reared together would also be studied, in a companion project, to serve as a basis for comparison.

The work has been under way for eight years. Bouchard's research crew had swelled from 3 to 18 and includes psychologists, psychiatrists, pathologists, geneticists, and dentists. Many of the twins who serve as subjects had already reunited before they volunteered for the program or were recruited by the researchers. Others have come individually to Minnesota hoping for help in locating a twin they know is out there. Once in the program, all the twins engage in a six-day testing marathon. They are wired with electrodes, placed on treadmills, hooked to round-the-clock portable devices that monitor temperature and activity. They are X-rayed, videotaped, and probed for everything from high blood pressure to heart murmurs to anxieties. In written tests and oral interviews they recount their sexual history, life stresses, schooling, and family history. They will answer 15,000 written questions alone.

To date, 77 sets of reunited twins—including Jerry Levey and Mark Newman—and 4 sets of reunited triplets have traveled to the Twin Cities to serve science and learn more about themselves. Several hundred sets of reared-together twins have also been studied. "The reared-apart pairs are coming in at about eight or ten per year," says psychophysiologist and team member David Lykken. "Since twins who are put up for adoption aren't being separated anymore at birth, we have a finite pool. I guess we'll study the ones there are until we retire."

Results, however, are beginning to appear. The team has already published some of its findings in professional journals, and other papers have been written and are awaiting publication. . . . With their work quickly coming to public light, the researchers have grown increasingly eager to talk about what they've discovered so far. The stories they tell are remarkable indeed.

There were the Jim twins of Ohio. That they had the same name was obviously a fluke. But the Jims also smoked the same brand of cigarettes, drove the same kind of car, held the same jobs, and engaged in the same hobby: woodworking. In fact, they had built identical white wood benches around trees in their yards. The Jims were both nervous nail-biters and both developed migraines at the same age.

Then there was Jack, a Jew who lived variously in Trinidad, California, and Israel. His twin, Oskar, grew up as a Catholic in Germany and belonged to the Hitler Youth. Despite their dramatically different backgrounds, the twins showed dramatically similar personalities when tested in Minnesota. They even shared the same eccentricities: both flushed the toilet before and after use, and both thought it funny to take a sneeze in a crowded elevator.

Also fascinating were Daphne and Barbara, a bubbly pair of Finnish twins. Despite growing up in opposite socioeconomic circumstances, they were both penny-pinchers. And both were stingy not just with their money but also with their opinions, refusing to take stands on even the most innocuous issues. Both had suffered miscarriages during their first marriage but went on to have three healthy children. The women shared a fear of heights. Shortly after meeting for the first time, they began finishing each other's sentences and answering questions in unison.

But such dramatic, even freakish similarities are by no means all the Minnesota team is after. Indeed, while the researchers understand the appeal of such anecdotes, they consider them little more than that—colorful stories that dress up their work but don't accurately represent it. The true focus of their studies, they explain, lies in the genes. What they hope to discover is the heritability of countless thousands of human traits and characteristics. "Heritable," they stress, does not mean "*in*heritable." What heritability addresses is percentages—how much of, say, our intelligence is bequeathed to us in our genes and how much we pick up from our upbringing and our surroundings.

To help answer these questions, Bouchard's group has made it a point to include fraternal twins as well as identical twins in the study. Both superficially and genetically, the difference between the two twin types is considerable. At the cellular level the conception of identical twins is a routine matter, taking place just like the conception of any singleton (as the rest of us are called): a solitary sperm fertilizes a solitary egg, creating a zygote. Ordinarily, the zygote immediately begins the nine-month process of maturing into a human being. But in the case of identical twins one step is added first: the zygote divides in two. Since both of the new cells originated from the same egg and the same sperm, they are perfectly identical, sharing 100 percent of their genetic material. The infants who appear nine months later—dubbed monozygotic (MZ) twins—will therefore usually be similarly indistinguishable.

Fraternal twins are a different matter. There, a glitch in the ovulation process causes not one egg to be released into the mother's fallopian tube, but two. This pair of completely separate ova are then fertilized by a pair of completely separate sperm, creating two completely discrete zygotes. Fraternal, or dizygotic (DZ), twins thus have an average of half of their genetic material in common, no more or less than any other pair of singleton siblings. With their often identical upbringing, however, they serve as a valuable control group against which the *genetic* similarities of identical twins can be measured.

Twin types are not taken for granted. A 20-part blood analysis is the ultimate test of whether a pair is monozygotic or dizygotic. There have been some surprises. One pair assumed to be fraternal because of their differing appearances and abilities turned out to be identical. Their differences came about because one was found to have had an environmentally induced neurological problem. This, says Bouchard, was a case of "environment overwhelming nature." Another case of mistaken zygosity involved two young women who were so physically similar that they first discovered each other when one was mistaken for the other. But their blood tests proved them fraternal.

The most puzzling case, however, involved two Japanese-born women reared by separate families in California. Though the twins looked almost indistinguishable, a few key markers, like the shape of their ears and face, were just different enough to get researchers wondering. Examinations and interviews revealed that both twins shared split nails on the same toes; both had had miscarriages; both suffered from a similar intestinal ailment. Yet one twin wore glasses and the other did not; one had a phobia of flying and the other did not; and one was reserved and traditional, the other more outgoing. It was not until the blood tests were completed that the answer was known: the twins were indeed identical. What then could account for the differences between them? "A whole host of things," says Lykken. "Environment, perhaps nutrition. Twins are also susceptible to all sorts of birth stresses, including the 'transfusion effect,' where one twin gets more than his share of blood. Twins are thus more likely than singletons to suffer from congenital birth anomalies that could distinguish them from each other."

Despite such occasional zygosity muddles, the Minnesota study is yielding a wealth of hard, empirical data—and not just on twins, but on the heritability of characteristics for the population at large. Most of the least controversial findings involve not psychological or temperamental traits, but physical ones. The researchers have observed that our capacity to ward off illness, for example, seems highly heritable. Monozygotic twins reared apart (MZA's) appear to have remarkably similar immune systems; researchers looked for nine key antibodies in the blood and found that these twins usually had at least seven in common. Dizygotic twins reared apart (DZA's) and singleton siblings share, on the average, only four. Genes also seem to govern susceptibility to heart and lung disease, as shown by the almost identical cardiac and pulmonary histories of the Minnesota MZA's.

More remarkable, however, is that not just the absence or presence of disease appears to be genetically encoded but also its timing. MZA's have developed everything from pancreatitis to diabetes to heart attacks within a short time of each other. Jerry and Mark both underwent a hernia operation during early childhood.

MZA's also seem to share the tendency to have or not have periodic disorders like cold sores or ear infections. William Knobloch, the chief ophthalmologist in the study, has found that identical twins are highly concordant in the timing of their need for glasses as well as in the onset of other eye problems like glaucoma.

The most striking example of biological timing Knobloch has seen was in the case of MZA triplets. "The men were in their fifties when they were reunited," he says. "One had just been diagnosed with glaucoma when he came to Minnesota. We then found that the other two were also glaucoma suspect. At the same time, one triplet had lost some vision in one eye from a different degenerative problem. And sure enough we found the same deterioration was beginning in the other brothers."

Researchers stress, that, in many cases, MZ twins do not simply inherit disease time bombs, set to go off at unchangeable, preset ages. Rather, like the rest of us, they inherit predispositions to illness. Other researchers suggests that a nonsmoking twin with a family history of lung cancer will still have a better chance of staying healthy than his identical sibling with a pack-a-day habit. Similarly, no matter what two twins' genes say about their hearts, the sibling who favors red meat and eggs is still at greater risk than the one who eats fish and salad. Indeed, even physical characteristics as seemingly predetermined as height can be profoundly influenced by environment: Identical twins reared apart may vary in stature if only one receives proper nourishment.

Other Minnesota findings suggest that predispositions to both severe and mild mental disorders might also have some genetic component. Schizophrenia, for instance, has long been known to be heritable; but the Minnesota study now suggests that such subtler problems as antisocial leanings, depression, and alcoholism might also involve genes. MZ's tend to share these problems far more frequently than do DZ's or singleton siblings. Many

> The Minnesota twin-researchers never use the word *inheritable*. They speak instead of "heritability" — the degree to which a trait or characteristic is caused by our genes rather than our environment.
>
> The heritability of a specific characteristic — say, height — can be judged by looking at pairs of monozygotic twins reared apart (MZA's). Since these siblings share 100 percent of their genetic material, any height difference must be due to environment. By comparing the typical amount of variation between one pair of twins and another with the typical amount of variation within a pair, the researchers come up with a ratio. In the case of height that ratio is 0.9, meaning that 90 percent of the variation in people's height is genetic and the remaining 10 percent is environmental. Researchers stress that the 0.9 figure applies not to individuals but to the population as a whole.
>
> "We don't say that ninety percent of *your* height is influenced by genetic factors and the other ten percent by environmental factors," says Minnesota psychologist Nancy Segal. "Rather, that ratio represents the proportion of differences among the people that can be explained by genes or by environmental influences."
>
> Monozygotic twins reared together (MZT's) have an even closer height correlation — 0.94. From this number, researchers conclude that an additional 4 percent of stature similarity can be caused by environmental experiences the siblings share — say, the balanced diet mom provided both her twins.
>
> And what of the remaining 6 percent *difference* in height that can distinguish MZT's from each other? This can be attributed to experiences unique to each sibling even when they're reared under the same roof. Maybe one twin poured his milk down the sink, while the other drank extra in hopes of making the basketball team. "Just because a characteristic is genetically influenced does not mean it can't be modified," says Segal. "By altering elements of our environment, we can alter genetic expression in any number of ways."

MZA's even display identical anxieties and phobias. One set of twins, for example, shared a terror of water that neither could trace to any triggering trauma. But both had learned to cope with their fear in the same unusual way: they always backed into a pool or lake.

It is in these areas of so-called soft science — personality and intelligence — that the Minnesota team has earned its most vocal critics. And perhaps understandably. Although blood type, immune function, and cardiac health can all be measured empirically, no one has ever been able to assign an irrefutable number to such vague characteristics as social skills, anxiety levels, and problem-solving abilities. Admits Lykken: "Psychological research is not exactly high-tech stuff."

Lykken's specialty is psychophysiology, meaning he deals with simple physiological responses that reflect psychological causes. He has found that identical twins reared apart have very similar brain-wave patterns, react alike to stimuli, and process information with comparable speed. MZA's also perform alike on tests of spatial perception, verbal fluency, and IQ. All this indicates that genes are at work, but no one seems to know just how.

"Genes do not fashion IQ or personality, they make proteins," Lykken says. "And those proteins are many biochemical steps removed from the complex traits and abilities we see in a person. Our study and others show that a good deal of what we are is heritable. But don't forget that heritability figures are estimates, not absolutes. Subsequent experience can sometimes overcome nature."

Nonetheless, Lykken believes that the testing techniques the Minnesota group uses come as close as any can to providing an accurate measure of twin intelligence and personality. The IQ methodology is a good example. "In the past," he says, "a single IQ test would sometimes be given by a single tester to both twins in turn." Bouchard and his team determined that just one day of testing was insufficient to judge IQ accurately. They also knew that the use of a single examiner could bias whatever scores the tests did yield.

So the Minnesota scientists do things differently. On one day of testing, the twins are taken into separate rooms by separate researchers who administer what is known as the WAIS (Wexler Adult Intelligence Scale), the standard method of evaluating IQ. On another day the subjects are given a second test, this one administered not by a psychologist but by a computer. A third test is also included, designed to evaluate such cognitive skills as spatial reasoning. Over the remaining week the twins participate in no fewer than 20 tests or interviews designed to measure other aspects of intellectual ability.

The grueling sessions have yielded some remarkable numbers, most supporting the findings of twin and adoption studies of the last half century. Identical twins reared in the same family usually have about an 86 percent level of correspondence. Fraternal twins hover at about 60 percent. But identical twins reared apart are generally much more similar than same-nest fraternals, with a 72 percent match. By contrast, garden-variety siblings reared together score 47 percent, and adopted children have only a 32 percent correspondence with their nonblood siblings.

Though the Minnesota researchers believe these findings indicate that mental ability is strongly affected by the genes, they do concede that there is no way to separate the development of an inherited trait from its environmental history. They stress, however, that if the environment does influence intellectual talents, the effect is subtle. Time after time in the Minnesota study, twins with very different schooling opportunities came out only a few points apart in intelligence. One memorable case involved two British twins with a lifetime of unequal opportunity behind them. "One had a cockney accent and the other one spoke like the queen," Lykken recalls.

The more privileged of the sisters was the daughter of a wealthy lawyer and had attended posh private schools; her sister was the daughter of a lower-middle-class East Londoner and had to give up formal education at age 16 in order to take a job. But when their scores were tallied, the two women were found to be just a single point apart in IQ. Lykken concludes that the upbringing of the disadvantaged twin was "plenty good enough" to allow her mind to flower. "Just because your father is from the lower middle class," he says, "doesn't mean he doesn't like books."

Most twins in the Minnesota study have come from the white Western world with backgrounds that meet Lykken's "plenty good enough" criterion. The Minnesota team acknowledges that its findings are therefore valid for only that segment of the population. But there is disagreement from other researchers about the findings from even this relatively thin demographic slice.

In 1981 psychologist Susan Farber of Columbia University reanalyzed the data from three smaller twin studies that preceded the Minnesota work and from a number of individual case studies. While she agrees generally with Bouchard's work, she feels more attention must be paid not just to how much genes affect the IQ of separated twins but also to the length and the timing of the separation. The earlier the siblings are taken from each other and the more years they spend apart, she suggests, the more dissimilar some of their IQ skills might be.

Bouchard disagrees. Working with the scores from the same studies, he found no such effect: Twins who had been "highly separated" had similar or identical IQ's an astonishing 76 percent of the time, while, paradoxically, "little separated" twins showed a far lower 65 percent correlation. Bouchard attributes these upside-down results to what researchers call the differentiation phenomenon, a theory to which Farber herself subscribes. Differentiation suggests that MZ's reared together may often try to distinguish themselves from their partners and thus—either consciously or unconsciously—create intellectual or personality differences. When reared under separate roofs, however, they feel no such pressure to differentiate themselves and so are more likely to become what they are genetically inclined to be.

Some of the controversies that bedevil the study of twin IQ also show up in the study of twin personality. Like intelligence, personality appears to be determined by a complicated interplay of both genes and upbringing. *Un*like intelligence, however, temperament traits do not appear to be rooted in the genes and merely influenced by environment. Rather, according to Minnesota psychologist Auke Tellegen, the formation of personality is closer to a fifty-fifty affair, with genetics and experience both holding considerable sway over what we become.

Though the twins under study go through a number of interviews and written tests during their stay in Minnesota, the most telling exam they take is a 300-question survey Tellegen developed, called the Multidimensional Personality Questionnaire. The MPQ is designed to provide a deep, 11-layer core sample of a twin's personality. Subjects are evaluated for impulsiveness; aggressiveness; need for achievement; traditionalism; stress reaction; sense of well-being; social potency, which includes such traits as leadership; social closeness or bonding ability; alienation; harm avoidance; and even absorption, or "proneness to imaginative activities."

In each of these areas, Tellegen found a heritability of about half. The figures range from 39 percent for achievement to 55 percent for harm avoidance; but Tellegen stresses that the significance of his findings is that heritabilities were found at all, and that they all hover at about 50 percent.

The other half of the psychological diversity—the half not accounted for by genetic diversity—is, of course, environmental. But it's environment broken down into two parts. One part is common family environment; the other is experiences unique to the individual. While in some areas all siblings may react in the same fashion to lessons taught by mom and dad, in other areas they may go their own way. The desire for achievement, for example, could be molded less by parental example than by the personal triumph of pitching a no-hitter in a

> Twins come in two varieties, right? Wrong. Geneticists have now proven that a third type of twin certainly exists and a fourth may be out there as well.
>
> The two most common twin types are identical twins, who share 100 percent of their genetic material, and fraternal twins, who share about 50 percent. However, a quirk in the way human eggs are manufactured makes a 75 percent twin at least a biological possibility.
>
> An immature ovum begins life as a 46-chromosome cell called an oocyte. During its development, the oocyte divides once, shedding a cell with enough genetic material for 46 chromosomes. This cell soon disintegrates; the surviving partner then divides again into a pair of 23-chromosome cells.
>
> Sometimes, though, the cell that *should* die, doesn't. Known as a polar body, this unusual egg is genetically identical to the ovum from which it separated. If both the ovum and the polar body are released during ovulation, and if both are fertilized by separate sperm (which usually have about half their genes in common), a pair of three-quarter twins could result.
>
> It is difficult to identify polar-body twins. However, Frederick Bieber, a geneticist at Harvard Medical School, reports one case in which a woman gave birth to a healthy twin with a normal 46 chromosomes and a badly deformed stillborn twin with 69 chromosomes. The stillborn baby, Bieber concludes, was the result of the fertilization of the first polar body shed by the oocyte, which contributed 46 chromosomes.
>
> "This tells us that fertilization of healthy, twenty-three-chromosome polar bodies is also theoretically possible," he says. "It is, however, probably rare, since a human polar body contains less cytoplasm than a mature ovum and is therefore less viable."
>
> Just as remarkable as polar-body twinning is an observed phenomenon known as heteropaternal dizygotic twinning—the conception of fraternal twins by separate fathers. "Sperm can survive for up to forty-eight hours in the female genital tract," says Bieber. "If a woman ovulates twice—as she would with ordinary fraternal twins—and has sex with two men within this period, the eggs can be fertilized by different men."
>
> Ordinarily, it takes a blood test to identify these unusual half-twins, but sometimes all that's needed is a simple look. "We've seen some cases," Bieber reports, "in which one twin was white and the other one black."

Little League game or by winning a school election.

Tellgen examined the common family environment and found that social closeness was the only personality trait that could really be attributed to it. Other traits seemed to depend on individual experiences. "Our findings don't show that families have no influence over their children," Tellegen says. "What we looked for was the 'common' family effect, the ways in which parents try to move all their children in the same direction. Families undoubtedly affect children, but not uniformly."

But Tellegen concedes that the architecture of personality—and the factors that shape it—can be only approximated by tests like his. Says psychiatrist Leonard Heston, another member of the Minnesota team: "It is utterly frustrating to try to pinpoint the environmental. We simply haven't got the tools to measure such effects."

Such caveats notwithstanding, the team has put forward a provocative hypothesis about an always controversial subject: the roots of homosexuality. So far, the findings suggest that while homosexuality may be heritable to a degree in males, it is probably based more on environment among females. Heston, along with psychiatrist Elke Eckert, was largely responsible for this branch of the research. Of the 55 separated MZ twins the two of them studied, six sets have contained homosexual or bisexual members. In one male pair, both brothers were homosexual; in another, only one was. In contrast with the men, none of the three female twins who said they were lesbian, nor a fourth who said she was bisexual, had an identical twin with a matching sexual orientation.

Curiously, the bisexual woman and the three lesbians were all taller and heavier than their heterosexual twins and all had started menstruation two years later than their sisters. Eckert thus speculates that lesbianism or female bisexuality may stem from a nongenetic endocrine change. She hastens to add, however, that this is just a possibility, since so few lesbian twins have been studied.

Though the Minnesota project is the first to investigate homosexual twins reared apart, a number of earlier studies have looked at the profiles of homosexual twins reared together. All these studies were of men, and all suggested that genetics plays a substantial role in the emergence of homosexuality. The largest previous survey showed a 100 percent sexual correlation in identical twins reared together, compared with only a 12 percent similarity in fraternal twins reared under the same roof. Heston himself, in a 1968 study, found a less striking but still significant 40 to 50 percent concordance in identical male twins reared together.

Until the Minnesota study is complete, most of the findings—from those regarding homosexuality to those that touch on personality and IQ—must remain indicators rather than answers. "We are in the long, arduous process of collecting data," Bouchard says. And data, he recognizes, can often lead to controversy. Bouchard recalls an argument he had with psychologist Leon Kamin of Princeton University over Kamin's claim that the similar environment of same-sex fraternal twins—particularly females, because they often share bedrooms—gives them IQ scores closer than those of ordinary siblings. Kamin cited a study showing that male fraternals showed an impressive 51 percent IQ concordance, and females a staggering 70 percent. Bouchard countered by citing 41 separate IQ studies embracing 3,670 same-sex fraternal pairs and 1,592 opposite-sex fraternal pairs. The statistics showed that same-sex fraternals had about the same IQ correlation (62 percent) as did opposite-sex fraternals (57 percent). While Bouchard insists the numbers are conclusive, Kamin points out that data are not accepted unless they fit the bias of the day.

"You can use data to prove anything you want," he says. "When I went to school, schizophrenia was laid to 'family dynamics.' Now we know genes play a part. But the new data are no better than the old, they're just better accepted."

And so the war between biology and culture grinds on. Lykken insists that the very concept of nature versus nurture is artificial because the two are totally interdependent: "I like to think of it as 'nature via nurture.'"

To the twins themselves, the whole debate seems pretty esoteric. They have something more fundamental on their minds: the sometimes easy, other times taxing job of readjusting to a world in which a living carbon of themselves has suddenly appeared after three or four decades of absence. Before even joining the study Mark and Jerry were comfortable declaring: "I'm him and he's me." And yet just as often they need their distance. Toward the end of their week in Minnesota, both said: "When this is over, we'll take a vacation from each other."

But like most twins who have gone to Minnesota, these two count their reunion as the greatest good luck of their lives. Again and again, twins who have found each other tell researchers that their only sadness is that they lost so many years together.

"I used to feel something was missing," Mark Newman confided in one of his interviews. "Now, it's back in place."

READING 11   JOAN ISENBERG
Societal Influences on Children

Today's youth live in a fast-paced, changing world characterized by social pressures that push them to grow up too fast. They are pressured to adapt to changing family patterns, to achieve academically at early ages, and to participate and compete in sports and specialized skills. Moreover, they are pressured to cope with adult information in the media before they have mastered the problems of childhood. Such pressure places increased responsibility and stress on children while simultaneously redefining the essence of childhood itself (Berns, 1985; Postman, 1985; Damon, 1983; Suransky, 1982; Elkind, 1981).

From Joan Isenberg, "Societal Influences on Children," *Childhood Education* (June 1987):341–348. Reprinted with permission of Joan Isenberg and the Association for Childhood Education International, 11141 Georgia Avenue, Suite 200, Wheaton, MD. Copyright © 1987 by the Association.

Both educators and psychologists are expressing concern over the impact of these changes on children. In examining the pressures of contemporary society, Elkind (1981) labels today's child "the hurried child," pushed by adults to succeed too soon thereby increasing the likelihood of failure. Others (Winn, 1983; Postman, 1982) contend that the media have contributed to the disappearance of childhood through "adultification" of children in television, films and literature. And Suransky (1982) believes the very concept of childhood is eroding through the institutionalization of early learning environments that deprive children of their right to discover, create and invent by imposing preschool curricula unrelated to their development and interests.

Because children are shaped and molded largely by the expectations of the institutions society creates for them, the social context in which they grow deeply affects their development. Erikson's (1963) theory of studying individuals in their social contexts illustrates the importance of children's interactions and interrelationships with critical agents in their social environment. Within these agents of the family, school, peer group and media, children acquire social skills and behaviors enabling them to participate in society. Recent changes in the patterns of these settings, however, push children out of childhood too fast and threaten their basic social needs at all ages and stages of development.

To best understand how today's youth are influenced by these societal agents, this article will identify children's basic social needs, describe the social pressures affecting those needs and provide suggestions for balancing social priorities for children.

CHILDREN'S SOCIAL NEEDS

Despite the fact that children have their own unique personalities, all children have basic social needs that must be adequately met to develop a healthy sense of self (Erikson, 1963; Bronfenbrenner, 1979). Such needs form the necessary and basic conditions for children from birth through the elementary years and enable them to better meet the lifelong challenges of productive social interaction. Table 1 outlines the critical ages and conditions for developing children's needs and their subsequent personality outcome.

SOCIAL PRESSURES AFFECTING CHILDREN'S NEEDS

Family

As the United States has moved toward urbanization, industrialization and the information age, significant changes have occurred in the structure and function of families (Bronfenbrenner, 1985a; Elkind, 1984; Umansky, 1983). We have witnessed a rise in single-parent homes, divorce, blended families and working mothers, as well as a decline in extended family homes and the birth rate. Today, approximately 20 percent of our youth live in single-parent families. Moreover, each year more than one million children experience divorce in their families (National Center for Health Statistics, 1983; Wallerstein & Kelley, 1980). Yet while the structure of families may have changed, the needs of children are still the same. The family remains their primary socializing agent.

TABLE 1 Social Needs

Need	Critical Age	Necessary Conditions	Personality Outcome
Love, Security, Stability	Infancy	Parents and caretakers provide consistent, regular and predictable care.	Develop strong sense of trust and belief in security of world. Foundation for self-confidence.
Independence	Toddlerhood	Parents and caretakers provide encouragement, freedom and choices for children to practice newly developed skills.	Grow self-confident and develop autonomy as they begin to find their own personality and self-will.
Responsibility	Preschool	All family members provide opportunities and encouragement for children to self-initiate exploration and discovery of their environment through projects, role-playing and taking time to answer "why" questions.	Develop sense of purpose, goal-directedness, willingness to try new things.
Competence and Success	Elementary School	Family, neighborhood and school provide opportunities for children to learn how things work and become competent and productive "tool-users" in their society.	Develop self-esteem and sense of self. Sense of competence and order.

Consequences

The dissolution of the family places additional pressures on children to adjust. Many of these children experience pressure to mature and assume increased adult responsibility (Berns, 1985; Elkind, 1981; Hetherington, 1979).

Preschool children, the most vulnerable to divorce, often do not understand the reasons given and have a strong need to identify with the absent parent. Consequently, they often feel guilty and responsible for the divorce and think that the parent left because they were bad. Elementary children may be very frightened, experience an acute sense of shame and display anger at one or both parents. They may engage in acting-out behavior (stealing, cheating) or develop physical symptoms (headaches, stomachaches). Early adolescents also feel anger and depression and may act out sexually or quickly assume adult roles and responsibilities (Wallerstein & Kelley, 1976). No matter what the age, children experiencing divorce often face additional challenges along with the usual tasks of growing up. Their ability to resolve these tasks depends, in part, on their own resilience and, in part, on parental handling of the separation issues (Papalia & Olds, 1986).

In addition to family changes precipitated by single parenting, the increase in women in the labor force has contributed to the pressure on children to grow up too early. A major problem for working mothers—and, therefore, children—is the availability of adequate child care. The lack of adequate child care has given rise to a group of unsupervised children, commonly referred to as "latchkey" children. At least 7–10 million children between the ages of 7 and 13 are left unattended after school (Seligson et al., 1983). These children spend part of each day alone and take responsibility for themselves. Such lack of supervision may lead to physical or psychological harm, contribute to delinquency, or produce feelings of abandonment and fear through lack of adult contact and security (Galambos & Gabarino, 1983; Herzog & Sudia, 1973). As the number of working mothers increases, the need for adequate child care also increases. Without adequate supervision, "latchkey" children are placed at risk.

Because the family is the child's first introduction to societal living, it has primary responsibility for children's socialization. How children learn to relate within the family context strongly affects their developing values, personalities and basic social needs.

Schooling

In addition to affecting the family, societal changes have affected the shape of early education. Today's parents are pushing their children to learn as much as they can earlier than ever (Spodek, 1986; *Newsweek*, 1983; Elkind, 1981). Anxious parents, influenced by mass media, believe that the earlier children begin learning academics, the more successful their school and life experience will be. Publishers are producing popular books such as *Teach Your Child To Read in 20 Minutes a Day* (Fox, 1986) and *Teach Your Child To Read in 60 Days* (Ledson, 1985), better baby videos and "teach your child at home" kits. All focus on developing children's intelligence at the expense of their personal and social adjustment. Advertisements promote anxiety in parents, which is then imparted to children: "And by the time they are 2 or 3 years old, another miracle can occur—if you allow it to. They can begin reading" (Moncure, 1985).

Today public kindergarten is available in every state. Moreover, increases in availability of preschool experiences have made the world of schooling available to children earlier (Spodek, 1986). Unfortunately, in many cases elementary school criteria and programming are being applied to programs for young children (Elkind, 1986; Suransky, 1982). Pressure to provide more formal learning and more rigorous academic content has resulted in refocusing early education: from meeting children's developmental needs in an environment generally free of social pressures to pressuring children to prepare for elementary school and later life. The notion of the "competent infant" fits into our changing lifestyles, along with the idea that children today are more sophisticated and advanced because of the nature of their experiences (Hunt, 1961; Bloom, 1964; Bruner, 1960). New importance has been attached to children's intellectual development as children are placed in high-pressure academic programs for "their own good" (Elkind, 1986).

Consequences

The pressure for early academic achievement has been criticized by child development experts not only because there is no research base to support it but also because it may impede development of other equally important skills (Spodek, 1986; Elkind, 1986; Seefeldt, 1985). Some argue that formal instruction at early ages makes unnecessary demands on children and places them in unnatural learning modes. Others argue that undue emphasis on early formal learning has the potential to diminish children's long-term motivation to learn by interfering with the natural development of their need for self-directed learning. It places children at intellectual risk by interfering with their developing reflective abstraction and at social risk by forcing them to rely on "adults for approval and . . . social comparison for self-appraisal" (Elkind, 1986, p. 636).

Pressure for academic achievement can encourage school failure. Maturity, one factor of development virtually ignored in past years, is now the subject of considerable attention. According to Friesen (1984), there is the "possibility that much of the failure in our schools is the result of overplacement, and that we might reduce the rate of failure by finding a better match between a youngster's grade assignment and his or her developmental age" (p. 14). Research supports the proposition that overplacement can be a significant cause of school failure.

"There is, of course, no evidence to support the value of such early pushing. There is, however, considerable evidence that children are showing more and more serious stress symptoms than ever before" (Elkind, 1984, p. viii). Attempting to force children at early ages to learn specific academic material or develop specific skills may produce a negative attitude toward learning in general, with serious long-term effects evidenced in increased drop-out rates and a high rate of cheating (Harris, 1986; Elkind, 1982).

Peers

Peer groups provide yet another critical agent of socialization. Historically, children have relied primarily on informal peer groups, formed and maintained by themselves, to develop social roles and cooperative interests. Today, however, more and more children are engaged in formal group activities, organized and maintained by adults. Activity markers such as organized sports, beauty contests, graduations and specialized arts training—once reserved for the teen years—are rapidly being pushed down to younger and younger children. Elkind (1984) suggests that much of this "premature structuring" stems from parental need rather than concern and understanding for the child. Children pushed too soon into formal and adult organized groups often raise questions in adolescence:

"Why am I doing this? Who am I doing this for? When seeking answers to these questions, children revolt in many ways when the answer is for the parent. Delinquency, school dropouts, drugs, alcohol and refusal to perform are some of the behaviors evidenced by children forced to achieve too early" (Elkind, 1982, pp. 178–179). The shift of these activity markers from adolescence to childhood creates unnecessary stress for children, causing them to develop parts of their personality and leaving other parts undeveloped (Elkind, 1984).

Consequences

Unsuccessful children pushed by parents into sports or specialized activities become discouraged and humiliated by not meeting parental expectations and may even end up hating the activity itself. Although the range of pressure is great, some feel rejected by both parents and peers for not achieving (McElroy, 1982).

The notion of competition carries with it negative aspects. Psychological damage can occur when adults stress competition over learning skills and view their children's victories, losses and performances as indicators of their personal successes or shortcomings.

Television

Because television-watching occupies more time than any other single activity except sleeping (Bee, 1985; Gerbner & Gross, 1978; Stein & Friedrich, 1975), it acts as a powerful socializing influence. By the end of high school, the average American child has watched over 20,000 hours of television, more than the number of hours spent in school (Comstock, 1975).

Television programs provide the same information to everyone, regardless of age (Postman, 1985). Information about violence, sexual activity, aggression, and physical and mental abuse is readily available and erodes the dividing line between childhood and adulthood. It places

> children and adults in the same symbolic world. . . . All the secrets that a print culture kept from children—about sex, violence, death and human aberration—are at once revealed by media that do not and cannot exclude any audience. Thus, the media forced the entire culture out of the closet. And out of the cradle. (Postman, 1981, p. 68)

Consequences

The content of prime-time television programming and advertising can cause children to increase their aggressive behavior in the short term (NIMH, 1982) and become desensitized to violence later in life (Thomas, 1982). Viewing violent content through images, characters and plots—whether on prime-time TV, cartoons, MTV or the nightly news—discourages children from cooperating to resolve problems because they come to accept what they see as appropriate behavior (Papalia & Olds, 1986; NIMH, 1982).

Advertisements, on the other hand, glorify instant gratification both explicitly and implicitly. New products and new fads constantly bombard viewers. Advertising directed explicitly at young children can create resentment when parents refuse to purchase products; for older children, it can create unrealistic fantasies that certain products will make them more popular.

Postman (1985) argues that children view one million commercials before age 18 at a rate of 1,000 per week, most of them perpetuating a youth culture, sex and materials as a way of solving problems instantaneously. Elkind (1981) suggests that by treating children as consumers before they are wage earners, children are pressured into a kind of "hucksterism," causing "adults to treat them as more grown-up than they are" and to assume they are able to see through the deceptions of advertising and to make informed choices (p. 79).

Thus, television programming and advertising continue to erode the dividing line between childhood and adulthood by opening secrets once only available to adults, eliminating the innocence of childhood, reducing the concept of childhood, and making the adult's and child's world homogeneous (Postman, 1985, p. 292). In a world where children view adult programming and advertising, how well are our youth being nurtured? Indeed, "the children of the 80's are growing up too fast, too soon. They are being pressured to take on the physical, emotional and social trappings of adulthood before they are prepared to deal with them" (Elkind, 1981, p. xii).

BALANCING PRIORITIES FOR CHILDREN

Pushing children to grow up too early affects the very core of the social fabric that develops, sustains and connects healthy, competent children. There is an urgent need to re-weave the unravelling social fabric of significant social influences (Bronfenbrenner, 1985a, p. 10). This can be accomplished by attending to the following critical agents of socialization at the family, school and policy levels.

Family

Balance concern for academic achievement with equal concern for developing feelings of competence, confidence and self-worth.
Children's successful adjustment to family life affects their ability to adjust to the outside world. The quality of parent/child relationships is built from the means of communication used. As the structure of families changes, there is greater need for positive communication about issues that affect children's self-respect and self-regard. Through empathic listening, talking and responding—setting realistic and honest expectations and talking about fears—families can build a strong foundation for children's positive feelings about themselves.

One context for this communication is the *family meeting*, which provides opportunities for parents and children to talk about concerns, make decisions and suggest ways to solve problems. Children can assume responsibility as family members as well as have a time for "hurried lives" to engage in constructive "family time."

Balance the need for structured and professionalized activity with opportunities for play.
Probably the least understood childhood need is the need for play. Play is vital to children's intellectual, social and physical development and is "seen as a primary mode for a child who is involved in becoming" (Suransky, 1982, p. 12).

Families contribute to children's optimal development by assuring opportunities for children to generate their own play with peers. In so doing, "they are fulfilling a fundamental human activity of intentionality and purposiveness" (Suransky, 1982, p. 173). Denying children the right to play denies them their primary means of learning about themselves and their world. Lack of adequate opportunities to engage in genuine play is evident in our hurried children today (Elkind, 1981, p. 193).

Help children become critical TV-viewers.
Children can develop proper TV-viewing habits with simple guidelines. Adults can view programs with children and talk with them about what they see. In viewing TV, adults should notice those behaviors children can imitate; for example, TV characters who model caring behaviors and programs that depict women as being competent. Moreover, adults should talk to children about the programs and note the differences between make-believe and reality. They should discuss alternate ways to solve problems they see on TV, as well as the effect of commercials.

School

Establish balanced curricula that meet children's needs.
Teachers, administrators and parents must be informed about what children are expected to learn and how they learn best. They need to set high but realistic expectations for children and encourage them to do their best work without pressuring them to perform beyond their level. We need to employ sensitive teachers who promote children's abilities and who recognize the power of their pedagogic task.

Provide inservice support for teachers and administrators about school and community resources.
Schools must take responsibility for educating school personnel about realistic expectations for children and changing family patterns. School counselors must be able to support teachers and help children and families through the varied transitions of schooling and family patterns. In providing this stability and support, counselors must understand current literature and research on the changing fabric of societal institutions.

Provide courses, workshops and training sessions for parents and educators.
Both colleges and communities must provide parenting courses and teaching courses in response to the stresses of contemporary society. Educating parents about parenting is no longer a luxury; it is an imperative.

Policy

Advocate for quality and appropriate child care.

Families with children must demand high quality child care that takes into account the needs of children and their families. Whether the care occurs in or out of the home, children's social patterns and behaviors continue to form in these settings. Young children need settings that integrate play naturally, encourage their active exploration and foster a sense of trust and security. They also need caregivers who enjoy working with young children, understand their growth and development, have realistic expectations for their behavior and are responsive to parents.

School-age children need safe and supervised care in which they are involved in activities appropriate to their stage of development. They also need teachers who understand them, their families and their needs.

Parents and community members must be advocates for quality, comprehensive child care settings. An informed community must develop appropriate programs for children, its most vulnerable group.

CONCLUSION

Pressured by each of the critical socializing agents in their lives, today's children are experiencing shortened childhoods. The sources and consequences of such pressures are clear. Also clear is the urgent need to direct our efforts toward balancing priorities for children at the family, school and policy levels.

REFERENCES AND OTHER READINGS

A healthy personality for each child. (1951). A digest of the factfinding report to the Midcentury White House Conference on Children and Youth. Raleigh, NC: Heath Publications Institute.

Bee, H. (1985). *The developing child,* (4th ed.). Cambridge, MA: Harper & Row.

Berns, R. M. (1985). *Child, family and community.* New York: Holt, Rinehart & Winston.

Bloom, B. (1964). *Stability and change in human characteristics.* New York: Wiley.

Bronfenbrenner, U. (1985a). The parent/child relationship and our changing society. In L. E. Arnold, (Ed.), *Parents, children and change.* Lexington, MA: Lexington Books.

Bronfenbrenner, U. (1985b). *The three worlds of childhood.* Principal, 64(5), 7–11.

Bronfenbrenner, U., & Crouter, A. C. (1983). Work and family through time and space. In S. B. Kamerman & C. D. Hayes, (Eds.), *Families that work: Children in a changing world.* Washington, DC: National Academy Press.

Bronfenbrenner, U. (1979). *The ecology of human development.* Cambridge, MA: Harvard University Press.

Bruner, J. (1960). *The process of education.* Cambridge, MA: Harvard University Press.

Coleman, M., & Skeen, P. (1985). *Play, games and sport. Their use and misuse.* Childhood Education, 61(3), 192–197.

Comstock, G. A. (1975). *Effects of television on children: What is the evidence?* Santa Monica, CA: The Rand Corp., #P5412.

Damon, W. (1983). *Social and personality development: Infancy through adolescence.* New York: W. W. Norton.

Elkind, D. (1986). Formal education and early childhood education: An essential difference. *Phi Delta Kappan, 67*(9), 631–636.

Elkind, D. (1984). *All grown up and no place to go: Teenagers in crisis.* Reading, MA: Addison-Wesley.

Elkind, D. (1982, March). Misunderstandings about how children learn. Today's Education, 24–25.

Elkind, D. (1981). *The hurried child.* Reading, MA: Addison-Wesley.

Erikson, E. (1963). *Childhood and society,* (2nd ed.). New York: W. W. Norton.

Fox, B. J. (1986). *Teach your child to read in 20 minutes a day.* New York: Warner.

Friesen, D. (1984). Too much too soon. *Principal, 6*(4), 14–18.

Galambos, N. L., & Garbarino, J. (1983). Identifying the missing links in the study of latchkey children. *Children Today, 40,* 2–4.

Gerbner, G., & Gross, N. (1978). Demonstration of Power. *Journal of Communication, 29,* 177–184.

Glick, P. C. (1979). Children of divorced parents in demographic perspective. *Journal of Social Issues, 35,* 170–182.

Harris, A. C. (1986). *Child development.* New York: West.

Helms, D. B., & Turner, J. S. (1986). *Exploring child behavior,* (3rd ed.). Belmont, CA: Wadsworth.

Herzog, E., & Sudia, C. E. (1973). Children in fatherless families. In B. Caldwell & H. N. Riccuti (Eds.), *Review of child development research, 3.* Chicago: University of Chicago Press.

Hetherington, E. M. (1979). Divorce: A child's perspective. *American Psychologist, 34,* 851–858.

Hetherington, E. M., Cox, M., & Cox, R. (1978). The aftermath of divorce. In J. H. Stevens, Jr. & M. Matthews (eds.), *Mother-child, father-child relations.* Washington, DC: National Association for the Education of Young Children.

Hofferth, S. L. (1979). Day care in the next decade, 1980–1990. *Journal of Marriage and the Family, 4,* 649–658.

Hoffman, L. W. (1974). Effects of maternal employment on the child: A review of the research. *Developmental Psychology, 10,* 204–228.

Hunt, J. McV. (1961). *Intelligence and experience.* New York: Ronald Press.

Ledson, S. (1985). *Teach your child to read in 60 days.* New York: Berkley.

Martens, R. (1978). *Joy and sadness in children's sports.* Champaign, IL: Human Kinetics.

McElroy, M. (1982). Consequences of perceived parental pressures on the self-esteem of youth sport participants. *American Corrective Therapy Journal, 36*(6), 164–167.

Moncure, J. (1985). *My first steps to reading.* Haddam, CT: Children's Reading Institute.

National Center for Health Statistics. (1983). *Report on marriage and divorce today, 7,* 3–4.

National Institutes of Mental Health. (1982). *Television and behavior: Ten years of scientific progress and implications for the eighties.* Washington, DC: U.S. Government Printing Office.

Newsweek. (1983, March). Bringing up superbaby, p. 62.

Papalia, D. E., & Olds, S. W. (1986). *Human development,* (3rd ed.). New York: McGraw-Hill.

Postman, N. (1985). The disappearance of childhood. *Childhood Education, 61*(4), 286–293.

Postman, N. (1983, March). The disappearing child. *Educational Leadership,* 10–17.

Postman, N. (1982). *The disappearance of childhood.* New York: Delacorte.

Postman, N. (1982). Disappearing childhood. *Childhood Education, 58*(2), 66–68.

Robinson, S. L. (1985). Childhood: Can it be preserved? An interview with Neil Postman. *Childhood Education, 61*(3), 337–342.

Santrock, J. W., & Wasnak, R. A. (1979). Father custody and social development in boys and girls. *Journal of Social Issues, 35,* 112–125.

Seefeldt, C. (1985). Tomorrow's kindergarten: Pleasure or pressure? *Principal, 64*(5), 12–15.

Seligson, M., Genser, A., Gannett, E., & Gray, W. (1983, December). *School-age child care: A policy report.* Wellesley, MA: Wellesley College Center for Research on Women.

Smith, R. E., & Smoll, F. L. (1978). Sport and the child: Conceptual and research perspectives. In F. L. Smoll & R. E. Smith (Eds.), *Psychological perspectives in youth sports.* New York: Wiley.

Spodek, B. (Ed.). (1986). *Today's kindergarten: Exploring the knowledge base, expanding the curriculum.* New York: Teachers College Press.

Stein, A., & Freidrich, L. (1975). Impact of television on children and youth. In E. M. Hetherington (Ed.), *Review of child development research, 5.* Chicago: University of Chicago Press.

Suransky, V. P. (1982). *The erosion of childhood.* Chicago: University of Chicago Press.

Thomas, M. H. (1982). Physiological arousal, exposure to a relatively lengthy aggressive film, and aggressive behavior. *Journal of Research in Personality, 16,* 72–81.

Umansky, W. (1983). On families and the re-valuing of childhood. *Childhood Education, 59*(4), 260–266.

Wallerstein, J. S., & Kelley, J. B. (1980). *Surviving the breakup: How children actually cope with divorce.* New York: Basic Books.

Wallerstein, J. S., & Kelley, J. B. (1975). The effects of parental divorce: Experiences of the child in later latency. *American Journal of Orthopsychiatry, 46,* 256–269.

Wallerstein, J. S., & Kelley, J. B. (1976). The effects of parental divorce: Experiences of the child in later latency. *Journal of the American Academy of Child Psychiatry, 14,* 600–616.

Winn, M. (1983). *Children without childhood.* New York: Pantheon.

PART TWO
Study and Discussion Questions

CHAPTER THREE Developmental Dynamics and Growth Outcomes

Reading 6 Children in a Changing Society

1. In what ways are children's lives changing when it comes to matters like single-parent families, television watching, sexual activities, drug use, suicide, and child abuse?

2. What does research suggest about how children's attitudes are changing?

3. If you were to develop proposals for ways to make life better for children, what recommendations would you make?

Reading 7 Those Gangly Years

1. Puberty may not have the overwhelming psychological impact that researchers thought it did, but it does have many effects on body image, moods, and relationships. Can you explain what some of these effects are?

2. Can you think of examples from your own adolescence that illustrate these effects?

3. Assume that a group of parents of adolescents asks you, "What can we expect in terms of change and behavior from our teenagers, and how should we respond?" What would you say to these parents?

Reading 8 Resilient Children

1. Are you able to identify and say something about the protective factors that help make resilient children resilient?

2. As adults, what can we do to promote greater resiliency in children?

Reading 9 Males and Females and What You May Not Know About Them

1. What special vulnerabilities does each sex have?

2. Can you identify the special intellectual strengths that have been associated with each sex?

3. Someone asks you, "Do men and women act differently because their brains are different?" How do you respond?

CHAPTER FOUR The Great Behavioral Shapers: Genetics and Environment

Reading 10 The Eerie World of Reunited Twins

1. Why is it that twin researchers do not like using the word *inheritable,* preferring, rather, the word *heritability*?

2. The Minnesota twin studies have shown that twins who have been "highly separated" had similar or identical IQs, whereas those twins who were "little separated" showed less IQ similarity. What is the probable reason for this finding?

Reading 11 Societal Influences on Children

1. The social pressures affecting children's needs originate from four primary sources. Can you identify those four sources and briefly describe their effects on children?

2. In what ways is exposure to heavy television viewing likely to be detrimental to children's psychological development?

3. Based on what you have read in Readings 10 and 11, what can you conclude about the relative effects of genes and environment on the development of intelligence and personality?

PART THREE

Brain Development and Intellectual Expressions

The three-pound mass lodged in the top of our heads is the grandest, most awesome computer of them all. It not only generates answers, but more important, it is able to ask questions. It can think about its own thinking; it can question its own questions. It is a vast intrapsychic network of interconnected neurons, which number about 10 billion, approximately the number of hairs on 100,000 people. In fact, the web of connections between neurons in the top layer of the brain—the neocortex—is so vast that it has been estimated to measure an incredible 10,000 miles per cubic inch. Research in the past 20 years or so has begun to unlock some of its deepest secrets. The articles in Part Three have been chosen with an eye to learning more about those secrets.

Chapter Five overviews some of the important advances made in understanding brain growth and functioning. In Reading 12, Kathleen McAuliffe explores why a child is so receptive to new information, and why adults seem to lose this capacity as they gain more knowledge of the world around them. There are, it appears, certain "critical periods" for learning that influence language development and even the disposition for certain social skills.

A great deal of press, not all of it accurate, has been given to "right brain" and "left brain" functions. In Reading 13, Jerre Levy sets the record straight as she discusses evidence indicating that the separate-hemisphere, "two brain" idea is largely a myth founded on an erroneous premise.

In Reading 14, Daniel Goleman summarizes recent research evidence suggesting that the brain's nerve cells continue to grow and develop in response to intellectual enrichment of all sorts: travel, puzzles, reading, anything that stimulates the brain with novelty and challenge. What is true for other parts of the body seems equally true for the brain: When we use it, we are less likely to lose it.

Chapter Six focuses on two exciting new views about the nature of human intelligence. In Reading 15, Howard Gardner offers what he calls a "theory of multiple intelligences," an idea that goes far beyond the usual "ability for abstract thinking" or "capacity to do school work" points of view. Gardner theorizes that there are really seven different kinds of "intelligences," ranging all the way from logical–mathematical intelligence to intrapersonal intelligence, an idea that has stirred considerable debate.

Robert Sternberg, on the other hand, theorizes that intelligence is composed of three different aspects, and in Reading 16, Robert J. Trotter explains the details of this viewpoint, known as the "triarchic theory." Both Gardner and Sternberg are broadening our definition of intelligence, something that seems long overdue.

Why is it that if the basics of language development are not learned at a certain age, they are so difficult to learn at a later time? Are the brain's two hemispheres as separate as they have been thought to be? Are brain growth and intellectual development possible even into one's later years? If so, what are the necessary conditions for this? Can an enriched environment later in life compensate for brain-cell deficiencies from earlier deprivation? Can intelligence be compartmentalized so that a person could be smart in math, but stupid in interpersonal relationships, or smart in analytical thinking, but notably lacking in what Sternberg calls "street-smartness"?

Chapters Five and Six will help you in your search for answers to these and related questions.

CHAPTER FIVE

How the Brain Develops and Functions

READING 12   KATHLEEN McAULIFFE
Making of a Mind

"Give me a child for the first six years of life and he'll be a servant of God till his last breath."
—JESUIT MAXIM

A servant of God or an agent of the devil; a law-abiding citizen or a juvenile delinquent. What the Jesuits knew, scientists are now rapidly confirming—that the mind of the child, in the very first years, even months, of life, is the crucible in which many of his deepest values are formed. It is then that much of what he may become—his talents, his interests, his abilities—are developed and directed. The experiences of his infancy and childhood will profoundly shape everything from his visual acuity to his comprehension of language and social behavior.

What underlies the child's receptivity to new information? And why do adults seem to lose this capacity as they gain more knowledge of the world around them? Why is it that the more we know, the less we *can* know?

Like a Zen koan, this paradox has led scientists down many paths of discovery. Some researchers are studying development processes in infants and children; others search the convoluted passages of the cortex for clues to how memory records learning experiences. Still others are studying the degree to which learning is hardwired—soldered along strict pathways in the brains of animals and humans.

Another phenomenon recently discovered: Long after patterns of personality have solidified, adults may tap fresh learning centers in the brain, new nerve connections that allow intellectual growth far after fourscore years.

Although much research remains to be done, two decades of investigation have yielded some dramatic —and in some instances unexpected—insights into the developing brain.

An infant's brain is not just a miniature replica of an adult's brain. Spanish neuroscientist José Delgado goes so far as to call the newborn "mindless." Although all the nerve cells a human may have are present at birth, the cerebral cortex, the gray matter that is the seat of higher intellect, barely functions. Surprisingly, the lower brain stem, the section that we have in common with reptiles and other primitive animals, dictates most of the newborn's actions.

This changes drastically in the days, weeks, and months after birth, when the cerebral cortex literally blossoms. During this burst of growth, individual brain cells send out shoots in all directions to produce a jungle of interconnecting nerve fibers. By the time a child is one year old, his brain is 50 percent of its adult weight; by the time he's six, it's 90 percent of its adult weight. And by puberty, when growth trails off, the brain will have quadrupled in size to the average adult weight of about three pounds.

How trillions of nerve cells manage to organize themselves into something as complex as the human brain remains a mystery. But this much is certain: As this integration and development proceeds, experiences can alter the

From Kathleen McAuliffe, "Making of a Mind," *Omni* (October 1985):62–66, 74. Copyright ©1985 by Kathleen McAuliffe and reprinted with permission of Omni Publications International, Ltd.

brain's connections in a lasting, even irreversible way.

To demonstrate this, Colin Blakemore, professor of physiology at Oxford University, raised kittens in an environment that had no horizontal lines. Subsequently, they were able to "see" only vertical lines. Yet Blakemore had tested their vision just before the experiment began and found that the kittens had an equal number of cells that responded to each type of line.

Why had the cats become blind to horizontal lines? By the end of the experiment, Blakemore discovered that many more cells in the animals' brains responded to vertical lines than horizontal lines.

As the human brain develops, similar neurological processes probably occur. For example, during a test in which city-dwelling Eurocanadians were exposed to sets of all types of lines, they had the most difficulty seeing oblique lines. By comparison, the Cree Indians, from the east coast of James Bay, Quebec, perceived all orientations of lines equally well. The researchers Robert Annis and Barrie Frost, of Queens University, in Kingston, Ontario, attributed this difference in visual acuity to the subjects' environments. The Eurocanadians grow up in a world dominated by vertical and horizontal lines, whereas the Indians, who live in tepees in coniferous forests, are constantly exposed to surroundings with many different types of angles.

The sounds—as well as the sights—that an infant is exposed to can also influence his future abilities. The phonemes *rah* and *lah*, for instance, are absent from the Japanese language, and as might be expected, adults from that culture confuse English words containing *r* and *l*. (Hence the offering of steamed "lice" in sushi bars.) Tests reveal that Japanese adults are quite literally deaf to these sounds.

Infants, on the other hand, seem to readily distinguish between speech sounds. To test sensitivity to phonemes, researchers measure changes in the infants' heartbeats as different speech sounds are presented. If an infant grows familiar with one sound and then encounters a new sound, his heart rate increases. Although the evidence is still incomplete, tests of babies from linguistic backgrounds as varied as Guatemala's Spanish culture, Kenya's Kikuyu-speaking area, and the United States all point to the same conclusion: Infants can clearly perceive phonemes present in any language.

The discovery that babies can make linguistic distinctions that adults cannot caused researchers to wonder at what age we lose this natural facility for language. To find out, Janet Werker, of Dalhousie University, in Nova Scotia, and Richard Tees, of Canada's University of British Columbia, began examining the language capabilities of English-speaking adolescents. Werker and Tees tested the subjects to see whether they could discriminate between two phonemes peculiar to the Hindi language.

"We anticipated that linguistic sensitivity declines at puberty, as psychologists have commonly assumed," Werker explains.

The results were surprising. Young adolescents could not make the distinction, nor could eight-year-olds, four-year-olds, or two-year-olds. Finally, Werker and Tees decided to test infants. They discovered that the ability to perceive foreign phonemes declines sharply by one year of age. "All the six-month-olds from English-speaking backgrounds could distinguish between the Hindi phonemes," Werker says. "But by ten to twelve months of age, the babies were unable to make this distinction."

The cutoff point, according to Werker, falls between eight and twelve months of age. If not exposed to Hindi by then people require a lot of learning to catch up. Werker found that English-speaking adults studying Hindi for the first time needed up to five years of training to learn the same phoneme distinctions any six-month-old baby can make. With further testing, Werker succeeded in tracking down one of the learning impairments that thwarted her older subjects. Although there is an audible difference, the adult mind cannot retain it long enough to remember it. "The auditory capabilities are there," Werker says. "It's the language-processing capabilities that have changed."

Even a brief introduction to language during the sensitive period can permanently alter our perception of speech. Werker and Tees tested English-speaking adults who could not speak or understand a word of Hindi, although they had been exposed to the language for the first year or two of life. They found that these adults had a major advantage in learning Hindi, compared with English-speaking adults who lacked such early exposure.

Werker and Tees's studies show that there is an advantage in learning language within the first year of life. But when it comes to learning a second tongue another study has revealed some startling findings: Adults actually master a second language more easily than school-age children do.

For four years Catherine Snow, of the Harvard Graduate School of Education, studied Americans who were learning Dutch for the first time while living in Holland. "When you control for such factors as access to native speakers and the daily exposure level to the language," Snow says, "adults acquire a large vocabulary and rules of grammar more quickly than children do. In my study, adults were found to be as good as children even in pronunciation, although many researchers contend that children have an advantage in speaking like natives."

Obviously not all learning stops when the sensitive period comes to a close. This observation has led some researchers to question the importance of early experiences. What would happen, for example, if a child did not hear a single word of any language until after one year of age? Would the propensity to speak be forfeited forever? Or could later exposure to language make up the deficit?

Because of the unethical nature of performing such an experiment on a child, we may never know the answer to that question. But some indications can be gleaned from animal studies of how early deprivation affects the development of social behavior.

> **I**t's probably fair to say that if you want bright kids, you should cuddle them a lot when they're babies because that increases the number of neural connections.

In *An Outline of Psychoanalysis,* Sigmund Freud refers to "the common assertion that the child is psychologically the father of the man and that the events of his first years are of paramount importance for his whole subsequent development." At the University of Wisconsin Primate Laboratory, the pioneering studies of Harry and Margaret Harlow put this belief to the test on our closest living relative—the rhesus monkey.

"Our experiments indicate that there is a critical period somewhere between the third and sixth month of life," write the Harlows, "during which social deprivation, particularly deprivation of the company of [the monkey's] peers, irreversibly blights the animal's capacity for social adjustment."

When later returned to a colony in which there was ample opportunity for interacting with other animals, the experimental monkeys remained withdrawn, self-punishing, and compulsive. Most significantly, they grew up to be inept both as sexual partners and parents. The females never became impregnated unless artificially inseminated. We don't know whether humans, like Harlow's monkeys, must establish close bonds by a certain age or be forever doomed to social failure. But an ongoing longitudinal study, the Minnesota Preschool Project, offers the encouraging finding that emotionally neglected four-year-olds can still be helped to lead normal, happy lives. To rehabilitate the children, the teachers in the project provide them with the kind of intimate attention that is lacking at home.

Perhaps one of the Harlows' observations sheds light on why the project was successful. During the critical period for social development, the Harlows found that even a little bit of attention goes a long way. During the first year of life, for example, only 20 minutes of playtime a day with other monkeys was apparently sufficient for the animals to grow into well-adjusted adults. L. Alan Sroufe, codirector of the Minnesota Project, tells the story of one four-year-old boy who was constantly defiant—the kind of child who would hit the other children with a toy fire truck. Instead of sending him to a corner, the teacher was instructed to remove him from the group and place him with another teacher. The message they hoped to impart: We are rejecting your behavior, but we're not rejecting you. Within a few months, the antisocial little boy learned to change his behavior.

If children aren't exposed to positive social situations until adolescence, however, the prognosis is poor. Like any complex behavior, human socialization requires an elaborate series of learning steps. So by adolescence, the teenager who missed out on many key social experiences as a child has a tremendous handicap to overcome.

Researchers are finding that each stage of life demands different kinds of competencies. This may be why sensitive learning periods exist. "When a baby is born it has to do two things at the same time," says biochemist Steven Rose of England's Open University. "One is that it has to survive as a baby. The second is that it has to grow into that very different organism, which is a child and then finally an adult. And it is not simply the case that everything the baby does is a miniature version of what we see in the adult."

For example, the rooting reflex, which enables the baby to suckle, is not a preliminary form of chewing: There's a transitional period in which the child must begin eating solid foods. And then other sorts of skills become necessary—the child must learn to walk, talk, form friendships, and when adulthood is reached, find a sexual partner. "But the child does not have to know all that at the beginning." Rose says. "So sensitive periods are necessary because we have to know how to do certain things at certain times during development."

During the course of a sensory system's development, several sensitive periods occur. In the case of human vision, for example, depth perception usually emerges by two months of age and after that remains relatively stable. But it takes the first five years of life to acquire the adult level of visual acuity that allows us to see fine details. And during that prolonged period, we are vulnerable to many developmental problems that can cause this process to go awry. For example, a drooping lid or an eye covered by a cataract—virtually anything that obstructs vision in one of the child's eyes for as few as seven days—can lead to a permanent blurring of sight. This condition, known as amblyopia, is one of the most common ophthalmological disorders. Treatment works only if carried out within the sensitive period, before the final organization of certain cells in the visual cortex becomes fixed. After five years of age, no amount of visual stimulation is likely to reorganize the connections laid down when the young nervous system was developing.

Like molten plastic, the nervous system is, at its inception, highly pliable. But it quickly settles into a rigid cast—one that has been shaped by experience. Just what neurological events set the mold is not known. Some suggestive findings, however, come from the research of John Cronly-Dillon, a professor of ophthalmic optics at the University of Manchester Institute of Science and Technology, in England.

Working with colleague Gary Perry, Cronly-Dillon studied growth activity in the visual cortex of rat pups reared under normal light conditions. To measure growth, researchers monitored the rate at which certain cells synthesized tubulin, a protein vital for forming and maintaining nerve connections. The researchers found that tubulin production in the visual cortex remained at a low level until day 13, which marks the onset of the sensitive period for visual learning. It coincides with the moment when the animal first opens its eyes. At that time, tubulin production soars, indicating a rise in growth activity.

Cronly-Dillon and Perry found that the rat's visual cortex continues to grow for the next week and then declines. By the end of the critical period, when the pup is roughly five weeks old, tubulin production drops to the level attained before the eyes open.

To Cronly-Dillon the surplus of tubulin at the beginning of the critical period and its subsequent cutback have profound implications. "It means that an uncommonly large number of nerve connections can exist at the peak of the critical period, but only a small fraction of them will be maintained at the end," he says. "So the question, of course, is which nerve connections will be kept?"

If Cronly-Dillon is correct, experience probably stabilizes those connections most often used during the sensitive period. "So by definition," he says, "what remains is most critical for survival."

Cronly-Dillon's work elaborates on a theory Spanish neurophysiologist Ramon y Cajal advanced at the turn of the century. According to this view, which has been gaining broader acceptance in recent times, brain development resembles natural selection. Just as the forces of natural selection ensure the survival of the fittest, so do similar forces preserve the most useful brain circuits.

The beauty of this model is that it could explain why the brain is as exquisitely adapted to its immediate surroundings, just as the mouthparts of insects are so perfectly matched to the sexual organs of the flowers they pollinate. The textures, shapes, sounds, and odors we perceive best may have left their imprint years ago in the neural circuitry of the developing mind.

There is also a certain economic appeal to this outlook: Why, for example, should Japanese adults keep active a neural circuit that permits the distinction between *r* and *l* sounds when neither of these linguistic components is present in their native tongue?

Yet another economic advantage of the theory is that it would explain how nature can forge something as intricate as the brain out of a relatively limited amount of genetic material. "It looks as though what genetics does is *sort of* make a brain," Blakemore says. "We only have about one hundred thousand genes—and that's to make an entire body. Yet the brain alone has trillions of nerve cells, each one forming as many as ten thousand connections with its neighbors. So imagine the difficulty of trying to encode every step of the wiring process in our DNA."

This vast discrepancy between genes and connections, according to Blakemore, can be overcome by encoding in the DNA the specifications for a "rough brain." "Everything gets roughly laid down in place," Blakemore says. "But the wiring of the young nervous system is far too rich and diffuse. So the brain overconnects and then uses a selection process to fine-tune the system."

The brain of an eight-month-old human fetus is actually estimated to have two to three times more nerve cells than an adult brain does. Just before birth, there is a massive death of unnecessary brain cells, a process that continues through early childhood and then levels off. Presumably many nerve connections that fall into disuse vanish. But that is only part of the selection process—and possibly a small part at that.

According to Blakemore, many neural circuits remain in place but cease to function after a certain age. "I would venture a guess," he says, "that as many as ninety percent of the connections you see in the adult brain are nonfunctional. The time when circuits can be switched on or off probably varies for different parts of the cerebral cortex—depending on what functions they control—and would coincide with the sensitive period of learning. Once the on-off switch becomes frozen, the sensitive period is over."

This doesn't mean however, that new circuits can't grow. There appears to be a fine-tuning of perception coinciding with these developmental events. And as the brain becomes a finer sieve, filtering out all but a limited amount of sensory input, its strategy for storing information appears to change.

"Studies indicate that as many as fifty percent of very young children recall things in pictures," says biochemist Rose. "And by the time we're about four or five, we tend to lose our eidetic [photographic] memory and develop sequential methods of recall."

To Rose, who is studying the neurological mechanisms that underlie learning, this shift in memory process may have an intriguing logic. "To be a highly adaptable organism like man, capable of living in a lot of different environments, one must start out with a brain that takes in everything," Rose explains. "And as you develop, you select what is important and what is not important to remember. If you went on remembering absolutely everything, it would be disastrous."

The Russian neurologist A. R. Luria had a patient cursed with such a memory—the man could describe rooms he'd been in years before, pieces of conversations he'd overheard. His memory became such an impediment that he could not hold even a clerk's job; while listing to instructions, so many associations for each word would arise that he couldn't focus on what was being said. The only position he could manage was as a memory man in a theatrical company.

"The crucial thing then," Rose says, "is that you must learn what to *forget*."

Some components of the brain, however, must retain their plasticity into adulthood—otherwise, no further learning would be possible, says neuroscientist Bill Greenough, of the University of Illinois, at Urbana-Champaign. While the adult brain cannot generate new brain cells, Greenough has uncovered evidence that it does continue to generate new *nerve connections*. But as the brain ages, the rate at which it produces these connections slows.

If the young brain can be likened to a sapling sprouting shoots in all directions, then the adult brain is more akin to a tree, whose growth is confined primarily to budding regions. "In the mature brain," Greenough says, "neural connections appear to pop up systematically, precisely where they're needed."

Early experience, then, provides the foundation on which all subsequent knowledge and skills build. "That's why it's extraordinarily difficult to change certain aspects of personality as an adult," says neuroscientist Jonathan Winson, of Rockefeller University. "Psychiatrists have an expression: 'insight is wonderful, but the psyche fights back.' Unfortunately, one of the drawbacks of critical-period learning is that a lot of misconceptions and unreasonable fears can become frozen in our minds during this very vulnerable period in our development."

Greenough acknowledges that the system isn't perfect; nevertheless, it works to our advantage because you can't build on a wobbly nervous system. "You've got to know who your mother is, and you've got to have perceptual skills," he explains. "These and other types of learning have to jell quickly, or all further development would halt."

Can these insights into the developing brain help educators to devise new strategies for teaching?

"We're a very long way from being able to apply the work of neurobiologists to what chalk-faced teachers are trying to do," says Open University's Rose.

But he can see the rough outline of a new relationship between neurobiology and education, which excites him. "We can now say with considerable certainty that there are important advantages to growing up in an enriched environment," he says. "That does not mean that you should be teaching three-year-olds Einstein's theory of relativity on the grounds that you will be turning them into geniuses later on. But it's probably fair to say that if you want bright kids, you should cuddle them a lot as babies because that increases the number of neural connections produced in the brain."

Although early learning tends to overshadow the importance of later experience, mental development never ceases. Recent studies indicate that our intellectual abilities continue to expand well into our eighties, provided the brain has not been injured or diseased. Most crucial for maintaining mental vigor, according to Greenough, is staying active and taking on new challenges. In his rat studies, he found that lack of stimulation—much more than age—was the factor that limited the formation of new neural connections in the adult brain.

As long as we don't isolate ourselves as we grow older, one very important type of mental faculty may even improve. Called crystallized intelligence, this ability allows us to draw on the store of accumulated knowledge to provide alternate solutions to complicated problems. Analyzing complex political or military strategies, for example, would exploit crystallized intelligence.

There is a danger in believing that because the brain's anatomical boundaries are roughly established early in life, all mental capabilities are restricted, too. "Intelligence is not something static that can be pinned down with an I.Q. test like butterflies on a sheet of cardboard," says Rose. "It is a constant interplay between internal processes and external forces."

To be sure, many types of learning do favor youth. As violinist Isaac Stern says, "If you haven't begun playing violin by age eight, you'll never be great." But in the opinion of Cronly-Dillon, the best time for learning other types of skills may be much later in life. Although he will not elaborate on this until further studies are done, he believes we may even have sensitive periods with very late onsets.

"There's a real need," Cronly-Dillon says, "to define all the different types of sensitive periods so that education can take advantage of biological optimums."

It is said that the ability to learn in later life depends on the retention of childlike innocence. "This old saw," insists Cronly-Dillon, "could have a neurological basis."

READING 13 JERRE LEVY
Right Brain, Left Brain: Fact and Fiction

I guess I'm mostly a right-brain person . . . my left side doesn't work long enough for me to figure it out," concludes a character in a *Frank and Ernest* cartoon. "It's tough being a left-brained person . . . in a right-brained world," moans a youngster in the cartoon *Wee Pals,* after perusing a tome on the "psychology of consciousness."

The notion that we are "left brained" or "right brained" has become entrenched in the popular culture. And, based on a misinterpretation of the facts, a pop psychology myth has evolved, asserting that the left hemisphere of the brain controls logic and language, while the right controls creativity and intuition. One best-selling book even claimed to teach people how to draw better by training the right brain and bypassing the left. According to the myth, people differ in their styles of thought, depending on which half of the brain is dominant. Unfortunately, this myth is often represented as scientific fact. It is not.

From Jerre Levy, "Right Brain, Left Brain: Fact and Fiction," *Psychology Today* (May 1985):38–39, 42–44. Reprinted with permission from *Psychology Today* magazine. Copyright © 1985 (PT Partners, L.P.).

As a researcher who has spent essentially her whole career studying how the two hemispheres relate to one another and to behavior, I feel obliged to set the record straight on what is known scientifically about the roles of the hemispheres. As it turns out, the brain's actual organization is every bit as interesting as the myth and suggests a far more holistic view of humankind.

People's fascination with relating mental function to brain organization goes back at least to Hippocrates. But it was René Descartes, in the 17th century, who came up with the notable and influential notion that the brain must act as a unified whole to yield a unified mental world. His specific mental mapping was wrong (he concluded that the pineal gland—now known to regulate biological rhythms in response to cycles of light and dark—was the seat of the soul, or mind). But his basic premise was on the right track and remained dominant until the latter half of the 19th century, when discoveries then reduced humankind to a half-brained species.

During the 1860s and 1870s, Paul Broca, a French neurologist, and Karl Wernicke, a German neurologist, reported that damage to the left cerebral hemisphere produced severe disorders of language, but that comparable damage to the right hemisphere did not. Neurology was never to be the same.

Despite their generally similar anatomies, the left and right cerebral hemispheres evidently had very different functions. Language appeared to be solely a property of the left side; the right hemisphere, apparently, was mute. The scientific world generalized this to conclude that the left hemisphere was dominant not only for language but for all psychological processes. The right hemisphere was seen as a mere relay station. Since each half of the brain is connected to and receives direct input from the opposite side of the body, the right hemisphere was needed to tell the left hemisphere what was happening on the left side of space and to relay messages to muscles on the body's left side. But the right hemisphere was only an unthinking automaton. From pre–19th century whole-brained creatures, we had become half-brained.

From the beginning, there were serious difficulties with the idea that the left hemisphere was the seat of humanity and that the right hemisphere played no role in thinking. In the 1880s, John Hughlings Jackson, a renowned English neurologist, described a patient with right-hemisphere damage who showed selective losses in certain aspects of visual perception—losses that did not appear with similar damage of the left hemisphere. He suggested that the right hemisphere might be just as specialized for visual perception as the left hemisphere was for language.

From the 1930s on, reports began to confirm Hughlings Jackson's findings. Patients with right-side damage had difficulties in drawing, using colored blocks to copy designs, reading and drawing maps, discriminating faces and in a variety of other visual and spatial tasks. These disorders were much less prevalent or serious in patients with left-hemisphere damage.

The investigators, quite aware of the implications of their findings, proposed that although the left hemisphere was specialized for language, the right hemisphere was specialized for many nonlinguistic processes. Nonetheless, these were voices in the wilderness, and their views hardly swayed the general neurological community. Until 1962, the prevalent view was that people had half a thinking brain.

Beginning in the early 1960s, Nobel Prize winner Roger W. Sperry and his colleagues and students demonstrated certain unusual characteristics in patients who, to control intractable epileptic seizures, had undergone complete surgical division of the corpus callosum, the connecting bridge between the two sides of the brain. These patients, like split-brain animals that Sperry had studied, couldn't communicate between the cerebral hemispheres. An object placed in the right hand (left hemisphere) could be named readily, but one placed in the left hand (nonverbal right hemisphere) could be neither named nor described. But these

> **A** myth: the left hemisphere controls logic and language, the right controls creativity and intuition.

same patients could point to a picture of the object the left hand had felt. In other words, the right hemisphere knew what it felt, even if it could not speak.

Outside the laboratory, the split-brain patients were remarkably normal, and within the laboratory, each cerebral hemisphere seemed to be able to perceive, think and govern behavior, even though the two sides were out of contact. In later split-brain studies, a variety of tasks were devised to examine the specialized functions of each hemisphere. These showed that the right hemisphere was superior to the left in spatial tasks but was mute and deficient in verbal tasks such as decoding complex syntax, short-term verbal memory and phonetic analysis. In brief, the split-brain studies fully confirmed the inferences drawn from the earlier investigations of patients with damage to one hemisphere.

These findings were further expanded by psychologist Doreen Kimura and others, who developed behavioral methods to study how functions of the hemispheres differed in normal people. These involved presenting visual stimuli rapidly to either the left or right visual fields (and the opposite hemispheres). Normal right-handers were more accurate or faster in identifying words or nonsense syllables in the right visual field (left hemisphere) and in identifying or recognizing faces, facial expressions of emotion, line slopes or dot locations in the left visual field (right hemisphere).

Another method was "dichotic listening," in which two different sounds were presented simultaneously to the two ears. The right ear (left hemisphere) was better at identifying nonsense syllables, while the left ear (right hemisphere) excelled at identifying certain nonverbal sounds such as piano melodies or dog barks.

By 1970 or soon thereafter, the reign of the left brain was essentially ended. The large majority of researchers concluded that each side of the brain was a highly specialized organ of thought, with the right hemisphere predominant in a set of functions that complemented those of the left. Observations of patients with damage to one side of the brain, of split-brain patients and of normal individuals yielded consistent findings. There could no longer be any reasonable doubt: The right hemisphere, too, was a fully human and highly complex organ of thought.

It was not long before the new discoveries found their way into the popular media and into the educational community. Some myth-makers sought to sell the idea that human beings had neither the whole and unified brain described by Descartes, nor the half brain of Broca and Wernicke, but rather two brains, each devoted to its own tasks and operating essentially independently of the other. The right hemisphere was in control when an artist painted a portrait, but the left hemisphere was in control when the novelist wrote a book. Logic was the property of the left hemisphere, whereas creativity and intuition were properties of the right. Further, these two brains did not work together in the same person. Instead, some people thought primarily with the right hemisphere, while others thought primarily with the left. Finally, given the presumed absolute differences between hemispheres, it was claimed that special subject matters and teaching strategies had to be developed to educate one hemisphere at a time, and that the standard school curriculums only educated the "logical" left hemisphere.

Notice that the new two-brain myth was based on two quite separate types of scientific findings. First was the fact that split-brain patients showed few obvious symptoms of their surgery in everyday life and far greater integrity of behavior than would be seen if two regions within a hemisphere had been surgically disconnected. Thus, it was assumed that each hemisphere could be considered to be an independent brain.

Second, a great deal of research had demonstrated that each hemisphere had its own functional "expertise," and that the two halves were complementary. Since language was the specialty of the left hemisphere, some people concluded that any verbal activity, such as writing a novel, depended solely on processes of the left hemisphere. Similarly, since visual and spatial functions were the specialties of the right hemisphere, some people inferred that any visuospatial activity, such as painting portraits, must depend solely on processes of that hemisphere. Even if thought and language were no longer synonymous, at least logic and language seemed to be. Since intuitions, by definition, are not accessible to verbal explanation, and since intuition and creativity seemed closely related, they were assigned to the right hemisphere.

Based, then, on the presumed independent functions of the two hemispheres, and on the fact that they differed in their specializations, the final leap was that different activities and psychological demands engaged different hemispheres while the opposite side of the brain merely idled along in some unconscious state.

The two-brain myth was founded

> **I**n the late 19th century we went from being whole-brained creatures to half-brained.

on an erroneous premise: that since each hemisphere was specialized, each must function as an independent brain. But in fact, just the opposite is true. To the extent that regions are differentiated in the brain, they must integrate their activities. Indeed, it is precisely that integration that gives rise to behavior and mental processes greater than and different from each region's special contribution. Thus, since the central premise of the mythmakers is wrong, so are all the inferences derived from it.

What does the scientific evidence actually say? First, it says that the two hemispheres are so similar that when they are disconnected by split-brain surgery, each can function remarkably well, although quite imperfectly.

Second, it says that superimposed on this similarity are differences in the specialized abilities of each side. These differences are seen in the contrasting contributions each hemisphere makes to all cognitive activities. When a person reads a story, the right hemisphere may play a special role in decoding visual information, maintaining an integrated story structure, appreciating humor and emotional content, deriving meaning from past associations and understanding metaphor. At the same time, the left hemisphere plays a special role in understanding syntax, translating written words into their phonetic representations and deriving meaning from complex relations among word concepts and syntax. But

there is no activity in which only one hemisphere is involved or to which only one hemisphere makes a contribution.

Third, logic is not confined to the left hemisphere. Patients with right-hemisphere damage show more major logical disorders than do patients with left-hemisphere damage. Some whose right hemisphere is damaged will deny that their left arm is their own, even when the physician demonstrates its connection to the rest of the body. Though paralyzed on the left side of the body, such patients will often make grandiose plans that are impossible because of paralysis and will be unable to see their lack of logic.

Fourth, there is no evidence that either creativity or intuition is an exclusive property of the right hemisphere. Indeed, real creativity and intuition, whatever they may entail, almost certainly depend on an intimate collaboration between hemispheres. For example, one major French painter continued to paint with the same style and skill after suffering a left-hemisphere stroke and loss of language. Creativity can remain even after right-hemisphere damage. Another painter, Lovis Corinth, after suffering right-hemisphere damage, continued to paint with a high level of skill, his style more expressive and bolder than before. In the musical realm, researcher Harold Gordon found that in highly talented professional musicians, both hemispheres were equally skilled in discriminating musical chords. Further, when researchers Steven Gaede, Oscar Parsons and James Bertera compared people with high and low musical aptitude for hemispheric asymmetries, high aptitude was associated with equal capacities of the two sides of the brain.

Fifth, since the two hemispheres do not function independently, and since each hemisphere contributes its special capacities to all cognitive activities, it is quite impossible to educate one hemisphere at a time in a normal brain. The right hemisphere is educated as much as the left in a literature class, and the left hemisphere is educated as much as the right in music and painting classes.

Finally, what of individual differences? There is both psychological and physiological evidence that people vary in the relative balance of activation of the two hemispheres. Further, there is a significant correlation between which hemisphere is more active and the relative degree of verbal or spatial skills. But there is no evidence that people are purely "left brained" or "right brained." Not even those with the most extremely asymmetrical activation between hemispheres think only with the more activated side. Rather, there is a continuum. The left hemisphere is more active in some people, to varying degrees, and verbal functioning is promoted to varying degrees. Similarly, in those with a more active right hemisphere, spatial abilities are favored. While activation patterns and cognitive patterns are correlated, the relationship is very far from perfect. This means that differences in activation of the hemispheres are but one of many factors affecting the way we think.

In sum, the popular myths are misinterpretations and wishes, not

> **I**t is impossible to educate one hemisphere at a time in a normal brain.

the observations of scientists. Normal people have not half a brain nor two brains but one gloriously differentiated brain, with each hemisphere contributing its specialized abilities. Descartes was, essentially, right: We have a single brain that generates a single mental self.

READING 14 DANIEL GOLEMAN
New Evidence Points to Growth of Brain Even Late in Life

Evidence is building that development and growth of the brain go on into old age. It was once thought that the brain was fixed by late childhood, according to innate genetic design.

As long ago as 1911, however, Santiago Ramón y Cajal, a pioneering neurobiologist, proposed that "cerebral exercise" could benefit the brain. But a scientific consensus that the brain continues to bloom if properly stimulated by an enriched environment was long in coming.

"Over the last decade, neuroscientists have become impressed

From Daniel Goleman, "New Evidence Points to Growth of Brain Even Late in Life," *New York Times* (July 30, 1985): C1, C7. Copyright © 1985 by The New York Times Company. Reprinted by permission.

by the degree to which the structure and chemistry of the brain is affected by experience," said Floyd Bloom, director of the division of neuroscience and endocrinology at the Scripps Clinic and Research Foundation in La Jolla, Calif. The new research seeks to provide a more detailed understanding of that phenomenon.

Investigations at several different laboratories have shown that environmental influences begin while the brain is forming in the fetus and are particularly strong in infancy and early childhood.

Among the most striking new evidence is a report published in a recent issue of Experimental Neurology showing that even in old age the

> **P**hysical changes linked to enriched environment.

cells of the cerebral cortex respond to an enriched environment by forging new connections to other cells. Marian Diamond, a professor of physiology and anatomy at the University of California at Berkeley, led the team of researchers who did the study.

In Dr. Diamond's study, rats 766 days old—the equivalent in human terms to roughly 75 years—were placed in an enriched environment and lived there until they reached the age of 904 days. For a rat, an impoverished environment is a bare wire cage a foot square with a solitary occupant; an enriched one is a cage a yard square where 12 rats share a variety of toys, such as mazes, ladders and wheels.

The elderly rats, after living in the stimulating environment, showed increased thickening of the cortex. This thickening, other research has shown, is a sign that the brain cells have increased in dimension and activity, and that the glial cells that support the brain cells have multiplied accordingly.

The brain cells also showed a lengthening of the tips of their dendrites, the branches that receive messages from other cells. This increase in the surface of the dendrites allows for more communication with other cells.

Previous studies have shown that enriched environments changed brain cells in a number of ways, these among them. While the specific effects differ from one region of the brain to another, in general the enriched environment has been generally seen to result in growth in the bodies of nerve cells, an increase in the amount of protein in these cells and an increase in the number or length of dendrites. In more fully developed dendritic spines, a part of the dendrite that receives chemical messages from other brain cells is induced to further growth.

Moreover, as in the new study, the thickness of the cortex was seen to increase, in part because of an increase in the numbers of glial cells needed to support the enlarged neurons. Dr. Diamond's studies on the older rats show that many, but not all, of these effects continue into old age.

These changes, in Dr. Diamond's view, mean that the cells have become more active, forming new connections to other brain cells. One sign of what the increased brain cell activity signifies for intellectual abilities is that the rats in the enriched environment became better at learning how to make their way through a maze. Indeed, Dr. Diamond and other researchers recently examined specimens from Einstein's brain. The tissue samples, from parts of the cortex presumed critical for mathematical skills, seemed to have unusually large numbers of glial cells.

MORE NEURAL FLEXIBILITY

What does all this mean for the aging brain? "There is much more neural flexibility in old age than we had imagined," said Roger Walsh, a psychiatrist at the University of California medical school at Irvine, who has done research similar to Dr. Diamond's. "The changes in brain cells have been found in every species investigated to date, including primates. They certainly should occur in humans as well."

"In my work," Dr. Walsh added, "I've found that an enriched environment in late life can largely compensate for brain cell deficiencies from earlier deprivations."

"We've been too negative in how we view the human brain," Dr. Diamond said in an interview. "Nerve cells can grow at any age in response to intellectual enrichment of all sorts: travel, crossword puzzles, anything that stimulates the brain with novelty and challenge."

Still, there seem to be limits to the degree to which the brain can respond to experience. Richard Lerner, in "On the Nature of Human Plasticity" (Cambridge University Press), notes, for example, that the impact of environmental enrichment on brain cells seems to diminish with age, although it continues into old age, an effect Dr. Diamond has noted in her research.

The effects of enriched environments on the brain are but part of a larger investigation of the impact of

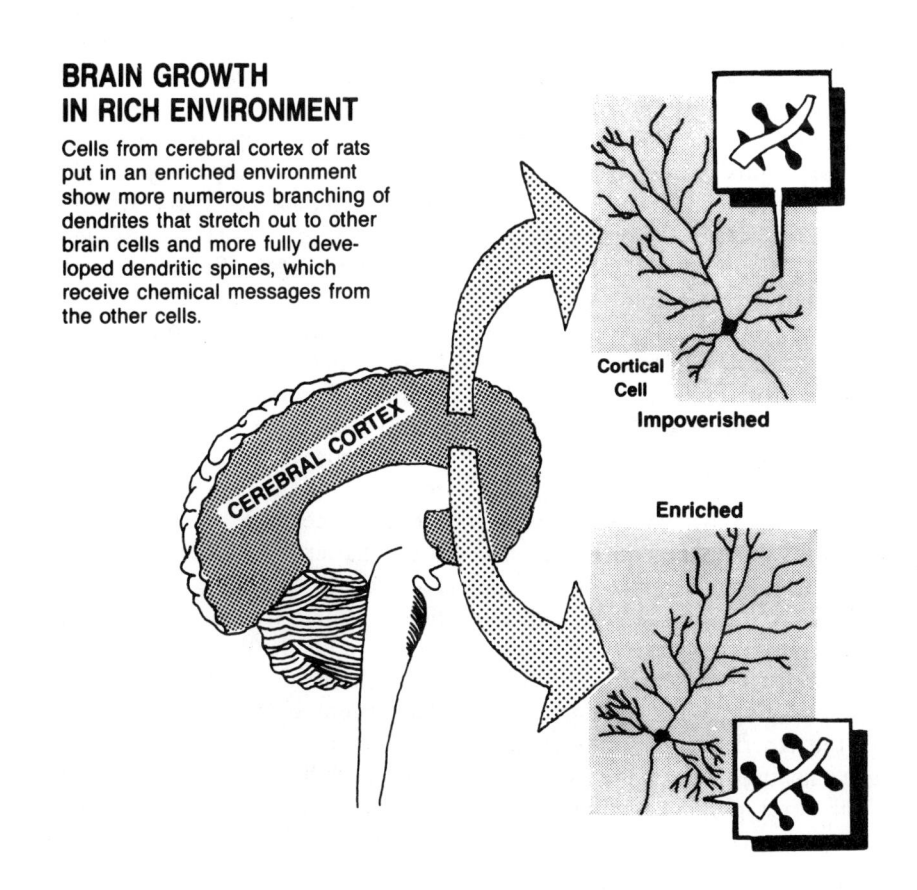

BRAIN GROWTH IN RICH ENVIRONMENT

Cells from cerebral cortex of rats put in an enriched environment show more numerous branching of dendrites that stretch out to other brain cells and more fully developed dendritic spines, which receive chemical messages from the other cells.

life's experiences on the brain, and the picture is not always positive.

"Brain plasticity can operate for better or for worse," said Jeannine Herron, a neuropsychologist at California Neuropsychology Services in San Rafael. . . .

TESTS ON VISION OF KITTENS

Perhaps the most frequently cited example of how experience—or the lack of it—can have a negative effect on the brain is the work of David Hubel, Dr. Hubel . . . won a Nobel Prize for his research on the visual cortex.

As part of his research, Dr. Hubel showed that if the eye of a growing kitten is kept shut so that it is deprived of its normal experience, the cells that would ordinarily register what that eye sees will develop abnormally.

> "There is much more neural flexibility in old age than we had imagined."

The notion that certain experiences go hand in hand with the growth and development of the brain has been demonstrated in other research, as well. For example, Arnold Scheibel, a professor of anatomy and psychiatry at the University of California at Los Angeles, has found that the cells in the speech centers of infants undergo a growth burst, in which they form many new connections to other cells, just at the time the infant is beginning to respond to voices, between 6 and 12 months. Between 12 and 18 months, as the infant begins to grasp that words have meanings, this growth accelerates.

Part of this explosion of growth, Dr. Scheibel proposes, may be primed by the infant's interactions with adults, who stimulate the centers for speech by talking to the infant.

The main changes that occur during this growth in the cells of the speech centers are in the dendrites ensemble, the projecting branches of the cell that spread to send and receive messages from other cells. "The dendritic projections are like muscle tissue," Dr. Scheibel said. "They grow more the more they're used."

"Even in adulthood," he added, "if you learn a new language, it's dendritic fireworks."

RESPONSES TO INJURY

The brain's ability to adapt to circumstances can also be seen in its response to injury. Patricia Goldman-Rakic, a neuroanatomist at Yale University medical school, is one of many researchers who have shown that brain cells, within limits, can rearrange themselves to compensate for a brain injury.

"The new connections that occur after an injury to the brain show that the brain's anatomy is not rigidly fixed," Dr. Goldman-Rakic said in an interview. "The uninjured cells reroute how they grow and interconnect. This ability is most prominent during infancy, when neurons are still growing. It doesn't go on forever, but we don't yet know precisely at what point in later life the brain no longer can compensate in this way. We need to more fully understand normal brain maturation first."

Norman Geschwind, a noted neuroanatomist at Harvard Medical School who died [in 1985], had been pursuing evidence suggesting that the experiences of a mother can have a lasting effect on the structure of the developing fetus's brain.

In a series of articles published posthumously in the most recent issues of Archives of Neurology, Dr. Geschwind, with Albert Galaburda, a colleague at Harvard Medical School, proposes that the infant brain is shaped in crucial ways by the level of testosterone, a male sex hormone, present in the intrauterine environment at different stages of fetal development.

At crucial points in the growth of the fetus, brain cells are formed and then migrate to the part of the brain ordained by a genetic plan. In certain parts of the brain these patterns of migration can be affected by the presence of sex hormones, particularly testosterone.

Testosterone levels in the fetus can vary with such factors as the amount of psychological stress the mother feels, maternal diet and possibly even the season of the year.

The main effects of testosterone, according to Dr. Geschwind and Dr. Galaburda, are in the areas of the brain that control such skills as speech, spatial abilities and handedness. One of the key effects of testosterone is in determining the side of the brain on which the centers that control such skills will be located.

When the process goes awry, according to the theory, the result can be problems such as dyslexia, on the one hand, or unusual talents, such as mathematical giftedness, on the other.

These effects are more marked among males, in part because the brains of males develop more slowly than those of females, and in part because testosterone plays a direct role in the growth of certain areas of the male brain. The unusual patterns of brain formation are most common, the theory holds, among left-handed males.

Before his death, Dr. Geschwind found from autopsies of people who had severe dyslexia in childhood that the parts of the cortex that control speech had abnormal cell development along the lines predicted by his theory.

CHAPTER SIX

Contemporary Views About the Nature of Intelligence

READING 15   HOWARD GARDNER
Developing the Spectrum of Human Intelligences

Allow me to transport all of us to the Paris of 1900—La Belle Epoque. Around 1900 the city fathers of Paris approached a psychologist named Alfred Binet with an unusual request: Could he devise some kind of measure which would predict which youngster would succeed and which would fail in the primary grades of Paris schools? As everybody knows, Binet succeeded. He produced a set of test items which could predict a child's success or failure in school. In short order, his discovery came to be called the "intelligence test"; his measure, the "IQ." Like other Parisian fashions, the IQ soon made its way to the United States, where it enjoyed a modest success until World War I. Then, it was used to test over one million American recruits, and it had truly arrived.

From Gardner, Howard, "Developing the Spectrum of Human Intelligences," *Harvard Educational Review*, 57:2, 187–193. Copyright © 1987 by the President and Fellows of Harvard College. All rights reserved.

From that day on, the IQ test has looked like psychology's biggest success—a genuinely useful scientific tool.

What is the vision that led to the excitement about IQ? At least in the West, people had always relied on intuitive assessments of how smart other people were. Now intelligence seemed to be quantifiable. You could measure someone's actual or potential height, and now, it seemed, you could also measure someone's actual or potential intelligence. We had one dimension of mental ability along which we could array everyone.

The search for the perfect measuring of intelligence has proceeded apace. Here, for example, are some quotations from an ad for a widely used test:

Need an individual test which quickly provides a stable and reliable estimate of intelligence in four or five minutes per form? Has three forms. Doesn't depend upon verbal production or subjective scoring. Can be used with the severely physically handicapped (even paralyzed) if they can signal yes or no, handles two-year-olds and superior adults with the same short series of items and the same format. Only $16.00 complete.

Now, that's quite a claim. Arthur Jensen suggests that we could look at reaction time to assess intelligence: a set of lights go on; how quickly can the subject react? Hans Eysenck suggests that investigators of intelligence should look directly at brain waves.

There are also, of course, more sophisticated versions of the IQ test. One of them is called the Scholastic Aptitude Test (SAT). It purports to be a similar kind of measure, and if you add up a person's verbal and math scores, as is often done, you can rate him or her along that dimension. Programs for the gifted,

89

for example, often use that kind of measure.

I want to suggest that along with this one-dimensional view of how to assess people's minds comes a corresponding view of school, which I will call the "uniform view." In the uniform school, there is a core curriculum, a set of facts that everybody should know, and very few electives. The better students, perhaps those with higher IQs, are allowed to take courses that call upon critical reading, calculation, and thinking skills. In the "uniform school," there are regular assessments, using paper and pencil instruments, of the IQ or SAT variety. They yield reliable rankings of people; the best and the brightest get into the better colleges, and perhaps—but only perhaps—they will also get better rankings in life. There is no question that this approach works well for certain people—Harvard is eloquent testimony to that. Since this measurement and selection system is clearly meritocratic in certain respects, it has something to recommend it.

But there is an alternative vision that I would like to present—one based on a radically different view of the mind and one that yields a very different view of school. It is a pluralistic view of mind, recognizing many different and discrete facets of cognition, acknowledging that people have different cognitive strengths and contrasting cognitive styles. I would also like to introduce the concept of an individual-centered school that takes this multifaceted view of intelligence seriously. This model for a school is based in part on findings from sciences that did not even exist in Binet's time: cognitive science (the study of the mind) and neuroscience (the study of the brain). One such approach I have called my "theory of multiple intelligences." Proceeding rapidly, I will now tell you something about its sources, its claims, and its educational implications for a possible school of the future.

Dissatisfaction with the concept of IQ and with unitary views of intelligence is fairly widespread—one thinks, for instance, of the world of L. L. Thurstone, J. P. Guilford, and other critics. From my point of view, however, these criticisms do not suffice. The whole concept has to be challenged; in fact, it has to be replaced.

I believe that we should get away altogether from tests and correlations among tests and look instead at more naturalistic sources of information about how peoples around the world develop skills important to their ways of life. Think, for example, of sailors in the South Seas, who find their way around hundreds, or even thousands, of islands by looking at the constellations of stars in the sky, feeling the way a boat passes over the water, and noticing a few scattered landmarks. A word for intelligence in a society of these sailors would probably refer to that kind of navigational ability. Think of surgeons and engineers, hunters and fishermen, dancers and choreographers, athletes and athletic coaches, tribal chiefs and sorcerers. All of these different roles need to be taken into account if we accept the way I define intelligence—that is, as the ability to solve problems or to fashion products that are valued in one or more cultural settings. For the moment I am saying nothing about whether there is one dimension, or more than one dimension, of intelligence; nothing about whether intelligence is inborn or developed. Instead I emphasize the ability to solve problems and to fashion products. In my work I seek the building blocks of the intelligences used by the aforementioned sailors and surgeons and sorcerers.

The science in this enterprise, to the extent that it exists, involves trying to discover the right description of the intelligences. What is an intelligence? To try to answer this question, I have, with my colleagues, surveyed a wide set of sources which, to my knowledge, have never been considered together before. One source is what we already know of the development of difficult kinds of skills in normal children. Another source, and a very important one, is information on the ways that these abilities break down under conditions of brain damage. When one suffers a stroke or some other kind of brain damage, various abilities can be destroyed, or spared, in isolation from other abilities. This research with brain-damaged patients yields a very powerful kind of evidence, because it seems to reflect the way the nervous system has evolved over the millennia to yield certain discrete kinds of intelligence.

My research group looks at other special populations as well: prodigies, idiot savants, autistic children, children with learning disabilities, all of whom exhibit very jagged cognitive profiles—profiles that are extremely difficult to explain in terms of a unitary view of intelligence. We examine cognition in diverse animal species and in dramatically different cultures. Finally, we consider two kinds of psychological evidence: correlations among psychological tests of the sort yielded by a factor analysis of a test battery and the results of efforts of skill training. When you train a person in skill A, for example, does that training transfer to skill B? So, for example, does training in mathematics enhance one's musical abilities, or vice versa?

Obviously, through looking at all these sources—information on development, on breakdowns, on special populations and the like—we end up with a cornucopia of information. Optimally, we would perform a factor analysis, feeding all the data into a computer and noting the kinds of factors or intelligences that are extracted. Alas, this kind of material didn't exist in a form that is susceptible to computation, and so we had to perform a more subjective factor analysis. In truth, we simply studied the results as best we could and tried to organize them in a way that made sense to us and, hopefully, to critical readers as well. My resulting list of seven intelligences is a preliminary attempt to organize this mass of information.

SEVEN INTELLIGENCES

I want now to mention briefly the seven intelligences we have located and to cite one or two examples of each intelligence. Linguistic intelligence is the kind of ability exhibited in its fullest form, perhaps, by poets. Logical-mathematical intelligence, as the name implies, is logical and mathematical ability, as well as scientific ability. Jean Piaget, the great developmental psychologist, thought he was studying *all* intelligence, but I believe he was studying the development of logical-mathematical intelligence. Although I name the linguistic and logical-mathematical intelligences first, it is not because I think they are the most important—in fact, I think all seven of the intelligences have equal claim to priority. In our society, however, we have put linguistic and logical-mathematical intelligences, figuratively speaking, on a pedestal. Much of our testing is based on this high valuation of verbal and mathematical skills. If you do well in language and logic you will do well in IQ tests and SATs, and you may well get into a prestigious college, but whether you do well once you leave is probably going to depend as much on the extent to which you possess and use the other intelligences, and it is to those that I want to give equal attention.

Spatial intelligence is the ability to form a mental model of a spatial world and to be able to maneuver and operate using that model. Sailors, engineers, surgeons, sculptors, and painters, to name a few examples, all have highly developed spatial intelligence. Musical intelligence is the fourth category of ability we have identified: Leonard Bernstein, Harvard Class of '39, has lots of it; Mozart, presumably, had even more. Bodily-kinesthetic intelligence is the ability to solve problems or to fashion products using one's whole body, or parts of the body. Dancers, athletes, surgeons, and craftspeople all exhibit highly developed bodily-kinesthetic intelligence.

> If you do well in language and logic, you will do well in IQ tests and SATs . . . but whether you do well once you leave is probably going to depend as much on the extent to which you possess and use the other intelligences.

Finally, I propose two forms of personal intelligence—not well understood, elusive to study, but immensely important. Interpersonal intelligence is the ability to understand other people: what motivates them, how they work, how to work cooperatively with them. Successful salespeople, politicians, teachers, clinicians, and religious leaders are all likely to be individuals with high degrees of interpersonal intelligence. Intrapersonal intelligence, a seventh kind of intelligence, is a correlative ability, turned inward. It is a capacity to form an accurate, veridical model of oneself and to be able to use that model to operate effectively in life.

These, then, are the seven intelligences that we have described in our research. This is a preliminary list, as I have said; obviously, each form of intelligence can be subdivided, or the list can be rearranged. The real point here is to make the case for the plurality of intellect. Also, we believe that individuals may differ in the particular intelligence profiles with which they are born, and that certainly they differ in the profiles they end up with. I think of the intelligences as raw, biological potentials, which can be seen in pure form only in individuals who are, in the technical sense, freaks. In almost everybody else the intelligences work together to solve problems, to yield various kinds of cultural endstates—vocations, avocations, and the like.

This is my theory of multiple intelligences in capsule form. In my view, the purpose of school should be to develop intelligences and to help people reach vocational and avocational goals that are appropriate to their particular spectrum of intelligences. People who are helped to do so, I believe, feel more engaged and competent, and therefore more inclined to serve the society in a constructive way.

These thoughts, and the critique of a universalistic view of mind with which I began, lead to the notion of an individual-centered school, one geared to optimal understanding and development of each student's cognitive profile. This vision stands in direct contrast to that of the uniform school that I described earlier.

The design of my ideal school of the future is based upon two assumptions. The first is that not all people have the same interests and abilities; not all of us learn in the same way. (And we now have the tools to begin to address these individual differences in school.) The second assumption is one that hurts: it is the assumption that nowadays no one person can learn everything there is to learn. We would all like, as Renaissance men and women, to know everything, or at least to believe in the potential of knowing everything, but that ideal clearly is not possible anymore. Choice is therefore inevitable, and one of the things that I want to argue is that the choices that we make for ourselves, and for the people who are under our charge, might as well be informed choices. An individual-centered school would be rich in assessment of individual abilities and proclivities. It would seek to match individuals not only to curricular areas, but also to particular ways of teaching those subjects. And after the first few grades, the school would also seek to match individuals with the various kinds of life and work options that are available in their culture.

I want to propose a new set of roles for educators that might make this vision a reality. First of all, we might have what I will call "assessment specialists." The job of these people would be to try to understand as sensitively as possible the abilities and interests of the students in a school. It would be very important, however, that the assessment specialists use "intelligence-fair" instruments. We want to be able to look specifically and directly at spatial abilities, at personal abilities, and the like, and not through the usual lenses of the linguistic and logical–mathematical intelligences. Up until now nearly all assessment has depended indirectly on measurement of those abilities; if students are not strong in those areas, their abilities in other areas may be obscured. Once we begin to try to assess other kinds of intelligences directly, I am confident that particular students will reveal strengths in quite different areas, and the notion of general brightness will disappear or become greatly attenuated. . . .

It is of the utmost importance that we recognize and nurture all of the varied human intelligences and all of the combinations of intelligences. We are all so different largely because we all have different combinations of intelligences. If we recognize this, I think we will have at least a better chance of dealing appropriately with the many problems that we face in the world. If we can mobilize the spectrum of human abilities, not only will people feel better about themselves and feel more competent; it is even possible that they will also feel more engaged and more readily able to join with the rest of the world community in working for the broader good. Perhaps if we can mobilize the full range of human intelligences and ally them to an ethical sense, we can help to increase the likelihood of our survival on this planet and perhaps even contribute to our thriving.

This article is based on an informal talk given on the 350th anniversary of Harvard University on September 5, 1986. It has been edited only in the interests of greater clarity. No formal references have been included. The reader interested in documentation of the theory of multiple intelligences is referred to Howard Gardner's book *Frames of Mind: The Theory of Multiple Intelligences* (New York: Basic Books, 1983). More recent articles, which treat educational implications of the theory, are:

Joseph Walters and Howard Gardner, "The Development and Education of Multiple Intelligences," in *Essays on the Intellect*, edited by Frances Link (Washington, DC: Curriculum Development Associates, 1985); and

Joseph Walters and Howard Gardner, "Multiple Intelligences: Some Issues and Answers," in *Practical Intelligences*, edited by Robert Sternberg and Richard Wagner (New York: Cambridge University Press, 1987).

The work reported in this article was supported by the Rockefeller Foundation, the Spencer Foundation, and the Bernard Van Leer Foundation.

READING 16 ROBERT J. TROTTER
Three Heads Are Better Than One

"I really stunk on IQ tests. I was just terrible," recalls Robert J. Sternberg. "In elementary school I had severe test anxiety. I'd hear other people starting to turn the page, and I'd still be on the second item. I'd utterly freeze."

Poor performances on IQ tests piqued Sternberg's interest, and from rather inauspicious beginnings he proceeded to build a career on the study of intelligence and intelligence testing. Sternberg, IBM Professor of Psychology and Education at Yale University, did his undergraduate work at Yale and then got his Ph.D. from Stanford University in 1975. Since then he has written hundreds of articles and several books on intelligence, received numerous fellowships and awards for his research and proposed a three-part theory of intelligence. He is now developing an intelligence test based on that theory.

Running through Sternberg's work is a core of common-sense practicality not always seen in studies of subjects as intangible as intelligence. This practical bent, which stems from his early attempts to understand his own trouble with IQ tests, is also seen in his current efforts to devise ways of teaching people to better understand and increase their intellectual skills.

Sternberg got over his test anxiety in sixth grade after doing so poorly on an IQ test that he was sent to retake it with the fifth-graders. "When you are in elementary school," he explains, "one year makes a big difference. It's one thing to take a test with sixth-graders, but if you're taking it with a bunch of babies, you don't have to worry." He did well on the test, and by seventh grade he was designing and administering his own test of mental abilities as part of a science project. In 10th grade he studied how distractions affect people taking mental-ability tests.

After graduating from high school he worked summers as a research assistant, first at the Psychological Corporation in New York, then at the Educational Testing Service in Princeton, New Jersey. These jobs gave him hands-on experience with testing organizations, but he began to suspect that the intelligence field was not going anywhere. Most of the tests being used were pretty old, he says, and there seemed to be little good research going on.

This idea was reinforced when Sternberg took a graduate course at Stanford from Lee J. Cronbach, a leader in the field of tests and measurements. Intelligence research is dead, Cronbach said; the psychometric approach—IQ testing—has run its course and people are waiting for something new. This left Sternberg at a loss. He knew he wanted to study intelligence, but he didn't know how to go about it.

About this time, an educational publishing firm (Barron's) asked Sternberg to write a book on how to prepare for the Miller Analogies Test. Since Sternberg had invented a scheme for classifying the items on the test when he worked for the Psychological Corporation, which publishes the test, he was an obvious choice to write the book. Being an impecunious graduate student, he jumped at the chance, but he had an ulterior motive. He wanted to study intelligence and thought that because analogies are a major part of most IQ tests, working on the book might help. This work eventually led to his dissertation and a book based on it.

At this stage, Sternberg was analyzing the cognitive, or mental, processes people use to solve IQ test items, such as analogies, syllogisms and series. His research gave a good account of what people did in their heads, he says, and also seemed to account for individual differences in IQ test performance. Sternberg extended this work in the 1970s and in 1980 published a paper setting forth what he called his "componential" theory of human intelligence.

"I really thought I had the whole bag here," he says. "I thought I knew what was going on, but that was just a delusion on my part." Psychology comes out of everyday experiences, Sternberg says. And his own experiences—teaching and working with graduate students at Yale—gave him the idea that there was much more to intelligence than what his componential theory was describing. He brings this idea to life with stories of three idealized graduate students—Alice, Barbara and Celia.

Alice, he says, is someone who looked very smart according to conventional theories of intelligence. She had almost a 4.0 average as an undergraduate, scored extremely high on the Graduate Record Exam (GRE) and was supported by excellent letters of recommendation. She had everything that smart graduate students are supposed to have and was admitted to Yale as a top pick.

"There was no doubt that this was Miss Real Smarto," Sternberg says, and she performed just the

From Robert J. Trotter, "Three Heads Are Better Than One: Triarchic Theory of Intelligence," Psychology Today (August 1986):56–62. Reprinted with permission from Psychology Today magazine. Copyright © 1986 (PT Partners, L.P.).

way the tests predicted she would. She did extremely well on multiple-choice tests and was great in class, especially at critiquing other people's work and analyzing arguments. "She was just fantastic," Sternberg says. "She was one of our top two students the first year, but it didn't stay that way. She wasn't even in the top half by the time she finished. It just didn't work out. So that made me suspicious, and I wanted to know what went wrong."

The GRE and other tests had accurately predicted Alice's performance for the first year or so but then got progressively less predictive. And what became clear, Sternberg says, is that although the tests did measure her critical thinking ability, they did not measure her ability to come up with good ideas. This is not unusual, he says. A lot of people are very good analytically, but they just don't have good ideas of their own.

Sternberg thinks he knows why people with high GRE scores don't always do well in graduate school. From elementary school to college, he explains, students are continuously reinforced for high test-smarts. The first year of graduate school is similar—lots of multiple-choice tests and papers that demand critical thinking. Then around the second year there is a transition, with more emphasis on creative, or synthetic, thinking and having good ideas. "That's a different skill," Sternberg says. "It's not that test taking and critical thinking all of a sudden become unimportant, it's just that other things become more important."

When people who have always done well on tests get to this transition point, instead of being continually reinforced, they are only intermittently reinforced. And that is the kind of reinforcement most likely to sustain a particular type of behavior. "Instead of helping people try to improve their performance in other areas, intermittent reinforcement encourages them to overcapitalize on test-smarts, and then try to use that kind of intelligence in situations in which it is not relevant.

"The irony is that people like Alice may have other abilities, but they never look for them," he says. "It's like psychologists who come up with a theory that's interesting and then try to expand it to everything under the sun. They just can't see its limitations. It's the same with mental abilities. Some are good in certain situations but not in others."

The second student, Barbara, had a very different kind of record. Her undergraduate grades were not great, and her GRE scores were really low by Yale standards. She did, however, have absolutely superlative letters of recommendation that said Barbara was extremely creative, had really good ideas and did exceptional research. Sternberg thought Barbara would continue to do creative work and wanted to accept her. When he was outvoted, he hired her as a research associate. "Academic smarts," Sternberg says, "are easy to find, but creativity is a rare and precious commodity."

Sternberg's prediction was correct. In addition to working full time as a research associate she took graduate classes, and her work and ideas proved to be just as good as the letters said they would be. When the transition came, she was ready to go. "Some of the most important work I've done was in collaboration with her," Sternberg says.

Barbaresque talent, Sternberg emphasizes, is not limited to psychology graduate school. "I think the same principle applies to everything. Take business. You can get an MBA based on your academic smarts because graduate programs consist mostly of taking tests and analyzing cases. But when you actually go into business, you have to have creative ideas for products and for marketing. Some MBA's don't make the transition and never do well because they overcapitalize on academic smarts. And it's the same no matter what you do. If you're in writing, you have to have good ideas for stories. If you're in art, you have to have good ideas for artwork. If you're in law. . . . That's where Barbaresque talent comes in."

The third student was Celia. Her grades, letters of recommendation and GRE scores were good but not great. She was accepted into the program and the first year, Sternberg says, she did all right but not great. Surprisingly, however, she turned out to be the easiest student to place in a good job. And this surprised him. Celia lacked Alice's super analytic ability and Barbara's super synthetic, or creative, ability, yet she could get a good job while others were having trouble.

Celia, it turns out, had learned how to play the game. She made sure she did the kind of work that is valued in psychology. She submitted her papers to the right journals. In other words, Sternberg says, "she was a street-smart psychologist, very street-smart. And that, again, is something that doesn't show up on IQ tests."

Sternberg points out that Alice, Barbara and Celia are not extreme cases. "Extremes are rare," he says, "but not good. You don't want someone who is incredibly analytically brilliant but never has a good idea or who is a total social boor." Like all of us, Alice, Barbara and Celia each had all three of the intellectual abilities he described, but each was especially good in one aspect.

After considering the special qualities of people such as Alice, Barbara and Celia, Sternberg concluded that his componential theory explained only one aspect of intelligence. It could account for Alice, but it was too narrow to explain Barbara and Celia. In an attempt to find out why, Sternberg began to look at prior theories of intelligence and found that they tried to do one of three things:

Some looked at the relation of in-

> Academic smarts are easy to find, but creativity is rare and precious.

telligence to the internal world of the individual, what goes on inside people's heads when they think intelligently. "That's what IQ tests measure, that's what information processing tasks measure, that's the componential theory. It's what I had been doing," Sternberg says. "I'd take an IQ test problem and analyze the mental processes involved in solving it, but it's still the same damned problem. It's sort of like we never got away from the IQ test as a standard. It's not that I thought the componential work was wrong. It told me a lot about what made Alice smart, but there had to be more."

Other theories looked at the relation of intelligence to experience, with experience mediating between what's inside—the internal, mental world—and what's outside—the external world. These theories say you have to look at how experience affects a person's intelligence and how intelligence affects a person's experiences. In other words, more-intelligent people create different experiences. "And that," says Sternberg, "is where Barbara fits in. She is someone who has a certain way of coping with novelty that goes beyond the ordinary. She can see old problems in new ways, or she'll take a new problem and see how some old thing she knows applies to it."

A third kind of theory looks at intelligence in relation to the individual's external world. In other words, what makes people smart in their everyday context? How does the environment interact with being smart? And what you see, as with Celia, is that there are a lot of people who don't do particularly well on tests but who are just extremely practically intelligent. "Take Lee Iacocca," Sternberg says. "Maybe he doesn't have an IQ of 160 (or maybe he does, I don't know), but he is extremely effective. And there are plenty of people who are that way. And there are plenty of people going around with high IQ's who don't do a damned thing. This Celiaesque kind of smartness—how you make it in the real world—is not reflected in IQ tests. So I decided to have a look at all three kinds of intelligence."

He did, and the result was the

THE TRIARCHIC THEORY

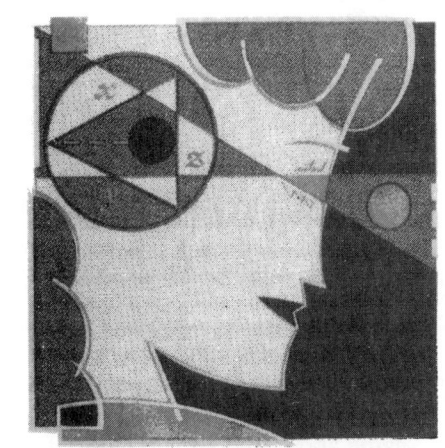

Componential

Alice had high test scores and was a whiz at test-taking and analytical thinking. Her type of intelligence exemplifies the componential subtheory, which explains the mental components involved in analytical thinking.

Experiential

Barbara didn't have the best test scores, but she was a superbly creative thinker who could combine disparate experiences in insightful ways. She is an example of the experiential subtheory.

Contextual

Celia was street-smart. She learned how to play the game and how to manipulate the environment. Her test scores weren't tops, but she could come out on top in almost any context. She is Sternberg's example of contextual intelligence.

triarchic theory. A triarchy is government by three persons, and in his 1985 book, *Beyond IQ*, Sternberg suggests that we are all governed by three aspects of intelligence: componential, experiential and contextual. In the book, each aspect of intelligence is described in a subtheory. Though based in part on older theories, Sternberg's work differs from those theories in a number of ways. His componential subtheory, which describes Alice, for example, is closest to the views of cognitive psychologists and psychometricians. But Sternberg thinks that the other theories put too much emphasis on measuring speed and accuracy of performance components at the expense of what he calls "metacomponents," or executive processes.

"For example," he explains, "the really interesting part of solving analogies or syllogisms is deciding what to do in the first place. But that isn't isolated by looking at performance components, so I realized you need to look at metacomponents—how you plan it, how you monitor what you are doing, how you evaluate it after you are done.

"A big thing in psychometric theory," he continues, "is mental speed. Almost every other group test is timed, so if you're not fast you're in trouble. But I came to the conclusion that we were really misguided on that. Almost everyone regrets some decision that was made too fast. Think of the guy who walks around with President Reagan carrying the black box. You don't want this guy to be real fast at pushing the button. So, instead of just testing speed, you want to measure a person's knowing when to be fast and when to be slow—time allocation—it's a metacomponent. And that's what the componential subtheory emphasizes."

The experiential subtheory, which describes Barbaresque talent, emphasizes insight. Sternberg and graduate student Janet E. Davidson, as part of a study of intellectual giftedness, concluded that what gifted people had in common was insight. "If you look at Hemingway in literature, Darwin in science or Rousseau in political theory, you see that they all seemed to be unusually insightful people," Sternberg explains. "But when we looked at the research, we found that nobody seemed to know what insight is."

> **A** big thing in IQ testing is speed, but almost everyone regrets some decision that was made too fast.

Sternberg and Davidson analyzed how several major scientific insights came about and concluded that insight is really three things: selective encoding, selective combination and selective comparison. As an example of selective encoding they cite Sir Alexander Fleming's discovery of penicillin. One of Fleming's experiments was spoiled when mold contaminated and killed the bacteria he was studying. Sternberg says most people would have said, "I screwed up, I've got to throw this out and start over." But Fleming didn't. He realized that the mold that killed the bacteria was more important than the bacteria. This selective encoding insight—the ability to focus on the really critical information—led to the discovery of a substance in the mold that Fleming called "penicillin." "And this is not just something that famous scientists do," Sternberg explains. "Detectives have to decide what are the relevant clues, lawyers have to decide which facts have legal consequences and so on."

The second kind of insight is selective combination, which is putting the facts together to get the big picture, as in Charles Darwin's formulation of the theory of natural selection. The facts he needed to form the theory were already there; other people had them too. But Darwin saw how to put them together. Similarly, doctors have to put the symptoms together to figure out what the disease is. Lawyers have to put the facts together to figure out how to make the case. "My triarchic theory is another example of selective combination. It doesn't have that much in it that's different from what other people have said," Sternberg admits. "It's just putting it together that's a little different."

A third kind of insight is selective comparison. It's relating the old to the new analogically, says Sternberg. It involves being able to see an old thing in a new way or being able to see a new thing in an old way. An example is the discovery of the molecular structure of benzene by German chemist August Kekule, who had been struggling to find the structure for some time. Then one night he had a dream in which a snake was dancing around and biting its own tail. Kekule woke up and realized that he had solved the puzzle of benzene's structure. In essence, Sternberg explains, Kekule could see the relation between two very disparate elements—the circular image of the dancing snake and the hexagonal structure of the benzene molecule.

Sternberg and Davidson tested their theory of insight on fourth-, fifth- and sixth-graders who had been identified through IQ and creativity tests as either gifted or not so gifted. They used problems that require the three different kinds of insights. A selective-encoding problem, for example, is the old one about four brown socks and five blue socks in a drawer. How many do you have to pull out to make sure you'll having a matching pair? It's a selective-encoding problem because the solution depends on selecting and using the relevant information. (The information about the 4-to-5 ratio is irrelevant.)

As expected, the gifted children were better able to solve all three types of problems. The less gifted children, for example, tended to get hung up on the irrelevant ratio information in the socks problem, while the gifted children ignored it. When the researchers gave the less gifted children the information needed to solve the problems (by underlining what was relevant, for example), their performance improved significantly. Giving the gifted children this information had no such effect, Sternberg explains, because they tended to have the insights spontaneously.

Sternberg and Davidson also found that insight skills can be taught. In a five-week training program for both gifted and less gifted children, they greatly improved children's scores on insight problems, compared with children who had not received the training. Moreover, says Sternberg, the gains were durable and transferable. The skills were still there when the children were tested a year later and were being applied to kinds of insight problems that had never appeared in the training program.

Sternberg's contextual subtheory emphasizes adaptation. Almost everyone agrees that intelligence is the ability to adapt to the environment, but that doesn't seem to be what IQ tests measure, Sternberg says. So he and Richard K. Wagner, then a graduate student, now at Florida State University, tried to come up with a test of adaptive ability. They studied people in two occupations: academic psychologists, "because we think that's a really important job," and business executives, "because everyone else thinks that's an important job." They began by asking prominent, successful people what one needs to be practically intelligent in their fields. The psychologists and executives agreed on three things:

First, IQ isn't very important for success in these jobs. "And that makes sense because you already have a restricted range. You're talking about people with IQ's of 110 to 150. That's not to say that IQ doesn't count for anything," Sternberg says. "If you were talking about a range from 40 to 150, IQ might make a difference, but we're not. So IQ isn't that important with regard to practical intelligence."

They also agreed that graduate school isn't that important either. "This," says Sternberg, "was a little offensive. After all, here I was teaching and doing the study with one of my own graduate students, and these people were saying graduate training wasn't that helpful." But Sternberg remembered that graduate school had not fully prepared him for his first year on the job as an academic. "I really needed to know how to write a grant proposal; at Yale, if you can't get grants you're in trouble. You have to scrounge for paper clips, you can't get students to work with you, you can't get any research done. Five years later you get fired because you haven't done anything. Now, no one ever says you are being hired to write grants, but if you don't get them you're dead meat around here." Sternberg, who has had more than $5 million in grants in the past 10 years, says he'd be five years behind where he is now without great graduate students.

"What you need to know to be practically intelligent, to get on in an environment," Sternberg says, is tacit knowledge, the third area of agreement. "It's implied or indicated but not always expressed, or taught." Sternberg and Wagner constructed a test of such knowledge and gave it to senior and junior business executives and to senior and junior psychology professors. The results suggest that tacit knowledge is a result of learning from experience. It is not related to IQ but is related to success in the real world. Psychologists who scored high on the test, compared with those who had done poorly, had published more research, presented more papers at conventions and tended to be at the better universities. Business executives who scored high had better salaries, more merit raises and better performance ratings than those who scored low.

The tacit-knowledge test is a measure of how well people adapt to their environment, but practical knowledge also means knowing when not to adapt. "Suppose you join a computer software firm because you really want to work on educational software," Sternberg says, "but they put you in the firm's industrial espionage section and ask you to spy on Apple Computer. There are times when you have to select another environment, when you have to say 'It's time to quit. I don't want to adapt, I'm leaving.'"

There are, however, times when you can't quit and must stay put. In such situations, you can try to change the environment. That, says Sternberg, is the final aspect of contextual, or practical, intelligence— shaping the environment to suit your needs.

One way to do this is by capitalizing on your intellectual strengths and compensating for your weaknesses. "I don't think I'm at the top of the heap analytically," Sternberg explains. "I'm good, not the greatest, but I think I know what I'm good at and I try to make the most of it. And there are some things I stink at and I either try to make

> There are plenty of people going around with high IQ's who don't do a damned thing.

them unimportant or I find other people to do them. That's part of how I shape my environment. And that's what I think practical intelligence is about—capitalizing on your strengths and minimizing your weaknesses. It's sort of mental self-management.

"So basically what I've said is there are different ways to be smart, but ultimately what you want to do is take the components (Alice intelligence), apply them to your experience (Barbara) and use them to adapt to, select and shape your environment (Celia). That is the triarchic theory of intelligence."

What can you do with a new theory of intelligence? Sternberg, who seems to have a three-part answer for every question . . . says, "I view the situation as a triangle." The most important leg of the triangle, he says, is theory and research. "But it's not enough for me to spend my life coming up with

> It's really important to me that my work has an effect that goes beyond the psychology journals, to bring intelligence into the real world and the real world into intelligence.

theories," he says. "So I've gone in two further directions, the other two legs of the triangle—testing and training."

He is developing, with the Psychological Corporation, now in San Antonio, Texas, the Sternberg Multidimensional Abilities Test. It is based strictly on the triarchic theory and will measure intelligence in a much broader way than traditional IQ tests do. "Rather than giving you a number that's etched in stone," he says, "this test will be used as a basis for diagnosing your intellectual strengths and weaknesses."

Once you understand the kind of intelligence you have, the third leg of the triangle—the training of intellectual skills—comes into play. One of Sternberg's most recent books, *Intelligence Applied,* is a training program based on the theory. It is designed to help people capitalize on their strengths and improve where they are weak. "I'm very committed to all three aspects," Sternberg says. "It's really important to me that my work has an effect that goes beyond the psychology journals. I really think it's important to bring intelligence into the real world and the real world into intelligence."

PART THREE
Study and Discussion Questions

CHAPTER FIVE How the Brain Develops and Functions

Reading 12 Making of a Mind

1. What do brain-research findings tell us about why it is easier to teach a new language to a developing infant than to an adult?

2. Research shows that although the adult brain cannot generate new brain cells, it does continue to generate new nerve connections. What are the implications of this finding for adult learning?

3. When researchers talk about "critical periods" in a brain's development for acquiring particular skills, what does this mean?

Reading 13 Right Brain, Left Brain: Fact and Fiction

1. Is the following statement true or false? "Since each brain hemisphere is specialized, each must function as a separate brain." What evidence supports your answer?

2. Consider this statement: "There is no evidence that either creativity or intuition is exclusively the property of the right hemisphere." True or false? Why?

Reading 14 New Evidence Points to Growth of Brain Even Late in Life

1. If someone asked you how living in a deprived or enriched environment affected brain growth, what would you say?

2. What does the following statement mean? "In adulthood, if you learn a new language it's dendritic fireworks."

CHAPTER SIX Contemporary Views About the Nature of Intelligence

Reading 15 Developing the Spectrum of Human Intelligences

1. How does Gardner's definition of intelligence differ from the usual views?

2. Can you name and briefly describe each of Gardner's "seven intelligences"?

3. Which of these "intelligences" do you feel is particularly well developed in you? Why do you think so?

4. If the educational system were to widely accept Gardner's idea of seven intelligences, how might this change the way we go about the business of schooling?

Reading 16 Three Heads Are Better Than One

1. Can you identify and briefly describe each of the three components of intelligence in Sternberg's "triarchic theory" of intelligence?

2. Why does Sternberg feel that his three-part theory of intelligence is better than the usual one-dimensional view?

3. When you line up your own intellectual skills alongside Sternberg's components of intelligence, where do you see your strengths?

PART FOUR

Learning: Process and Strategies

In this section we will examine the reason why schools exist in the first place—learning. We will look at what learning involves, strategies for encouraging it, metacognitive and information-processing strategies behind it, and how grouping, class size, and retention practices may influence its outcomes.

Discovery learning, around since Jerome Burner introduced the idea in the 1960s, has been one of the major staples on the approaches-to-learning menu for teachers. In Reading 17, Ray T. Wilcox details some practical suggestions for revitalizing discovery methods in the classroom.

Benjamin Bloom's mastery learning concepts can also be found among the available learning menu options from which teachers can choose. In Reading 18, Thomas R. Guskey overviews the effectiveness of this approach as a mode of learning in terms of its impact on both students and teachers in the past twenty-five years.

In Reading 19, Robert E. Slavin outlines the major advantages of using cooperative methods as a means of promoting school learning. He is careful to point out, however, that although cooperating groups must have a group goal that is important to them, there still must be *individual accountability* when it comes to assessing learning within those groups.

It is not possible to discuss school learning without also considering the increasing role that computers are playing in this process. In Reading 20, M. D. Roblyer provides an overview of the rationale for using computers and discusses a number of ways computers can be used as aids to learning in school situations.

Although we learn many things without any particular conscious awareness of what we are learning, the kind of formal learning that goes on in the classroom is more likely to occur when there is a plan for how to go about it. In Reading 21, Sharon J. Derry discusses some strategies teachers can use to help students develop their own plans for learning.

Chapter Eight deals with processes that are central to learning—metacognition (the way we think about our thinking), components of critical thinking, and information processing (the way we deal with information in our minds and memories). Annemarie Sullivan Palincsar and Kathryn Ransom suggest that all students should be provided with knowledge about factors that affect learning and taught strategies that allow them to take charge of their learning. A plan for doing this is found in Reading 22.

In Reading 23, Matthew Lipman contrasts the differences between ordinary thinking and critical thinking and suggests ways to encourage more critical thinking in classroom situations.

Without our capacity for memory there would, of course, be no learning. In Reading 24, Robert Sylwester discusses the basic processes involved in long-term and short-term memory and suggests ways to enhance the effectiveness of memory.

Chapter Nine overviews the effects that grouping, class size, and retention can have on learning. In Reading 25, Robert E. Slavin synthesizes what research teaches us about students' learning when they are grouped according to different kinds of ability. Grouping students is not the panacea it was once thought to be.

Class size can dramatically affect learning for better or worse. As shown by Mary Lee Smith and Gene V. Glass in Reading 26, class size affects the quality of the learning environment, the students' attitudes, and the morale of teachers. A strong case is made for the advantages of smaller classes.

It is an age-old question: Does holding students back a year help their learning? As discussed by Gary Cooke and John Stammer in Reading 27, the evidence is equivocal. Suggestions are offered for programs and solutions that go beyond keeping in the same grade children who have trouble learning.

Is one strategy better than others for promoting learning? Are cooperative learning approaches to learning better than individual efforts? How can teachers use both discovery and mastery learning approaches to encourage learning? What metacognitive strategies should students use to help the learning process? How can we tell the difference between ordinary and critical thinking? What can teachers do to help students retain new learning in long-term memory?

It is questions of this sort that will occupy our attention in Part Four.

CHAPTER SEVEN
Strategies for Promoting Learning

READING 17   RAY T. WILCOX
Rediscovering Discovery Learning

Ever since the 1960s, when Jerome Bruner focused attention on the process of learning by discovery, teachers have been bombarded with suggestions to forsake direct, expository teaching in favor of indirect, discovery methods. Along with many teachers, I used to be fearful about holding back answers and possibly abandoning students to their own devices so that they might discover meanings for themselves. Discovery methods seemed risky, much like throwing youngsters into the deep end of a swimming pool so they would learn to swim. Furthermore, discovery methods appeared to be complicated and overly time-consuming.

It was only recently that I began rereading a few articles and books about discovery teaching, where I found some suggestions that motivated me to try again. Now, I have introduced discovery methods into my own classes with excellent results. Most of the techniques have not proven to be complicated or unusually time-consuming. And I have had good feedback from my students. They really like these discovery methods, which are a diversion from the steady routine of show and tell, tell, tell, and they seem to have an increased excitement for learning.

I hasten to add that I have not abandoned expository approaches. Current curriculum requirements and my own lack of ingenuity do not afford me that choice. Instead, I use discovery methods to supplement regular direct, frontal teaching. By using techniques from both ends of the expository-discovery continuum, there is more variety in my classroom, and I have proven to myself that teaching does not have to be an either/or situation. Educators can use many teaching approaches to suit their own requirements. This article discusses ten of the discovery methods that I have found to be the most helpful supplements.

WARM-UPS

Warm-ups are short practice exercises to get students in the mood to participate fully in indirect, discovery-type lessons. Warm-ups represent an anticipatory set—an obvious shifting of gears from expository-type lessons. Students are given responsibility for asking questions and are invited to take an active part in each warm-up activity.

"Twenty questions" is an excellent warm-up. This activity is like the parlor game in which a riddle is given and the students must figure out the answer by asking the teacher only yes/no questions. An example is the following riddle: "The man who made it didn't want it. The man who bought it didn't need it. The man who used it didn't know it. What is it?" Answer: "A coffin." Variations of this exercise are "Animal, vegetable, or mineral?" or "I'm thinking of a noun."

Public interviews are also good warm-ups. A student is selected to be interviewed, and the class is al-

From *The Clearing House*, October 1987, pp. 53–56. Reprinted with permission of the Helen Dwight Reid Educational Foundation. Published by Heldref Publications, 4000 Albemarle St., N.W., Washington, D.C. 20016. Copyright © 1987.

lowed to ask questions about his or her personal life and past experiences. If the interviewee does not want to answer a particular question, he or she simply says, "I pass," and another question is asked. After the allotted time is gone, the teacher concludes the session.

Incomplete sentences provide a warm-up that can be done individually, like the public interview, or with the entire class as a group. Incomplete sentences such as "If I were president, the first thing I would do is . . . ," "I like people who . . . ," or "The one thing I want most to accomplish is . . . ," are given out for completion; completed versions may be read aloud later.

Class meetings have been recommended by William Glasser to involve the teacher and individual class members. I like to use such meetings as warm-up activities. In a circle, students talk to me and to each other about a variety of topics. The subject is relatively unimportant as long as all students participate. Thus they learn from each other as well as from the teacher. They also practice taking increased responsibility for their own learning.

Another warm-up activity is working simple problems in rapid-fire order. The teacher starts the process by putting a math problem on the board, giving a spelling word, or asking a question. A student is called on at random for the answer. The teacher quickly presents another problem. The student who correctly answered the preceding problem chooses another student. This process continues until someone makes a mistake. Then the chain can be started again by the teacher calling on another student. The object of the game is to see how many problems can be worked correctly in a given period of time. Variations are to divide the class into two teams that compete against each other, or to have students come up with the problems.

STUDENT QUESTIONS

In using the "ask me about . . ." method, once a topic has been introduced, the teacher answers only those questions that students ask. If the pump has been primed through various warm-up activities, students quickly recognize that they have a responsibility for how the lesson develops. "Ask me about behavioral objectives," I might begin. The rest is up to the students. I have found that students are usually quite willing to ask relevant questions once they understand they control how much I tell them and, thus, how much they learn. Sometimes I am disappointed with how little they want to know, and so I revert to telling or try another discovery method, but often I am impressed with the quality and quantity of the questions asked. Occasionally, questions come up that I cannot answer without doing additional reading. In those cases, I try to bring back more information the next day, which usually prompts even further questions.

> **I**f all the student needs to do is follow a "recipe" and fill in the blanks, discovery opportunities will be minimal.

EXAMPLES AND NON-EXAMPLES

For different concepts or important generalizations, a list of examples and corresponding non-examples can usually be identified in advance of the planned teaching episode. By simply presenting these examples and non-examples and nothing more, I have been pleasantly surprised at how often students can discover the concept I am trying to teach. They usually have trouble naming the concept, so I either tell them or play the game of "hangman," in which all the letters are represented by short lines on the chalkboard and the students guess letters that go on the lines.

Examples should be broad enough to include special cases unless inclusion of the exceptional case would confuse students and detract from correct identification and naming of the concept. Normally, if students can succeed in discovering the concept, special cases can be pointed out later through more traditional expository approaches.

A variation on providing examples and non-examples is to give good examples and bad examples. In a speech class, for instance, an oration is presented using clear organization, proper English, and attractive gestures. A second oration follows, and this time the speaker uses improper organization, poor English, and distracting gestures. Without any preaching at all, it is relatively easy for the class to discover that proper organization, use of English, and suitable gestures add to the persuasiveness of an oration.

CLASS DISCUSSION

There can be several forms of class discussion. On a continuum, these forms will range from narrow, teacher-directed questions and answers to freewheeling, almost out-of-control, shoot-the-breeze sessions with everyone asking questions and interjecting opinions. The closer a teacher can come to conducting the latter type of class discussion without totally losing control, the better the opportunity for discovery learning to take place.

Open-ended or divergent questions usually stimulate more student involvement in the discussion.

I've started class sessions by saying, "What is learning?" English teachers might ask, "What is poetry?" and so on.

SET INDUCTION

Set induction is used mainly to teach an object lesson. The attention of the class is focused on a physical object or an experience that is common to all class members. Then the lesson shifts to an abstract concept. Through the use of analogy and student discovery, the abstraction is interpreted as being like the physical object or the common experience. This comparison to what is already known and perceived by the students makes the abstraction more meaningful and understandable to them.

For example, by comparing a group of people to a pile of books, it is possible to show that one cannot really judge people by their appearance any more than one can judge a book by its cover.

SOLVING PROBLEMS

Almost any kind of problem will do to begin the process of student thinking, whether the problem be mathematical, scientific, creative, or value-laden.

Mathematical problem solving will not always be relevant outside of science and mathematics classes. However, regardless of subject, many teachers will find that judicious use of story problems and puzzles may serve to set the stage and develop an interest in the general mechanics of problem solving.

In solving a mathematical problem, students discover that it is important to classify the problem so it can be related to similar problems with known solutions. Or they find that it is usually appropriate to draw a picture and then work forward or even backward. They might even learn that it is best to widen the conditions or to simply guess and test the answer.

Scientific problem solving helps students learn that they must gather and analyze relevant information, formulate a hypothesis, test the hypothesis, draw conclusions, and make possible recommendations. For example, a homemaking teacher might ask students to vary the amount of water added to one cup of pancake flour and observe the product under standard cooking conditions.

Creative problem solving begins with raising new questions and possibilities, or by viewing old problems from a different angle. For example: "How can educators have quality education programs without asking for more money?" "Please find another way of doing long division other than the one taught in the textbook." A good brainstorming session in which all ideas are welcomed is beneficial in delving into these kinds of problems.

Value-laden problem solving deals with examining both sides of any controversial issue. Debates might be conducted in class to make sure that both sides of the issue get a fair hearing. Or students might be charged with the responsibility of investigating both sides in an issue probe and then reporting their findings to the class. The teacher may need to play the devil's advocate if students are leaning completely to one side or the other.

Student discovery is encouraged as they listen to the differing opinions expressed. The disequilibrium that normally follows an issue probe requires students to do some cognitive restructuring, which might take the form of a new awareness or a new value different from what they have believed in the past. Or it might take the form of confirming already established values.

Some value-laden problems I have used in my classes are: "Should senior high school students be required to pass a minimum competency test for graduation from high school?" "Should schools allow students to rate teachers?" "Should parents be permitted to teach their children at home rather than send them to the public schools?" "Should special education students be mainstreamed?"

SOCRATIC QUESTIONS

Since this style of questioning began with Socrates, teachers should read some of the dialogues attributed to him to get a feel for the kinds of questions he asked.

Socratic questioning, as it is used today, leads the students to recognize a predetermined concept by focusing on a few carefully selected examples. Then, when the students believe they have discovered the intended generalization, the teacher surprises them with a mind-boggling counter-example. Thus trapped by the teacher, students are left to extricate themselves from the dilemma as best they can. After the discussion has ended, it is hoped the students begin to recognize the larger dimensions of the concept or debate. Perhaps they will conclude that the dilemma has no pat answers, as they might have expected, for example, from a discussion of the question, "Who is the educated man or woman?"

APPROPRIATE LABORATORY EXERCISES

Unfortunately, simply conducting an exercise in a laboratory does not ensure discovery. If all the student needs to do is follow a "recipe" and fill in the blanks, discovery opportunities will be minimal.

To make a laboratory exercise become a discovery experience, the teacher must hold something back, either answers or directions or both. The student must then try to figure out what has been left out.

Ideally, the student should be given the opportunity to form his or her own hypothesis and design an experiment to test this hypothesis. The student must then conduct the experiment, analyze data, and accept or reject the hypothesis.

Laboratory exercises are designed to be a part of most science classes, but other subject teachers, with a little forethought, can use this approach also. For example, I asked my students to keep a "teaching journal" for a one-week period in which they recorded an assignment to teach a friend about the concepts they were learning in my class. I then asked them to let me check their journals, which I deliberately kept for almost a full week. After the second week, I gave them a test that was divided equally between the concepts taught during the first week and the second week. I scored the papers and returned them along with the question, "Which concepts were learned the best, those for week one or those for week two?" Considering the time factor, those for week two should have been remembered the best. But it turned out that the concepts taught when the students had been forced to teach them to another person were remembered the best. Although the difference was not large, the class members nonetheless concluded that teaching a concept to another person helped them learn the concept better.

SUITABLE CLASS DEMONSTRATIONS

The same principle applies to class demonstrations as to laboratory exercises. Something must be held back if students are to discover. Teachers must show and not tell. Or, they must show and not tell all.

As the teacher conducts the demonstration, students are provided clues to help them recognize and hence find regularities and solutions that fit the experiment or demonstration. The teacher carefully directs the students so they discover the main concepts. Actual generalizations might even be left for students to formulate, the teacher eventually endorsing them as correct.

For example, I observed a student teacher in a junior high school general science class who conducted a discovery-oriented demonstration. He had filled a number of coke bottles (which are hard to break) with varying proportions of oxygen and hydrogen by displacing water from the bottles by bubbling gas into them from two compressed tanks, one of oxygen and the other of hydrogen. He set each bottle upside-down in a pan of water to keep the gases from escaping. He then refreshed the students' memories by recording on the chalkboard the exact percentage of oxygen and the exact percentage of hydrogen in each coke bottle. Finally, he asked the class members to predict which bottle would make the loudest noise and spray the contents the farthest. The students voted for the winning bottle and served as judges when the teacher aimed each bottle at the class and held it to an open candle flame. The bottle with 67 percent hydrogen and 33 percent oxygen was declared the actual winner. The class members went on to determine that they had discovered the formula for water, H_2O.

Some of the students told me they really liked the student teacher's lesson and thought he was doing a great job.

INDIVIDUALIZED STUDY ASSIGNMENTS

In this type of activity, each student works at his or her own speed on a planned assignment that is common to the class or designed solely for the single student.

Individualized study assignments are given to heighten student activity levels both in and out of class. To make a study assignment a discovery activity, the student's activity must be focused and meaningful. The teacher might ask a student to do almost any of the things already suggested: to find out about a particular subject, to look for examples or even non-examples, to compare an abstract concept with a physical object, to solve problems, or to conduct a special laboratory exercise.

The purpose of a discovery study assignment should be to expand on what students have already learned and to integrate new insight with previous information and knowledge. There probably will be built-in opportunities for students to experience insightful moments when they see for themselves what is right or wrong, how something works, or what the solution to a problem may be ("Ah hah, I get it!").

For example, I have asked my students to view and evaluate their previously made micro-teaching videotapes and tell me what they liked and disliked about their teaching and what they would change if they were able to reteach that particular lesson. Most students discover some things they would like to change.

CONCLUSION

Undoubtedly there are still other excellent discovery approaches that I have not mentioned. However, these ten methods have been the most useful for me.

Robert M. Gagné has defined discovery learning as "something the student does, beyond merely sitting in his [sic] seat and paying attention" (1966, p. 135). Ideally, students accept increased responsibility for their own education, discovering and learning through their own activities, both mental and physical, and not necessarily through the teacher's activities.

Today, we are living through an incredibly accelerated and unprecedented explosion of knowledge. That fact, along with the frighteningly complex economic, social, and political problems our world faces, leave educators no logical alternatives but to try to produce students who can think for themselves, who see education as a process and not merely a product, who know how to learn, and who are adept at solving problems. Are not these kinds of students the ones for whom discovery methods are designed?

By whatever name, we need these methods in today's schools: warm-ups, student questions, examples and non-examples, class discussions, set induction, problem solving, Socratic questions, laboratory exercises, class demonstrations, and individualized study assignments. All of us need to rediscover discovery learning.

REFERENCE

Gagné, R. M. 1966. Varieties of learning and the concept of discovery. In *Learning by discovery: A critical appraisal*, edited by L. S. Shulman and E. R. Keislar. Chicago: Rand McNally.

READING 18 THOMAS R. GUSKEY
Bloom's Mastery Learning: A Legacy of Effectiveness

Walk into a third-grade classroom and ask any child, "Who are the brightest students in this class?" After a brief moment, you will undoubtedly hear two or three names. Then ask, "Well, who are the slowest students in the class?" Again, after a brief moment, you will probably hear two or three different names. Finally, ask the child, "If we were to put everyone in the class in order, from the very brightest to the very slowest, where would *you* stand?" Within a very short period of time you are likely to hear a fairly accurate estimate of that child's relative standing among his or her classmates.

It does not trouble me that most children in the third grade are able to do this. Third-graders are, after all, unusually clever people. I am troubled, however, that this relative standing among children in third grade does not change very much from third to fifth grade, to eighth grade, or to the eleventh grade in high school. In fact, by measuring children in the third grade, we can predict their achievement in the eleventh grade with better than 80% accuracy.[1] All that seems to change in those eight years is the comparative distance between the brightest and slowest children—each year that distance grows a little larger.

My point is that educators need to ask whether this high degree of predictability is an inevitable part of the education process, or are there other choices? Is such determinism in students' learning unavoidable, or can we alter these results?

The problems that educators confront today in their struggle to improve the quality of education for all students are the same issues Benjamin S. Bloom confronted 20 years ago when he developed the theory of mastery learning.

HISTORICAL CONTEXT

The theory of mastery learning was proposed at a time when the general perspective toward education was rather pessimistic. During the 1960s, much of the research seemed to indicate that the potential of teaching and the power of teachers to influence the learning of *all* students was very slight. Differences in students' ability to learn were thought to be determined primarily by factors outside the control of educators. The first Coleman Report,[2] for example, stressed the strong influence of social factors in determining school learning, and other evidence presented at the time seemed to support this conclusion.[3]

But then, based on his research on human variability and the reasons for that variability, Bloom suggested another perspective—a perspective that was bold and challenging and at the same time very optimistic. He granted that social variables are important in school

From Thomas R. Guskey, "Bloom's Mastery Learning: A Legacy for Effectiveness," *Education Horizons* (Winter 1986):80–86. Reprinted with permission of the author and *Educational Horizons* quarterly journal published by Pi Lamda Theta national honor and professional association, Bloomington, IN 47407-6626.

learning, especially under the conditions that seemed to exist in most classrooms. But he emphasized how these conditions could be altered and suggested that instruction be organized into smaller, sequentially ordered units and that teachers provide students with regular and specific feedback on their progress through the use of diagnostic "formative" tests. This feedback was to be paired with alternative corrective activities, designed to help students remedy their learning errors and reach a high standard of learning before moving on to the next unit. Bloom theorized that perhaps 80% or more of students in a class could reach the same high standard of learning that is attained by only the top 20% of students under more traditional methods of instruction.[4] He labeled these more favorable learning conditions *mastery learning*.

This alternative perspective gave educators new optimism at a very critical time. It suggested that individual differences in school learning were not fixed and that determinism in education outcomes was not inevitable.

EARLY RESEARCH

Most of the early research on mastery learning was conducted on a relatively small scale. The majority of the studies were of short duration, involved only with a small number of classes, and were limited primarily to mathematics and science.[5] These initial, relatively modest efforts did two very important things:

- They served to operationalize mastery learning and showed how teachers could apply the theory in a variety of settings.
- They demonstrated that under these more favorable conditions the vast majority of students could learn quite well.

Mastery learning was not to be considered an educational panacea. It was not going to solve all the classroom problems that teachers face. These studies provided strong evidence, however, that with relatively minor changes in their instructional procedures, teachers could help nearly all students in their classes learn very well those things they set out to teach.

Today, mastery learning is being used in classrooms across the U.S. and throughout the world.[6] We have come a long way since those early applications. But what has the impact of all this really been? What changes in education have been brought about? What contributions has mastery learning made?

EFFECTS ON STUDENTS

When mastery learning is carefully implemented, students do far better on teacher-made tests, they earn higher course grades, and they attain higher scores on standardized examinations.[7] Students in mastery learning classes also are able to learn well the more complex and abstract ideas related to a particular subject, they can apply these ideas to new problems, and they retain the ideas longer.[8]

This was dramatically illustrated in a recent study conducted in the New York City Public Schools.[9] The Mastery Learning Program in New York City is jointly sponsored by the Board of Education, the United Federation of Teachers, and the Economic Development Council of New York City. Since 1978, groups of teachers have been meeting together in workshops and seminars to learn about the theory of mastery learning and develop materials for implementing it in their classes.[10] Two years ago the Division of High Schools commissioned an independent group of evaluators to assess the effectiveness of this effort. A major portion of the evaluation was based on comparisons of achievement on examinations given annually to high school honor students throughout New York State. The tests are designed primarily to measure higher level skills, such as problem solving application, analyzing, and synthesizing. Students who score above a very high criterion on these exams in three different subject areas qualify for a Regents Diploma, which is a special honors diploma.

The evaluation of the program showed that mastery learning classes scored three to four times higher than similar classes of the same subject in the same school. That is the 20% to 80% difference Bloom originally hypothesized. And, keep in mind, this difference was attained on examinations that focus primarily on higher level skills.

But measures of achievement are not the only student outcomes that mastery learning has been found to affect. Other studies have shown that mastery learning also helps to bring about more positive attitudes and greater interest in the subject being learned. We find that students in mastery learning classes tend to spend more time involved in learning[11] and tend to assume greater personal responsibility for their learning,[12] have greater confidence in themselves and in their ability to do well in that subject, and tend to be more highly motivated for further learning.[13]

For example, several years ago three teachers from one junior high school in Brooklyn took part in a summer training workshop after which they began to implement mastery learning in their seventh-grade language arts, mathematics, and social studies classes. The following spring the entire seventh-grade class presented a petition to the school principal asking that he require their eighth-grade teachers to use mastery learning. Asked why they liked mastery learning and why they wanted their other teachers to use mastery learning, they responded that they liked having a "second chance" on quizzes and tests. Many said that before mastery learning, a quiz or test always marked "the end." It was their one and only chance to do well, and often they did not. With mastery learning, however, they got a second chance. They could use their quizzes and tests as learning tools, study what they got wrong, and improve their marks. They also indicated that they liked mastery learning because, "It helps us learn better." The principal also received phone calls from over 30 parents asking that mastery learning be continued for their children.[14]

Students in mastery learning classes frequently gain valuable "learning to learn" skills that they are able to use throughout their lives. A teacher in one New York City high school, for example, introduces mastery learning to her remedial classes as a strategy for succeeding in the "school game." She first explains mastery learning by asking the students what they usually do with a test or a quiz after the teacher marks and returns it. The typical answer is, "Well, I look at it, then throw it in the waste can as I leave the room." Then she asks them to think about what students who always get good grades do with a test or quiz when it is returned. Again, the response is, "They always save it. They usually look up the answers to the questions they got wrong." Finally, with great conviction, she says to the class,

> The only difference between you and the others who always get the good grades is that they know how to play the "school game" and you don't! What I am going to teach you in this class is how to play that game just as well as they do, so that you can succeed in this class and in your other classes as well. The strategy I am going to use is called "mastery learning."

The dropout rate among students in this teacher's classes has been cut in half in the four years since she began using mastery learning.

EFFECTS ON TEACHERS

Although they sincerely strive to provide appropriate instruction for all their students, the vast majority of teachers find they are able to reach only about one-third of the students in their classes.

In spite of the problems, most teachers continue to nurture a strong commitment to helping all their students learn. Such commitment was apparent in the Rand Corporation's Change Agent Study. These researchers found that the primary reason teachers participate in staff development and inservice education activities is because they want to become better teachers, which to them means helping more of their students learn well.[15]

Mastery learning offers teachers a way to provide more appropriate instruction for a larger proportion of students. The use of mastery learning does not require great cost or major changes in current instructional practice. By incorporating relatively minor changes in instructional procedures, most teachers are able to help many more of their students learn well.

But how does this really affect teachers? First, we find that when teachers use mastery learning and gain evidence of improvement in their students' learning, they experience a profound sense of professional renewal.[16] Second, we find that teachers tend to feel much better about teaching and about themselves as teachers. They also develop a strong sense of personal responsibility for students' learning.[17] For example, as teachers gain direct evidence of the effectiveness of mastery learning, they often begin to use mastery learning in all class sections. When asked to explain, they state simply that students in the mastery section were doing better and that it would have been "immoral" for them not to offer mastery learning to their other students as well.[18]

Third, mastery learning also brings about a significant change in the teacher's role. Under more traditional approaches to instruction, students must compete among themselves for a few scarce rewards (high grades) to be distributed by the teacher. With mastery learning, however, learning is a much more cooperative endeavor. The teacher and students are all on the same side, out to master what is to be learned. Students do not compete against each other, but rather work together to attain a shared goal. The teacher thus becomes an instructional leader and learning facilitator, who helps all students reach a high standard of learning.[19]

Probably the most appealing aspect of mastery learning is that it provides teachers with a way to pass along to more students the very special benefits of learning success. The more successful students are in learning situations, the better they feel about themselves, the more confident they are of their ability to learn, the more likely they are to become involved in additional learning activities. For example, college students have been found to put forth unusual effort in order to acquire simple certificates that verified attainment of mastery criterion on a formative test.[20] Although the certificates were only photocopies, they represented tangible evidence of learning success—success that many of these students had seldom attained.

EFFECTS ON EDUCATION

If there is a central theme to the now vast literature on mastery learning, and particularly such hallmark works as Bloom's *Human Characteristics and School Learning*[21] and *All Our Children Learning,*[22] it is the tremendous power of education and the fantastic potential available to educators. Mastery learning has helped raise the expectations of educators in this country and throughout the world. Goals such as "all students learning excellently," once considered only in dreams and lofty imaginings, are today discussed and debated, and even included in some educational plans.

This new perspective has forced curriculum developers to ask new questions about what is truly worth learning when they are faced with the possibility, and indeed the probability, that *all* students will learn quite well. These questions are seldom considered when only a few students in each class learn that which is taught.

The probability that all students can learn well is threatening to some people and societies, as shown in James Block's *Schools, Society and Mastery Learning*.[23] Would we in the U.S., a highly developed, technologically advanced country, know how to deal with an exceptionally effective educational system that graduated many more able and highly motivated students? We are accustomed to an educational system that separates and categorizes students by accentuating their differences. But while our educational system might do this quite well, it grants the benefits of learning success to only a select few.

FUTURE DIRECTIONS

In recent years, considerable attention has been focused on ways to improve teaching and learning. This has been accompanied by a preponderance of research on the elements of effective instruction. Moreover, if one combines the elements shown to be consistently related to improved student learning, that combination looks very much like mastery learning. In fact, it is becoming evident to many educators today that the mastery learning process Bloom outlined nearly 20 years ago captures the essence of very effective teaching.

Mastery learning also has opened the door to an entirely new set of questions for educational researchers. Today we have very strong evidence that indicates that the average student in a mastery class achieves at a level attained by only the top 15% of students in more traditionally taught classes. These results have stimulated several researchers to ask questions about whether the mastery learning process can be further enhanced or improved. Among these researchers is James Block, who has helped to define and refine critical aspects of the process.[24] Lorin Anderson has investigated the use of time under mastery learning conditions and how initial instruction can be better adapted to the specific needs of students.[25] The use of feedback and corrective procedures in mastery learning to improve students' learning of higher level skills has been the focus of research by Zamira Mevarech.[26] The effects of direct instruction on learning prerequisites prior to the implementation of mastery learning have been assessed in the research of F. Leyton.[27] Recently, Joanne Anania has considered what can be done under group-based instruction to more closely approach the positive results attained under individual tutoring.[28] In my own research I have sought to identify ways teachers can implement critical aspects of the mastery learning process more easily and with greater efficiency.[29] These are only a few examples of research that have helped extend our thinking about mastery learning. In addition, rather than identifying barriers or limitations on what might be possible, this research has made us more keenly aware of the very great potential available to us.

NOTES

1. B. S. Bloom, *Stability and Change in Human Characteristics* (New York: John Wiley & Sons, 1964).
2. J. S. Coleman, E. W. Campbell, C. J. Hobson, J. McPartland, A. M. Mood, F. D. Weinfeld, and R. L. York, *Equality of Educational Opportunity* (Washington, D.C.: U.S. Government Printing Office, 1966).
3. A. R. Jensen, "How Much Can We Boost IQ and Scholastic Achievement?," *Harvard Educational Review* 39(1969): 1–123.
4. B. S. Bloom, "Learning for Mastery," UCLA–CSEIP *Evaluation Comment* 1(1968): 1–12.
5. J. H. Block, ed., *Mastery Learning: Theory and Practice* (New York: Holt, Rinehart & Winston, 1971).
6. E. B. Fiske, "New Teaching Method Produces Impressive Results," *New York Times*, 30 March 1980, 1.
7. J. H. Block and R. B. Burns, "Mastery Learning," in *Review of Educational Research*, edited by L. Schulman, vol. 4, 3–49 (Itasca, Ill.: F. E. Peacock, 1976); and B. S. Bloom, *Human Characteristics and School Learning* (New York: McGraw-Hill, 1976).
8. Z. R. Mevarech, "The Role of Teaching-Learning Strategies and Feedback and Corrective Procedures in Developing Higher Cognitive Achievement," Ph.D. diss., University of Chicago, 1980; "Attaining Mastery on Higher Cognitive Achievement," paper presented at the annual meeting of the American Educational Research Association, Los Angeles, 1981; and G. Yildiran, "The Effects of Level of Cognitive Achievement on Selected Learning Criteria under Mastery Learning and Normal Classroom Instruction," Ph.D. diss., University of Chicago, 1977.
9. F. J. McDonald, *Mastery Learning Evaluation: Interim Report* (New York: New York City Board of Education, 1982).
10. L. M. Cooke, "Why Business Supports Mastery Learning," *Educational Leadership* 37(1979): 124–125; and T. R. Guskey, "Mastery Learning: Applying the Theory," *Theory Into Practice* 19(1980a): 104–111.
11. L. W. Anderson, "Time and School Learning," Ph.D. diss., University of Chicago, 1973; and "Student Involvement in Learning and School Achievement," *California Journal of Educational Research* 26(1975): 53–62.
12. P. B. Duby, "An Investigation of the Mediating Role of Causal Attributions in School Learning," Ph.D. diss., University of Chicago, 1980; and "Attributions and Attribution Change: Effects of a Mastery Learning Instructional Approach," paper presented at the annual meeting of the American Educational Research Association, Los Angeles, 1981.
13. G. Yildiran, "The Effects of Level of Cognitive Achievement on Selected Learning Criteria under Mastery Learning and Normal Classroom Instruction."
14. D. DelSeni, "Mastery Learning from

the Perspective of an Intermediate School Principal," *IMPACT on Instructional Improvement* 17(1981): 25–31.
15. M. W. McLaughlin and D. D. Marsh, "Staff Development and School Change," *Teachers College Record* 80(1978): 69–93.
16. T. R. Guskey, "What Is Mastery Learning," *Instructor* 90(1980b): 80–86.
17. T. R. Guskey, "The Effects of Change in Instructional Effectiveness on the Relationship of Teacher Expectations and Student Achievement," *Journal of Educational Research* 75(1982): 345–349; and "The Influence of Change in Instructional Effectiveness upon the Affective Characteristics of Teachers," *American Educational Research Journal* 21(1984): 245–259.
18. T. R. Guskey, "Inservice Education, Classroom Results, and Teacher Change," Ph.D. diss., University of Chicago, 1979.
19. T. R. Guskey, "The Theory of Practice of Mastery Learning," *The Principal* 27(1982): 1–12.
20. T. R. Guskey and J. A. Monsaas, "Mastery Learning: A Model for Academic Success in Urban Junior Colleges," *Research in Higher Education* 11(1979): 263–274.
21. See B. S. Bloom, *Human Characteristics and School Learning*.
22. B. L. Bloom, *All Our Children Learning* (New York: McGraw-Hill, 1981).
23. J. H. Block, ed., *Schools, Society and Mastery Learning* (New York: Holt, Rinehart & Winston, 1974).
24. J. H. Block, ed., *Mastery Learning: Theory and Practice* (New York: Holt, Rinehart & Winston, 1971).
25. L. W. Anderson, "An Empirical Investigation of Individual Differences in Time to Learn," *Journal of Educational Psychology* 68(1976): 226–233; and "Adaptive Education," *Educational Leadership* 37(1979): 140–143.
26. See Z. R. Mevarech, "The Role of Teaching-Learning Strategies and Feedback and Corrective Procedures in Developing Higher Cognitive Achievement"; and "Attaining Mastery on Higher Cognitive Achievement."
27. F. Leyton, "The Extent to Which Group Instruction Supplemented by Mastery of Initial Cognitive Prerequisites Approximates the Learning Effectiveness of One-to-One Tutorial Methods," Ph.D. diss., University of Chicago, 1983.
28. J. Anania, "The Effects of Quality of Instruction on the Cognitive and Affective Learning of Students," Ph.D. diss., University of Chicago, 1981.
29. T. R. Guskey, *Implementing Mastery Learning* (Belmont, Calif.: Wadsworth, 1985).

READING 19 ROBERT E. SLAVIN
Cooperative Learning and Student Achievement

In recent years, cooperative learning has been proposed as a solution to a staggering array of problems. Cooperative learning methods have been offered as an alternative to ability grouping, special programs for the gifted, Chapter I pullouts, and special education. They have been suggested as a means of introducing higher-level skills into the curriculum, of ensuring students an adequate level of basic skills, of mainstreaming academically handicapped students, and of giving students the collaborative skills necessary in an increasingly interdependent society. Further, cooperative learning methods have been proposed as a major component of bilingual and ESL programs and as a way to improve relationships among students of different racial or ethnic backgrounds.

There is evidence that cooperative learning can in fact, under certain circumstances, accomplish many of these goals. However, I am becoming increasingly concerned about a widespread belief that *all* forms of cooperative learning are instructionally effective. This is emphatically not the case.

TWO ESSENTIAL CONDITIONS

Two conditions are essential if the achievement effects of cooperative learning are to be realized. First, the cooperating groups must have a *group goal* that is important to them. For example, groups may be working to earn certificates or other recognition, to receive a few minutes extra of recess, or to earn bonus points on their grades (although I am philosophically opposed to having grades largely determined by team performance). Second, the success of the group must depend on the individual learning of all group members. That is, there must be *individual accountability* as well as group accountability. For example, groups might be rewarded based on the average of their members' individual quiz scores.

We can only hypothesize reasons that group goals and individual accountability are essential to the achievement effects of cooperative

From Robert E. Slavin, "Cooperative Learning and Student Achievement," *Educational Leadership* (October 1988): 31–33. Reprinted with permission of the Association for Supervision and Curriculum Development. Copyright © 1988 by ASCD. All rights reserved.

learning. Some plausible explanations are that group goals are necessary to motivate students to help one another learn; they give students a stake in one another's success. Without group goals, students are not likely to engage in the elaborate explanations that have been found to be essential to the achievement effects of cooperative learning (Webb 1985). Further, group goals may help students overcome their reluctance to ask for help or provide help to one another; that is, without an overriding group goal, they may be embarrassed to ask for or offer help. In addition, without individual accountability, one or two group members may do all the work; group members perceived to be low achievers may be ignored if they contribute ideas or ask for help.

ACHIEVEMENT EFFECTS OF VARIOUS METHODS

Table 1 presents data from a recent review of the cooperative learning literature (Slavin 1988). In the studies from which the table was derived, cooperative learning groups were compared to randomly selected or matched control groups on fair measures of the objectives pursued equally by both groups. Study durations were at least four weeks, with a median length of 10 weeks.

> I am becoming increasingly concerned about a widespread belief that *all* forms of cooperative learning are instructionally effective. This is emphatically not the case.

TABLE 1 Achievement Effects of Alternative Forms of Cooperative Learning

	Median Effect Size	No. of Studies
Group Goals and Individual Accountability	+.30	32
Group Goals Only	+.04	8
Individual Accountability Only (Task Specialization)	+.12	9
No Group Goals or Individual Accountability	+.05	2

Note: Effect sizes are the difference between cooperative learning and control classes on achievement measures divided by the post-test standard deviation. Only methodologically adequate studies of at least four weeks' duration are included.

Table 1 shows that the success of cooperative learning in increasing student achievement depends substantially on the provision of group goals and individual accountability. Methods that incorporate group goals and individual accountability include Student Teams–Achievement Divisions (Slavin 1986), Teams–Games–Tournament (DeVries and Slavin 1978), Cooperative Integrated Reading and Composition (Stevens et al. 1987), and Team Assisted Individualization–Mathematics (Slavin et al. 1984).

In contrast to the relatively positive effects of methods that use both group goals and individual accountability, those that use group goals but not individual accountability have been ineffective in increasing student achievement. For example, in Johnson and Johnson's (1987) Learning Together methods, students work together to complete a single work sheet and are praised, rewarded, and/or graded on the basis of this common worksheet. On fair measures of achievement these methods have produced no better achievement than individualistic or traditional methods (e.g., Johnson et al. 1978). Two studies did find positive achievement effects for a form of this approach in which students were graded not on the basis of one worksheet, but on the average of individual quiz scores, which ensures individual accountability (Humphreys et al. 1982, Yager et al. 1986). However, it is important to note that these studies are highly artificial experiments in which teachers did not present lessons to students. Rather, teachers only helped individuals with worksheets, so that in the "individualistic" control groups students had no resources other than the worksheets to help them understand the material.

Another major category of cooperative learning methods uses task specialization, which means that each student has a unique task within an overall group objective. For example, Jigsaw Teaching (Aronson et al. 1978) assigns each student a topic on which he or she is to become an "expert." This method has not generally been instructionally effective. A much more effective form of cooperative learning that uses task specialization is Group Investigation (Sharan and Shachar, in press), in which students take on subtasks within an overall group task. In contrast to Jigsaw, Group Investigation bases individuals' evaluations on the group's product or report, so this method may in actuality be an instance of group goals and individual accountability.

Finally, studies of methods that provide neither group goals nor individual accountability find few achievement benefits for this approach. One example is the Groups of Four mathematics program in which students work together to solve complex math problems (Burns 1981).

Comparing the achievement effects of the various cooperative learning methods, we see that those incorporating both group goals and individual accountability are considerably more effective than other methods (see, for example, the following reviews of the literature: Slavin 1983a, b; Davidson 1985; Newmann and Thompson 1987). The misconception that all forms of cooperative learning are equally effective can perhaps be attributed to a meta-analysis by Johnson and colleagues (1981) that claimed that 122 studies supported the effectiveness of cooperative learning in all its forms. However, this meta-analysis was not restricted to *school* achievement; it included playing golf, card playing, swimming, block stacking, solving mazes, and other performance outcomes. Most of these were laboratory studies of a few hours' duration, and most allowed the groups to work together on the task that constituted the outcome measure while the "individualistic" students had to work alone. Obviously, individuals will score better when they can give each other answers than when they work in isolation, but they may or may not *learn* more from the experience (see Slavin 1984).

CONSIDER THE RESEARCH

I'm delighted to see the enthusiasm with which school districts have embraced cooperative learning. Regardless of its effects on achievement, cooperative learning has many positive effects, for example, on self-esteem, intergroup relations, and the ability to work with others (see Slavin 1983a). However, when schools adopt cooperative learning methods with the primary intention of increasing student achievement, they must take the research into account. There is no reason to expect that if teachers simply allow students to work together or reward them based on a single group product or task, they will learn more.

Future research may identify effective forms of cooperative learning that do not require group goals and individual accountability; but schools that use such programs now must do so with a clear understanding that, at present, nothing in the literature promises that they will increase student achievement.

REFERENCES

Aronson, E., N. Blaney, C. Stephan, J. Sikes, and M. Snapp. *The Jigsaw Classroom.* Beverly Hills, Calif.: Sage, 1978.

Burns, M. "Groups of Four: Solving the Management Problem." *Learning* (September 1981): 46–51.

Davidson, N. "Small-Group Learning and Teaching in Mathematics: A Selective Review of the Research." In *Learning to Cooperate, Cooperating to Learn,* edited by R. E. Slavin, S. Sharan, S. Kagan, R. Hertz-Lazarowitz, C. Webb, and R. Schmuck, New York: Plenum, 1985.

DeVries, D. L., and R. E. Slavin. "Teams–Games–Tournament (TGT): Review of Ten Classroom Experiments." *Journal of Research and Development in Education* 12 (1978): 28–38.

Humphreys, B., R. Johnson, and D. W. Johnson. "Effects of Cooperative, Competitive, and Individualistic Learning on Students' Achievement in Science Class." *Journal of Research in Science Teaching* 19 (1982): 351–356.

Johnson, D. W., and R. T. Johnson. *Learning Together and Alone.* 2nd ed. Englewood Cliffs, N.J.: Prentice-Hall, 1987.

Johnson, D. W., R. T. Johnson, and L. Scott. "The Effects of Cooperative and Individualized Instruction on Student Attitudes and Achievement." *Journal of Social Psychology.* 104; (1978): 207–216.

Johnson, D. W., G. Marayuma, R. Johnson, D. Nelson, and L. Skon. "Effects of Cooperative, Competitive and Individualistic Goal Structures on Achievement: A Meta-Analysis." *Psychological Bulletin* 89 (1981): 47–62.

Newmann, F. M., & J. Thompson. *Effects of Cooperative Learning on Achievement in Secondary Schools: A Summary of Research.* Madison, Wis.: University of Wisconsin, National Center on Effective Secondary Schools, 1987.

Sharan, S., and H. Shachar. *Language and Learning in the Cooperative Classroom.* New York: Springer-Verlag, in press.

Slavin, R. E. *Cooperative Learning.* New York: Longman, 1983a.

Slavin, R. E. "When Does Cooperative Learning Increase Student Achievement?" *Psychological Bulletin* 94 (1983b): 429–445.

Slavin, R. E. "Meta-Analysis on Education: How Has It Been Used?" *Educational Researcher* 13, 8 (1984): 6–15, 24–27.

Slavin, R. E. *Using Student Team Learning.* 3rd ed. Baltimore: Center for Research on Elementary and Middle Schools, Johns Hopkins University, 1986.

Slavin, R. E. "Cooperative Learning and Student Achievement." In *School and Classroom Organization,* edited by R. E. Slavin. Hillsdale, N.J.: Erlbaum, 1988.

Slavin, R. E., N. A. Madden, and M. Leavey. "Effects of Team Assisted Individualization on the Mathematics Achievement of Academically Handicapped Students and Nonhandicapped Students." *Journal of Educational Psychology* 76 (1984): 813–819.

Stevens, R. J., N. A. Madden, R. E. Slavin, and A. M. Farnish. "Cooperative Integrated Reading and Composition: Two Field Experiments." *Reading Research Quarterly* 22 (1987): 433–454.

Webb, N. "Student Interaction and Learning in Small Groups: A Research Summary." In *Learning to Cooperate, Cooperating to Learn,* edited by R. E. Slavin, S. Sharan, S. Kagan, R. Hertz-Lazarowitz, C. Webb, and R. Schmuck, 147–172. New York: Plenum, 1985.

Yager, S., R. T. Johnson, D. W. Johnson, B. Snider. "The Impact of Group Processing on Achievement in Cooperative Learning." *Journal of Social Psychology* 126 (1986): 389–397.

Author's note: This paper was written under funding from the Office of Educational Research and Improvement, U.S. Department of Education (No. OERI-G-86-0006). However, any opinions expressed are mine and do not represent OERI positions or policy.

READING 20   M. D. ROBLYER
Courseware: A Practical Revolution

INTRODUCTION

Instructional computing ... is a democratic country. Nearly every educational philosophy and ideology is represented. There's something for everyone, which also means there's something for everyone to criticize. Just as it's popular nowadays to condemn "government waste," it's become fashionable to criticize courseware which does not "enhance the intellect" or promote "powerful ideas." Educators who have been around for awhile will recognize yet another attempt to revolutionize educational goals. Having just barely survived the microcomputer revolution, many of us may already be reluctant to participate in another violent attack on traditional values. But there are other, even better reasons for rejecting the position that courseware must have revolutionary methods to be instructionally useful.

A RATIONALE FOR USING COMPUTERS

The battle to improve courseware quality would probably have been won by now if we educators had presented publishers with a clearcut message of what we expect products to do. However, there continue to be conflicting signals. The source of much of this disagreement is differing educational philosophies underlying the use of courseware. Some say that computers should not be doing things that teachers can do, and thus all "traditional" modes of instructional computing, such as tutorial and drill programs, are archaic. In the same revolutionary vein, some contend that the methods used in these kinds of traditional computer products serve to continue outmoded educational goals. Dyed-in-the wool systems people tend to scoff at these views, observing that the only "powerful ideas" inherent in the new unstructured approaches are those of the products' inventors, who are themselves trained with the very traditional methods they abjure. There are, however, moderates in the field who feel there is room for all kinds of computer-based approaches, since each addresses a different kind of instructional need.

Recent syntheses of research results (Kulik, 1985; Roblyer, 1985) indicate that neither structured-traditional nor unstructured-innovative computerized methods are setting the world on fire. Use of computer products may not even come close to producing the same results as the more mundane strategies such as decreasing class size and peer tutoring. What, then, can serve as a rationale for continuing the use of computer-based methods? If one accepts the position that the classroom teacher is the single most prevalent delivery system in schools today and that this situation is not likely to change in the foreseeable future, it is easy to come to the conclusion that we should be looking for ways to support teachers and improve their productivity. The benefits of computers as productivity tools have been widely acknowledged in other areas of society. Some examples of how computer products can enhance teacher activities may help illustrate how this can and is working, when computer software is effectively integrated into instructional situations.

EXAMPLES OF COURSEWARE USES

It is tempting to hypothesize that the five primary genres of computer products have evolved as a direct result of the most common instructional needs. Even if this is not completely true, the different product types usually catalogued by instructional computing experts do seem to serve different events of instruction (as outlined by Gagné) and help address different logistical problems in the classroom:

1. Tutorials

These products are scarce as hens' teeth in the field, presumably because they are difficult to develop and require more instructional time on computers than is usually feasible. Yet they could be useful aids to teachers if enough computer time were available and the teacher knew how to employ them. When structured as they should be, tutorials include most of Gagné's instructional events which, taken together, constitute "teaching" as a teacher would do it: gaining attention, informing students of the objective, reviewing prerequisite skills, delivering new information, providing learning guidance, giving items to respond to and provide feedback, and even giving formal tests. They rarely contain sufficient additional items and explanations to provide for retention and transfer. However, it may not be essential that they do so, since other computer products may better fulfill this function.

From M. D. Roblyer, "Courseware: A Practical Revolution," *Educational Technology* (February 1986): 34–35, 57. Reprinted by permission of M. D. Roblyer, Professor, Florida A. M. University, College of Education, Tallahassee, FL, and Educational Technology Publications, Englewood Cliffs, NJ.

> **N**either structured-traditional nor unstructured-innovative computerized methods are setting the world on fire. Use of computerized products may not even come close to producing the same results as the more mundane strategies such as decreasing class size and peer tutoring.

Why let tutorials take the place of teachers in delivering instruction? There are perhaps three different situations when it would be productive. The first two are really additions to, rather than replacements for, teacher delivery. First, a tutorial can sometimes be a good follow-up to a topic the teacher has just covered. Some students may need a little more review of the concepts; some may use it as a refresher before a nine-week test; still others may need remedial work which the teacher has insufficient time to provide. Second, a teacher can use a tutorial as an initial introduction to the concepts for those who were absent for whatever reason (e.g., band trips, transfer from another school, illness). After the tutorial, a test over the concepts can indicate to the teacher if further instruction is required, and, if so, in which specific areas of the topic. Tutorials would seem especially important in parts of the curriculum which are critical to learning other, later skills.

A third role for tutorials is strictly replacement, but it is only an option when no teacher is available to deliver the course and when students are capable of learning on a self-instructional basis. Many courses are already offered for credit in a self-teaching format via textbooks and instructional television, and computer tutorials could enhance the usefulness of these units.

2. Drills

That most reviled of courseware types, drill and practice, is, without a doubt, still the most utilitarian for teachers. They normally provide only two of the instructional events: giving items for student response and providing feedback on correctness. Yet these often turn out to be the most essential to debugging what one is learning and remembering it after it is understood. Courseware drills also take the place of several on-paper devices which teachers frequently use to accomplish these purposes, but that they hate to deal with because they are time-consuming and boring: in-class worksheets and homework. These are usually assigned for drill purposes, but there are two problems. First, they take a lot of teacher time to prepare and grade, time which could be better spent diagnosing students' problems and providing individual help. Second, the time lapse between the students' completion on the worksheet and the feedback on its correctness is often so long as to make the assignment virtually useless. Given adequate computer resources and well-designed lessons, it seems likely that courseware drills can raise student and teacher productivity, as well as motivation for both.

3. Simulations

While computer models of real systems should not be expected to stand by themselves to teach concepts, they can be extremely helpful as a form of learning guidance. Some concepts can be introduced through discussion and non-interactive tools, but a clear understanding of the workings of the system under study can only come with demonstrations. Sometimes these demonstrations are better done with real materials. But, very often, it is simply too time-consuming, dangerous, expensive, or otherwise unfeasible to use real-life examples. In these cases, simulations fit very nicely into the teacher's instructional framework. They can even be done with groups of students to promote discussion and explication of the important principles.

4. Instructional Games

When courseware games are not related to specific curricular skills but serve the purpose of "brain-teasers," they are lumped in with "problem-solving tools" (described below). But games which provide review of skills in a drill and practice way can meet an important in-

> **I**nstructional tools which promote divergent responses may be important in promoting creativity and building healthy attitudes about learning and control over one's environment. But other, more traditional kinds of learning will probably always be just as important.

structional need. Very often, teachers recognize the necessity of providing intermittent drill on already-learned skills, perhaps with a variety of item types, to assure long-term retention and transfer to other skills (Gagné's ninth event of instruction). Yet this means more worksheets and further practice on skills students may be tired of seeing. A motivational, competitive format can give teachers just the mechanism they need to get students to keep going.

5. "Problem-solving Tools"

This is the "other" category into which everything is thrown which does not fit into one of the previous four. When courseware has specific content skills as its objectives, even if it seems unstructured in its internal format, it is usually a simulation or game and can be integrated into teacher-delivered instruction as learning guidance or some kind of practice. However, courseware which addresses generalized problem-solving abilities or encourages exploration into fantasy worlds serves a different purpose than those described above. The designers of these unstructured products often advocate "turning the student loose" with the courseware for discovery learning and unplanned insights. This strategy, of course, steps outside the events of instruction, which are offered as a pattern for systematic teaching. Even these tools may, as their promoters claim, enhance later learning of curricular skills or may provide important preparation for dealing with the act of learning itself. But, clearly, computer-based discovery methods take a long time to achieve results and have uncertain benefits to students who want to be promoted to the next grade or get into college. For these students, discovering skills may be a luxury they cannot afford. The delights of "problem-solving tools" must remain an addition to the sometimes boring, but absolutely essential basic and advanced skills in the curriculum. In this country's educational system of the present and the future, traditional instruction will be as necessary and inevitable as taxes.

CONCLUSION

Described here are some ways courseware can increase the productivity of teachers, as well as the quality of student learning. It is important to recognize that computers may make classroom instruction more expensive—admittedly a fiscally controversial direction to advocate—but it would ultimately be more cost-effective. And, although the contribution of a computerized delivery system to learning is difficult to measure, it is a cinch in comparison with calculating cost-effectiveness. Yet comparative cost-effectiveness is fast becoming the central issue when we debate the usefulness of computer-based methods and products. From the data we have at this point, it seems likely that increased teacher productivity will have to be a primary reason for using computers in education. For this to happen, software must be more responsive to teacher needs.

Perhaps it is time for us to send a message to courseware publishers on behalf of teachers that rote memorization will never go out of style; neither will the drills that facilitate it. Even computer products which duplicate some of what teachers are capable of doing may have a vital role to play in improving the overall quality of education. Instructional tools which promote divergent responses may be important in promoting creativity and building healthy attitudes about learning and control over one's environment. But other, more traditional kinds of learning will probably always be just as important, if not more so, because they provide the support knowledge and skills that students need in order to make use of their sharpened creative powers.

There is room in education for high-quality drills and tutorials in selected topics, as well as simulations, games, and unstructured learning tools. This seems a more practical "party line" for us to begin developing as a general outlook for the future of instructional computing. And, surely, a practical approach to taking advantage of the microcomputer revolution is something we can all vote for.

REFERENCES

Kulik, J. A. Consistencies in Findings on Computer-Based Education. Symposium presented at the American Educational Research Association Conference, Chicago, Illinois, April 1985.

Roblyer, M. D. *Measuring the Impact of Computers in Education: A Non-technical Review of Research for Educators.* Washington, D.C.: The Association for Educational Data Systems, 1985.

READING 21   SHARON J. DERRY
Putting Learning Strategies to Work

Recent research in cognitive and educational psychology has led to substantial improvements in our knowledge about learning. Researchers have identified certain mental processing techniques—learning strategies—that can be taught by teachers and used by students to improve the quality of school learning. Let me illustrate.

As a professor of educational and cognitive psychology, I often begin the semester with a simulation exercise designed to illustrate major principles about the role of learning strategies in classroom instruction. For example, recently I presented my students with the following scenario:

> You are a high school student who has arrived at school 20 minutes early. You discover that your first-period teacher is planning to give a test covering Chapter 5. Unfortunately, you have prepared the wrong chapter, and there is no one around to help you out. Skipping class is not the solution, since this results in an automatic "F," and you would never dream of cheating. So you open your book and use the next 15 minutes as wisely as you can.

I gave my students 15 minutes to study. They then took a quiz with eight main idea questions and two application questions. At the end of the quiz, I asked them to write in detail exactly what they did when they studied. Quizzes (without names) were collected and then distributed randomly to the class for scoring and for analyzing the study strategies reported in them.

Few people performed well on this test. A student who did wrote the following:

> There wasn't enough time for details. So I looked at the chapter summary first. Then I skimmed through the chapter and tried to understand the topic paragraphs and the summary paragraphs for each section. I also noticed what the headings said, to get the organization, and I noticed certain names that went with each heading, figuring they did something related to each topic, a study or something. I started to do some memory work on the heading, but time was up before I finished.

By comparison, most students answered only two or three of the main idea questions, reporting a study strategy something like the following.

> Panic. There was not enough time! I started going over the chapter and got as far as I could, but it was hopeless. I assume you do not plan to grade this quiz, because that would be unfair!

Learning is a form of problem solving that involves analyzing a learning task and devising a strategy appropriate for that particular situation.

As illustrated in these two examples, the differences between successful and unsuccessful learning strategies often are clear and striking. Whereas the successful learners assessed the learning situation and calmly developed a workable plan for dealing with it, the less successful learners were occupied with fruitless worries and vague strategies but little planning effort.

Such an exercise serves to introduce the following important principles about self-directed learning:

1. The plan that one uses for accomplishing a learning goal is a person's learning strategy. Learning strategies may be simple or complex, specific or vague, intelligent or unwise. Obviously, some learning strategies work better than others.
2. Learning strategies require knowledge of specific learning skills, or "tactics" (e.g., Derry and Murphy 1986), such as skimming, attending to chapter structure, and memorization techniques. The ability to devise appropriate learning strategies also requires knowledge about when and when not to use particular types of learning tactics.
3. Learning is a form of problem solving that involves analyzing a learning task and devising a strategy appropriate for that particular situation. Different learning situations may call for different strategies.

Further, I asked my students to determine whether any reported learning strategy had produced useful knowledge. Alas, no participant had applied the knowledge acquired in the 15-minute study session to

From Sharon J. Derry, "Putting Learning Strategies to Work," *Educational Leadership* (December 1988/January 1989):4–10. Reprinted with permission of the Association for Supervision and Curriculum Development. Copyright © 1988/1989 by ASCD. All rights reserved.

the two application questions on the quiz. Even when learning strategies are apparently successful according to one form of measurement, the resultant learning is not necessarily usable later in problem solving. Thus, we added a fourth principle to our list:

4. In most school learning situations, strategies should be devised with the aim of creating usable, rather than inert, knowledge. Clearly, not all learning strategies will lead to the formation of usable knowledge structures.

Next I will elaborate these principles in greater detail, suggesting how they can influence classroom practice.

STRATEGIES AS LEARNING PLANS

There is much confusion about the term *learning strategy*. The term is used to refer to (1) specific learning tactics such as rehearsal, imaging, and outlining (e.g., Cook and Mayer 1983, Levin 1986); (2) more general types of self-management activities such as planning and comprehension monitoring (e.g., Pressley et al. in press a); and (3) complex plans that combine several specific techniques (e.g., Derry and Murphy 1986, Snowman and McCown 1984).

To clarify the uses of the term, I distinguish between the specific tactics and the learning strategies that combine them. Thus, a learning strategy is a complete plan one formulates for accomplishing a learning goal; and a learning tactic is any individual processing technique one uses in service of the plan (Derry and Murphy 1986, Snowman and McCown 1984). That is, a learning strategy is the application of one or more specific learning tactics to a learning problem. Within this definition, the plethora of learning techniques (popularly called "strategies") being promoted by various researchers and practitioners can be viewed as potentially useful learning tactics that can be applied in various combinations to accomplish different learning jobs.

This definition points to the need for two distinct types of strategies instruction: specific tactics training and training in methods for selecting and combining tactics into workable learning plans. Teachers can incorporate both types of training into regular classroom instruction by thoughtfully combining different study tactics—outlining plus positive self-talk, for example—and assigning them along with regular homework.

LEARNING STRATEGIES EMPLOY SPECIFIC LEARNING TACTICS

In this section I discuss tactics in three major categories: (1) tactics for acquiring verbal knowledge, that is, ideas and facts fundamental to disciplines such as science, literature, and history; (2) tactics for acquiring procedural skills such as reading, using language, and solving problems that underlie various curriculum disciplines; and (3) support tactics for self-motivation, which are applicable to all types of learning situations. (For a more thorough treatment of these topics, see the reviews by Derry and Murphy 1986, Weinstein and Mayer 1985, Levin 1986, and Pressley et al. in press b.)

Verbal Learning Tactics

Strategies aimed at improving comprehension and retention of verbal information should build upon tactics that enhance these mental processes: (1) focusing attention on important ideas, (2) schema building, and (3) idea elaboration (see Table 2).

Attentional Focusing

Two types of attention-focusing tactics are simple focusing and structured focusing. In the simple focusing category, highlighting and

TABLE 2 Tactics for Learning Verbal Information

Category	Examples	Some Conditions of Use	Strengths or Weaknesses
Attentional Focusing			
Simple focusing	Highlighting. Underlining.	Structured, easy materials. Good readers.	No emphasis on importance or conceptual relations of ideas.
Structured focusing	Looking for headings, topic sentences. Teacher-directed signaling.	Poor readers. Difficult but considerate materials.	Efficient, but may not promote active elaboration, deep thinking.
Schema Building	Use of story grammars, theory schemas. Networking.	Poor text structure. Goal is to encourage active comprehension.	Inefficient, but develops higher-order thinking skills.
Idea Elaboration	Some types of self-questioning. Imagery.	Goal is to comprehend and remember specific ideas.	Powerful, easy to combine. Difficult for some students unassisted. Will not ensure focus on what is important.

> A learning strategy is a complete plan one formulates for accomplishing a learning goal; and a learning tactic is any individual processing technique one uses in service of the plan.

underlining are common examples. Unfortunately, the use of simple focusing procedures does not necessarily ensure identification of important information. I have often confirmed this point by requesting to see the textbooks of students who are having academic problems. Frequently I find almost every word in their texts highlighted.

Students, weaker ones in particular, should be taught to combine simple focusing with structured focusing, whereby the learner directs primary attention to headings, topic sentences, or other signals provided by the instructional presentation. The teaching of structured focusing is a well established practice in English classes, and it can profitably be reinforced in other courses to help students identify information they need to learn. However, the success of structured focusing depends heavily on well-structured, considerate instructional presentations (as well as on considerate teachers who test for the main idea). And the use of these tactics does not ensure that the ideas identified will actually be remembered.

Schema Building

A more powerful type of verbal-learning tactic is schema building, which encourages active analysis of an instructional presentation and formation of a synthesizing framework. One well-known form of schema building is networking (Dansereau 1985, Dansereau et al. 1979), whereby a student draws a node-link map representing the important ideas in a text and the interrelationships among them. This technique is powerful, but it is difficult to teach and time-consuming to apply (McKeachie 1984). Simpler forms of schema building include the use of teacher-suggested schemas, such as the well-known tactic of requiring students to analyze stories in English literature by identifying the theme, setting, plot, resolution, and so on. Similar assignments can facilitate verbal learning in other courses of study. For example, Dansereau (1985) improved students' performance on science tests by teaching them to use a theory schema as a study aid for scientific text.

Schema building encourages in-depth analysis and is particularly useful if instruction is inconsiderate or unclear. Schema-building strategies are generally employed as comprehension aids; however, they also aid memory through the organization and elaboration of ideas.

Idea Elaboration

Idea elaboration is a memory-enhancing process whereby students link each important new idea with prior knowledge so as to connect them. These linkages can be based on an image, a logical inference, or on anything else that serves to connect new ideas to prior knowledge (Gagne 1985).

Many elaboration tactics capitalize on imagery, a powerful memory-enhancing technique. For example, the key-word method for acquiring foreign vocabulary involves creating a mental image (prior knowledge) representing the sound of a foreign word (new information), and relating that image to another image (prior knowledge) representing the meaning of the word's English equivalent. Many types of elaboration tactics facilitate memorization (e.g., Bransford and Stein 1984), and these can be employed to great advantage in many courses.

Procedural Learning Tactics

Most learning strategies research has examined tactics for acquiring verbal information. However, some strategy researchers are developing techniques for acquiring procedural skills. Procedural learning has three aspects (Anderson 1983, Gagne 1985): (1) learning how to carry out basic actions such as performing long division or executing a tennis lob; (2) learning to recognize the conceptual patterns that indicate when it is appropriate to perform particular actions (such as recognizing that a word problem is a division situation or that a tennis lob is required); and (3) learning to combine many pattern-action pairs into a smooth overall system of response. Consider, for example, the complex combining of subskills that underlies the actual playing of a tennis match.

Based on this view, Table 3 presents three categories of mental tactics for procedural learning: (1) tactics for learning conceptual patterns that cue applicability of associated actions; (2) tactics for acquiring the component actions (performance subskills) themselves; and (3) tactics for perfecting and tuning complex overall performance.

Pattern-Recognition Tactics

Pattern recognition plays an important role in the development of procedural performance; however, students are probably not aware of this. Thus, developing students' procedural learning abilities includes both conveying the important function of pattern recognition and helping students develop tactics for acquiring performance-related patterns.

TABLE 3 Tactics for Learning Procedural Knowledge

Category	Examples	Some Conditions of Use	Strengths or Weaknesses
Pattern Learning			
Hypothesizing	Student reasons and guesses why particular pattern is or isn't example of concept.	Goal is to learn attributes of concepts and patterns.	Inefficient unless feedback given. Encourages independent thinking.
Seeking reasons for actions	Student seeks explanations why particular actions are or are not appropriate.	Goal is to determine which procedures are required in which situations.	Develops meta-cognitive knowledge. Inefficient if not guided. If too guided, might not promote thinking skills.
Reflective Self-Instruction	Student compares reification of own performance to expert model.	Goal is to tune, improve complex skill.	Develops understanding of quality performance. May increase self-consciousness, reduce automaticity.
Practice			
Part practice	Student drills on one specific aspect of performance.	A few specific aspects of a performance need attention.	Develops subskill automaticity. Doesn't encourage subskill integration.
Whole practice	Student practices full performance without attention to subskills.	Goal is to maintain or improve skill already acquired or to integrate subskills.	May consolidate poorly executed subskills. Helps develop smooth whole performance.

Examples of tactics in the patterns-acquisition category include hypothesizing and seeking reasons for actions. In applying these tactics, the learner attempts to discover the identifying features of a pattern or concept through guesswork, reasoning, and investigation. For example, while watching a tennis pro at work, the student might hypothesize about the features of play that cause the pro to execute a lob or a groundstroke. Hypotheses are confirmed or altered through continued observation, until the pattern features are known. Alternatively, the student might seek reasons by consulting the tennis pro directly. Seeking information overcomes the major weakness of the hypothesizing tactic, inefficiency. However, the virtue of hypothesizing is that it can be used in situations where expert advice is not available.

Practice Tactics

Other aspects of procedural learning include the acquisition of basic component actions (subskills) and, ultimately, the development of smooth complex performances that combine those subskills. There are learning tactics that can help students derive maximum benefits from their practice sessions. One example is part practice, whereby the student attempts to improve a complex performance by perfecting and automating an important subcomponent of that performance. For example, a student might greatly improve performance on mathematics tests by memorizing and practicing square-root tables. Or performance in tennis might be improved by concentrating practice on service and smashes. Part practice should be alternated with whole practice (Schneider 1985), whereby the student practices the full complex performance with little attention to individual subskills.

Reflective Self-Instruction

Another class of procedural learning tactics is reflective self-instruction, whereby the student attempts to improve personal performance by studying an expert model. For example, a student might videotape her tennis swing and compare that to a tape of an expert's swing. Or the student might critically compare her homework solution for a geometry proof to the teacher's expert solution presented on the board. Reflective self-instruction can concentrate either on specific component subskills or on whole complex performances. One key to successful self-instruction is the availability of adequate performance models. By providing models of expert performance and guiding students in how to benefit from those models while learning, teachers can provide training in the valuable technique of reflective self-instruction.

Mental Support Tactics

Acquiring useful knowledge in school is a lengthy and difficult process demanding a great investment of time and effort on the part of the student. Thus, tactics are needed for helping learners maintain a positive attitude and a high state of motivation during learning and practice. Researchers (e.g., Dansereau et al. 1979, 1985; Meichenbaum 1980; McCombs 1981–82) recommend several types of support tactics: (1) behavioral self-management, (2) mood management, and (3) self-monitoring (see Table 4).

The behavioral self-management category includes such tactics as breaking a complex learning chore into subgoals, developing a schedule for meeting subgoals, devising a reporting procedure for charting progress, and devising a self-reward system for completing major subgoals. Mood management tactics include concentration and relaxation techniques (useful for combating test anxiety); and positive self-talk, used to establish and maintain a positive frame of mind before and during learning and performance (e.g., Meichenbaum 1980). Finally, an example of self-monitoring is the technique of stopping periodically during learning and practice to check and, if necessary, readjust strategy, concentration, and mood.

Frequently used by professional athletes, mental support tactics can also be used by students to increase academic performance and motivation and to decrease tension associated with evaluation. They are applicable to all types of learning situations and can be combined with both verbal and procedural learning tactics in study assignments. For example, to study for a history test, a student might devise a learning strategy that orchestrates several specific tactics, such as positive self-talk with self-checking (to maintain motivation), networking (to help organize facts in a meaningful way), and use of imagery or mnemonics (to help with memorization).

TABLE 4 Tactics for Developing Motivation

Category	Examples	Some Conditions of Use	Strengths or Weaknesses
Behavioral Self-Management	Student breaks task into subgoals, creates goal-attainment plan, rewards.	Complex, lengthy task; low motivated students.	Promotes extrinsic, rather than intrinsic, motivation. Very powerful.
Mood Management			
Positive self-talk	Student analyzes, avoids negative self-statements, creates positive self-statements.	Preparation for competitive or difficult performance; presence of negative ideas.	Good intrinsic motivator; requires conscious attention during performance.
Relaxation techniques	Student uses deep breathing, counting, other clinical relaxation methods.	Text anxiety; highly anxious students.	Techniques controversial in some districts.
Self-Monitoring	Student stops self during performance to consciously check mood, progress, etc.	Goal is to increase conscious awareness and control of thinking process.	May interrupt concentration.

> Verbal information is likely to be called into service only if it is understood when learned and only if it is stored in memory within well-structured, well-elaborated networks of meaningfully related ideas.

STRATEGY-BUILDING AS PROBLEM SOLVING

The ultimate aim of tactics training is to provide students with tools that will enable them, as autonomous learners, to devise their own strategies. Unfortunately, a persistent problem in strategy training has been students' failure to apply tactics in situations outside the class in which they were learned originally.

However, several training techniques can alleviate these problems. A large number of researchers (e.g., Baron 1981, Bransford and Stein 1984) suggest teaching students to respond to all learning tasks using a general problem-solving model. For example, Derry, Jacobs, and Murphy (1987) taught soldiers to use the "4C's" to develop plans for study reading. The 4C's stood for: clarify learning situation, construct a learning strategy, carry out the strategy, and check results.

One presumed advantage of such plans is that they remind students to stop and think reflectively about each learning situation prior to proceeding with the task (Baron 1981). Also, such plans may serve as mnemonic devices that help students recall previously learned tactics associated with each step. There is some empirical support for the idea that problem-solving models enhance tactics transfer (Belmont et al. 1982).

Another procedure for inducing tactics transfer is informed training (Campione et al. 1982, Pressley et al. 1984). This procedure enhances direct tactics instruction with explicit information regarding the effectiveness of various tactics, including how and when they should be used. As Levin (1986) points out, there are different learning tools for different learning jobs. With informed training, students learn that tactics selection is always influenced by the nature of the instructional material as well as the nature of the learning goal. For example, if a text is not highly structured and the primary aim of study is to comprehend and remember important ideas, a strategy that combines networking with idea elaboration would be appropriate. However, if the aim is primarily comprehension rather than retention, a schema-building technique alone would suffice. Informed training is superior to "blind training" in producing transfer and sustained use of specific learning tactics (Pressley et al. 1984, Campione et al. 1982).

Previously I suggested that teachers can help develop students' learning skills by devising, assigning, and explaining learning strategies and by providing feedback on strategy use. Such established classroom practices are excellent vehicles for informed training.

LEARNING STRATEGIES SHOULD PRODUCE USEFUL KNOWLEDGE

Cognitive psychology has taught us much about the nature and structure of usable knowledge. Verbal information is likely to be called into service only if it is understood when learned and only if it is stored in memory within well-structured, well-elaborated networks of meaningfully related ideas. Procedural skills, on the other hand, are likely to be accessed and accurately executed only if they have been developed through extensive practice and only if the environmental patterns that indicate their applicability are well learned. If the primary aim of schooling is the creation of useful knowledge, then strategy application should result in the deliberate creation of a well-structured knowledge base, whether verbal, procedural, or both.

It is unlikely that reliance on any single learning tactic alone will ensure the creation of well-constructed knowledge. Rather, multiple tactics are usually required. For example, if an elaboration technique is applied for the purpose of enhancing individual ideas, another schema-building tactic may be needed to tie related ideas together. Or if practice is used to perfect a specific aspect of procedural performance, a pattern-learning tactic may still be needed to ensure that the skill is executed only when appropriate. Thus, useful knowledge is most likely to evolve through a dynamic process requiring, first, an informed analysis of each learning problem, then selection and combining of all the learning tactics needed to produce a well-formed mental structure.

Not every learning strategy produces useful knowledge. Some strategies lead to isolated, unstructured bits of learning that will remain forever inert. For this reason, both teachers and students should be aware of the nature and form of useful knowledge and of learning strategies that are likely to facilitate its creation.

STRATEGY TRAINING FOR LIFELONG LEARNING

Students who receive good strategy training during their years in school can acquire a form of knowledge especially useful in coping with the wide variety of learning situations they will encounter throughout their lives. Given the amount of time that people spend in school, in job-related training, and in acquiring knowledge associated with their interests and hobbies, the ability to find good solutions to learning problems may be the most important thinking skill of all.

REFERENCES

Anderson, J. R. (1983). *The Architecture of Cognition.* Cambridge, Mass.: Harvard University Press.

Baron, J. (1981). "Reflective Thinking as a Goal of Education." *Intelligence* 5: 291–309.

Belmont, J. M., E. C. Butterfield, and R. P. Ferretti. (1982). "To Secure Transfer of Training Instruct Self-Management Skills." In *How and How Much Can Intelligence Be Increased,* edited by D. K. Detterman and R. J. Sternberg, pp. 147–154. Norwood, N.J.: ABLEX.

Two distinct types of strategies instruction are needed: specific tactics training and training in methods for selecting and combining tactics into workable learning plans.

Bransford, J. D., and B. S. Stein. (1984). *The Ideal Problem Solver: A Guide For Improving Thinking, Learning, and Creativity.* New York: Freeman.

Campione, J. C., A. L. Brown, and R. A. Ferrara. (1982). "Mental Retardation and Intelligence." In *Cognitive Strategy Research: Educational Applications,* edited by R. J. Sternberg, pp. 87–126. New York: Springer-Verlag.

Cook, L. K., and R. E. Mayer. (1983). "Reading Strategies Training for Meaningful Learning from Prose." In *Cognitive Strategy Research: Educational Applications,* edited by M. Pressley and J. R. Levin, pp. 87–126. New York: Springer-Verlag.

Dansereau, D. F. (1985). "Learning Strategy Research." In *Thinking and Learning Skills,* edited by J. W. Segal, S. F. Chipman, and R. Glaser, vol. 1, pp. 209–240. Hillsdale, N.J.: Erlbaum.

Dansereau, D. F., K. W. Collins, B. A. McDonald, C. D. Holley, J. C. Garland, G. M. Diekhoff, and S. H. Evans. (1979). "Development and Evaluation of an Effective Learning Strategy Program." *Journal of Educational Psychology* 79: 64–73.

Derry, S. J., J. Jacobs, and D. A. Murphy, (1987). "The JSEP Learning Skills Training System." *Journal of Educational Technology Systems* 15, 4: 273–284.

Derry, S. J., and D. A. Murphy. (1986). "Designing Systems That Train Learning Ability: From Theory to Practice." *Review of Educational Research* 56, 1: 1–39.

Gagne, E. D. (1985). *The Cognitive Psychology of School Learning.* Boston: Little, Brown and Company.

Levin, J. R. (1986). "Four Cognitive Principles of Learning-Strategy Instruction." *Educational Psychologist* 21, 1 and 2: 3–17.

McCombs, B. L. (1981–82). "Transitioning Learning Strategies Research in Practice: Focus on the Student in Technical Training." *Journal of Instructional Development* 5: 10–17.

McKeachie, W. J. (1984). "Spatial Strategies: Critique and Educational Implications." In *Spatial Learning Strategies: Techniques, Applications, and Related Issues,* edited by C. D. Holley and D. F. Dansereau, pp. 301–312. Orlando, Fla.: Academic Press.

Meichenbaum, D. H. (1980). "A Cognitive-Behavioral Perspective on Intelligence." *Intelligence* 4: 271–283.

Pressley, M., J. G. Borkowski, and J. T. O'Sullivan. (1984). "Memory Strategy Instruction Is Made of This: Metamemory and Durable Strategy Use." *Educational Psychologist* 19: 94–107.

Pressley, M., J. G. Borkowski, and W. Schneider. (In press a). "Cognitive Strategies: Good Strategy Users Coordinate Metacognition and Knowledge." In *Annals of Child Development,* edited by R. Vasta and G. Whitehurst, vol. 4. Greenwich, Conn.: JAI Press.

Pressley, M., F. Goodchild, J. Fleet, R. Zajchowski, and E. D. Evans. (In press b). "The Challenges of Classroom Strategy Instruction." In *The Elementary School Journal.*

Schneider, W. (1985). "Training High-Performance Skills: Fallacies and Guidelines." *Human Factors* 27: 285–300.

Snowman, J., and R. McCown. (April 1984). "Cognitive Processes in Learning: A Model for Investigating Strategies and Tactics." Paper presented at the annual meeting of the American Educational Research Association, New Orleans.

Weinstein, C. E., and R. E. Mayer. (1985). "The Teaching of Learning Strategies." In *Handbook of Research on Teaching,* 3rd ed., edited by M. C. Wittrock. New York: Macmillan.

CHAPTER EIGHT

Understandings About Metacognition, Critical Thinking, and Information-Processing

READING 22

ANNEMARIE SULLIVAN PALINCSAR AND KATHRYN RANSOM

From the Mystery Spot to the Thoughtful Spot: The Instruction of Metacognitive Strategies

There is a popular tourist attraction called The Mystery Spot where one experiences a giddy sensation of disorientation. The floor seems to be moving under foot, the room appears to be getting smaller and yet as you walk through, it never really changes in size; water even appears to flow uphill.

For many, the Mystery Spot is a fun place to be. The cognitive dissonance created by the phenomena poses a challenge. But there are others for whom The Mystery Spot holds little intrigue and in fact some find the confusion to be downright unpleasant.

In many respects, classrooms are "mystery spots" with the same potential for amusement and challenge or disquiet and confusion. This is especially true for poor readers. What determines children's responses to the mysteries of learning is their awareness of the variables important to learning as well as their ability to respond to and take control of their learning environment.

In this article, we will discuss the role of the teacher in providing all children in the classroom, but particularly poor readers, with knowledge of the variables important to learning as well as knowledge of the strategies that facilitate control of learning. We will embed our examples in a discussion of learning from text.

METACOGNITION DEFINED AND ILLUSTRATED

Metacognition refers to knowledge of the factors that affect learning activity, including reading, as well as control of these factors (Baker and Brown, 1984). Three sets of factors that act and interact in reading are knowledge of oneself as a reader, the demands of reading tasks, and the strategies one can employ in reading activity (Garner, 1987).

Consider the following scenario in which 2 children are given the same task but proceed in very different ways, perhaps because of differences in their metacognitive knowledge.

From Annemarie Sullivan Palincsar and Kathryn Ransom, "From the Mystery Spot to the Thoughtful Spot: The Instruction of Metacognitive Strategies," *The Reading Teacher* (April 1988):784–789. Reprinted with permission of Annemarie Sullivan Palincsar and the International Reading Association.

Sam and Barry are preparing for an essay test concerning the events that led to World War I and World War II. Sam bemoans the fact that essay tests are hard for him, revealing his knowledge of himself as a learner. He decides that he will prepare for the test by organizing the information about the two wars. This decision reflects the manner in which Sam's knowledge of himself and strategies interact to influence his study plans.

He skims the unit and, demonstrating his knowledge of task, decides that the best way to organize the information is in terms of comparisons and contrasts. Sam recalls that he does better when he writes while studying so he draws a line down the middle of his paper, writes "WWI" at the top of one column, "WWII" at the top of the other as well as subheadings in the margins that correspond to the subheadings in the text, and proceeds to outline the chapter. The manner in which Sam takes control of his reading activity is testimony to the interaction of knowledge of self, task, and strategy.

Barry is also unhappy about the essay format, because he knows he does better on multiple choice tests. He too demonstrates knowledge of himself as a learner. In fact, he did so well on the last multiple choice test that he decides to study in the same manner. Unfortunately, he has failed to consider the demands of the task. He turns to the "fact finding" questions at the end of the chapter and skims the material to locate the answers. Barry's failure to use the knowledge of self and to consider the task demands, perhaps in hand with a limited repertoire of strategies, leads him to select an inappropriate strategy. This scenario illustrates the highly interactive nature of metacognitive knowledge and the manner in which metacognitive knowledge affects the selection of strategies or activities that facilitate the attainment of goals.

Many teachers reading this scenario are probably struck by the fact that Sam's study strategy was so "effortful," and might question the extent to which motivation was the real issue and not metacognition. Motivation, or will to learn, is an important issue in that effective strategy use necessitates both *skill* and *will* (Paris, Lipson, and Wixson, 1983). The research to date suggests that the beliefs we hold about ourselves as learners and the value we attribute to strategy use influence our motivation to acquire and use strategies. Reciprocally, instruction in the use of strategies can serve to enhance motivation.

THE METACOGNITIVE KNOWLEDGE OF POOR READERS

One way in which students experiencing reading difficulty can be distinguished from those who are not is by examining their metacognitive knowledge as well as their strategic behavior during reading. A number of interesting differences have emerged. For example, poor readers indicate less awareness of the "meaning getting" nature of reading, more often identifying the purpose of reading as "knowing all the words."

Provided an array of strategies, some that are effective and others that impede comprehension, less skilled readers have difficulty accurately evaluating these strategies. When presented with the various purposes for which we read, less skilled readers have difficulty identifying the approach to the reading activity that best fits the purposes for which one is reading.

These differences in the metacognitive knowledge of readers are reflected in their reading activities as well (cf. Ryan, 1981). To illustrate, skilled readers are more likely than less skilled readers to reread when they discern comprehension difficulty. Skilled readers also adjust study time by allocating more time when they are studying difficult stories. As Brown (1980) suggests, if readers are unaware of the purposes and goals of reading, it is unlikely that they will employ successful strategies to meet the demands of reading.

INSTRUCTIONAL IMPLICATIONS

In the introduction to this article we suggested that, for many children, especially poor readers, classroom learning poses a mystery—not a mystery with the positive features of suspense and discovery but rather a mystery that perplexes, confounds, and in time renders it difficult to maintain attention and engagement. We have reported that children's success with learning is, in part, a function of their metacognitive knowledge and strategy use. In the remainder of this article, we will describe how teachers can increase poor readers' metacognitive knowledge and use of strategies.

During the past 6 years in our collaborative research with Brown regarding reading comprehension instruction (Palincsar and Brown, 1986), a number of questions have arisen repeatedly. We would like to use these questions to structure our discussion of the instruction of strategies.

Assuming It Is Helpful to Know About Students' Metacognitive Knowledge and the Strategies They Use in Learning, How Do You Find this Out?

There are several ways in which teachers can become informed regarding their students' metacognitive knowledge and strategy use. One is simply to ask the children questions. For example, what do you do when you want to be sure to understand and remember a chapter in your history book? Why is reading the science book sometimes difficult? What is the thing to do when you are having difficulty reading the science book? (See Wixson et al., 1984, for a sample interview.)

Another way of assessing this knowledge is by asking a student to tutor another child, particularly a younger child. By noting the directions the student gives, the hints suggested, and the cautions provided, the teacher is provided a glimpse of the strategies the student thinks are important to success with the task.

A variation on tutoring is to share vignettes in which children are taking certain approaches to a reading activity and ask the students to discuss in an evaluative manner these approaches. For example, the story of Sam and Barry that was presented earlier might be used.

A final approach is the use of "think alouds." Just as the term suggests, children are asked to "think aloud" while completing an activity.

How Do You Decide What Reading Strategies to Teach Children?

One of the abiding sources of frustration to the teachers with whom we have worked is that there is already so much to teach and too little time. In our own selection of reading strategies, we have used 3 criteria: (1) The strategies should have the potential to be used flexibly across a range of reading situations; (2) the strategies should serve the dual functions of promoting students' interaction with the text as well as students' monitoring of how successfully they are understanding the material; and (3) the cost/benefit ratio should favor the instruction of the strategy.

To illustrate the application of these criteria, consider the instruction of 2 strategies: summarization and making up mental images. Summarizing is a strategy in which readers identify and integrate the gist of what they are reading. Imaging is a process by which readers construct a "picture in the mind" of what they are reading.

Imaging lends itself particularly well to memorizing those high imagery features or events in the text that can be stored in the memory in picture form. Summarizing is not restricted by the necessity of high imagery material and, therefore, is the more flexible strategy.

With regard to the second criterion, if a student is unable to paraphrase information to form a summary, this may well be an indication that the material was not understood; hence summarizing serves as a valuable means of monitoring understanding. Once again, imaging can be a useful monitoring strategy with high imagery material.

Finally, considering the third criterion, summarizing is a difficult strategy to teach, while imaging is probably less difficult. However, in light of the benefits of teaching summarizing (as assessed by criteria 1 and 2), the extra time spent on teaching it is justified.

The instruction of strategies should be thought of as an integral part of the curriculum. Strategy instruction should not assume the dimensions of an added course or even added content.

How Does One Go About Conducting Strategy Instruction?

To answer this question, we will use the example of teaching students question generating as a strategy. In introducing students to a strategy, the teacher answers the questions "what," "why," and "where" regarding the strategy. Thus, attention is paid to identifying the strategy to be taught, discussing the reasons why it is being taught, and the contexts in which the strategy will be useful.

For example, in introducing the students to self questioning as a strategy, the teacher might begin by asking the students how they generally prepare for a test in which they will be asked to answer a number of questions. The teacher would explain that the students are going to be taught to generate their own questions as a means of studying.

The teacher would lead students in a discussion regarding the value of learning to self question: to identify the kind of information they think might be covered in the test, to frame that information in the form of a question, and to self-test by answering their own questions. Next, the teacher would point out that it is a useful strategy since it would lend itself to preparing for tests and reading text in many content areas.

Having introduced the students to the strategy, the teacher might then determine the students' initial competence with this activity. Given a short piece of text, the students might be asked to generate several questions that reflect the most important information provided by the text. Now the teacher has some idea as to how extensive the instruction and support will be in teaching these students question generating.

Instruction proceeds by sharing with the students the steps that are useful to executing the strategy. To determine these processes, teachers might reflect on the way in which they would proceed to execute the strategy. In the case of questioning, teachers may begin by teaching or reviewing with students the words that trigger questions: who, why, how, etc.

Teachers could explain how they go about making decisions about what is important in the text; for example, "I ask myself what the section is all about (the topic) and what the author is telling me about that topic. Having decided this, I will ask a question regarding that information." Explanation is followed by the teacher modeling the process.

Duffy, Roehler, and Herrmann . . . discuss very cogently what they refer to as the "mental modeling" which occurs at this point in the sequence.

If the strategies are to come under the ownership of the learner, then it is critical that the students receive guided practice in the use of the strategy. This is particularly crucial for poor readers. Guided practice might best be distinguished from practice by thinking of guided practice as a collaborative phase of learning. The teacher and students collaborate in the acquisition of the strategy. Each student is given the support he or she needs to successfully execute the strategy but no more. For example, some children will need guidance in identifying the substance of the question while others will simply need to be reminded how they might phrase the question. The support is removed as the students indicate increased competence with the strategy.

Following the guided practice, the students are given the opportunity for independent practice. To promote maintenance of the strategy and to promote use of the strategy across content areas, this independent practice can be provided using a variety of texts and if possible in a variety of classroom situations.

Throughout strategy instruction, it is imperative that the students be involved in monitoring the success with which they are learning and applying the strategy. This might be accomplished in a variety of ways. For example, the students could compare the quality of the questions they generated when given the "preteaching assessment" with the quality of the questions they are now generating. They might discuss those situations, outside of reading instruction, in which they have successfully used the strategy or attempted to use the strategy.

Finally, of course, they can monitor the results of using the strategy in testtaking situations. Monitoring the success of strategy use is a key to motivating students to expend the extra effort that strategy use demands.

SUMMARY

The purpose of metacognitive strategy instruction is to increase students' awareness of themselves as learners and place students in control of their own learning activity. Strategy instruction is facilitated when teachers are attentive to the processes in which students engage while learning and are more reflective regarding their own cognitive processing. This suggests that teachers inquire about students' metacognitive knowledge and strategy use as well as make public the activity they, as adults, engage in while learning.

The outcomes of strategy instruction are different for various children; however, strategies equip all students, including poor readers, so that they can become more skillful participants in the mystery spots we call classrooms.

REFERENCES

Baker, Linda, and Ann Brown. "Metacognitive Skills and Reading." In *The Handbook of Reading Research,* edited by P. David Pearson. New York: Longman, 1984.

Brown, Ann. "Metacognitive Development and Reading." In *Theoretical Issues in Reading Comprehension,* edited by Rand Spiro, Bertram Bruce, and William Brewer. Hillsdale, NJ: Erlbaum, 1980.

Garner, Ruth. *Metacognition and Reading Comprehension.* Norwood, NJ: Ablex, 1987.

Palincsar, Annemarie, and Ann Brown. "Interactive Teaching to Promote Interactive Reading from Text." *The Reading Teacher,* vol. 39 (April 1986), pp. 771–77.

Paris, Scott, Marjorie Lipson, and Karen Wixson. "Becoming a Strategic Reader." *Contemporary Educational Psychology,* vol. 8 (July 1983), pp. 293–316.

Ryan, Ellen, "Identifying and Remediating Failures in Reading Comprehension: Toward an Instructional Approach for Poor Comprehenders." In *Reading Research: Advances in Theory and Practice,* edited by George MacKinnon and T. Gary Waher. New York: Academic Press, 1981.

Wixson, Karen, Anna Bosky, N. Nina Yochum, and Donna Alverman, "An Interview for Assessing Students' Perceptions of Classroom Reading Tasks." *The Reading Teacher*, vol. 37 (January 1984), pp. 346–53.

READING 23 MATTHEW LIPMAN
Critical Thinking—What Can It Be?

If we are to foster and strengthen critical thinking in schools and colleges, we need a clear conception of what it is and what it can be. We need to know its defining features, its characteristic outcomes, and the underlying conditions that make it possible.

THE OUTCOMES OF CRITICAL THINKING ARE JUDGMENTS

Let's begin with outcomes. If we consult current definitions of critical thinking, we cannot help being struck by the fact that the authors stress the *outcomes* of such thinking but generally fail to note its essential characteristics. What is more, they specify outcomes that are limited to *solutions* and *decisions*. Thus, one writer defines critical thinking as "the mental processes, strategies, and representations people use to solve problems, make decisions, and learn new concepts."[1] Another conceives of critical thinking as "reasonable reflective thinking that is focused on deciding what to believe and do."[2]

These definitions provide insufficient enlightenment because the outcomes (solutions, decisions, concept-acquisition) are too narrow, and the defining characteristics (reasonable, reflective) are too vague. For example, if critical thinking is *thinking that results in decisions,* then selecting a doctor by picking a name at random out of a phone book would count as critical thinking. *We must broaden the out-*

From Matthew Lipman, "Critical Thinking—What Can It Be?" *Educational Leadership* (September 1987):38–43. Reprinted with the permission of the Association for Supervision and Curriculum Development. Copyright © 1987 by ASCD. All rights reserved.

comes, identify the defining characteristics, and then show the connection between them.

Our contemporary conception of education as inquiry combines two aims—the transmission of knowledge and the cultivation of wisdom. But what is wisdom? Consulting a few dictionaries will yield such phrases as "intelligent judgment," "excellent judgment," or "judgment tempered by experience." But what is judgment?[3] Here again, recourse to dictionaries suggests that judgment is "the forming of opinions, estimates, or conclusions." It therefore includes such things as solving problems, making decisions, and learning new concepts; but it is more inclusive and more general.

The line of inquiry we are taking shows wisdom to be the characteristic outcome of good judgment and good judgment to be the characteristic of critical thinking. Perhaps the point where we are now, where we want to know how ordinary judgment and good judgment differ, is a good place to consider some illustrations.

Wherever knowledge and experience are not merely possessed but *applied to practice,* we see clear instances of judgment. Architects, lawyers, and doctors are professionals whose work constantly involves the making of judgments. It is true of any of us when we are in moral situations: we have to make moral judgments. It is true of teachers and farmers and theoretical physicists as well: all must make judgments in the practice of their occupations and in the conduct of their lives. There are practical, productive, and theoretical judgments, as Aristotle would have put it. Insofar as we make such judgments well, we can be said to behave wisely.

> **C**ritical thinking is thinking that both employs criteria and that can be assessed by appeal to criteria.

It should be kept in mind that good professionals make good judgments about their own practice as well as about the subject-matter of their practice. A good doctor not only makes good diagnoses of patients and prescribes well for them, but also makes good judgments about the field of medicine and his or her ability to practice it. Good judgment takes everything into account, including itself.

A judgment, then, is a determination—of thinking, of speech, of action, or of creation. A gesture, such as the wave of a hand, can be a judgment; a metaphor, like "John is a worm," is a judgment; an equation, like $E = mc^2$, is a judgment. They are judgments because, in part, they have been reached in certain ways, relying on certain instruments or procedures in the process. They are likely to be *good* judgments if they are the products of *skillfully* performed acts guided by or facilitated by appropriate instruments and procedures. If we now look at the process of critical thinking and identify its essential characteristics, we can better understand its relationship to judgment. I will argue that critical thinking is *skillful, responsible thinking that facilitates good judgment because it (1) relies upon criteria,*[4] *(2) is self-correcting, and (3) is sensitive to context.*

CRITICAL THINKING RELIES ON CRITERIA

We suspect an association between the terms *critical* and *criteria* because they have a common ancestry. We are also aware of a relationship between criteria and judgments, for the very meaning of *criterion* is "a rule or principle utilized in the making of judgments." A criterion is an instrument for judging as an ax is an instrument for chopping. It seems reasonable to conclude, therefore, that there is some sort of logical connection between "critical thinking" and "criteria" and "judgment." The connection, of course, is to be found in the fact that judgment is a skill, critical thinking is skillful thinking, and skills cannot be defined without criteria by means of which allegedly skillful performances can be evaluated. So critical thinking is thinking that both employs criteria and that can be assessed by appeal to criteria.

The fact that critical thinking relies upon criteria suggests that it is well-founded, structured, and reinforced thinking, as opposed to "uncritical" thinking, which is amorphous, haphazard, and unstructured. Critical thinking seems to be defensible and convincing. How does this happen?

Whenever we make a claim or utter an opinion, we are vulnerable unless we can back it up with *reasons*. What is the connection between reasons and criteria? Criteria *are* reasons: they are one kind of reason, but it is a particularly *reliable* kind. When we have to sort things out descriptively or evaluationally—and these are two very important tasks—we have to use the most reliable reasons we can find, and these are classificatory and evaluational criteria. Criteria may or may not have a high level of public acceptance, but they have a high level of acceptance and respect in the community of inquiry. The competent use of such respected criteria is a way of establishing the objectivity of our prescriptive, descriptive, and evaluative judgments. Thus, architects will judge a building by employing such criteria as *utility*, *safety*, and *beauty*; and presumably, critical thinkers rely upon such time-tested criteria as *validity*, *evidential warrant*, and *consistency*. Any area of practice—architectural, cognitive, and the like—should be able to cite the criteria by which that practice is guided.

The intellectual domiciles we inhabit are often of flimsy construction; we can strengthen them by learning to reason more logically. But this will help little if their foundations are soft and spongy. We need to rest our claims and opinions—all of our thinking—upon footings as firm as bedrock. One way of putting our thinking upon a solid foundation is to rely upon sound criteria.

Here, then, is a brief list of the sorts of things we invoke or appeal to and that therefore represent specific kinds of criteria:

- standards;
- laws, by-laws, rules, regulations;
- precepts, requirements, specifications;
- conventions, norms, regularities;
- principles, assumptions, presuppositions, definitions;
- ideals, goals, objectives;
- tests, credentials, experimental findings;
- methods, procedures, policies.

All of these instruments are part of the apparatus of rationality. Isolated in categories in a taxonomy, as they are here, they appear inert and sterile. But when they are at work in the process of inquiry, they function dynamically—and critically.

As noted, by means of logic we can validly extend our thinking; by means of reasons such as criteria we can justify and defend it. The improvement of student thinking—from ordinary thinking to good thinking—depends heavily upon students' ability to identify and cite good reasons for their opinions (see Table 1). Students can be brought to realize that, for a reason to be called good, it must be *relevant* to the opinion in question and *stronger* (in the sense of being more readily accepted, or assumed to be the case) than the opinion in question.

Critical thinking is a sort of *cognitive accountability*.[5] When we openly state the criteria we employ —for example, in assigning grades to students—we encourage students to do likewise. By demonstrating models of *intellectual responsibility*, we invite students to assume responsibility for their own thinking and, in a larger sense, for their own education.

When we have to select among criteria, we must of course rely on other criteria to do so. Some criteria serve this purpose better than others and can therefore be said to operate as *meta-criteria*. For example, when

---

TABLE 1 Comparing Ordinary Thinking to Good Thinking

Ordinary Thinking	Critical Thinking/Reasoning
Guessing	Estimating
Preferring	Evaluating
Grouping	Classifying
Believing	Assuming
Inferring	Inferring logically
Associating concepts	Grasping principles
Noting relationships	Noting relationships among other relationships
Supposing	Hypothesizing
Offering opinions without reasons	Offering opinions with reasons
Making judgments without criteria	Making judgments with criteria

I pointed out earlier that criteria are especially reliable reasons and that good reasons are those that reveal strength and relevance, I was saying that *reliability, strength,* and *relevance* are important meta-criteria. *Coherence* and *consistency* are others.

Some criteria have a high level of generality and are often presupposed, explicitly or implicitly, whenever critical thinking takes place. Thus the notion of knowledge presupposes the criterion of *truth*, and so wherever scientific knowledge is claimed, the concomitant claim being made is that it is true. In this sense, philosophical domains such as epistemology, ethics, and aesthetics do not dictate the criteria relevant to them; rather, the criteria define the domains. Epistemology consists of judgments to which truth and falsity are the relevant criteria; ethics comprises judgments to which right and wrong are relevant; and aesthetics contains judgments to which beautiful and not-beautiful are relevant. *Truth, right, wrong, just, good, beautiful*—all of these are of such vast scope that we should probably consider them *mega-criteria*. And they in turn are instances of the great galactic criterion of *meaning*.

One of the primary functions of criteria is to provide a basis for comparisons. When a comparison is made and no basis or criterion is given (for example, "Tokyo is better than New York"), confusion results. On the other hand, if several competing criteria might be applicable (as when someone says, "Tokyo is larger than New York" but does not specify whether in size or in population), the situation can be equally confusing. Just as opinions should generally be backed up with reasons, comparisons should generally be accompanied by criteria.

Sometimes criteria are introduced "informally" and extemporaneously, as when someone remarks that Tuesday's weather was good compared with Monday's, while Wednesday's weather was bad compared with Monday's. In this case, Monday's weather is being used as an informal criterion. Even figurative language can be understood as involving the use of informal criteria. Thus, an open simile such as "The school was like an army camp" suggests the regimentation of an army camp as an informal criterion against which to measure the orderliness of the school.

On the other hand, when criteria are considered by an authority or by general consent to be a basis of comparison, we might speak of them as "formal" criteria. When we compare the quantities of liquid in two tanks in terms of gallons, we are employing the unit of the gallon on the say-so of the Bureau of Weights and Measures. The gallon measure at the Bureau is the institutionalized paradigm case to which our gallon measure is comparable.

So things are compared by means of more or less formal criteria. But there is also the distinction between comparing things with one another and comparing them with an ideal standard, a distinction Plato addresses in *The Statesman*.[6] For example, in grading test papers, we may compare a student's performance with the performances of other students in the class (using "the curve" as a criterion); or we may compare it with the standard of an error-free performance.[7]

Standards and *criteria* are terms often used interchangeably in ordinary discourse. Standards, however, represent a vast subclass of criteria. It is vast because the concept of *standard* can be understood in many different ways. There is the interpretation cited in the preceding paragraph, where we are talking about a standard of perfection. There are, in contrast, standards as *minimal* levels of performance, as in the oft-heard cry, "We must not lower our standards!" There is a sense in which standards are conventions of conduct: "When in Rome, do as the Romans do." There is also the sense in which standards are the units of measurement defined authoritatively by a bureau of standards.

There is, of course, a certain arbitrariness about even the most reliable standards, such as units of measurement, in that we are free to define them as we like. We could, if we liked, define a yard as containing fewer inches than it presently does. But the fact is that, once defined, we prefer such units to be unchanging: they are so much more reliable that way.

Perhaps we can sum up the relationship between criteria and standards by saying that criteria specify general requirements, while standards represent the degree to which these requirements need be satisfied in particular instances. Criteria—and particularly standards among them—are among the most valuable instruments of rational procedure. Teaching students to use them is essential to the teaching of critical thinking (see Figure 1).

CRITICAL THINKING IS SELF-CORRECTING

The most characteristic feature of inquiry is that it aims to discover its own weaknesses and rectify what is at fault in its own procedures. Inquiry, then, is *self-correcting*.[8]

Much of our thinking unrolls impressionistically, from association to association, with little concern for either truth or validity, and with even less concern for the possibility that it might be erroneous. Among the many things we may reflect

---

——— Reasons ———▶
Reasons are offered to support or justify opinions.

◀——— Criteria ———▶
Criteria disclose why we consider an object to be of a particular kind.

◀——— Standards ———▶
Standards disclose the degree to which a particular object satisfies given criteria.

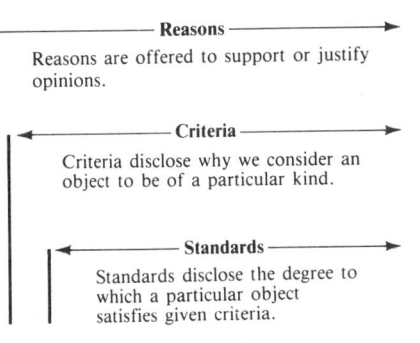

FIG. 1 Relationship of Standards to Criteria to Reasons

upon is our own thinking, yet we can do so in a way that is still quite uncritical. And so, "meta-cognition," or thinking about thinking, need not be equivalent to critical thinking.

One of the most important advantages of converting the classroom into a community of inquiry (in addition to the improvement of moral climate) is that the members of the community not only become conscious of their own thinking but begin looking for and correcting each other's methods and procedures. Consequently, insofar as each participant can internalize the methodology of the community as a whole, each participant is able to become self-correcting in his or her own thinking.

CRITICAL THINKING IS SENSITIVE TO CONTEXT

Just as critical thinking is sensitive to uniformities and regularities that are generic and intercontextual, it is sensitive to situational characteristics that are holistic or context-specific. Thinking that is sensitive to context takes into account:

(a) *exceptional or irregular circumstances and conditions*—for example, a line of investigation ordinarily considered *ad hominem* and therefore fallacious might be found permissible in a trial;

(b) *special limitations, contingencies, or constraints*—for example, the rejection of certain Euclidean theorems, such as that parallel lines never meet, in non-Euclidean geometries;

(c) *overall configurations*—for instance, a remark taken out of context may seem to be flagrantly in error but in the light of the discourse taken as a whole appears valid and proper, or vice versa;

(d) *the possibility that evidence is atypical*—for example, a case of overgeneralizing about national voter preferences based on a tiny regional sample of ethnically and occupationally homogeneous individuals.

(e) *the possibility that some meanings do not translate from one context or domain to another*—there are terms and expressions for which there are no precise equivalents in other languages and whose meanings are therefore wholly context-specific.

With regard to *thinking with criteria* and *sensitivity to context*, a suitable illustration might be an exercise involving the application of a particular criterion to a set of fictional situations. Suppose the criterion in question is *fairness* (which is itself a way of construing the still broader criterion of justice). One form that fairness assumes is *taking turns*. Table 2 is an exercise taken from *Wondering at the World*,[9] the instructional manual accompanying *Kio and Gus*,[10] a Philosophy for Children program for children 9 to 10 years of age.

In performing this exercise, students apply the criterion of *turn-taking* (i.e., *fair play* or *justice*) to six situations requiring sensitivity to context. Classroom discussion should distinguish between those situations in which the procedure of turn-taking is appropriate and those in which it is dubious. Using exercises like these in a community of inquiry sets the stage for critical thinking in the classroom. It is not the only way to accomplish this, but it is one way.

THE PROMISE OF INTELLECTUAL EMPOWERMENT

What, then, is the relevance of critical thinking to the enhancement of elementary school, secondary school, and college education? Part of the answer lies in the gradual shift that is occurring in the focus of education—the shift from *learning* to *thinking*. We want students to think for themselves and not merely to learn what other people have thought.

But another part of the answer lies in the fact that we want students who can do more than merely think: it is equally important that they exercise good judgment. It is good judgment that characterizes the sound interpretation of written text; the well-balanced, coherent composition; the lucid comprehension of what one hears; and the persuasive argument. It is good judgment that enables one to weigh and grasp what a statement or passage states, assumes, implies, or suggests. And this good judgment cannot be operative unless it rests upon proficient reasoning skills that can assure competency in inference, as well as upon proficient inquiry, concept-formation, and translation skills. Students who are *not* taught to use criteria in a way that is both sensitive to context and self-corrective are *not* being taught to think critically. If teaching critical thinking can improve education, it will be because it increases the quantity and quality of meaning that students derive from what they read and perceive and that they express in what they write and say.

Last, a word about the employment of criteria in critical thinking that facilitates good judgment. Critical thinking, as we know, is skillful thinking, and skills are proficient performances that satisfy relevant criteria. When we think critically, we are required to orchestrate a vast variety of cognitive skills, grouped in families such as reasoning skills, concept-formation skills, inquiry skills, and translation skills. Without these skills, we would be unable to draw meaning from written text or from conversation, nor could we impart meaning to a conversation or to what we write.

We all know that an otherwise splendid musical performance can be ruined if so much as a single instrumentalist performs below acceptable standards. Likewise, the mobilization and perfection of the cognitive skills that make up critical thinking cannot omit any of these skills without jeopardizing the process as a whole. We cannot be content, then, to give students practice

TABLE 2 "Taking Turns" Exercise

Taking Turns

To the teacher: There are times when people engage in sharing. For example, they go to a movie and share the pleasure of looking at the movie together. Or they can share a piece of cake by each taking half.

In other cases, however, simultaneous sharing is not so easily accomplished. If two people ride a horse, someone has to ride in front. They can take turns riding in front, but they can't both ride in front at the same time. Children understand this very well. They recognize that certain procedures must be followed in certain ways.

For example, ask your students to discuss the number of ways they "take turns" in the classroom during the ordinary day. They take turns washing the blackboard, going to the bathroom, going to the cloakroom, and passing out the papers. On the playground, they take turns at bat, they take turns lining up for basketball, and they take turns at the high bar.

Ask your students what they think the connection is between "taking turns" and "being fair." The resulting discussion should throw light on the fact that sometimes being fair involves the way children are to be treated simultaneously, while at other times it involves the way they are to be treated sequentially. For example, if it is one child's birthday and there is going to be a party with cupcakes, there should be at least one cupcake for every child. This is being fair simultaneously. Later, if you want to play "Pin the Tail on the Donkey," children should sequentially take turns in order to be fair. (The prospect of everyone *simultaneously* being blindfolded and searching about with a pin boggles the mind.)

Exercise: When Is It Appropriate to Take Turns?

	Appropriate	Not Appropriate	?
1. Pam: "Louise, let's take turns riding your bike. I'll ride it Mondays, Wednesdays, and Fridays, and you ride it Tuesdays, Thursdays, and Saturdays."	☐	☐	☐
2. Gary: "Burt, let's take turns taking Louise to the movies. I'll take her the first and third Saturday of every month, and you take her the second and fourth Saturday."	☐	☐	☐
3. Jack: "Louise, let's take turns with the dishes. You wash and I'll dry."	☐	☐	☐
4. Chris: "Okay, Louise, let's take turns with the TV. You choose a half-hour program, then I'll choose one."	☐	☐	☐
5. Melissa: "Louise, what do you say we take turns doing our homework? Tonight I'll do yours and mine, and tomorrow you can do mine and yours."	☐	☐	☐
6. Hank: "Louise, I hate to see you struggle to school each day, carrying those heavy books! Let me carry yours and mine today, and you can carry yours and mine tomorrow."	☐	☐	☐

Reprinted from Matthew Lipman and Ann Margaret Sharp. *Wondering at the World.* Lanham, Md.: University Press of America and IAPC, co-publishers, 1986.

> The improvement of student thinking —from ordinary thinking to good thinking—depends heavily upon students' ability to identify and cite good reasons for their opinions.

in a handful of cognitive skills while neglecting all the others necessary for the competency in inquiry, in language, and in thought that is the hallmark of proficient critical thinkers. Instead of selecting and polishing a few skills that we think will do the trick, we must begin with the raw subject matter of communication and inquiry—with reading, listening, speaking, writing, and reasoning—and we must cultivate all the skills that the mastery of such processes entails. It is only when we do this that we realize that the philosophical disciplines alone provide both the skills and the criteria that are presently lacking in the curriculum.

NOTES

1. Robert Sternberg, "Critical Thinking: Its Nature, Measurement, and Improvement" in *Essays on the Intellect*, ed. Frances R. Link (Alexandria, Va.: Association for Supervision and Curriculum Development, 1985), p. 46.
2. Robert H. Ennis, "A Taxonomy of Critical Thinking Dispositions and Abilities" in *Teaching Thinking Skills: Theory and Practice*, ed. Joan Boykoff Baron and Robert J. Sternberg (New York: W. H. Freeman and Co., 1987), p. 10.
3. For a penetrating discussion of judgment, see Justus Buehler, *Toward a General Theory of Human Judgment* (New York: Columbia University Press, 1951).
4. Useful discussions of the nature of criteria are to be found in Michael Anthony Slote, "The Theory of Important Criteria," *The Journal of Philosophy* LXIII, 8 (April 1966): 221–224; and Michael Scriven, "The Logic of Criteria," *The Journal of Philosophy* 56 (October 1959): 857–868; and Stanley Cavell, *The Claim of Reason* (Oxford: The Clarendon Press, 1979), pp. 3–36.
5. I see no inconsistency between urging "cognitive accountability" and urging the development of intellectual autonomy among students. There are times when we cannot let other people do our thinking for us; we must think for ourselves. And we must learn to think for ourselves by thinking for ourselves: no one can instruct us in how to do it, although a community of inquiry makes it relatively easy. The point is that students must be encouraged to become reasonable for their own good (i.e., as a step toward their own autonomy) and not just for our good (i.e., because the growing rationalization of the society requires it).
6. The Stranger remarks to young Socrates, "We must posit two types and two standards of greatness and smallness. . . . The standard of relative comparison will remain, but we must acknowledge a second standard, which is a standard of comparison with the due measure." *Statesman* (283e) in *Plato: The Collected Dialogues*, ed. Edith Hamilton and Huntington Cairns (Princeton: Princeton University Press, 1961), p. 1051.
7. For a contemporary interchange regarding comparison of things with one another vs. comparison of things with an ideal, see Gilbert Ryle, "Perceiving" in *Dilemmas* (London: Cambridge University Press, 1966), pp. 93–102; and D. W. Hamlyn, *The Theory of Knowledge* (London: Doubleday and Company and Macmillan, 1970), pp. 16–21.
8. Charles Peirce, in "Ideals of Conduct," *Collected Papers of Charles Sanders Peirce*, ed. by Charles Hartshorne and Paul Weiss (Cambridge, Mass.: Harvard University Press, 1931–35), discusses the connection between self-correcting inquiry, self-criticism, and self-control.
9. Matthew Lipman and Ann Margaret Sharp, *Wondering at the World* (Lanham, MD.: University Press of America and IAPC, co-publishers, 1986), pp. 226–299.
10. Matthew Lipman. *Kio and Gus* (Upper Montclair, N.J.: IAPC, 1982).

READING 24   ROBERT SYLWESTER
Research on Memory: Major Discoveries Major Educational Challenges

Memory and its handmaiden, learning, have always been central to education, but we have never really understood their underlying cognitive mechanisms—and neither have the people who investigated them. Indeed, after 30 years of study, the noted memory researcher Lashley (1950) wrote somewhat wryly, "In reviewing the evidence on the localization of the memory trace, I sometimes feel that the necessary conclusion is that learning is just not possible." More recently, Neisser (1982) concluded that years of extensive psychological research studies have led to major generalizations about memory that the average middle class American 3rd grader already knows through personal experience.

That situation is changing dramatically. New research technologies have vastly increased our understanding of brain functions, and scientists are moving closer to an understanding of memory, perhaps the most complex cognitive system. Their discoveries probably won't immediately affect educational practice, however, because of the great distance that has unfortunately always existed between laboratory research and classroom practice. Further, knowing that cognitive processes function basically through the manufacture and release of neural chemicals that affect the permeability of the membranes of other neurons is a far cry from knowing why most of the students in a class missed a given item on a recall test—or why I can remember a trivial childhood event, but not where I left an important file yesterday.

Still, memory is so important that educators ought to begin to monitor current theory and research for new developments that could affect the teaching and learning process. This article provides a nontechnical introduction to current memory theory and research, identifies potential curricular issues and challenges, and suggests general study resources.

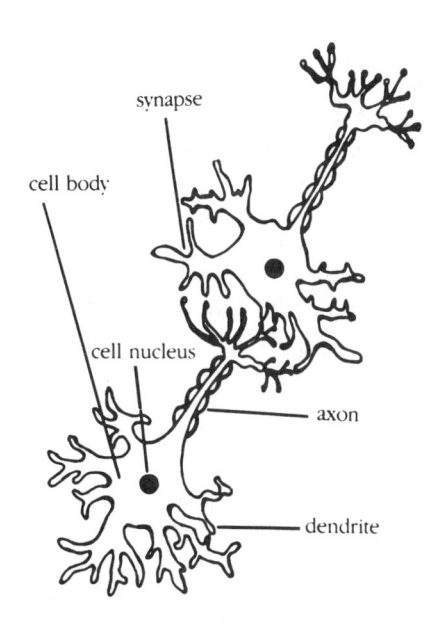

From Robert Sylwester, "Research on Memory: Major Discoveries, Major Educational Challenges," *Educational Leadership* (April 1985):69–75. Reprinted with permission of the Association for Supervision and Curriculum Development. Copyright © 1985 by ASCD. All rights reserved.

HUMAN MEMORY MECHANISMS

Memory mechanisms appear to be more localized and specialized than previously thought and probably involve physical changes in the neural network. . . .

The process of remembering begins within our limited-capacity sensory and short-term memory systems, which briefly hold incoming sensory information that captures our attention. It's possible to hold such information longer within memory feedback loops that require continued conscious attention or verbalization, but almost any distraction will erase it. For example, the memory trace of an unfamiliar phone number undergoes electrochemical disintegration within seconds if we don't dial it or consciously retain it.

When such transitory information is no longer needed, we fortunately forget it—in this case, to be replaced immediately with the sensory input that now competes for our attention, the voice answering the phone.

> Visualization and mapping seem to be especially effective as memory strategies—not surprising since over 10 percent of the human brain is devoted to processing visual data.

Important and emotion-laden information that should be retained longer is entered and consolidated within two separate but interrelated

...rm, educationally significant memory systems that probably develop some type of physical manifestation of memories. The *declarative* system processes explicit who/what/where/when/why facts and symbols that are relatively easy to learn and to forget—a car's license number. The *procedural* system processes automatic motor and problem-solving skills that are relatively difficult to learn and to forget —how to drive the car.

Think of *short-term memory* (or the working brain) as the collection of things that arrive on your desk and compete briefly for your attention. Consider *long-term memory* to be everything you've organized for later use within your desk and files, and *forgetting* as all the things you processed and then threw into the wastebasket—or as information hopelessly lost in your files.

Declarative Memory

The fingersize hippocampus, located within the temporal lobes, plays a major role in consolidating the factual declarative memories that are probably stored in the neocortex, the large, deeply folded top layer of the human brain that occupies about 85 percent of its mass. The hippocampus has been compared to a telephone switchboard— connecting new phones to the existing network, locating and coordinating messages (but not storing them). The nearby interconnected amygdala appears to process the important emotional overtones of declarative memory.

Since the declarative memory storage area is vast, efficient storage and retrieval strategies are crucial to an effective memory of all the labels and locations that keep us in touch with our environment. This suggests that we should store declarative material at multiple sensory and logical levels, much as a business that depends on phone contacts would list its phone number under several phone book classifications.

Researchers have discovered that we can enhance the potential for retrieval of an important item we want to remember by consciously examining it to determine all the ways we could describe it, define it, and use it. This conscious effort will help to create rich, logical, and emotional interconnections with easily retrieved, related items already stored in our memory. When we want to locate and retrieve the item later, these connections will help lead us to it.

The hippocampus and amygdala appear to work together to continually compare incoming sensory data with our memory's vast store of related prior experience. They then efficiently direct the limited-capacity working brain to ignore things that occur within normal predictable limits, and to attend to unusual, intense, and emotional stimuli—potential problem areas that will require conscious attention. Mass media capitalize on this mental tendency by focusing on the uncommon, the bizarre. Conversely, schools try to provide students with a rich complex of experiences, formulas, and algorithms that give them the sense of factual normality and predictability they will need to recognize abnormality and error when they experience it. This focus on normality might explain why maintaining student interest is such a constant challenge to teachers.

We seem to know what we know and don't know. Ask someone what George Washington's telephone number was, and you'll get an immediate, surprised laugh—and no effort to recall it. On the other hand, people will make agonizing searches through their declarative memory labyrinth in search of a trivial bit of information they can't immediately recall that they know is in there somewhere. *Metamemory* is the knowledge people have about their own memory storage and retrieval strategies. Pressley and others (1984) report on the type of research that educators ought to examine to design curriculums that develop this significant form of knowledge in students.

Novelty and multiple storage are important factors in most mnemonic devices and memory improvement programs. Such programs ask people to visualize and locate the item to be remembered, and to peg it to some (even artificially) related but easily remembered item—linking everything together into a memory chunk. Recalling any segment of the chunk will then generally lead the mind through the related information to the specific item sought.

Visualization and mapping (mentally locating objects in space) seem to be especially effective as memory strategies—not surprising since over 10 percent of the human brain is devoted to processing visual data. It's much easier to recognize something than it is to recall it.

We tend to lose our memory of *specific* examples of recurring information (holidays, students) as we incorporate earlier information into the more recent. Thus, over time we develop a *general* memory of former Christmas celebrations, students, and so on and tend to remember only the first, the last, the norm, and those that deviated significantly. This important consolidation process reduces and simplifies the information held in our memory. Unfortunately, it can also lead to oversimplifying complex issues, bigotry, forgetting the names of people we're supposed to know, and other assorted memory lapses. So it goes. The declarative memory system is excellent, but it's not perfect.

Procedural Memory

The cerebellum, the large bump at the lower back of the head, appears

The Biochemistry of Memory

The Basic Mechanism

The human brain is composed of tens of billions of neurons and glial cells. Neurons regulate communication and action; and the smaller and more numerous glial (glue) cells support, nourish, and insulate neurons.

A neuron is shaped to interact with thousands of other neurons. It's composed of (1) the main cell body, the chemical factory where communication decisions are made; (2) many branched (and often modifiable) dendrite extensions that receive chemical information from other neurons; and (3) a longer axon extension that sends electrochemical information to dendrites of related neurons.

Protein molecules called neurotransmitters are the chemical agent of neural communication. The neuron's RNA uses coded genetic instructions (DNA) to assemble amino acids into neurotransmitters in the cell. Estimates of the number of types of neurotransmitters in the human brain range from eight to over 50, and it appears that each neuron generally manufactures a single type that is keyed to its communicative network. The neurotransmitters glutamate, GABA, serotonin, and acetylcholine have been related to memory networks.

A neurotransmitter's basic message is either to enhance (excite) or inhibit the further transmission of a unit of information. The chemical composition of the neurotransmitter in interaction with its target dendritic receptor determines the nature of the message. Many drugs mimic the action of these neural chemicals and thus can affect the brain's decision-making and communication activities.

Cognitive behavior depends on the rapid movement of neurotransmitters among related neurons. Since a neuron's related neurons may be located at some distance, neurotransmitters move down the tubular axon after assembly to holding sacs in the axon's terminals, where they can rapidly move to adjacent target neurons when directed to do so. (Think of a factory that sensibly moves its products to stores located near its target consumer group.)

Neural communication is a complex electro-chemical process.

1. Neurotransmitters released from related neurons attach to chemically compatible receptor sites (synapses) on a target neuron's dendrites and cell membrane.
2. The target neuron integrates its continuous and competing excitatory/inhibitory input. If inhibitory input is greater, the communication sequence stops. On the other hand, if the combined input favors excitation and reaches the neuron's excitatory threshold, changes occur in the permeability of the axon's membrane.
3. This causes the neuron, which normally has a slight negative charge, to become positively charged, and an electric current moves rapidly to the end of the axon.
4. Here the current triggers the release of stored neurotransmitters into the narrow synaptic gap between axon terminals and target dendrites.
5. The neurotransmitters attach themselves to appropriate dendritic receptor sites, provide their excitatory or inhibitory input, and the communicative decision process continues within the next neuron(s) in the sequence.
6. The neurotransmitters then detach from the receptor sites and are broken down by enzymes so they can be recycled within the neural system.

to be the place where important procedural skill sequences are processed. The cerebellum could be considered the brain's automatic pilot, in that routine actions such as walking, talking, typing, and bicycling are carried out almost unconsciously—thus freeing the limited-capacity working brain to focus on novel and complex things that require conscious attention.

Mastery of a procedure or skill often begins at the declarative memory level. We begin by consciously learning and executing the appropriate rules, sequences, and terminology. Continued successful practice moves the process into the procedural memory and automatic proficiency that often includes a clear, overall mental representation of the skill. This expert level permits successful improvisation within the basic skill patterns and sequences—the smooth and imaginative transitions between conscious and automatic actions that are so interesting to observe in creative people.

Sequence is a significant component of many mastered skills. Try to whistle a tune or write a memorized poem backwards. It appears that the assemblies of neurons that process such skills develop sequential firing patterns that habituate in only one direction. Language is an example of a skill that requires proficiency at several levels of sequential rigidity—from rigid spelling sequences to less rigid syntax to the quite flexible design of a unit of conversation or exposition.

Researchers recommend that people who are learning a skill frequently observe experts performing it, practice it often, receive continual constructive feedback followed by immediate further practice, gradually increase the number of actions they view as a single behavioral unit, and integrate mastered prerequisite skills into the mastery of the more advanced skill. Many instructional programs already follow these recommended procedures—and more should.

It's difficult to recall a skill except through its execution. It's also difficult to explain or discuss a skill. Skilled performers often so internalize their skills that they can't effectively verbalize them or teach them to others. The best athletes don't necessarily become the most successful coaches. Effective teaching may well arise out of a teacher's ability to make smooth and effective transitions between the declarative and procedural thought processes—to create clear explanations and powerful metaphors, to model effectively.

The declarative and procedural systems combine marvelously to enhance human life. Our ability to consciously analyze and label skill sequences permits us to develop valued skills at the expert level. Our ability to execute most skill behaviors automatically frees our conscious brain to explore and remember much of the complex social environment in which we live.

Psychologists have done much to enhance memory skills; and neuroscientists are close to understanding the biochemistry of memory and of memory-related maladies, such as learning disabilities, amnesia, and Alzheimer's Disease. Memory research is truly at the edge of exciting developments that will profoundly affect our profession.

CURRICULAR CHALLENGES

Recent developments in memory suggest four major areas of educational challenge.

1. *What knowledge and skills should students commit to memory?* The first challenge arises out of the recent development of memory technologies that store information outside the human brain (print and electronic reference and schedule materials, audio and video recorders, calculators and computers). These technologies exponentially expand human long-term memory and free our brains from actively remembering much of the large quantity of data they must continually process.

Educational issues abound. Most educators are already aware of the inevitable curricular impact that the increased availability of calculators will have on the memorization of arithmetic facts and skills. Much more is waiting in the wings. Developments such as software that corrects spelling and grammatical errors are readily available. When today's students are adults, they will probably use word processors with such programs for any writing that requires an extensive spelling vocabulary. What impact should that probability have on the size and composition of the spelling list students memorize today? What impact should such memory and information processing technology have right now on the education of students with dyslexia and other learning disabilities? Further, what instruction in external memory technologies should schools provide now (understanding, creating, and using electronic data banks)?

> **O**ur ability to execute most skill behaviors automatically frees our conscious brain to explore and remember much of the complex social environment in which we live.

The Biochemistry of Memory

The Memory Mechanisms

Neural decisions occur hundreds of times a second, and most of them are appropriately inhibitory. At any given moment, our attention tends to be focused, our activity limited, and most of our memories stored. Imagine life with a brain that attended to everything, carried out all possible actions, and had continual open access to all prior experiences! *Selective* access to the present and past is essential to life as we know it. Without memory, all new experiences would be novel. Without selective memory and forgetting, past memories would totally dominate the present.

Researchers are investigating changes in a neuron's normal state that might constitute the basic mechanism of a memory trace. These changes could involve (1) the rate at which neurons fire in the memory sequence; (2) the number and type of neurotransmitters released; and (3) the number, characteristics, and location of available receptor sites on a target neuron. It's possible that several or all of these are involved in the dynamic conscious/unconscious process that selectively determines the probability that a unit of information will be retained, recalled, and transmitted.

At another level of investigation, researchers are studying the behavior of aggregates of neurons — larger brain areas that seem to be involved in memory and in memory-related illness and injury. For example, malfunctions in the hippocampus have recently been linked to Alzheimer's Disease.

Current theories suggest that short-term memories (such as telephone numbers) probably involve chemical adaptations and patterns of electrical reverberation, since this would be consistent with the normal quick disintegration of such memories. Long-term memories probably involve physical changes that firmly establish and enhance preferred neural communicative routes — probably the addition and modification of specialized receptor spines on dendrites and the development of networks of cell assemblies.

All this suggests a dynamic memory mechanism that undergoes continual modification through experience. Intellectual stimulation and nutrition play obviously significant roles in both learning and memory — and scientists have already related some substances to enhanced learning and memory (for example, lecithin, vasopressin). Although it's quite premature to suggest specific dietary adaptations that will improve classroom learning and memory, research into the biochemistry of these processes ought to be of continuing interest to the education profession.

The general curricular principle might be that students should continue to memorize anything that they could normally process entirely in their minds (such as basic multiplication facts), but that they should learn to use the *most efficient available* external memory technology for anything they can't easily process mentally (such as complex multiplication problems). Unfortunately, it's easier to state such a principle than it is to implement it — in a system currently oriented to working with paper, pencil, and printed reference sources.

2. How can we help students move from memorizing random facts to creating useful concepts? Our society is fascinated by relatively useless random facts — TV game shows, crossword puzzles, trivia games, gossip magazines, sports statistics. The mind functions best when it has created rich connecting patterns (semantic networks, schema) among related units of useful information. The continuous barrage of diverse facts in isolation that can characterize classroom activity diminishes the effectiveness of memory in conscious thought.

Memory research suggests that a major curricular challenge ought to be to help students develop (a) patterns that create and connect concepts in the materials they study, and (b) memory search strategies that can effectively locate factual information, examine mental images, and draw inferences from limited information within their memory.

3. How can we teach students to use memory effectively in problem solving? The great increase in the amount and nature of information available to the human mind, and the complexity of contemporary life, suggest an increased emphasis on the development of problem-solving skills. Our working brain's limited capacity requires us to solve complex problems by breaking

Highlights from Research on Memory

Remembering begins in our limited-capacity sensory and *short-term* memory systems. We briefly hold information that catches our attention until it is no longer needed and then fortunately forget it when new input competes for our attention. More significant information is attended to by two separate but interrelated *long-term* memory systems—declarative and procedural.

1. *Declarative Memory.* The hippocampus (which consolidates factual memories) and the interconnected amygdala (which processes the important emotional aspects of declarative memory) together consolidate incoming sensory data within our vast store of related experiences. Specific examples of recurring information are integrated into general memories; we tend to remember only the first, the last, the norm, and those that deviated substantially. This remarkable consolidation process can lead, though, to oversimplification and assorted memory lapses. Mastery of a skill or procedure often begins at the declarative memory level; continued successful execution of the appropriate rules, sequences, and terms moves the process into the procedural level.
2. *Procedural Memory.* Important skills *sequences* are processed in the cerebellum—the brain's automatic pilot—which permits us to carry out routine actions almost unconsciously. Our limited-capacity working brain is free to concentrate on new and complex things that require more attention and to effectively improvise or experiment within the basic skill patterns and sequences.

Memory theory and research have implications for educators in four areas:

1. Deciding how to effectively use new memory technologies that store information outside the brain in order to free up students' memories for more quality learning.
2. Helping students to develop patterns that create and connect concepts studied and to make use of memory search strategies.
3. Teaching students to use memory effectively in problem solving.
4. Monitoring neuroscience research for developments in understanding and dealing with learning and memory disabilities.

Effective teaching may be related to a teacher's capacity to make smooth, meaningful transitions between the declarative and procedural thought processes—to create vivid explanations and powerful metaphors, to model successfully. A continually stimulating classroom environment can enhance the creation of physical connections among related brain regions, which in turn is positively related to cognitive development. Curriculums should be reevaluated as discoveries in the fields of memory and neuroscience offer new possibilities to invigorate teaching and enhance learning.

them into subproblems that we can solve through the interaction of conscious and automatic mental processes—and by farming out difficult segments to paper and electronic technologies, and to other people's brains. Inserting memorized routines, formulas, algorithms, and computer software (that don't require conscious attention) into the problem-solving process permits the working brain to focus on those factors that require conscious attention.

Fredricksen's (1984) extensive analysis of cognitive and curricular issues inherent in the development of memory and problem-solving skills provides a thought-provoking and useful introduction to the area and to available problem-solving programs.

4. *How can we use neuroscience research to enhance the effectiveness of students' memory?* We can anticipate that neuroscience research will continue to move closer to an understanding of the learning and memory disabilities that affect students. But it's one thing to diagnose

a malady and another to know how to remedy the situation. For example, memory problems associated with an over- or under-production of certain neurotransmitters might be solved one day through dietary adaptations, chemical therapy, or neural transplants—but such solutions are fraught with numerous technical and ethical issues and don't appear to be on the immediate horizon.

We do know that continual intellectual stimulation enhances the development of physical connections among related brain areas and that this is positively related to mental development. Thus, it's worth the effort to maintain a stimulating classroom environment. Further, psychologists have learned much about the development of effective memory and problem-solving strategies over the years, even though they didn't completely understand the neural organization of the system.

Schools can draw on this knowledge to create curriculums that teach effective memory skills, but that also teach students how to effectively use the many external memory technologies being developed. Students need to know what to attend to in a very busy environment, how to tie that information to their past experiences, and how to retrieve and use that integrated knowledge to enhance their present and future lives.

So we've gone beyond Lashley's lament that maybe "learning is just not possible," but we're a long way from simple solutions. All this suggests a dynamic memory mechanism that undergoes continual modification through experience. It's an important time for educators to get into the rapidly developing literature and to begin to think about the curricular challenges that will most certainly emerge.

SUGGESTED RESOURCES

Anderson, J. R. *The Architecture of Cognition.* Cambridge: Harvard, 1983. A major challenging theoretical work.

Campbell, Jeremy. *Grammatical Man: Information, Entropy, Language, and Life.* New York: Simon and Schuster, 1982. Fascinating, soaring, mind-expanding.

Computer Lab in Memory and Cognition (1982). Conduit, The University of Iowa, Iowa City, IA 52242. A fine three disk and manuals program that recreates ten classic memory and cognition research studies for serious students.

The Einstein Memory Trainer (1983). Avant Garde Publishing Corp., P.O. Box 30160, Eugene, OR 97403. A fine two disk and manual memory improvement software program.

Gallant, Roy. *Memory: How It Works and How To Improve It.* New York: Four Winds Press, 1980. Good junior high level book.

Gardner, Howard. *Frames of Mind: The Theory of Multiple Intelligences.* New York: Basic Books, 1983. Fascinating, controversial theory—memory implications.

Kent, Ernest. *The Brains of Men and Machines.* New York: McGraw-Hill, 1981. An interesting, challenging book: extensive comparison of human and computer memory.

Lerner, Eric J. "Why Can't a Computer Be More Like a Brain?" *High Technology* (August 1984): 34–41. Electrical theory of memory.

Loftus, Elizabeth. *Memory.* Reading, Mass.: Addison-Wesley, 1980. Excellent, readable introduction to memory and memory improvement.

Luria, A. R. *The Mind of a Mnemonist.* New York: Basic Books, 1968. A classic study in memory research—of a man who remembered everything.

Luria, A. R. *The Working Brain.* New York: Basic Books, 1973. Contains an excellent chapter on memory that expands on the earlier book.

McKean, Kevin. "Memory." *Discover Magazine* (November 1983): 19–28. Good description of current neuroscience theory and research.

Melnechuk, Theodore. "The Dream Machine." *Psychology Today* (November 1968): 22–34. Interesting explanation of Francis Crick's theory that dreams help us to forget information that we no longer need.

"Memory." *Science Digest* (November 1983): 72–77. Good description of current theory and research.

Norman, Donald. *Learning and Memory.* New York: Freeman, 1982. A simple introduction to memory systems.

Rand McNally Atlas of Body and Mind. Chicago: Rand McNally, 1976. Excellent reference work with well-illustrated sections on learning and memory.

Reason, James, and Mycielska, K. *Absent-Minded? The Psychology of Mental Lapses and Everyday Errors.* Englewood Cliffs, N.J.: Prentice-Hall, 1982. Interesting, informative book on a common problem.

Restak, Richard. *The Brain.* New York: Bantam, 1984. Based on the recent PBS TV series; an excellent introduction to the brain, with a good chapter on memory and learning.

Seamon, John. *Memory and Cognition: An Introduction.* New York: Oxford, 1980. College text.

Wingfield, Arthur, and Byrnes, D. *The Psychology of Human Memory.* New York: Academic Press, 1981. College text.

Young, J. Z. *Programs of the Brain.* New York: Oxford, 1978. A classic, readable work, with excellent sections on learning and memory.

REFERENCES

Frederiksen, Norman. "Implications of Cognitive Theory for Instruction in Problem Solving." *Review of Educational Research* 54, 3 (Fall 1984): 363–407. An excellent survey, analysis, and discussion; describes and discusses current programs; extensive bibliography.

Lashley, Karl. "In Search of the Engram." In *Society for Experimental Biology Symposium #4: Mechanisms in Animal Behavior.* New York: Cambridge University Press, 1950.

Neisser, Ulrich. *Memory Observed: Remembering in Natural Contexts.* New York: Freeman, 1982, p. 6. A fascinating collection of reading about the ecological and cultural aspects of memory.

Pressley, Michael; Borkowsky, J.; and O'Sullivan, J. "Memory Strategy Instruction Is Made of This: Metamemory and Durable Strategy Use." *Educational Psychologist* 19, 2 (Spring 1984): 94–107.

CHAPTER NINE

The Effects of Grouping, Class Size, and Retention on Learning

READING 25   ROBERT E. SLAVIN
Synthesis of Research on Grouping in Elementary and Secondary Schools

One of the most difficult decisions school administrators have to make, yet one of the most important, is how to group students for instruction. Should students be assigned to classes heterogeneously or according to ability? What kinds of grouping strategies, if any, should be used *within* classes? Should schools be departmentalized, self-contained, or some mix of the two? These questions are at the heart of school and classroom organization, and debates about them have gone on since the 19th century.

Decisions about grouping may be made on many grounds, from concerns about students' self-concepts and behavior to concerns about equity to concerns about efficiency or teacher morale. However, any discussion of grouping must consider the effects of alternative grouping plans on student achievement. My purpose here is to summarize what is known about the achievement effects of various forms of grouping at the elementary and secondary levels. I draw primarily on a "best-evidence synthesis" of research on ability grouping in elementary schools (Slavin 1987a,b), plus additional evidence concerning ability grouping at the junior and senior high school levels and evidence relating to alternatives to ability grouping at the elementary and secondary levels.

BACKGROUND AND RATIONALE FOR GROUPING

The study of alternative grouping arrangements has a long and distinguished pedigree. As early as 1929, Luther Purdom referred to the "great mass of literature" on the topic dating back to 1917. He complained that grouping decisions were too often based on personal impressions rather than hard evidence—a complaint that remains applicable 60 years later. The considerable interest in research on grouping in the 1920s was stimulated in part by a concern that since schools were serving a larger number of immigrants and children of the poor, they needed to differentiate instruction to meet the needs of a more diverse student body (see Billett 1932). This too has a distinctly modern ring.

The principal rationale for various forms of grouping has been basically the same since grouping was first proposed. Ability grouping exists to deal with one central fact of mass education: students differ in knowledge, skills, developmental stage, and learning rate. If a teacher is to present a lesson to a class, then it seems intuitively obvious that the lesson should be neither too easy nor too difficult for the students. If the class is highly heterogeneous,

From Robert E. Slavin, "Synthesis of Research on Grouping in Elementary and Secondary Schools," *Educational Leadership* (September 1988):67–77. Reprinted with permission of the Association for Supervision and Curriculum Development. Copyright © 1988 by ASCD. All rights reserved.

then one lesson will of necessity be easier than would be optimal for some students and more difficult than would be optimal for others. For the sake of instructional efficiency, students should be grouped so that they will profit from one lesson.

Yet virtually every means of grouping students by ability or performance level has drawbacks that may be serious enough to offset any advantages. Ability grouping plans may stigmatize low achievers, put them into classes or groups for which teachers have low expectations, or lead to the creation of academic elites (Persell 1977, Oakes 1985). Grouping may doom children who are not in the top tracks to second-class instruction and, ultimately, second-class futures. It may deprive students of the examples and stimulation provided by heterogeneous classes. Methods of dealing with student heterogeneity within the classroom, such as use of reading or math groups, create problems in terms of the management of multiple groups and reduction in the direct instruction received by individual students.

> **I**nstructionally effective cooperative learning methods provide group rewards based on the individual learning of all group members.

TYPES OF GROUPING

The principal types of grouping arrangements fall into two major categories: between-class and within-class. Between-class plans are school-level arrangements by which students are assigned to classes. Several means of assigning students to classes by ability fall into this category, as does departmentalization. Within-class grouping arrangements may attempt to reduce the heterogeneity of instructional groups, as in the use of within-class ability grouping or mastery learning. Finally, cooperative learning is a within-class grouping strategy that uses heterogeneous rather than homogeneous subgroups.

The following sections define the various grouping plans and summarize the research on each.

BETWEEN-CLASS ABILITY GROUPING

Perhaps the most controversial form of grouping is assignment of students to groups according to ability or performance. Arguments about the desirability of between-class ability grouping have raged from the 1920s (e.g., Miller and Otto 1930) to the present (e.g., Good and Marshall 1984; C. L. Kulik and J. A. Kulik 1982, 1984). Proponents have argued that ability grouping lets high achievers move rapidly and gives low achievers attainable goals and extra help. Opponents have countered that ability grouping is unfair to low achievers, citing the problems of poor peer models, low teacher expectations, and slow instructional pace.

Yet ability grouping is not a single practice but has many fundamentally different forms that have different educational as well as psychological effects. The most important forms of between-class ability groupings are discussed in the following sections.

Ability-Grouped Class Assignment

In many elementary schools, students are assigned to self-contained classes on the basis of a general achievement or ability measure. This method might produce, for example, a high-achieving 4th grade class, an average-achieving class, and a low-achieving class, with students assigned to classes according to some combination of a composite achievement measure, IQ scores, and/or teacher judgment. Students remain with the same ability-grouped classes for all academic subjects. At the secondary level, ability-grouped class assignment usually means that students are assigned to a particular track within which they receive all, or almost all, instruction (e.g., advanced, general, and remedial or academic, general, and vocational).

The achievement effects of ability-grouped class assignment (compared to heterogeneous grouping) are essentially zero. I identified 14 methodologically adequate studies of this practice at the elementary level and found the median effect size on standardized achievement measures to be approximately .00 (Slavin 1987a). Research at the junior high school level also fails to find consistent positive effects of between-class ability grouping (Borg 1965, Stoakes 1964, Peterson 1966). High school research is relatively rare, but even at this level controlled studies find few benefits of tracking (Borg and Perpich 1966, Billett 1932, Purdom 1929). There is some evidence that high achievers may gain from ability grouping at the expense of low achievers (e.g., Borg 1965, Flair 1965, Tobin 1966), but most studies find no such trend (see, e.g., Morgenstern 1963, Peterson 1966, Bremer 1958, Hartill 1936). Overall, the effects of ability grouping cluster closely around zero for students of all achievement levels.

One probable reason that ability-grouped class assignment has little effect on student achievement is that this plan typically has only a limited impact on the heterogeneity of the class. For example, Goodlad (1960) estimated that dividing a

> The mechanisms by which different grouping plans may have their effects are not at all clear. Yet we do know enough to dispel the notion that simply grouping students by ability will in itself accelerate their achievement.

group of elementary students into two ability groups on the basis of IQ reduced total variability in each class by only 7 percent. With three groups, heterogeneity was reduced by 17 percent, still not likely to be enough to have a measurable impact. Even though a student's performance in any one subject is correlated with performance in other subjects, this correlation is far from perfect. This means that grouping students on any one criterion is sure to leave substantial heterogeneity in any specific skill domain. On the other hand, assigning students to "high" and "low" ability classes may have a stigmatizing effect on low achievers and may evoke low expectations for student achievement and behavior even if the grouping has a minimal impact on class heterogeneity. Thus, ability-grouped class assignment may be enough to produce psychological drawbacks but does not do enough to reap the potential educational benefits of reducing student heterogeneity in any particular skill. Nonetheless, it is interesting that ability grouping is ineffective even at the secondary level, where student heterogeneity may be extreme.

Regrouping for Reading and/or Mathematics

Another commonly used ability grouping arrangement has students remain in heterogeneous classes most of the day but regroup for selected subjects. For example, three 4th grade classes in an elementary school might have reading scheduled at the same time. At reading time, students might leave their heterogeneous homerooms and go to a class organized according to reading levels. At the secondary level, students might be grouped for some subjects, but not for others.

Regrouping for selected subjects has three important advantages over ability-grouped class assignment. First, students remain in a heterogeneous setting most of the day, so they are likely to identify with that group, thereby reducing the labeling effect of all-day grouping. Second, students are grouped solely on the basis of their achievement in the particular subject, not by general achievement or ability level, so a meaningful reduction in heterogeneity in the skill being taught is possible. Third, elementary regrouping plans tend to be more flexible in operation than ability grouped class assignment, because changing students between reading or mathematics classes is less disruptive than changing basic class assignments. For this reason, any errors in assignment can be easily remedied, and any changes in student performance level can be accommodated with a change in grouping.

The limited research on regrouping plans suggests that regrouping can be instructionally effective if: (1) instructional level and pace are completely adapted to student performance level, and (2) the regrouping is done for only one or two subjects so that students stay in heterogeneous placements most of the day (Slavin 1987b). Studies at the elementary level that met these conditions have generally found positive effects on student achievement in reading (Berkun et al. 1966), in mathematics (Provus 1960), and in reading and mathematics taken together (Balow and Ruddell 1963, Morris 1969). On the other hand, when regrouping has been done in elementary schools without adapting the pace or level of instruction (Moses 1966, Davis and Tracy 1963) or in more than two different subjects (Koontz 1961), no benefits have been found. At the junior high school level, grouping in one subject has been no more successful than ability grouped class assignment (Bicak 1962, Fick 1963), and similar results have been obtained in high school studies (Drews 1963, Holy and Sutton 1930, Thompson 1974).

> There is some evidence that high achievers may gain from ability grouping at the expense of low achievers, but most studies find no such trend. Overall, the effects of ability grouping cluster closely around zero for students of all achievement levels.

Joplin Plan

One interesting form of regrouping applicable primarily to elementary schools is the Joplin Plan (Floyd 1954), in which students are regrouped for reading without regard for grade levels. That is, a reading class at 4th grade–first semester level (4–1) might contain some 3rd, some 4th, and some 5th graders.

One important consequence of this grouping plan is that it allows for the reduction or elimination of within-class grouping for reading, as students in each reading class may all be at the same reading level. Thus, teachers can spend more of the reading class time doing direct instruction, reducing the time during which students must do unsupervised follow-up seatwork.

Effects of the Joplin Plan and closely related forms of nongraded plans have been quite positive overall. In a recent review, I (Slavin 1987a) estimated the median effect size for Joplin and Joplin-like nongraded plans at +.44 for reading achievement, and one study (Hart 1962) found similar effects for mathematics. Two of the studies I reviewed (Morgan and Stucker 1960, Hillson et al. 1964) used random assignment of students and teacher to treatments, and most of the others were good-quality matched equivalent studies.

Nongraded Plans

Nongraded plans (Goodlad and Anderson 1963) are elementary grouping arrangements in which formal grade levels are abolished in favor of flexible cross-age groupings for different subjects. Many different forms of nongrading have been evaluated. In some cases (e.g., Hillson et al. 1964, Ingram 1960) where nongrading is done in reading or mathematics only, it is essentially identical to the Joplin Plan. At the other extreme, nongraded plans may involve many subjects, constant and flexible regrouping within and between classes, extensive use of individualized instruction, team teaching, and other features more in line with forms of the open classroom than with the still quite traditional Joplin Plan (see, e.g., Bowman 1971, Ross 1967).

I found achievement effects of comprehensive nongraded plans to be inconsistent but generally positive (Slavin 1987a, b). However, most of the studies that failed to find positive effects of nongraded plans either took place in laboratory schools (e.g., Otto 1963, Ross 1967) or found few implementation differences between nongraded and traditional programs (e.g., Carbone 1961, Hopkins et al. 1965). Studies in regular classrooms in which the nongraded program was used conscientiously usually found positive effects on student achievement (e.g., Bowman 1971, Machiele 1965).

Gifted Programs

Gifted programs may be offered in only one subject (often mathematics), or separate classes for high achieving or otherwise exceptional students may be provided. Most research on special programs for the gifted contains a serious systematic bias. Much of this research (e.g., Simpson and Martison 1961) compares students in gifted programs to students in the same schools who did not participate in the gifted program, matching on IQ or other measures. However, if two students have IQs of 130 and one is accepted for a gifted program while the other is rejected, then we can be sure that there were other factors, such as motivation, achievement, and so on, that also differentiate these students, all of which are likely to work to the advantage of the students accepted for the special program. Nonrandomed comparisons across schools with and without gifted programs (e.g., West and Sievers 1960, Baldauf 1959) are somewhat better, but also suffer from this systematic selection bias. Studies of acceleration (see J. A. Kulik and C. L. Kulik 1984), exposing gifted students to higher levels of information in some subjects or skipping them to higher grades, share the same problems of selection bias, with the additional problem that the accelerated students are exposed to material not seen by regular students, making comparisons difficult.

> **E**ffects of the Joplin Plan and closely related forms of nongraded plans have been quite positive overall.

The literature on gifted programs at the elementary level is small, inconclusive, and methodologically inadequate for the reasons described above and others. A few studies have reported achievement benefits of special programs for the gifted (e.g., West and Sievers 1960, Bell 1957, Atkinson and O'Connor 1963), while others found no significant advantages (e.g., Baldauf 1959, Cluff 1964, Becker 1963). Generally, acceleration programs (e.g., providing Algebra I to 6th or 7th graders) produce better achievement outcomes than enrichment programs (see Fox 1979, Justman 1954, Passow et al. 1961).

Special Education

Assignment to full- or part-time special education programs for learning problems can also be seen as a form of between-class ability grouping. Unfortunately, most research on the efficacy of special education has the same type of methodological flaws characteristic of studies of gifted programs. Matched comparisons between students assigned to special education and those remaining in regular classes are biased toward regular class assignment because of the likelihood of systematic differences between students of, for example, the same IQ assigned to regular or special classes (Madden and Slavin 1983).

However, there are a few randomized studies at the elementary level of special education vs. mainstreaming (regular class placement) for students with moderate academic handicaps, such as learning disabilities and mild retardation. For example, Goldstein and colleagues (1966) found that students randomly assigned to a high-quality special education program learned no more than did students who remained in regular classes. Calhoun and Elliott (1977) found that mildly retarded and emotionally disturbed students randomly assigned to regular classes that used individualized instruction gained substantially more in achievement than did students who experienced the same individualized program with the same teacher in self-contained special education classes. Overall, evidence from studies of special education and mainstreaming supports accommodating student differences within the regular classrooms rather than separating students into special classes (Madden and Slavin 1983).

Summary and Conclusions: Between-Class Ability Grouping

Evidence from studies of various forms of between-class ability grouping in elementary schools indicates that achievement effects depend on the types of programs evaluated. In general, ability grouping plans are beneficial for student achievement when they incorporate the following features (adapted from Slavin 1987b):

1. Students remain in heterogeneous classes most of the day and are regrouped by performance level only in such subjects as reading and mathematics in which reducing heterogeneity is particularly important.
2. The grouping plan reduces heterogeneity in the specific skill being taught.
3. Group assignments are flexible and are frequently reassessed.
4. Teachers adapt their level and pace of instruction in regrouped classes to accommodate students' levels of readiness and learning rates.

The between-class grouping plan that most completely incorporates these four principles is the Joplin Plan. Evidence on the Joplin Plan strongly supports the effectiveness of this arrangement and of within-grade regrouping plans and nongraded plans that most resemble it.

In contrast, ability grouped class assignment, special programs for the gifted, and special education for students with learning problems do not generally meet the four criteria. Typically, they segregate students all or most of the day, are based on general ability or achievement rather than skill in a specific subject, and tend to be highly inflexible. Teachers may or may not adjust their level and pace of instruction to adapt to students' needs in these plans. Evidence at all levels shows no benefits for ability-grouped class assignment or special education assignment and only inconsistent and flawed evidence in favor of special programs for the gifted.

DEPARTMENTALIZATION

One between-class grouping plan that is nearly universal in secondary schools and increasingly seen in elementary schools is some form of departmentalization, in which teachers teach one or a few (but not all) subjects to multiple class groups. At the secondary level, departmentalization usually implies that students change classes for all subjects. Alternatively, in elementary or middle schools, one teacher might see classes for more than one, but not all subjects; for example, teaching combined reading and language or mathematics and science blocks. Semi-departmentalized plans may have all teachers teach a set of subjects to students in their homeroom groups in the morning, while other subjects are departmentalized in the afternoon.

> **A**bility grouping is ineffective even at the secondary level, where student heterogeneity may be extreme.

The main advantage of departmentalization is that it allows teachers to specialize, teaching subjects they are most able and willing to teach. However, departmentalization risks diffusing responsibility for individual children, making it difficult for a student to identify with a single caring adult. In elementary schools, it may represent an unhealthy intrusion of the "subject-centered" secondary organization into the more typically "child-centered" elementary program.

Unfortunately, there is very little research on departmentalization. However, that which does exist fails to support the practice. Ward (1970) found that students in grades 4–6 learned reading and science significantly better in self-contained classes than in departmentalized classes, and there were no differences in mathematics and social studies. Hosley (1954) also found that 6th graders' achievement was higher in self-contained K-6 schools than in semi-departmentalized junior high schools. Jackson (1953) found no achievement differences between departmentalized and nondepartmentalized plans at the elementary or junior high school levels, and Spivak (1956) found higher achievement for 7th and 8th graders in self-contained than in departmentalized settings. Only one study, a dissertation by Case (1971), discovered an achievement benefit of departmentalization, comparing 5th graders in a new middle school to matched control students remaining in self-contained elementary classrooms. Becker (1987) found the achievement effects of departmentalization in 6th grades to vary by socioeconomic status. That is, students from the wealthiest backgrounds gained slightly, middle-income students lost slightly, and lower-class students lost substantially from departmentalized arrangements.

WITHIN-CLASS ABILITY GROUPING

Within-class ability grouping is the practice of assigning students to homogeneous subgroups for instruction within the class. In general, each subgroup receives instruction

---

Highlights of Research on Grouping in Elementary and Secondary Schools

Reviewers of the 1960s and 1970s (e.g., Borg 1965, NEA 1968, Passow 1962, Esposito 1973) often failed to distinguish between different types of grouping plans (i.e., between-class and within-class), combining studies of programs for the gifted with comprehensive between-class ability grouping, regrouping for selected subjects, and within-class ability grouping. Yet when we separate the research on these different plans, the picture becomes relatively clear.

Within-Class Grouping

- Little methodologically adequate research exists on *mastery learning* at the elementary level, and research has provided little support for this practice, despite its widespread use (Slavin 1987c).
- A great deal of research is available on *cooperative learning methods,* which involve students working in small, heterogeneous learning groups. If the groups are rewarded on the basis of the individual learning of all group members, then cooperative learning can consistently increase student achievement in the elementary grades (Slavin in press).

Between-Class Grouping

- Wholesale between-class grouping plans, such as *ability-grouped class assignment, special classes for the gifted,* and *self-contained special education,* do not generally affect student achievement. One exception: acceleration programs *may* benefit gifted students.
- Many elementary schools have introduced *departmentalization* to enable teachers to specialize in their strongest or favorite subjects. The advent of the middle school has also introduced departmentalization to students at earlier ages than was once the case. The small amount of research comparing departmentalized and self-contained arrangements for students in the upper elementary and middle grades recommends against early departmentalization.
- Ability-grouping plans such as the *Joplin Plan* and certain forms of *nongraded* and *regrouping plans* can be instructionally effective. They all: (1) leave students in heterogeneous classes most of the school day, (2) regroup only for reading and/or mathematics according to student performance in these skills, (3) flexibly change student placements, and (4) adapt the level and pace of instruction to the needs and preparedness of the regrouped classes. (Within-class ability grouping in mathematics also meets these four criteria and also increases student achievement.)
- Ability grouping can be a useful tool in elementary school organization; but it must be used sparingly, precisely, and with careful planning if it is to enhance student achievement.

—Robert E. Slavin

at its own level and progresses at its own rate. Within-class ability grouping is virtually universal in elementary reading instruction and is common in elementary mathematics, but it is rarely seen in secondary schools (Hallinan and Sorensen 1983, Barr and Dreeben 1983).

Within-class grouping plans generally conform to the four requirements for effective ability grouping proposed earlier. They involve only reading and/or mathematics, leaving students in relatively heterogeneous classes the rest of the school day. They group students in specific rather than general skills; and, at least in principle, within-class groupings are easy to change. Most teachers do adapt their level and pace of instruction to meet students' needs (Barr and Dreeben 1983). However, within-class ability grouping introduces a problem not characteristic of between-class grouping plans: management of multiple groups. When the teacher is instructing one reading group, for example, the remaining students must work independently on seatwork activities, which may be of questionable value (see Anderson et al. 1985). Supervising multiple groups and the transitions between them are major classroom management problems (Anderson et al. 1979).

Methodologically adequate research on within-class ability grouping has unfortunately been limited to the study of mathematics grouping, perhaps because few teachers would be willing to participate in an experiment in which they had to teach heterogeneous classes without breaking students into reading groups. However, the research on within-class grouping in mathematics clearly supports this practice. Every one of eight studies of within-class ability grouping in mathematics that I identified (Slavin 1987a), including five randomized studies, favored the grouped treatment (median effect size = +.34). Effects of within-class grouping were somewhat higher for low achievers (median effect size = +.65) than for average and high achievers. There was some trend for effects to be more positive when the number of ability groups was two or three rather than four.

Effects of within-class grouping on mathematics achievement cannot be assumed to hold for reading. In mathematics, students need to work problems independently, so there is an appropriate place for independent seatwork. The corresponding need for independent seatwork in grading is less compelling. The universality of within-class grouping in reading in North America provides at least some indications that this form of ability grouping is also instructionally necessary, although it is interesting to note that European schools do not generally use this type of grouping in reading.

Mastery Learning

Mastery learning is a form of within-class grouping in which grouping decisions are constantly changed to reflect student performance. In group-based mastery learning (Bloom 1976, Block and Burns 1976), students receive a lesson as a whole class and then take a formative test. Those whose test scores exceed a present mastery criterion (e.g., 80 percent) then do enrichment activities; those who do not achieve this criterion receive corrective instruction. Group-based forms of mastery learning are by far the most commonly used in elementary and secondary schools.

I recently reviewed the research on the achievement effects of group-based mastery learning (Slavin 1987c). In methodologically adequate studies of at least four weeks' duration, mastery learning had no significant effect on standardized achievement measures and only moderate effects on experimental-made measures. However, there are examples of successful continuous progress forms of mastery learning, in which students proceed through a hierarchy of skills at their own rate and are frequently assessed and regrouped (see Slavin 1987d).

Cooperative Learning

Cooperative learning (Sharan 1980; Slavin 1983, in press) refers to various instructional methods in which students work in small heterogeneous learning groups toward some sort of group goal. Cooperative learning differs from within-class ability grouping not only in that cooperative learning groups are small and heterogeneous, but also in that these groups are expected to engage in a great deal of task focused interaction, such as studying together or completing group assignments. Cooperative learning methods vary considerably in their basic structures. Some, such as Jigsaw Teaching (Aronson et al. 1978) and Group Investigation (Sharan and Sharan 1976) assign students specific tasks with a larger group task. In others (e.g., Johnson and Johnson 1975) students work together to complete a common group worksheet or other group product. A third category consists of methods in which students study together and are rewarded on the basis of the achievement of all group members (e.g., DeVries and Slavin 1978, Slavin 1983). For example, in Student Teams–Achievement Divisions, or STAD, students are assigned to four-member heterogeneous teams. The teacher presents a lesson, and then students study worksheets together in their teams, attempting to ensure that all team members master the material. Finally, the students are individually quizzed, and teams are rewarded with certificates or other recognition based on the average of their members' quiz scores.

The idea behind cooperative learning is that if students are re-

> Grouping may doom children who are not in the top tracks to second-class instruction and, ultimately, second-class futures.

warded on the basis of group or team performance, they will be motivated to help and encourage one another to achieve (Slavin 1983, in press). In a heterogeneous learning group, students among themselves are expected to be able to solve problems or organize material presented by the teacher and to transmit the group's understanding to each individual.

Research on cooperative learning in elementary schools has found that its effectiveness depends on how it is organized. Instructionally effective cooperative learning methods provide group rewards based on the individual learning of all group members. Student Teams–Achievement Divisions (Slavin 1983), Teams–Games–Tournaments (DeVries and Slavin 1978), Team Assisted Individualization (Slavin 1985), and related methods all provide group rewards based on the sum or average of individual student learning performances. If students wish to succeed as a group, then, they must ensure that every group member has mastered the material being studied. Studies of these methods have consistently found that they increase student achievement in a variety of subject areas and grade levels (see Slavin in press).

A MATTER OF BALANCE

While there is much we can learn from the research on grouping, there is still much to understand. For example, basic questions about the effects of within-class ability grouping in reading, of mastery learning, and of various forms of departmentalization remain unanswered. The mechanisms by which different grouping plans may have their effects are not at all clear.

Yet we do know enough to dispel the notion that simply grouping students by ability will in itself accelerate their achievement. Certain forms of grouping may be effective as part of a coherent plan for adapting instruction to meet individual needs, but the costs and benefits of each form of grouping must be carefully weighed.

REFERENCES

Anderson, L. M., N. L. Brubaker, J. Alleman-Brooks, and G. G. Duffy. "A Qualitative Study of Seatwork in First Grade Classrooms." *Elementary School Journal* 86 (1985): 123–140.

Anderson, L. M., C. Evertson, and J. Brophy. "An Experimental Study of Effective Teaching in First-Grade Reading Groups." *Elementary School Journal* 79 (1979): 193–223.

Aronson, E., N. Blaney, C. Stephan, J. Sikes, and M. Snapp. *The Jigsaw Classroom*. Beverly Hills, Calif.: Sage, 1978.

Atkinson, J. W., and P. O'Connor. *Effects of Ability Grouping in Schools Related to Individual Differences in Achievement-Related Motivation*. Final Report, Cooperative Research Project No. OE-2-10-024. Washington, D.C.: U.S. Department of Health, 1963.

Baldauf, R. S. "A Comparison of the Extent of Educational Growth of Mentally Advanced Pupils in the Cedar Rapids Experiment." *Journal of Educational Research* 52 (1959): 181–183.

Balow, I. H., and A. K. Ruddell. "The Effects of Three Types of Grouping on Achievement." *California Journal of Educational Research* 14 (1963): 108–117.

Barr, R., and R. Dreeben. *How Schools Work*. Chicago: University of Chicago Press, 1983.

Becker, H. J. *Addressing the Needs of Different Groups of Early Adolescents: Effects of Varying School and Classroom Organizational Practices on Students from Different Social Backgrounds and Abilities*. Technical Report No. 16. Baltimore: The Johns Hopkins University, Center for Research on Elementary and Middle Schools, 1987.

Becker, L. J. "An Analysis of the Science and Mathematics Achievement of Gifted Sixth Grade Children Enrolled in Segregated, Partially Segregated, and Non-Segregated Classes." Doctoral diss., Syracuse University, 1963.

Bell, M. E. "A Comparative Study of Mentally Gifted Children Heterogeneously and Homogeneously Grouped." Doctoral diss., Indiana University, 1957.

Berkun, M. M., L. W. Swanson, and D. M. Sawyer. "An Experiment on Homogeneous Grouping for Reading in Elementary Classes." *Journal of Educational Research* 59 (1966): 413–414.

Bicak, L. J. "Achievement in Eighth Grade Science by Heterogeneous and Homogeneous Classes." Doctoral diss., University of Minnesota, 1962.

Billett, R. O. *The Administration and Supervision of Homogeneous Grouping*. Columbus: Ohio State University Press, 1932.

Block, J. H., and R. B. Burns. "Mastery Learning." In *Review of Research in Education*, Vol. 4, edited by L. S. Shulman. Itasca, Ill.: Peacock, 1976, pp. 3–49.

Bloom, B. S. *Human Characteristics and School Learning*. New York: McGraw-Hill, 1976.

Borg, W. R. "Ability Grouping in the Public Schools: A Field Study." *Journal of Experimental Education* 34 (1965): 1–97.

Borg, W. R., and T. Perpich. "Grouping of Slow Learning High School Pupils." *Journal of Secondary Education* 41 (1966): 231–238.

Bowman, B. L. "A Comparison of Pupil Achievement and Attitude in a Graded School with Pupil Achievement and Attitude in a Nongraded School 1968–69, 1969–70 School Years. *Dissertation Abstracts* 32 (1971): 86-A (University Microfilms No. 71-20, 958).

Bremer, N. "First Grade Achievement under Different Plans of Grouping." *Elementary English* 35 (1958): 324–326.

Calhoun, G., and R. Elliott. "Self-Concept and Academic Achievement of Educable Retarded and Emotionally Disturbed Children." *Exceptional Children* 44 (1977): 379–380.

Carbone, R. F. "A Comparison of Graded and Non-Graded Elementary Schools." *Elementary School Journal* 62 (1961): 82–88.

Case, D. A. "A Comparative Study of Fifth Graders in a New Middle School with Fifth Graders in Elementary Self-Contained Classrooms." *Dissertation Abstracts* 32 (1971): 86-A (University Microfilms No. 71-16, 770).

Cluff, J. E. "The Effect of Experimentation and Class Reorganization on the Scholastic Achievement of Selected Gifted Sixth Grade Pupils in Wichita, Kansas." *Dissertation Abstracts* 24

(1964) (University Microfilms No. 64-10, 059).

Davis, O. L., and N. H. Tracy. "Arithmetic Achievement and Instructional Grouping." *Arithmetic Teacher* 10 (1963): 12–17.

DeVries, D. L., and R. E. Slavin. "Teams-Games-Tournament: Review of Ten Classroom Experiments." *Journal of Research and Development in Education* 12 (1978): 28–38.

Drews, E. M. *Student Abilities Grouping Patterns and Classroom Interaction.* Cooperative Research Project No. 608. Washington, D.C.: U.S. Department of Health, Education, and Welfare, 1963.

Esposito, D. "Homogeneous and Heterogeneous Ability Grouping: Principal Findings and Implications for Evaluating and Designing More Effective of Educational Environments." *Review of Educational Research* 43 (1973): 163–179.

Fick, W. W. "The Effectiveness of Ability Grouping in Seventh Grade Core Classes." *Dissertation Abstracts* 23 (1963): 2753.

Flair, M. D. "The Effect of Grouping on Achievement and Attitudes Toward Learning of First Grade Pupils." *Dissertation Abstracts* 25 (1965): 6430 (University Microfilms No. 64-03, 259).

Floyd, C. "Meeting Children's Reading Needs in the Middle Grades: A Preliminary Report." *Elementary School Journal* 55 (1954): 99–103.

Fox, L. H. "Progress for the Gifted and Talented: An Overview." In *The Gifted and Talented: Their Education and Development,* edited by A. H. Passow. Chicago: University of Chicago Press, 1979.

Goldstein, H., J. Moss, and J. Jordan. *The Efficacy of Special Class Training on the Development of Mentally Retarded Children.* Cooperative Research Project No. 619. Washington, D.C.: U.S. Office of Education, 1966.

Good, T., and S. Marshall. "Do Students Learn More in Heterogeneous or Homogeneous Groups?" In *Student Diversity and the Organization, Process, and Use of Instructional Groups in the Classroom,* edited by P. Peterson and L. Cherry Wilkinson. New York: Academic Press, 1984.

Goodlad, J. I. "Classroom Organization." In *Encyclopedia of Educational Research,* 3rd ed., edited by C. W. Harris. New York: Macmillan, 1960, pp. 221–225.

Goodlad, J. I., and R. H. Anderson. *The Nongraded Elementary School.* Rev. ed. New York: Harcourt, Brace, and World, 1963.

Hallinan, M., and A. Sorensen. "The Formation and Stability of Instructional Groups." *American Sociological Review* 48 (1983): 839–851.

Hart, R. H. "The Nongraded Primary School and Arithmetic." *The Arithmetic Teacher* 9 (1962): 130–133.

Hartill, R. "Homogeneous Grouping as a Policy in the Elementary Schools in New York City." *Teachers College, Columbia Contributions to Education,* #690. New York: Teachers College Press, 1936.

Hillson, M., J. C. Jones, J. W. Moore, and F. Van Devender. "A Controlled Experiment Evaluating the Effects of a Nongraded Organization on Pupil Achievement." *Journal of Educational Research* 57 (1964): 548–550.

Holy, T. C., and D. H. Sutton. "Ability Grouping in the Ninth Grade." *Educational Research Bulletin* 9 (1930): 419–422.

Hopkins, K. D., O. A. Oldridge, and M. L. Williamson. "An Empirical Comparison of Pupil Achievement and Other Variables in Graded and Nongraded Classes." *American Educational Research Journal* 2 (1965): 207–215.

Hosley, C. T. "Learning Outcomes of Sixth Grade Pupils under Alternative Grade Organization Patterns." *Dissertation Abstracts* 14 (1954): 490–491 (University Microfilms No. 7484).

Ingram, V. "Flint Evaluates Its Primary Cycle." *Elementary School Journal* 61 (1960): 76–80.

Jackson, J. "The Effect of Classroom Organization and Guidance Practice upon the Personality Adjustment and Academic Growth of Students." *Journal of General Psychology* 83 (1953): 159–170.

Johnson, D. W., and R. T. Johnson. *Learning Together and Alone.* Englewood Cliffs, N.J.: Prentice-Hall, 1975.

Justman, J. "Academic Achievement of Intellectually Gifted Accelerants and Nonaccelerants in Junior High School." *School Review* 62 (1954): 142–150.

Koontz, W. F. "A Study of Achievement as a Function of Homogeneous Grouping." *Journal of Experimental Education* 30 (1961): 249–253.

Kulik, C.-L., and J. A. Kulik. "Effects of Ability Grouping on Secondary School Students: A Meta-analysis of Evaluation Findings." *American Educational Research Journal* 19 (1982): 415–428.

Kulik, C.-L., and J. A. Kulik. "Effects of Ability Grouping on Elementary School Pupils: A Meta-analysis." Paper presented at the annual convention of the American Psychological Association, Toronto, August 1984.

Kulik, J. A., and C. L. Kulik. "Effects of Accelerated Instruction on Students." *Review of Educational Research* 54 (1984): 409–425.

Machiele, R. B. "A Preliminary Evaluation of the Non-Graded Primary at Leal School, Urbana." *Illinois School Review* 1 (1965): 20–24.

Madden, N. A., and R. E. Slavin. "Mainstreaming Students with Mild Academic Handicaps: Academic and Social Outcomes." *Review of Educational Research* 53 (1983): 519–569.

Miller, W. S., and H. J. Otto. "Analysis of Experimental Studies in Homogeneous Grouping." *Journal of Educational Research* 21 (1930): 95–102.

Morgan, E. F., and G. R. Stucker. "The Joplin Plan of Reading vs. a Traditional Method." *Journal of Educational Psychology* 51 (1960): 69–73.

Morgenstern, A. "A Comparison of the Effects of Heterogeneous (Ability) Grouping on the Academic Achievement and Personal-Social Adjustment of Sixth Grade Children." *Dissertation Abstracts* 23 (1963): 1054 (University Microfilms No. 63-6560).

Morris, V. P. "An Evaluation of Pupil Achievement in a Nongraded Primary Plan after Three and also Five Years of Instruction." *Dissertation Abstracts* 29 (1969): 3809-A (University Microfilms No. 69-7352).

Moses, P. J. "A Study of Inter-class Ability Grouping on Achievement in Reading." *Dissertation Abstracts* 26 (1966): 4342.

National Education Association. *Ability Grouping Research Summary.* Washington, D.C.: NEA, 1968.

Oakes, J. *Keeping Track: How Schools Structure Inequality.* New Haven, Conn.: Yale University Press, 1985.

Otto, H. J. *Nongradedness: An Elementary School Evaluation.* Austin: University of Texas, 1963.

Passow, A. H. "The Maze of Research on Ability Grouping." *Educational Forum* 26 (1962): 281–288.

Passow, A. H., M. L. Goldberg, and F. R. Link. "Enriched Mathematics for Gifted Junior High School Students." *Educational Leadership* 18 (1961): 442–448.

Persell, C. *Education and Inequality: The Roots and Results of Stratification in America's Schools.* New York: Free Press, 1977.

Peterson, R. L. "An Experimental Study of the Effects of Ability Grouping in Grades 7 and 8." Unpublished doctoral diss., University of Minnesota, 1966.

Provus, M. M. "Ability Grouping in Arithmetic." *Elementary School Journal* 60 (1960): 391–398.

Purdom, T. L. *The Value of Homogeneous Grouping.* Baltimore: Warwick and York, 1929.

Ross, G. A. "A Comparative Study of Pupil Progress in Ungraded and Graded Primary Programs." *Dissertation Abstracts* 28 (1967): 2146-A. (University Microfilms No. 67-16, 428, 462–470.).

Sharan, S. "Cooperative Learning in Small Groups: Recent Methods and Effects on Achievement, Attitudes, and Social Relations." *Review of Educational Research* 50 (1980): 241–271.

Sharan, S., and Y. Sharan. *Small-Group Teaching.* Englewood Cliffs, N.J.: Prentice-Hall, 1976.

Simpson, R., and R. Martison. *Educa-

tional Programs for Gifted Pupils: A Report to the California Legislature Pursuant to Section 2 of Chapter 2385. Statutes of 1957. (ERIC No. ED 100 072, 1961).

Slavin, R. E. *Cooperative Learning.* New York: Longman, 1983.

Slavin, R. E. "Team-Assisted Individualization: Combining Cooperative Learning and Individualized Instruction in Mathematics." in *Learning to Cooperate, Cooperating to Learn,* edited by R. E. Slavin, S. Sharan, S. Kagan, R. Hertz Lazarowitze, C. Webb, and R. Schmuck. New York: Plenum. 1985.

Slavin, R. E. "Grouping for Instruction in the Elementary School." *Educational Psychologist* 22 (1987a): 109–127.

Slavin, R. E. "Ability Grouping and Student Achievement in Elementary Schools: A Best Evidence Synthesis." *Review of Educational Research* 57 (1987b): 213–336.

Slavin, R. E. "Mastery Learning Reconsidered." *Review of Educational Research* 57 (1987c): 175–213.

Slavin, R. E. "Making Chapter I Make a Difference." *Phi Delta Kappan* 69 (1987d): 110–119.

Slavin, R. E. "Cooperative Learning and Student Achievement." In *School and Classroom Organization,* edited by R. E. Slavin. Hillsdale, N.J.: Erlbaum, in press.

Spivak, M. L. "Effectiveness of Departmental and Self-contained Seventh- and Eighth-grade Classrooms." *School Review* 64 (1956): 391–396.

Stoakes, D. W. "An Educational Experiment with the Homogeneous Grouping of Mentally Advanced and Slow Learning Students in the Junior High School." Doctoral diss., University of Colorado, 1964.

Thompson, G. W. "The Effects of Ability Grouping upon Achievement in Eleventh Grade American History." *Journal of Experimental Education* 42 (1974): 76–79.

Tobin, J. F. "An Eight Year Study of Classes Grouped within Grade Levels on the Basis of Reading Ability." *Dissertation Abstracts* 26 (1966): 3621A (University Microfilms No. 66–345).

Ward, P. E. "A Study of Pupil Achievement in Departmentalized Grades, Four, Five, and Six." *Dissertation Abstracts* 30 (1970): 4749a (University Microfilms No. 70–1201).

West, J., and C. Sievers. "Experiment in Cross Grouping." *Journal of Educational Research* 54 (1960): 70–72.

READING 26 — MARY LEE SMITH AND GENE V. GLASS
The Effect of Class Size on What Happens in Classrooms

Among techniques designed to improve education, decreasing class size is the most controversial. Teachers have lauded the benefits of smaller classes. Administrators have demonstrated their high cost. Because of the costs of decreasing class size, policymakers have demanded that it be justified on the basis of increased achievement. Yet researchers have, through many studies, been unable to resolve the controversy by providing an unequivocal answer to the class-size question.

Teachers have always been frustrated by this failure of research to confirm what, from their personal experience and tacit knowledge, seems so obvious. They feel that it is more difficult to work when confronted with greater numbers of students. It is harder to know each student. The range of possible teaching strategies is restricted in large classes. With greater numbers it is harder to be effective and, hence, in the teacher's view, the pupils learn less.

But anecdotal evidence is not honored by policymakers. In the present political climate, one must demonstrate "scientifically" that decreasing class size has social utility—that it produces higher achievement test scores at a reasonable cost.

In 1978 and 1979 we presented the results of a statistical integration of the research—drawing from 80 studies—on the relationship between class size and achievement, and we demonstrated a substantial relationship between class size and achievement. Those studies which employed rigorous control yielded results that—taken together—showed that the difference in being taught in a class of 20 versus a class of 40 is an advantage of 10 percentile ranks.

Improved academic achievement, however, is not the only justification for decreasing class size: In a climate less influenced by the systems approach to evaluation, one might argue that achievement is not even the best criterion for judging the value of decreasing class size. After all, it is not class size *per*

From Mary Lee Smith and Gene V. Glass, "The Effect of Class Size on What Happens in Classrooms." Reprinted with permission of *The Education Digest,* March 1980 issue, pp. 16–18.

se which directly affects achievement, nor is class size the sole determinant of achievement. Achievement reflects the pupils' intellectual abilities and levels of effort as well as the classroom processes to which they are exposed. Furthermore, an assessment of school effectiveness based on achievement tests ties us to all the limitations inherent in such tests. Achievement is at best a distal effect, several steps removed from class size. More directly affected by varying class sizes, so the argument goes, are the opportunities the teacher has for doing different things. This is not to say that each teacher will avail himself of these opportunities or that those teaching strategies chosen will inevitably be more propitious. But on the average, the environment and teaching processes afforded by decreased class size may produce, in turn, higher achievement test results.

Differing class sizes may affect the workload, morale, and perceptions of teachers, thus producing differences in teaching performance, which again lead to variation in achievement. Furthermore, pupils' self-esteem, their satisfaction with school, and a favorable affective and social climate in the classroom are desirable effects in themselves. They may also produce or be produced by improved achievement. To the extent that decreased class size is related to a favorable affective climate, one may defend class size as an important condition, and one that is within the power of educators to manipulate.

OPPOSING POSITIONS

Against these arguments for the benefits of small classes, the opposing positions must be weighed. First is the notion that teaching processes do not change as class size decreases—some teachers lecture even with a class size of 10. Nor is teacher knowledge of pupil characteristics necessary for pupil learning to take place. Second is that the positive effects of small classes on teachers merely reflect laziness or worse—a political ploy to make teaching less work, or to increase the number of teachers and hence the power of teachers unions. The third argument is that small classes actually harm students by, for example, reducing their independence and self-discipline.

These arguments were interesting enough for us to pursue the question of whether decreasing the size of classes produces improvements on nonachievement outcomes—teaching processes, and student and teacher effects in the affective domain. As before, we addressed the question with meta-analysis—a synthesis of extant studies; and also, as in the previous study, we found an affirmative answer. On all measures, reduction in class size is associated with higher quality schooling and more positive attitudes.

In the achievement study it was shown that more than 30 percentile ranks exist between the achievement of a pupil taught individually and a pupil taught in a class of 40. In this most recent study, the difference in the quality of the educational environment between a class size of one and a class size of 40 was measured at 46 percentile ranks.

POSITIVE EFFECTS

The class-size effect is positive, no matter how that effect was measured. The most dramatic effects were those relating to teachers; smaller but still substantial were affective effects on pupils and effects on the instructional process. The class-size effects were related to age of pupils, with effects most notable for children 12 years and under, and least apparent for pupils 18 or over.

Some features of the study interacted with the class-size effect. Well-controlled studies produced slightly smaller class-size effects than uncontrolled studies. But the difference in effects produced between the two sets of studies amounts to only about 10 percentile ranks even at the extreme points (fewer than 5 or more than 50 pupils) of the class-size scale. Studies produced before 1968, or from sources other than dissertations, produced higher class-size effects than later studies or studies gleaned from dissertations. Even with these few qualifications made, however, one may still have confidence that class size is related to pupil and teacher affect and to instructional processes.

Class size affects the quality of the classroom environment. In a smaller class there are more opportunities to adapt learning programs to the needs of individuals. Chances are good that the climate is friendlier and more conducive to learning. Students are more directly and personally involved in learning.

Class size affects pupils' attitudes, either as a function of better performance or as contributing to it. In smaller classes, pupils have more interest in learning. Perhaps there is less distraction. There seems to be less apathy, friction, frustration.

Class size affects teachers. In smaller classes their morale is better; they like their pupils better and have time to plan and diversify; they are more satisfied with their performance. Does this mean that class size is merely a selfish, political issue for teachers? Or is the happier teacher the one who performs better? This we cannot unravel, except to cite the other evidence—that the smaller the class is, the greater is the effect on the instructional process, on pupil affect, and on achievement.

READING 27
Grade Retention and Social Promotion Practices

GARY COOKE AND JOHN STAMMER

INTRODUCTION

According to Department of Health, Education and Welfare statistics, over one million students were retained in American schools during 1972. Nothing has transpired over the past decade that indicates a decline in this number. To the contrary, the "back-to-basics" movement and the more recent pronouncements about "excellence in education" have intensified concerns about student shortcomings. (The report of the National Commission on Excellence in Education in April of 1983 has put additional pressures on classroom teachers to maintain stringent academic standards. The commission report and others like it will result in a new epidemic of student retentions at all grade levels.)

Failing, retained, "socially promoted" or inappropriately placed students are symptoms of an educational system that is suffering from serious malfunctions. It is a system where retention practices habitually focus on the child as the problem rather than looking at the shortcomings of the system as a possible contributing factor in the problem.

The purpose of this article is to remind educators that "... schools should be made to fit the student, not the students made to fit the schools" (Koons, 1977, p. 701).

Without an awareness of and responsiveness to this reality, the losers will be those children who, for whatever reasons, do not meet arbitrary standards and are retained, often to spend another 40 weeks redoing the same work, or moved ahead to spend another year in ego-reducing failure experiences. One teacher expressed it this way: "They'll (the students) stay there until they get it right."

This means that school systems, and especially classroom teachers who are closest to the children, must resist getting caught up in the contest to maintain standards and "look good" to the public by retaining low-achieving students year after year. As increased pressure is applied for accountability in classrooms, it is imperative that teachers familiarize themselves with research regarding the effects of retention and promotion. With this research knowledge, thoughtful and intelligent decisions can be initiated about appropriate placement policies and procedures, and effective choices made about student placement which address all elements of the learning environment. Common sense tells us that students having difficulty learning in school need special attention through carefully designed and individualized programs. When students are failing, educators should examine teaching (effective methodology), curriculum (its appropriateness) and learning (the progress of the child toward goals) as a source of the problem instead of automatically blaming student "shortcomings."

The foundation for decisive educational change must be built on what research tells us. In examining promotion and retention, a number of questions must be asked: What do we know about the effectiveness of grade retention and so-called social promotion? Does an extra year to complete work automatically help a low-achieving student? Do social promotions really bolster children's self-esteem by keeping them with their age and peer group? Do social promotions just result in another year of continued failing experiences? Does the extra year really let children catch up?

RESEARCH FINDINGS

These and other questions have been the concern of teachers since schools began the practice of grading in the mid-1800s. The following research section encapsulates retention and promotion practices within schools over the past 65 years.

Major Reviews

The most impressive summary of research on retention and promotion practices appeared in the *Review of Educational Research* (Jackson, 1975). The author surveyed over 100 studies related to retention and promotion. From this extensive analysis 44 studies were scrutinized closely, since they met the primary criterion of having been original research.

Among Jackson's conclusions was the suggestion that "... those educators who retain pupils in a grade do so without valid research evidence to indicate that such treat-

From Gary Cooke and John Stammer, "Grade Retention and Social Promotion Practices," Childhood Education 61 (1985):302–310. Reprinted by permission of Gary Cooke and the Association for Childhood Education International, 11141 Georgia Avenue, Suite 200, Wheaton, MD. Copyright © 1985 by the Association.

ment will provide greater benefits to students with academic or adjustment difficulties than will promotion to the next grade" (p. 627).

Jackson further concluded that there were four weaknesses commonly found among the 44 studies which reduced both their validity and reliability:

1. Failing to sample from varied populations of students, severely limiting the researcher's ability to generalize.
2. Failing to carefully define the treatments or procedures for children in retained or socially promoted classrooms.
3. Failing to conduct longitudinal research, thus severely limiting statements about long-term effects of retention and promotion practices.
4. Failing to investigate the interactive effects between treatments, the general characteristics of students, the conditions for which they were considered for retention, and the nature of their schools.

A 1977 review (Bocks) discussed the results of 20 studies and suggested the following conclusions:

1. Grade retention was not an effective device to ensure greater mastery of elementary school subject matter.
2. Grade repetition produced many harmful consequences.
3. Social promotion did not create a wider range of abilities for upper-grade teachers to deal with.

Reiter (1973) in another extensive research review reported that retention appeared to produce long-term damaging effects and did not help schools maintain high achievement standards.

Individual Studies

In addition to confusing or contradictory results, other studies suffer from what might best be termed "fuzzy" definitions and questionable comparisons. Reinherz and Griffin (1970) followed 57 boys of normal intelligence who were repeating for the first time in grades 1 to 3. They found that children who were judged to be "immature" made the most significant gains in the retained year. In addition, they found that children with good peer relationships and good emotional adjustment also did well in the retained year. But we are forced to ask just what *is* "immature"? And how would these children have done had they been socially promoted? These imponderables raise serious questions about the authors' findings.

Not all studies, however, reveal negative or necessarily ambiguous outcomes regarding retention. Two studies frequently quoted in the literature, Owen and Ranick (1977) and Finlayson (1977), lend support to the notion that retention can be an effective educational decision for some students. The difficulty is finding out which students could benefit most from such a decision to retain. Studies by Strigner (1960) and Sandoval and Hughes (1981) have attempted to isolate and define more carefully the characteristics of students which would help teachers, parents and administrators decide whether retaining or promoting a marginal student would be most appropriate. By making decisions based on more specific learner and environmental characteristics, educators hope to accomplish a higher rate of success and more positive outcomes for retained students. Some guidelines for making these decisions are discussed in the literature.

DECISION-MAKING MODELS

Light (1977) and Lieberman (1980) constructed models to assist teachers and administrators in the task of making promotion and retention decisions. The Decision-Making Model for In-Grade Retention (Nonpromotion) by Lieberman uses a rational, problem-solving approach. The model asks the decision-maker (e.g., teacher, counselor, principal) to consider characteristics within three important categories.

Examples of elements within these categories are as follow:

Child Factors

physical disability
academic potential
chronological age

School Factors

System attitude on retention
teacher attitude on retention
program services

Family Factors

geographical moves
attitude toward retention
age of siblings

There are a total of 16 child factors, 5 family factors and 7 school factors. Each of the elements can be rated in one of four categories: for retention, against retention, undecided and not applicable.

Light's Retention Scale uses a numerical scale applied to 19 criteria. These criteria include factors such as school attendance, intelligence, age, emotional background, physical size and sex. Each criterion has a point system and a child is assigned points depending on the evaluation. In the "physical size" category, for example, the child may receive 0, 2, 4 or 5 points depending on the child's size in relationship to grade and age peers. The sum of the 19 categories provides a figure that helps place a student in one of five classifications for retention: excellent, good, fair, marginal, poor, or as a student who should not be retained.

Light cautions the user of the instrument that the score is only an indication (of what is best for the child), and should not — by itself —

be used as the final word in regard to retention decisions. It appears that the value of both the Light and Lieberman approaches lies in the careful and systematic posture that forces decision-makers into attempting to determine what is most appropriate for a child.

IMPLICATIONS AND RECOMMENDATIONS

Research studies have accomplished little toward providing data that would lead to a fool-proof formula for teachers and administrators in making decisions about retention or promotion of marginal children. From Cook (1941) to Dobbs and Neville (1967) and Lehr (1982), a central theme is reiterated:

> The crucial issue appears to be not whether the slow-learning pupil is passed or failed but how adequately his needs are met wherever he is placed (Cook, 1941).

Low achievers continue to experience failure whether promoted or retained unless classroom activities are adjusted to the ability of the individual child (Dobbs and Neville, 1967).

The reason for imposing or changing school policy (regarding retention and promotion practices) should be that it benefits students, not that it quiets criticism (Lehr, 1982).

It appears that neither grade retention nor social promotion necessarily solves the academic difficulties of the low-achieving students. We believe that the retention versus social promotion debate be considered as only one aspect of resolving the larger issue: the child's successful education. Teachers, administrators and parents should concentrate more energy and resources on positive approaches to solving each child's problem. The most important consideration is not to pass or fail the student but to meet the child's needs *in whatever environment that child is placed.* This means carefully considering the other elements in an instructional model such as the curriculum, the teaching and the learning. We seriously question that "recycling" children through the same or similar curriculum has substantive value to either the child or society. Alternatives to retention and social promotion should be considered. Some of the possibilities that permit alteration of curriculum, teaching and learning are:

- *Transitional Classrooms* that offer the child in the kindergarten or 1st grade (traditionally) a move to a new classroom environment—and teacher—while getting an opportunity to mature both socially and intellectually in a less-advanced and specially designed curriculum. Under such circumstances, the child generally meets the requirements of kindergarten and 1st grade in three years instead of two, but under positive environmental and learning conditions.
- *Continuous Progress/Ungraded Classes* that allow the child to acquire skills according to his or her own timetable. In such a program, the curriculum is clearly designed to meet the needs of the child.
- *Intensive Remedial Instruction*, where teaching is based on specific learner characteristics. The child with a specific modality strength receives instruction that is best suited to his/her learning style.
- *Individual Tutoring Programs* that occur on a year-round basis. Such programs offer content-specific instruction beyond that normally occurring in the school.
- *Home Assistance Programs* that offer help to parents in learning to build positive psychological climates. A major thrust of such programs is to provide opportunities for parents to help foster improved self-images in children.

Beyond formal program structures, three other considerations come to mind. First, smaller class size, particularly in the primary grades, seems crucial to improved learning climates. An accurate measure of pupil-teacher ratios must be based on calculations using classroom teachers and pupils only. Second, it seems important that specialized inservice and professional growth programs for personnel be an ongoing part of any school system to lend both vitality and improved functioning to such a system. Finally, better funding is crucial to permit the development of more lively, positive and relevant learning environments.

In addition to seeking alternatives to help children be more successful in school, we seek successes that evolve naturally from the improvement of curriculum and teaching. We believe that each school district should develop and institute policies that articulate promotion and retention standards. It is critical that systems establish guidelines for making decisions which address both the needs of teachers and parents in coming to grips with questions of effective promotion or retention and the eventual appropriate placement of the child.

When one attempts to answer the questions posed at the beginning of this article, two things are clear. First, there are no definitive or unambiguous answers. Second, and more important, the questions traditionally asked manage to avoid the real issues—analyzing the effect—instead of examining the roots of the problem. There really is only one question in regard to the problem of promotion, retention and pupil placement: How may this child's needs best be served?

REFERENCES

"A Nation at Risk: The Imperative for Educational Reform." *The Chronicle of Higher Education* (May 1983): 11–16.

Bloom, Benjamin S. "Affective Outcomes of School Learning," *Phi Delta Kappan* (Nov. 1977): 193–98.

Bocks, William. "Non-promotion. A Year to Grow?" *Educational Leadership* (Feb. 1977): 379–83.

Cook, Walter. *Grouping and Promotion in the Elementary School.* Minneapolis: University of Minnesota Press, 1941.

Dobbs, V., and D. Neville. "The Effect of Nonpromotion on the Achievement of Groups Matched from Retained First Graders and Promoted Second Graders." *The Journal of Educational Research* (July/Aug. 1967).

Farley, E. "Regarding Repeaters—Sad Effects of Failure upon the Child." *Nation's Schools* 18,4 (1936): 37–38.

Finlayson, Harry. "Nonpromotion and Self-concept Development." *Phi Delta Kappan* (Nov. 1977).

Jackson, Gregg. "The Research Evidence on Effects of Grade Retention." *Review of Educational Research* (Fall 1975): 613–35.

Klene, V., and E. Branson. Reported in *The Elementary School Journal* 29 (1929): 564–66.

Koons, C. I., "Nonpromotion: A Dead End Road." *Phi Delta Kappan* (May 1977): 701–02.

Lehr, Fran. "Grade Repetition vs. Social Promotion." *The Reading Teacher* (Nov. 1982).

Leiberman, Laurence M. "A Decision-making Model for In-grade Retention (Nonpromotion)." *Journal of Learning Disabilities* 13 (May 1980): 268–72.

Light, Wayne. *Light's Retention Scale and Recording Form.* Novato, CA.: Academic Therapy Publications, 1977.

Lindvig, Elise Kay. "Grade Retention: Evolving Expectations and Individual Differences." *The Clearing House* (Feb. 1983): 253–56.

Owen, Samuel, and Deborah Ranick. "The Greenville Program: A Common Sense Approach to Basics." *Phi Delta Kappan* (Mar. 1977): 213–18.

Reinherz, Helen, and Carol Griffin. "The Second Time Around: Achievement and Progress of Boys Who Repeated One of the First Three Grades," *The School Counselor* (Jan. 1970): 213–18.

Reiter, Robert. *The Promotion/Retention Dilemma: What Research Tells Us.* Report #7416, Philadelphia: Philadelphia School District Office of Research and Evaluation, 1973 (ED 099 412).

Sandoval, J., and G. P. Hughes. *Success in Non-promoted First Grade Children: A Final Report.* Davis, CA: University of California, Department of Education. 1981 (E1) 212–371).

Stringer, Lorene. "Report on Retentions Program." *The Elementary School Journal* (Apr. 1960): 370–75.

PART FOUR
Study and Discussion Questions

CHAPTER SEVEN Strategies for Promoting Learning

Reading 17 Rediscovering Discovery Learning

1. Discovery learning is a way of encouraging students to learn on their own without being taught directly. Can you explain how the suggestions for learning in this Reading promote this process?

Reading 18 Bloom's Mastery Learning: A Legacy of Effectiveness

1. What is the main idea behind mastery learning?
2. When the point is made about mastery learning that "students get a second chance," what does this mean?
3. How does using the mastery learning model change the role of teachers?

Reading 19 Cooperative Learning and Student Achievement

1. What two essential conditions must exist in order for cooperative learning to work?
2. Why is individual accountability so important for the success of cooperative learning?
3. Would you prefer working in a cooperative group format, or would you choose to work by yourself? Why?

Reading 20 Courseware: A Practical Revolution

1. What is the basic rationale for using computers as learning aids?
2. Identify and briefly describe the five ways that were discussed as ways to use computers to enhance learning outcomes.

Reading 21 Putting Learning Strategies to Work

1. How does a learning "strategy" differ from a learning "tactic"?
2. Can you explain how pattern learning differs from reflective self-instruction?
3. How can behavioral self-management, mood management, and self-monitoring be used to develop motivation?

158 *Part Four: Study and Discussion Questions*

CHAPTER EIGHT   Understandings About Metacognition, Critical Thinking, and Information-Processing

Reading 22   From the Mystery Spot to the Thoughtful Spot: The Instruction of Metacognitive Strategies

1. How would you explain the concept of metacognition to someone unfamiliar with it?

2. How is it advantageous for teachers to know about the metacognitive strategies of their students?

3. How can teachers go about getting this knowledge?

Reading 23   Critical Thinking—What Can It Be?

1. In what basic ways does critical thinking differ from ordinary thinking?

2. The point was made that critical thinking is self-correcting. What does this mean, and how does it work?

3. What suggestions do you have for teachers who want to promote more critical thinking among students?

Reading 24   Research on Memory: Major Discoveries, Major Educational Challenges

1. Can you explain the functional differences between short-term and long-term memory? That is, how does each work?

2. How can we help students (and ourselves) learn how to store new information into long-term memory so that it can be retrieved when needed?

3. What is the difference between declarative memory and procedural memory?

4. How can teachers use what is known about declarative and procedural memory processes to make teaching more successful?

CHAPTER NINE   The Effects of Grouping, Class Size, and Retention on Learning

Reading 25   Synthesis of Research on Grouping in Elementary and Secondary Schools

1. What are the advantages and disadvantages of grouping practices?

2. How does between-class grouping differ from within-class grouping?

3. What is it about the Joplin plan that has contributed to its success as a strategy for grouping?

4. If you had a child of your own who wasn't doing particularly well in elementary school, would you want him or her to be in a room where within-class ability grouping was followed? Why or why not?

Reading 26   The Effect of Class Size on What Happens in Classrooms

1. What does research say about the relationship between class size and school achievement?

2. What does research say about *why* class size affects achievement?

Reading 27 Grade Retention and Social Promotion Practices

1. What does research suggest about the effectiveness of social promotion and retention as ways to encourage learning?
2. If you had a child who did poorly in one of the elementary grades, would you argue for or against grade retention for your child? Why?

PART FIVE

An Overview of What It Takes to Be a Good Teacher

Chances are very good that each of us shares a very important experience: Somewhere along the way we experienced a remarkable teacher. It no doubt was a person who blended wisdom, warmth, enthusiasm, and positive energy into a memorable classroom experience. We not only learned from that teacher, but we felt good about ourselves and our possibilities. What is it about good teachers that makes them "good" in the first place? Are they good because they were born that way, or are there particular skills and personal qualities that can be acquired through training and experience?

Research has been clear in pointing out that good teaching involves a mixture of knowledge, personal experiences, careful planning, the development of routines, and, of course, the characteristics of the class. In Reading 28, Jere Brophy has synthesized some of the important findings that have emerged in recent years regarding teacher behaviors that are most commonly associated with positive achievement outcomes. The point is well made that good teachers are knowledgeable, flexible professionals committed to a broad array of teaching strategies to accomplish their goals.

In Reading 29, Carolyn Sweers, a high-school teacher, explores the possibility of helping students think critically about their lives through the use of Socratic questioning. It is an example of the sort of creative approaches to teaching frequently seen in good teachers. And in Reading 30, we will examine the psychodynamics of teachers' expectations in an effort to understand why and how they are such a powerful force in shaping achievement outcomes. In an expression of personal gratitude in Reading 31, Mark Medoff, who wrote *Children of a Lesser God*, sensitively describes how certain teachers made a positive difference in his life. You will see in those teachers the very characteristics described in research investigating good teachers.

The three Readings in Chapter Eleven focus on motivational strategies teachers can use to encourage student achievement. Research is abundant in this area, and in Reading 32 Jere Brophy presents a highly readable synthesis of some of the major motivational strategies teachers can use on an everyday basis. In Reading 33, Madeline Hunter and George Barker make a strong case for the idea that students will be better learners if they believe that their success depends more on effort than on luck or ability. Ways are suggested to help students develop a greater sense of control over their fate. In Reading 34, Sylvia Rimm addresses one of the toughest motivational challenges teachers face: How to reach the underachiever. Suggestions are made for both identifying and helping students who fit this mold.

Classroom management—keeping things running smoothly, disciplining when necessary—is another challenge confronting teachers. Fortunately, there are many positive ways for doing this fairly and effectively. Thomas McDaniel leads off Chapter Twelve with ten principles, distilled from many studies, that can serve as general disciplinary guidelines for teachers to use.

Jere Brophy follows this up in Reading 36 with suggestions for giving students a greater capacity for "self-guidance," an approach to classroom management that builds upon the idea that students are generally willing to cooperate and behave once they are "socialized" or taught how to behave appropriately.

In Reading 37, Lorrie Shepard spells out the differences between norm-referenced and criterion-referenced evaluation and discusses the strengths and weaknesses associated with each. Recognizing that teachers (and other people, too) are not likely to do research if they are terrorized by what seems to be a web of complex procedures, Robert Gable and Vincent Rogers attempt to "take the terror out of research" in their wonderfully lucid explanation of the basic mechanics and methodologies associated with quantitative and qualitative research in Reading 38.

What is research teaching us about good teachers and good teaching? What can teachers do to challenge students to think critically about their behavior and beliefs, to, in effect, examine their lives? How do teachers communicate high or low expectations to students? What are some of the ways positive reinforcement can be used as a motivator? What are the essential preconditions a teacher can establish to motivate students' learning? How can teachers use intervention techniques and assertive discipline to help maintain classroom discipline? What are the guidelines for deciding whether to use norm-referenced or criterion-referenced tests?

The Readings in this section will help you understand why teaching is such an enormously challenging, demanding, and fulfilling professional activity. A teacher friend of mine, in a moment of deep insight, once said that teaching can be one of the easiest jobs in the world . . . but not when it is done right.

CHAPTER TEN

The Many Faces of Good Teaching

READING 28 JERE BROPHY
Research on Teacher Effects: Uses and Abuses

Ideally, teaching is a technology for producing learning, informed by scientific data linking teacher behaviors to student achievement measures. Schools will fulfill their missions most effectively when teachers are trained to follow scientifically developed guidelines for instruction and then monitored to ensure compliance enforced through rigorous accountability procedures.

On the contrary, teaching is and always will be an art. Attempts to legislate instruction and turn teaching into a technology are doomed to failure. Schools work best when individual teachers use their professional knowledge and experience to decide what to teach and how to teach it to the particular students in their class.

These are two perspectives that might be taken on questions

From Jere Brophy, "Research on Teacher Effects: Uses and Abuses," *The Elementary School Journal* (September 1988):3–21. Published by The University of Chicago. © 1988 by The University of Chicago.

concerning the relevance and use of scientific data linking teacher behavior to students outcomes. In my view, they are inappropriate perspectives—each contains grains of truth but is too extreme and rigid to fit the facts. This article offers a more balanced and differentiated perspective on the same issues, focusing specifically on how research linking teacher behavior to student achievement might be used in educating teachers and evaluating their instruction. Using the role and functioning of the public school teacher to provide a context, it considers a variety of application issues and then addresses implications concerning preservice teacher education, induction programs for new teachers, and teacher evaluation. . . .

These findings will be familiar to most readers, so they are summarized only briefly here (see Brophy & Good, 1986, for extended review and discussion). The most consistently reported and replicated of these findings concern the quantity of academic instruction that stu-

dents receive from their teachers. Amount learned is determined in part by opportunity to learn (exposure to content). In turn, opportunity to learn is determined by the degree to which teachers: (1) are businesslike and task oriented, emphasize instruction as basic to their role, expect students to master the curriculum, and allocate most classroom time to activities with academic objectives rather than to activities with other objectives or no clear objectives at all; (2) use classroom organization and management strategies that maximize the time that students spend engaged in academic activities and minimize the time spent getting organized, handling transitions, or dealing with misconduct; (3) pace the students briskly through the curriculum, but also see that they make continuous progress all along the way, moving through small steps with high or at least moderate rates of success and minimal confusion or frustration; and (4) spend most of their time actively instructing their students in group lessons or supervising their work on assignments rather than expecting them to learn primarily on their own through independent reading and seatwork.

In addition to these findings concerning quantity of instruction, there are findings concerning the quality of instruction indicating that achievement gains are greater when teachers: (1) not only make frequent presentations and demonstrations but do so in ways that include sufficient enthusiasm of delivery, clarity and specificity of language, logical sequencing of the content, and structuring of the content in ways that help students recognize it as an integrated whole and appreciate the relationships among its parts (through advance organizers, outlining, signaling of transitions, calling attention to main ideas, and summarizing); (2) ask clear questions at appropriate levels of difficulty (so that most students can understand and respond adequately to them) and allow students sufficient time to process and begin to formulate answers before calling on one of them to respond; (3) provide clear and informative feedback to students' answers; (4) seek to elicit improved responses when students answer incorrectly or fail to answer at all; (5) answer or redirect relevant student questions and incorporate relevant student comments into the lesson; (6) prepare students for follow-up assignments by reviewing the instructions and working through practice examples with them until they are clear about what to do and how to do it; (7) circulate to provide supervision and help to students as they work on assignments (or if this is not possible, make sure that assignments are challenging enough to constitute meaningful learning experiences yet easy enough to allow students to attain high levels of success if they put forth reasonable effort, and make sure that those who still need help know when and how to get it).

PROFESSIONAL KNOWLEDGE AS POTENTIAL POWER

What are the potential uses and abuses of these findings linking teacher behavior to student achievement gain? What is an appropriate stance that educators (including not only classroom teachers but school administrators and teacher educators) might take with respect to them? The remainder of this article addresses these issues. . . .

Knowledge about teacher effects can be either empowering or limiting to teachers, depending on how it is used. Educators who view teachers as autonomous artists tend to see such knowledge as restricting teachers' freedom and thus resist it. Two points must be made in response to this attitude. First, it is neither realistic nor appropriate to expect teachers to exercise total autonomy in defining and doing their work. Like other professionals, teachers are subject both to formal laws and to informal expectations and codes of conduct based on professionally accepted standards for good practice. Furthermore, teachers are (appropriately) subject to additional regulation because they work in institutions (schools) that are established and maintained by social communities (not by teachers as individuals or even by education as a profession). Communities establish schools to educate their youth, so decisions about educational policy and practice should be made with input not only from teachers but from society at large (as represented by federal and state agencies, local school boards, and school administrators). Furthermore, the primary consideration that should determine such decisions is the degree to which proposed policies or practices further the primary goals of schooling. It is desirable and important that teachers obtain personal gratification and professional self-actualization from their work, but this must occur (to the extent possible) within the context of providing the best possible education for the students whom the schools were established to educate in the first place.

The second point is that if it is used appropriately, information about the effects of teaching practices is much more empowering than limiting to teachers because it allows them to act confidently on the basis of well-established principles rather than to have to rely on trial and error learning or on whatever techniques they have seen modeled during visits to other teachers' classes. An analogy to the medical profession illustrates this point. As my colleague Charles W. (Andy) Anderson points out, if we had the choice of going to our regular physicians or to reincarnations of historically prominent physicians such as Galen or Hippocrates, we would stick with our regular physicians because they give us access to the vital medical knowledge and technology that have been developed since Galen or Hippocrates lived. Far from oppressing modern physicians or turning them into deskilled technicians, the proliferation of the knowledge base that undergirds the practice of medicine has had primarily empowering effects. Modern physicians can confidently follow safe and efficient routines for doing things that were once chancy and dangerous, and they can do a great many things that were unknown to medical pioneers. These advances have brought responsibilities as well (physicians can be sued for malpractice), but their primary effects have been to improve the quality of medical practice and to increase physicians' success rates in responding to medical problems. As much as ever before, modern medical practice demands professional judgment and offers opportunities for artistry and creativity, but in addition to, rather than in the absence of, systematic application of scientific knowledge and technical skill. Teachers can look forward to similar developments in the quality and effects of educational practice as the knowledge base undergirding their profession expands.

Some such developments are already in evidence. For example, just 20 years ago teachers interested in learning about classroom management strategies were offered only vague and often conflicting advice that usually was not based on systematic research in classrooms. Since then, however, research on classroom organization and management has produced a stable and informative knowledge base (reviewed in Doyle, 1986, and Good and Brophy, 1987) offering principles that teachers can adopt with confidence, knowing that they are associated not only with better student engagement in classroom activities but ultimately with better student achievement. Teachers who may have wondered whether it was worth spending significant time early in the school year making sure that students learned and followed basic classroom rules and procedures now know that such allocation of their time is not only worthwhile but vital to successful establishment of a management system that will function effectively throughout the year. Similarly, teacher-effects research enables teachers to proceed with confidence in knowing that their interactive instruction of students provides important information and opportunities for clarification and elaboration of learning that students do not get consistently from reading texts or working on assignments, that time spent orienting students through advance organizers and calling their attention to important structuring elements will enhance their understanding of and memory for information, that it is usually better to address questions to the class as a whole (and then call on an individual to respond) than it is to designate a respondent before asking the question, and that it is important to wait for a response (and if necessary to probe or rephrase the question) when students do not respond (rather than to quickly give the answer or move on to someone else for fear of putting the student "on the spot").

In summary, because of the direct relevance and potentially empowering effects of information linking teacher behavior to student outcomes, it is counterproductive, if not unprofessional, to dismiss it out of hand on the basis of misguided notions about teacher artistry or autonomy. On the contrary, all teachers should be made aware of this information and stimulated to think about how it might apply to their practice. The information must be formulated accurately, however, and presented to teachers in appropriate ways. I recognize (and as one of the researchers who has generated the information, I am very troubled by) the fact that such information can be misused in ways that not only fail to empower teachers but limit their effectiveness by subjecting them to overly rigid or otherwise inappropriate prescriptions. Such misuse of this information stems in part from failure to recognize the limitations of scientific data in general and of teacher-effects data in particular.

LIMITATIONS OF THE NATURE AND USE OF SCIENTIFIC DATA ON TEACHER EFFECTS

As a first principle, it is important to recognize that neither teacher-effects data nor any other scientific data can directly prescribe guidelines for practice. Scientific findings can identify effective ways to attain given sets of prioritized educational objectives, but they cannot make decisions for educators about what the objectives should be or how they should be prioritized. These are policy decisions to be made on the basis of moral, social, and political values. In effect, those who attempt to finesse these decisions by prescribing teacher behavior strictly on the basis of teacher-effects data are using achievement-test gain as their sole educational objective, to the exclusion of all other considerations.

This is why I refer to "teacher-effects" data rather than to "teacher-effectiveness" data in discussing research linking teacher behavior to student achievement. "Teacher effectiveness" is a broad term that has meaning only in reference to a set of prioritized educational objectives, and most educators would want to consider several other objectives besides achievement-test gain in defining and assessing teacher effectiveness (developing student interest in subject matter, fostering the personal adjustment and mental health of individual students, developing a prosocial, cooperative group atmosphere in the class, etc.).

As an example illustrating the fact that teacher-effects data cannot be translated directly into prescriptions for practice, consider the debates over length of the school day or school year. Research has shown that amount learned is related to time spent learning. Although this relationship is less direct and powerful than most would suppose, it is clear that students would achieve more if they attended school for more time per day or more days per year. By itself, however, this scientific information does not constitute an argument that time spent in school should be increased. To construct such an argument, it would be necessary to convince others that: (a) what students are learning at present is "not enough" by some persuasive criterion; and (b) lengthening the time spent in school is a necessary response to this problem, or at least is preferable to other potential responses (toughening standards, improving curricula, improving teaching, etc.). Clearly, this would require consideration of values, cost/benefit trade-offs, and a great many other things in addition to data on teacher effects. . . .

Another limitation on teacher-effects data is that they are much more informative about the quantity of instruction (how much active teaching occurs) than about its quality (what forms it takes and how well it is implemented). This is because, although it has made important contributions, most of the process-outcome research that has been done so far has been designed in ways that inherently limit the nature and degree of specificity of the findings that it is capable of producing. Three limitations in particular should be noted. First, the samples usually included teachers who were poor classroom managers or who for whatever reason did not spend much time actively instructing their students or keeping them profitably engaged in academic activities. This virtually ensured that quantitative measures such as active instruction time or student engaged time would emerge as the most powerful correlates of achievement gain. Second, the process data usually were collected using methods that emphasized how often teachers did things rather than how well they did them. This minimized the likelihood that subtle qualitative differences in teacher behavior would be studied in the first place. Third, the data typically were analyzed by correlating teacher behavior scores averaged across many classroom observations with class average scores on standardized achievement tests. This made it likely that reliable but subtle effects of qualitative differences in teacher behavior, even if measured, would be masked by the much more powerful effects associated with differences in active teaching time and other quantitative measures.

As a result of these limitations, process-outcome data say more about the amount than about the quality of instruction associated with student achievement gains. A related point is that these data mostly reflect the differences between (a) the 25% or so of teachers who are the least successful in eliciting student achievement gain and (b) all other teachers. That is, these data identify key differences between teachers who instruct their students poorly or not at all and teachers who instruct their students adequately or better. Not much information is available yet on the differences between teachers who are outstanding instructors and those who are merely adequate or average. Such information is beginning to be accumulated, however, by researchers who have begun to exert more control over the range of classroom management skills and time-allocation preferences of the teachers in their studies, to include more qualitative measures of instruction, and to search for more specific and context-bound relationships between teaching and learning of particular content or skills.

In summary, the principles that can be derived from the teacher-effects research are mostly limited to general guidelines that focus on achievement gain to the exclusion of other potential objectives, focus on basic fundamentals rather than on more sophisticated fine points of instruction, and focus on quantitative rather than qualitative aspects of instruction. Consequently, these principles have limited value for those in-service teachers who routinely elicit impressive achievement gains from their students, but they should be valuable for educating preservice teachers and reeducating those in-service teachers who have not enjoyed much success in eliciting student achievement gain. The principles imply four possible reasons for low achievement gain in some in-service teachers' classes.

Two of the reasons are suggested by the findings indicating that high achievement gain is associated with placing high priority on achievement gain as a goal and adopting congruent definitions of the teacher's role, adopting high but realistic expectations about the students' ability to master the curriculum and the teacher's ability to teach it to them, and allocating most of the available time to academic activities so as to maximize content coverage and student opportunity to learn. By implication, these findings identify two types of teachers who will be relatively unsuccessful in eliciting achievement gains from their students: (1) teachers who are burned out or who for whatever reason are not committed to any clear-cut educational goals (those who devote a great deal of classroom time to busy-work or noneducational pastimes), and (2) teachers who place a high priority on affective or social outcomes but a low priority on achievement outcomes (so that less of the available time is spent instructing the students in the formal curriculum).

Given the complexity of teachers' work and the many demands and frustrations that are sometimes associated with it, burned out or apathetic teachers may need better administrative support, improvements in the quality of the workplace, or personal counseling more than they need in-service education concerning instructional goals and strategies. However, to the extent that such teachers have become burned out or apathetic due to a history of failure and frustration, exposure to teacher-effects data might help them to break out of their "learned helplessness" and become willing to invest effort in self-improvement programs. After all, most teacher-effects findings are based on studies of ordinary teachers working under typical classroom conditions, and experiments based on these findings have shown that teachers can learn to follow guidelines for classroom management and instruction that enable them to elicit significant increases in their students' achievement gains.

Teachers who place high priority

on affective or social outcomes but low priority on achievement outcomes may be less interested than other teachers in principles derived from teacher-effects research, but even these teachers should be interested in getting maximum benefit out of the time that they do devote to academic objectives and in developing confidence that they can pursue these objectives reliably and efficiently. Furthermore, there is some reason to believe that improvements in the instruction that they do target to cognitive goals may enhance the effectiveness of their efforts to achieve affective goals. Prawat (1985) reports that teachers who were balanced in emphasizing both cognitive and affective goals were more successful in achieving *both* sets of goals with their students than were teachers who placed high priority on affective goals but low priority on cognitive goals.

The findings concerning classroom management effectiveness and student engaged time identify a third class of teachers who tend to be unsuccessful in eliciting student achievement gain: those whose success is limited by their own poor classroom management skills. Such teachers could benefit from research-based classroom management in-service programs, which have proven effective in enabling teachers to increase their students' engagement rates and ultimately their achievement levels (Evertson, 1985).

The findings on active instruction identify a fourth class of teachers who stand to benefit from exposure to principles derived from teacher-effects research: teachers who expect their students to learn mostly on their own by reading and doing assignments or by working their way through sequences of individualized learning modules, rather than expecting to spend considerable time personally carrying the content to the students through active whole-class or small-group instruc-tion. Materials-based approaches can work in special resource rooms and other settings featuring low student/teacher ratios, but they usually do not work well in ordinary classrooms where one teacher must work with 20–40 students. The problem is not with the *theory* of individualized instruction that calls for beginning where students are and moving them along at their own pace. Instead, the problem is that *in practice,* individualized instruction in the typical classroom: (*a*) shifts a great deal of responsibility for planning and managing learning from the teacher to the students themselves, and (*b*) shifts a great deal of responsibility for carrying the content to the students from the teacher to the materials. This can succeed and may even have certain advantages when the teacher is continually available to provide close supervision and immediate help when needed, but it does not work well when students must work on their own for extended periods of time and try to learn by using the curriculum materials without getting much guidance or help from the teacher....

DERIVING INSTRUCTIONAL PRINCIPLES FROM RESEARCH FINDINGS

Research findings do not translate directly into guidelines for practice. Instead, the meanings and implications of the findings must be *interpreted.* This is why, when speaking of educating teachers, I have referred more often to *principles* derived from teacher-effects findings than to the findings themselves. Even where findings are well established and no one disputes the basic facts, there may be considerable disagreement about how the findings should be interpreted and what they imply about effective teaching.

Responsibility for sensible interpretation of scientific data begins with the researchers who originally collect the data and the editors and referees of the journals in which they publish their findings. It is vital that these individuals see that clear and complete information is given about the contexts within which data were collected, the measuring instruments, and the procedures followed in processing and analyzing the obtained scores; that the findings themselves are described clearly; and that statements of fact are distinguished from interpretations or opinions when discussing the data. Commonly made errors of interpretation (to be described below) should be avoided....

First, it is unwise to try to make too much of the findings of a single study. Not all reported findings have been replicated, and even replicated findings may apply only to certain situations (such as small-group reading instruction in the early grades). Also, even well-replicated *correlations* between a teacher behavior and student achievement do not necessarily indicate that the teacher behavior *causes* the achievement gain. It is possible, instead, that student behavior causes the teacher behavior (high rates of praise, low rates of criticism, and low rates of intrusive disciplinary interventions all are more likely in classes full of bright and well-motivated students than in classes full of alienated low achievers). Even more likely, it is possible that both student achievement gain and certain correlated teacher behaviors are caused by other, more fundamentally important, teacher behaviors (rates of teacher praise of student answers to recitation questions tend to correlate with achievement gain, but these correlations probably exist not so much because such teacher praise actually causes student achievement but because it occurs during recitation activities and thus indicates indirectly that the teacher spends a good deal of time actively instructing the students during group lessons....

The most extreme error is to leap

from a correlational finding to an extreme all-or-nothing prescription. Those who make this mistake end up urging teachers to always wait at least 3 seconds for a response to a question, to always praise and never criticize their students, or to always assign homework but never schedule independent seatwork. Such prescriptions stem from failure to recognize that a correlation reflects only the variation within the observed range of the teacher behavior in question, so that prescriptions for application must remain within this range. For example, suppose that rates of teacher praise (not mere positive feedback, but more personal and intensive praise) of students' correct answers to recitation questions correlate positively with student achievement gain, and that these average 10%, but range from 0% to 40% (e.g., at least one teacher never praised a correct answer and at least one praised 40% of the correct answers that his or her students produced). Do such data imply that teachers should always praise their students' correct answers? Clearly not — the data are silent concerning rates of praise above 40%, because such rates were not observed. Therefore, it would be a mistake to simple-mindedly extrapolate beyond this range (concluding from these data that teachers should always praise their students' correct answers would be akin to concluding that if 15 minutes of homework per night are good, 2 hours of homework per night are eight times better!).

Do the data support a recommendation that teachers praise 40% of their students' correct answers? Possibly, but probably not. This might be true if there were an extremely high correlation (.90 or above) reflecting a nearly one-to-one correspondence between the measures, so that teachers who praised at or near the 40% rate were those who got the highest achievement gains from their students, and teachers who praised at or near the 0% rate were those who got the least achievement gains. Such data would support a 40% guideline and would even provide reason to believe that the optimal percentage would be higher than 40% if teachers could be persuaded to praise even more often. However, teacher-effects research does not yield such high correlations between process measures and outcome measures. Instead of being at or above .90, even the correlations that do reach statistical significance tend to range between about .20 and .40, indicating only weak to moderate relationships between teacher behaviors and student outcomes. Such relationships reveal a general tendency for teachers who get high achievement gains to praise more often than teachers who get low achievement gains, but with many exceptions in both directions (e.g., many frequent praisers nevertheless get low achievement gains and many infrequent praisers nevertheless get high achievement gains). Thus, even though the observed rates of praise ranged from 0% to 40%, the average praise rate for the teachers who got poor achievement gains (say, the lowest quartile) might have been 6%, and the average praise rate for the teachers who got the highest achievement gains (the upper quartile) might have been 12%.

Given this information, a sensible guideline for optimal rate of praise would appear to be about 10% to 15% rather than some higher figure. This would be a useful guideline for communicating to teachers if it proved to be robust (e.g., if it stood up to replication attempts). . . . Also, the guideline is merely a frequency norm — it tells teachers roughly how often to praise correct recitation responses but says nothing about which students to praise, which responses to praise, or what kinds of praise would be most effective (see Brophy, 1981, on these issues).

In summary, a positive correlation between the frequency of a teacher behavior and student achievement gain usually does *not* mean that teachers should engage in that behavior at every possible opportunity, and a negative correlation between the frequency of a teacher behavior and student achievement gain usually does *not* mean that teachers should avoid that behavior entirely. To develop sensible norms, one must stay within the range of variance in the teacher behavior that was actually observed in the data and identify a target number or range that seems to reflect optimal teacher behavior given everything known about the nature of the process-outcome relationship and the reasons why it occurs. Usually, the average score for the most successful teachers or the range within which these teachers' scores are clustered will be the best guidelines that can be developed from the data.

This has been the approach taken by Stallings (1980) to develop guidelines for reading instruction based on previous process-outcome research. These guidelines suggest, for example, that observations of good reading instruction will reveal that about 20% of class time is spent informing students (presenting new information), 2% on drill and practice, 9% on oral reading, 25% on individual written work, and so on. Such guidelines are probably better than guidelines developed on the basis of untested theoretical assumptions, and they are certainly better than the all-or-nothing guidelines criticized above. Still, they are too rigid, and if mandated as required teacher behavior rather than merely presented to teachers as food for thought, they can be counterproductive (Myers, 1986). The problem is that the guidelines are based on observational data taken at particular grade levels and averaged across repeated observations. Even as averages, these data might not generalize to other grade levels (more oral reading might be appropriate in the early grades, for example, and less in the later grades). Furthermore, even when the guidelines hold up as averages, they fail to take into account shifts in the nature and length of activities that ordinarily should occur as the teacher and class move through an academic unit (e.g., there is usually more presentation of information and development of concepts early in a unit but more practice and application activities later in the unit). . . .

As the knowledge base available to inform teacher education expands, the professional work of teachers should become more like that of physicians in several respects (although it should be recognized that teachers concentrate on developing their clients' cognitive structure rather than on repairing damage in their physical structures). In particular, if teachers are to function as true professionals, it will be necessary for the education profession to develop a broad and integrated knowledge base concerning classroom functioning that would be capable of informing educational diagnosis and treatment the way the knowledge base concerning body functions informs medical diagnosis and treatment. For this to occur, there needs to be not only a proliferation of relevant process-outcome research, but also better recognition of some fundamental principles that are routinely violated at present by those who misuse research findings.

One is that *teacher behaviors are not ends in themselves but means toward ends. Usually, they cannot be labeled simply as good or bad but must be evaluated according to whether or not they foster accomplishment of the intended objectives.* For example, strategies for structuring and sequencing content are most relevant to situations in which the teacher is presenting new content to the students (especially abstract or otherwise complex content). They are less relevant to brief demonstrations of specific skills, and not relevant at all to activities that do not involve presentation of content. Similarly, information about the value of wait time following questions or about simplifying questions in the attempt to elicit improved responses is most relevant to discussions involving higher-level questions, less relevant to recitations involving lower-level questions, and not relevant at all to activities that do not involve questioning the students. These considerations should be intuitively obvious to anyone, yet it is not hard to find teacher educators or program developers who suggest that a single lesson format is appropriate for all academic activities, or to find local administrators or state officials suggesting that a classroom observation form that assumes a particular lesson format be used for assessing instruction in all classrooms and for every kind of academic activity. Although such individuals sometimes cite selected process-outcome research findings in attempting to justify their actions, process-outcome research considered as an integrated body of information (see Brophy & Good, 1986) provides no such support.

Rather than committing themselves to a single approach and using it in all situations (which is akin to a physician prescribing aspirin for all ills), curriculum designers and teachers should plan instruction by beginning with clear objectives, surveying known or proposed methods for accomplishing these objectives, and prescribing the method that appears to be the "treatment of choice" under the circumstances (to the extent that information is available to inform such decisions). Similarly, those who attempt to evaluate instruction should assess the degree to which the teacher selected and implemented a method appropriate for accomplishing the intended objectives, not the degree to which the teacher conformed to some supposedly generic model of good teaching.

Even if all of the data needed to implement this seemingly straightforward approach were available, however, it would be important to implement it flexibly with attention to context-specific circumstances. For one thing, teachers are always simultaneously working toward multiple objectives and trying to meet the differing needs of different students. Consequently, classroom teaching always involves dilemmas and trade-offs. Physical proximity and frequent questioning are effective nondisruptive techniques for keeping inattentive students involved in lessons, but consistent use of these techniques causes the teacher to pay less attention to and provide a lower-quality educational experience for the more attentive students who are seated farther away (Lampert, 1985). Moving at a slower pace and taking time to try to elicit improved responses following incomplete or incorrect answers is helpful for low achievers, but it reduces content coverage and may produce boredom or loss of concentration in higher achievers.

Furthermore, even generally applicable principles usually have exceptions. Confirmatory feedback is usually advisable but can be omitted when it is obvious to everyone that an answer was correct. In order to alert an anxious or inattentive student, it is sometimes better to deviate from common practice by calling the student's name before asking a question. Sometimes (such as when asking opinion questions or other divergent questions that do not have single right answers) it may be appropriate to allow students to call out answers, even though this is usually not a good idea. Thus, even relevant and valid guidelines need to be understood and used as general principles rather than as rigid rules.

In summary, research findings linking teacher behavior to student achievement gain have relevance and potential usefulness as a basis for developing prescriptions for practice, but valid use of the findings requires interpretation by educators who are knowledgeable about classroom functioning and mindful of the limitations and qualifications that must be placed on any guidelines induced from such research. Many purveyors of advice presumably based on process-outcome research have been rightly criticized for mindless empiricism or faulty generalization of findings. However, readers should note that these problems are in the use of the research rather than in the research itself. The research findings can be used to induce valid principles of instruction, and these principles can be strung together into a useful model or theory of what classroom teaching is all about and how it functions well. Much such consolidation and interpretation of the findings have been going on lately, and this process will continue.

Given that most findings were developed from research on teachers working under typical classroom conditions, there is good reason to believe that principles derived from these findings will be both relevant to and feasible for implementation by the majority of classroom teachers. For the most part, these findings underscore the important role of teachers (not just curriculum materials) in stimulating student achievement gains and the validity of most of the instructional practices that teachers have developed through intuition or reflection on their own practice. However, they also lay the groundwork for developing concepts and principles describing effective classroom teaching that should make it possible for preservice teachers to learn professional knowledge and skills more systematically than they do now and for in-service teachers to practice their profession with better-integrated knowledge and more reality-based confidence. . . .

CONCLUSION

Among its other contributions, recent research on teaching belies the notion that "those who can, do, and those who can't teach." It shows that although most reasonably competent adults could survive in the classroom, most could not teach effectively. Teaching well is a complex and difficult task, demanding a blend of energy, motivation, and knowledge of subject matter, pedagogy, and students that many teachers, let alone other adults, do not possess. Most educational professionals realize this at some level, yet many who should know better continue to act as if teaching were something that could be reduced to a single prescription and evaluated accordingly.

One more medical analogy is apropos here: Those (including licensed physicians) who would prescribe a single treatment for all ills or claim benefits to a particular practice that go far beyond any proof to support such claims are scorned as quacks. Educators who behave the same way deserve similar scorn.

Research on teaching, and research on teacher effects in particular, has a great deal to offer by contributing to the development of a knowledge base to inform professional practice. However, it is a misuse of such research to use it as a basis for developing simpleminded and rigid guidelines of the "behavior X correlates with student achievement gain, so teachers should always use behavior X" variety. To use the information appropriately, it is necessary first to synthesize it with other relevant information in order to develop explanations for observed process-outcome relationships, then derive instructional principles from this knowledge base, and then encourage teachers to apply these principles during relevant instructional situations. Development and appropriate use of a knowledge base to inform educational practice will lead to better professional decision making and more confident and systematic professional practice, but without oppressing or deskilling teachers. On the contrary, in the long run, the development and appropriate use of an educational knowledge base can be expected to have parallel benefits for teachers to the benefits that the medical knowledge base has had for physicians.

Note

This work is sponsored in part by the Institute for Research on Teaching, College of Education, Michigan State University. The institute is funded from a variety of federal, state, and private sources, including the U.S. Department of Education and Michigan State University. The opinions expressed in this publication do not necessarily reflect the position, policy, or endorsement of the funding agencies. I wish to thank W. John Crawford for his comments on an earlier version on this article, and June Smith for her assistance in manuscript preparation.

REFERENCES

Anderson, C. W., & Smith, E. (1987). Teaching science. In V. Richardson-Koehler (Ed.), *Educators' handbook: A research perspective* (pp. 84–111). New York: Longman.

Brophy, J. (1981). Teacher praise: A functional analysis. *Review of Educational Research, 51*, 5–32.

Brophy, J., & Good, T. (1986). Teacher behavior and student achievement. In M. C. Wittrock (Ed.), *Handbook of research on teaching* (3d ed., pp. 328–375). New York: Macmillan.

Cuban, L. (1984). *How teachers taught.* New York: Longman.

Doyle, W. (1986). Classroom organization and management. In M. C. Wittrock (Ed.), *Handbook of research on teaching* (3d ed., pp. 392–431). New York: Macmillan.

Duffy, G., Roehler, L., Meloth, M., Vavrus, L., Book, C., Putnam, J., & Wesselman, R. (1986). The relationship between explicit verbal explanations during reading skill instruction and student awareness and achievement: A study of reading teacher effects. *Reading Research Quarterly, 21*, 237–252.

Evertson, C. (1985). Training teachers in classroom management: An experimental study in secondary school classrooms. *Journal of Educational Research, 79,* 51–58.

Good, T., & Brophy, J. (1987). *Looking in classrooms* (4th ed.). New York: Harper & Row.

Lampert, M. (1985). How do teachers manage to teach? Perspectives on problems in practice. *Harvard Educational Review, 55,* 178–194.

Myers, M. (1986). When research does not help teachers. *American Educator,* 10(2), 18–23, 46.

Paris, S., Cross, D., & Lipson, M. (1984). Informed strategies for learning: A program to improve children's reading awareness and comprehension. *Journal of Educational Psychology, 76,* 1239–1252.

Prawat, R. (1985). Affective versus cognitive goal orientation in elementary teachers. *American Educational Research Journal, 22,* 587–604.

Romberg, T. A., & Carpenter, T. P. (1986). Research on teaching and learning mathematics: Two disciplines of scientific inquiry. In M. C. Wittrock (Ed.), *Handbook of research on teaching* (3d ed., pp. 850–873). New York: Macmillan.

Schoenfeld, A. (1979). Explicitly heuristic training as a variable in problem-solving performance. *Journal for Research in Mathematics Education, 10,* 173–187.

Stallings, J. (1980). Allocated academic learning time revisited, or beyond time on task. *Educational Researcher,* 8(11), 11–16.

READING 29   CAROLYN J. SWEERS
Teaching Students to Examine Their Lives

The importance of teaching Socratically has been a topic of much discussion in recent years. Mortimer Adler, perhaps the most famous advocate of this method, defines it as "questioning students about something they have read so as to help them improve their understanding of basic ideas and values" (1984, pp. 15–16). Over and over again, Adler makes the point that it is *books* that are being examined, not actual lives, although he admits that this is not exactly what Socrates did. He makes no mention of the fact that what was important to Socrates is the self-examination of an individual's life.

Reading Adler, I do not get a sense of the flesh-and-blood adolescents I teach who squirm and curse their way to truth and who think

From Carolyn J. Sweers, "Teaching Students to Examine Their Lives," *Educational Leadership* (May 1988):20–22. Reprinted with permission of the Association for Supervision and Curriculum Development. Copyright © 1988 by ASCD. All rights reserved.

they are critical thinkers just because they disagree with their parents. If we are to help young people deal constructively with the actual problems of their lives, we must, without sacrificing intellectual vigor for "relevance," make their problems a vital part of the curriculum. It is Socrates himself, I think, who can best show us how to do that.

Genuine Socratic questioning, the kind of questioning Socrates did, has to do with getting actual people, who have specific and often strong opinions, to examine carefully what they think they know. To Socrates this was important so that humans did not confuse their wisdom with the wisdom of the gods (an error that seems to have been made by the participants in "Irangate" and various other "gates" we've witnessed in recent years). Or, to say it another way, Socrates wanted people to recognize and revere the limits of human knowing. Such reverence, he said, will assist people in making the wisest possible choices about the conduct of their lives.

How, then, can we teach in such a way that students will think critically about their lives? There are two steps in doing this. The first has to do with a type of prereading exercise that taps into students' actual lives, the second with learning how to let the text itself function Socratically.

BEGINNING SOCRATIC QUESTIONING

Before the class discusses a topic from the text, the teacher should ask students to state their points of view about the topic *in writing*. Writing down their opinions gives people a vested interest in the topic; they have committed themselves. Students may change their original opinions, but there can be no denying the points from which they began.

There are direct and indirect ways of eliciting students' opinions. If the text's central issue is "power," either *political* (as perhaps in a social studies class) or *personal* (as in a novel or play dealing with human interactions), an example of a direct way would be to ask students to write their answers to questions such as: What is power? More specifically, who or what has power over you? Why? Do you have power over anyone or anything? If so, give specific examples. A Socratic examination of the examples could follow to discover what, in fact, a power issue is and to discover guidelines for dealing with such issues. (To prepare themselves for this process, teachers should study carefully one or more examples of Socratic dialogue.)

A less direct, less personal way of evoking students' views would be to show excerpts from a movie or television program and ask: Who has the power in this situation? What kinds of power? How is it used? With what success? Why? The point is that the focus of the prereading exercise should be on specific "true to life" examples before students proceed to consider an issue theoretically.

> **B**y his questions and by his example, Socrates showed how difficult self-examination is.

After one or more of these prereading exercises has been completed and after the teacher has elicited some common insights, it is time to proceed to the next step of the process: classroom discussion of the assigned text material.

USING A TEXT SOCRATICALLY

Preparing to teach a text Socratically is more than a matter of reading the text, underlining key points, and coming up with a set of questions to ask. That, in fact, is the easy part. The difficult but essential part of preparing for Socratic teaching is for each teacher to allow himself or herself to be questioned *by the text*. In confronting the text in this way, teachers submit their own lives and opinions to be questioned. Teachers who have engaged in this process will be better able to guide their students similarly.

To see how this process can be accomplished on the subject of power, study *Crito,* the dialogue in which Socrates tells why he cannot choose exile as punishment. The situation itself is fraught with power issues. The dialogue takes place in a courtroom, where Socrates has been found guilty of corrupting the young and not believing in the gods. The power of the state has tried him; the power of the state has found him guilty; the power of the state will determine punishment.

Does Socrates have any power? Apparently, or he would not be on trial. Although Socrates' own questioning renders the charges against him ridiculous, the state clearly regards him as a threat and wants him silenced. The state does not want to put Socrates to death. His accusers simply want him to go away and not bother them anymore. This he will not do. Socrates says if he is guilty of treason, he should be put to death. He says that the state is like a parent to him: its laws have governed the conditions of his life since his birth, have guided him in what to do and how to do it. If the state finds him guilty, he, as an individual, is not in a position to act as judge. The law is superior to the will of any and every individual.

The text of *Crito* functions as Socrates by challenging both teacher and students to answer questions such as the following: Has anyone in the class, the teacher included, ever regarded himself or herself as an exception to a rule? Has anyone ever stolen something (but not wished by so doing that everyone should steal)? In answering yes to these questions, are we saying by our actions that the "power" of the individual, by which we mean ourselves, is superior to the "power" that determines what other people should do? Can a government, or even a school for that matter, be run that way? Socrates did not think so. On the other hand, should we always do what our superiors tell us just because their decrees have the weight of tradition and law? Are there cases in which an exception is *right* and not just convenient?

The example of Socrates himself emphasizes individual courage and responsibility. This concept gives rise to such life-examining questions as: Has anyone in the class, the teacher included, failed to speak up on matters of conscience because of fearing the consequences? Has anyone, the teacher included, ever done or said something for the primary purpose of avoiding responsibility? Socrates was willing to die rather than be silent about matters which he regarded important. Thus, the example of his life, as recorded in *Crito,* confronts and questions us.

FULFILLING THE PURPOSE OF EDUCATION

"The unexamined life is not worth living," said Socrates. By his questions and by his example, he also showed how difficult self-examination is. Is the difficulty worth it? Yes, if as a result of our teaching, lives can improve and if thereby our students learn to be responsible citizens. After all, isn't that what we say is the purpose of education?

REFERENCE

Adler, Mortimer J. "The Conduct of Seminars." In Chapter I of *The Paideia Program: An Educational Syllabus.* New York: Macmillan, 1984.

READING 30 DON HAMACHEK
Psychodynamics of Teachers' Expectations

Predicting rain or sunny skies doesn't affect tomorrow's weather, but a Harris poll predicting victory or defeat for a certain political candidate can have a definite effect on the outcome. Betting on the flip of a coin doesn't change the odds, but letting an athlete know you've bet on him or her can considerably affect the performance. When Roger Bannister began training for the four-minute mile, almost no one believed it could be done. Bannister himself wasn't sure, but he has said many times, "I knew my trainer believed in me and I couldn't let him down." Thus, in 1954 he became the first person in the world to break the four-minute barrier with a 3'59.4" mile, something that today is done routinely by top-flight runners in competition. Charles E. Wilcox, former General Motors president, was fond of saying that one of the differences between good bosses and poor bosses is that "good bosses make their workers feel that they have more ability than they think they have so that they consistently do better work than they thought they could." More than hundred years ago Goethe observed, "Treat people as if they were what they ought to be and you help them to become what they are capable of being."

One person's expectancy of another person's behavior somehow becomes realized—not always, but enough so that increasing attention in recent years has been given to the idea of how self-fulfilling prophecies work in the classroom. Eliza Doolittle, who was changed from an awkward Cockney flower girl into an elegant lady in George Bernard Shaw's famous play *Pygmalion,* described the process involved quite simply: "The difference between a lady and a flower girl is not how she behaves, but how she is treated." Although it does not work quite so simply in the classroom, there is increasing evidence to suggest that perhaps one difference between poor students and good students is not how they behave but how they are treated. Like Eliza, students in school—whether in first grade or twelfth—have a tendency to perform as they are expected to perform.

A teacher's expectations for how any given student will perform academically is an essentially private prediction about the potential of that student. Although these expectations are not necessarily conscious, they nonetheless can act as powerful mediators between how students feel about themselves and how they perform academically. Before a student ever enters a classroom, he or she has been subjected to a myriad of inputs that have shaped his or her self-concept, behavior, and attitudes in certain directions. Acting on the information that is before them, real or imagined (perhaps a bit of both), teachers develop certain expectations for how well or how poorly certain students will do in their classrooms. It is a continuous cycle of inputs and outputs (see Figure 1). Notice the many input variables that influence who a student is as a total person. These variables influence a teacher's expectations, which in turn influence how a teacher interacts with any given student, which affects how the student responds to the teacher—and the cycle begins.

BENEFITS OF EXPLICIT, POSITIVE EXPECTATIONS

How and why do positive, clearly defined expectations influence students' behavior and performance? First, teachers' expectations make it clear to students that they cannot do what they want just because they want to do it. Having the opportunity to choose their own outside reading or writing on a topic of their choice or participating in class or not are important rights that all students should have opportunities to exercise. However, if that's all there is, they may seldom be stretched beyond the safety of their own choices. I say safety of their own choices because evidence exists to indicate that when people do only what they choose to do, they feel less successful and competent, even if they succeed, than those who accomplish a task that they did not choose and that represents another person's expectations.

Luginbuhl[1] noted, for example, that if people succeed at a problem that they choose from a number of problems, their feelings of success may be blunted by the knowledge that *they influenced the situation to make success more possible.* Thus it may not be wise for a teacher to permit students to have their own way (e.g., choose the number or kinds of books to read or the kind of paper to write) *all the time.* Living up to a teacher's expectations (e.g., writing a report on an assigned topic and handing it in on time) is another way students can feel suc-

Excerpted selection from Chapter 10 in *Encounters with the Self,* Third Edition, by Don Hamachek, copyright © 1987 by Holt, Rinehart and Winston, Inc., reprinted by permission of the publisher.

can successfully handle these on an everyday basis.

Expectations perform another important function: They relay the message that students have the ability to do what is required of them. When set at reasonable, reachable levels, expectations represent a positive vote of confidence. Expectations say, "This is what needs to be done and I know you can do it."

EXPECTATIONS MAY BECOME SELF-FULFILLING PROPHECIES

Although merely wishing for something is not likely to make it come true, our expectations do influence the way we behave, and the way we behave affects how other people respond. In fact, the expectations we have about people can cause us to interact with them so that they respond just as we thought they would. This justifies our original expectations (predictions), and thus a self-fulfilling prophecy is born.

For example, suppose you were considering taking a course from an instructor you knew nothing about and wanted to talk to him about course requirements. You ask a friend about him and you are told, "Mr. Brown is a terrific person. He knows his stuff, he has a sense of humor, he's a warm sort of person and he's easy to talk to—someone you'll like." After this, how do you think you would respond to Mr. Brown when meeting him for the first time? However, suppose your friend had said, "You're thinking of taking a course with Brown? Well, I'd be careful if I were you. It's hard to feel comfortable with him. He seems so... well, cold and abrupt. I never had the feeling that he enjoyed talking to people." If you heard this, how would you react to Mr. Brown?

If you are like most people, your response to Mr. Brown would be quite different depending on which of these contrasting characteriza-

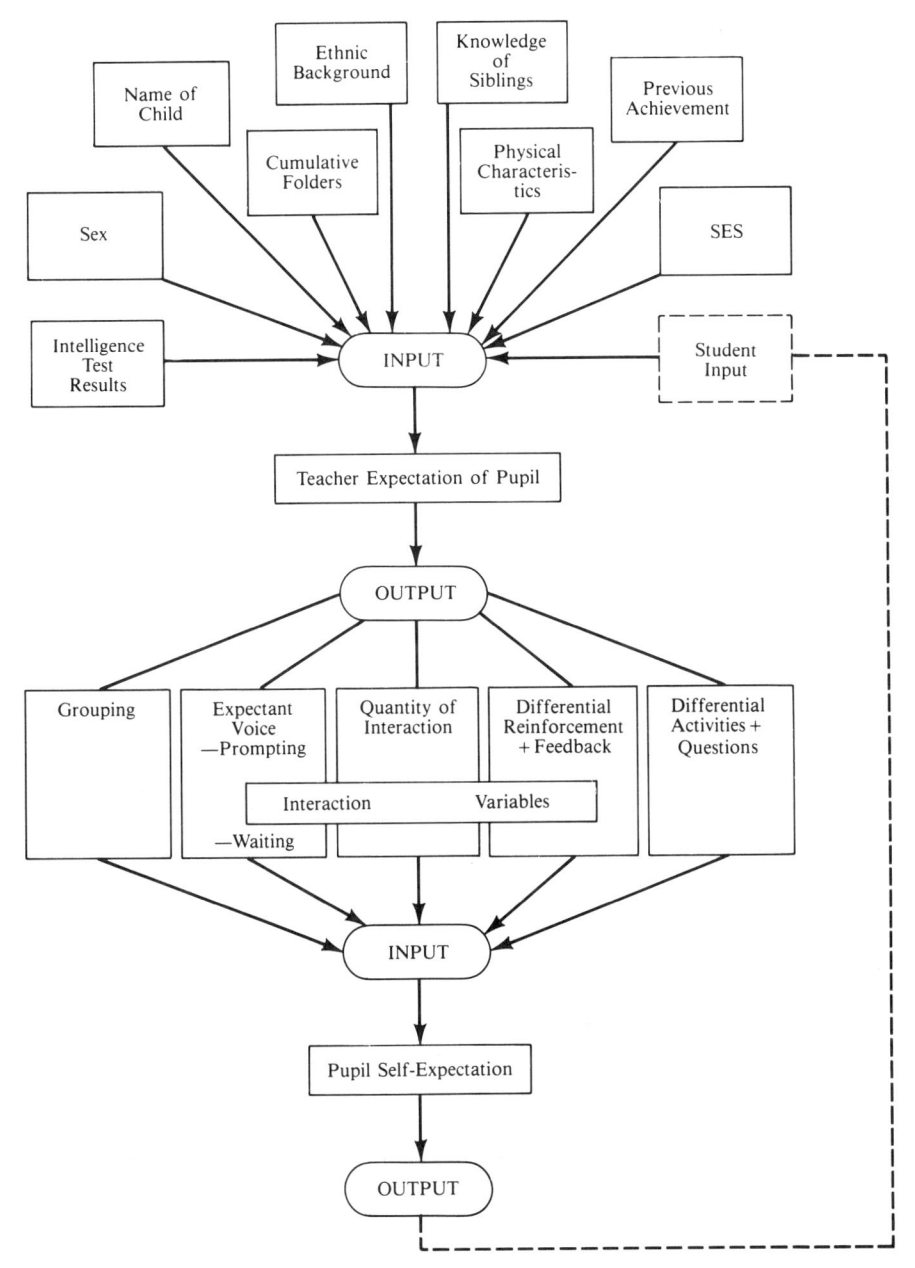

FIG. 1. The Behavioral Cycle of Pupil Behavior, Teacher Expectations, and Student Achievement.
Adapted from C. Braun, "Teacher Expectations: Sociopsychological Dynamics," *Review of Educational Research*. 1976, No. 46:413. Copyright 1976, American Educational Research Association, Washington, D.C.

cessful and thereby add to their feelings of competence and self-esteem.

Clearly defined teachers' expectations can serve as an important framework of students' self-evaluation. For instance, if Johnny is supposed to keep quiet when someone is talking and does it, he *knows* he's successful. If Janice knows she's expected to participate in class discussion and does it, she *knows* she tried her best. If Cathy is supposed to have a book report in by Friday and she does it, she *knows* she successfully lived up to an expectation. In other words, expectations let students know that a definition of their school environment is possible, that the world does impose restrictions and make demands, and that they

tions you had heard. If you had heard the first description, you would probably look forward to your visit with him; you might tell him that you had heard he was a fine instructor and someone with whom students liked to talk. You might further say that you were looking forward to taking his course and would ask if he could tell you a bit about it. If, on the other hand, you had heard the second description, you might approach your appointment with apprehension and hesitancy. You might look somewhat serious and guarded and present yourself in a more formal, businesslike manner.

Now, put yourself in Mr. Brown's shoes. He knows nothing about you as a person and reacts solely on the basis of his impressions of you during that initial meeting. Consider for a moment how he might respond to the person you present yourself as being in the two approaches just described. Learning in the first instance that you heard he was a fine instructor, that students liked him, and that you were looking forward to taking his class, he probably would feel good about himself and you. Your behavior might help him feel comfortable with you and perhaps even more willing to spend a little extra time answering your questions. What you see in his behavior would tend to confirm what you thought about him in the first place.

If you approached Mr. Brown somewhat nervously and formally, as in the second instance, no doubt he would respond in kind. If he were not already a somewhat nervous and formal person, he might soon become one. Sensing your cautious mood, he might feel that you really didn't want to spend a lot of time with him, even that you didn't like him. In light of your behavior, he might conclude that attempts at small talk would be risky, so he would give you the information you wanted, you would be on your way, and you would think to yourself, "My friend was right—he *is* cold; he really *doesn't* enjoy talking to people."

Thus a self-fulfilling prophecy is not the outgrowth of an expectation; rather, it is an outgrowth of the behavior that the expectation produces. This behavior has an effect on other people, which increases the likelihood that they will act in expected ways. Expectations not only cause us to notice some things and not to notice others but also affect the way we *interpret* what we notice. In the classroom the process involved may work something like this:

1. Based on what the teacher has read about or heard from others regarding particular students, he or she develops certain ideas and expectations about their achievement.
2. As a result of different expectations, the teacher behaves differently with different students.
3. The students infer from the teacher's behavior that they either are or are not good students, which has an effect on their self-concepts of ability and levels of aspiration.
4. If the teacher's behavior is consistent, and if students are susceptible to its input, it will affect their achievement in the direction of the expectations. High-expectation students will be more likely to achieve at high levels, and low-expectation students will be more likely to achieve at low levels.

These changes do not occur automatically, nor do they occur with all students because a teacher may not have explicit expectations for them. A high-school English teacher in one of my graduate classes said, "I try to make it a point *not* to expect that my students have to end up at a certain level at the end of my course. I do have the general hope —call it an expectation if you like —that they will improve their English skills, but I try not to have any specific expectations for particular students as to how *much* they will or should improve." Also, a student might prevent expectations from becoming self-fulfilling by offering a steady resistance to their effects. I have heard many accounts from students who said they were subjected to teachers' negative expectations, but refused to bend. As one college senior said, "I had a math teacher who told me more times than I can count that I was one of his 'slower' students and that I may want to consider going to a trade school to learn a specific skill rather than to college, which was my dream. On more than one occasion I remember thinking, 'You're wrong and I'll show you.'"

TEACHERS' EXPECTATIONS AND STUDENTS' ACHIEVEMENT

Rosenthal and Jacobson's book *Pygmalion in the Classroom*[2] was the first major research showing that a teacher's expectations can influence students' performance and behavior in school. Within each of the six grades in a particular school were classrooms in which children performed at above-average, average, and below-average levels of scholastic achievement. In each of these classes, an average of 20 percent of the children were identified to the teachers as having scores on the *Test for Intellectual Blooming* that suggested they would show unusual academic gains during the academic year. Actually, the children had been picked at random from the total population of children taking the same test. Eight months after the experimental conditions were instituted, all children were retested with the same IQ test.

For the school as a whole, those children from whom the teacher had been led to expect greater intellectual gain showed significantly greater gain in IQ score than did other children in the school. In fact, the lower the grade level, the greater the IQ gain. Apparently teachers interacted with the "brighter" children more positively and more favorably, and the children responded in kind, showing greater gains in IQ. One reason there was more change in the lower grades is that younger children are generally more malleable, less fixed, and more capable of change. Also, younger children do not have firmly established reputations, which can be passed on from one teacher to the next. It may be erroneous to suggest that as students get older, teachers' interactions with them are determined to some extent by the kind of "reputation" (good student or poor, delinquent or well-behaved) they have established.

A typical Pygmalion effect is illustrated in Figure 2, which shows the results of a study by Keshock[3] involving inner-city black boys aged seven to eleven in second to fifth grades, most of whom were not doing well in school. The teacher in each grade was given the actual ability test scores for a randomly chosen half of the class and ability test scores that were artificially raised one standard deviation higher than the actual scores for the other half of the class. As in the Rosenthal and Jacobson experiment, teachers were led to believe that half of their students were much more capable than their actual test scores would have suggested. At the end of the year the students the teachers believed were brighter (the experimental groups) showed larger gains on reading and arithmetic tests than those whose true ability scores had been given to the teachers (the control groups). You can see in Figure 2 that the experimental groups in grades two and three made significant gains, although the experimental group in the fifth grade barely held its own. As in the Rosenthal and Jacobson study, the younger children were more affected by positive expectations, perhaps for the same reasons. The control group in the fifth grade actually lost ground, suggesting that whatever factors affected the performance of the experimental group also affected the controls. Still, the overall results show that if teachers think certain pupils are smarter, those pupils tend to perform better.

The Rosenthal and Jacobson and Keshock research is somewhat unique in that it involves the artificial manipulation of test scores to influence teachers' expectations. Later studies[4,5] have done the same thing and have come up with somewhat similar conclusions. What happens, however, when teachers form their *own* expectations based on their own experiences?

Seaver[6] studied teachers' "natural expectancies" by analyzing the performance of 27 elementary-school students who had older siblings precede them in school by no more than three grade levels and who, in addition, had the same teachers. Seaver reasoned that teachers who had taught a student's older brother or sister would have a built-in expectancy for the younger child, high if the older child did well and low if he or she did poorly. In addition, the school environment provided a natural control group of students whose older siblings had different teachers. Seaver found that teachers' expectations did, indeed, make a difference. When the older siblings' performance had been high, the performance of children in the high-expectancy group was higher than that of the control group on eight different measures of academic achievement. When the older siblings' performance had been low, the expectancy group scored lower than the controls on seven of the eight tests. Research proves what we may always have suspected: The reputation that older siblings in a family establish in school is passed on to their brothers and sisters, and teachers tend to expect—and therefore get—from the younger members of the family what they had learned to expect from the older ones.

Additional support for the power of naturally induced expectations comes from an investigation by Palardy,[7] who found that if first-grade teachers believed boys would achieve as well as girls in reading, the boys did, in fact, perform better than boys having teachers who be-

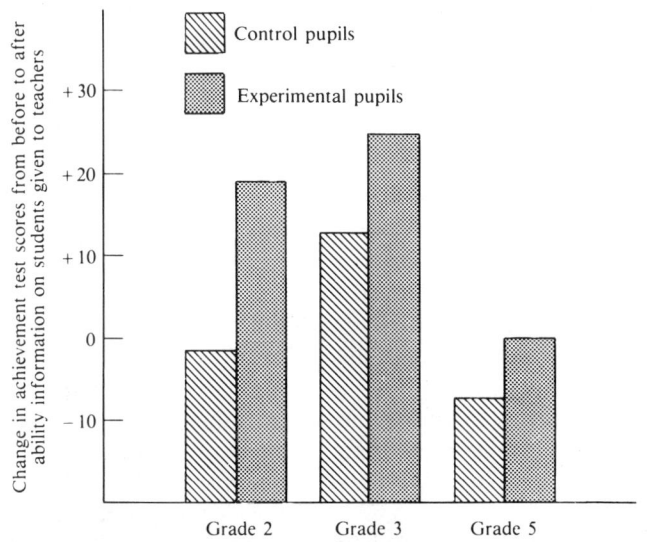

FIG. 2 Effects on Pupil Achievement Test Scores of Telling Teachers Their Actual Ability Scores (Control Pupils) or Scores Considerably Higher than Actually Attained (Experimental Pupils).

From J. D. Keshock, "An Investigation of the Effects of the Expectation Phenomenon Upon the Intelligence, Achievement, and Motivation of Inner City Elementary School Children." Unpublished doctoral dissertation. Case Western Reserve University, 1970.

lieved girls were better readers. Another study along this vein by Doyle and his associates[8] found that elementary school teachers have a tendency to overestimate the IQs of girls and underestimate the IQs of boys. The revealing aspect is that even though there was no *actual* IQ difference between boys and girls, the girls showed higher reading achievement. Not only that, *but within both sexes, the children whose IQs had been overestimated by teachers showed higher reading achievement.* Remember, actual IQ is not the important factor here. What seems to make a difference is the teacher's *perceptions or beliefs* about a particular student's IQ, which in turn sets in motion certain expectancies.

Although Rosenthal's original expectancy research has been criticized by some researchers[9,10,11] for shortcomings in design and methodology, none of those criticisms denied the possibility that teachers' expectations may be a crucial variable in students' learning. Since the first trickle of studies related to expectations in the mid-1960s, a plethora of expectancy research has been done and, for that matter, is still going on. Not all research supports the expectancy phenomenon, but much of it does. For example, Rosenthal[12] reviewed 242 studies and found that in 84 of them the experimenter's or teacher's expectations made a significant difference in how subjects performed in various situations. Eighty-four may not seem like a large number of supporting studies. However, if we apply the rules of statistical significance, we would expect that only about 5 percent of those 242 studies (about 12) would have occurred when predicted just by chance. The fact that we have 84, seven times more than chance would dictate, suggests that expectations do indeed affect performance in certain circumstances. Several large-scale reviews[13,14,15] of expectancy research tend to confirm this conclusion.

On the basis of the evidence, there seems little question that teachers' expectations make a difference. However, as Brophy and Good[16] noted, these effects are far from universal. Not all teachers will become Pygmalions, nor will all students be affected by their expectations. Teachers' expectations contain no magic. Students will not do better or work as hard as they are able just because a teacher "expects" or "believes" that they can do good work. This is not what is meant when teachers' expectations are referred to as self-fulfilling prophecies. Expectations have the potential to be self-fulfilling because teachers (and others) do certain things to communicate their expectations, an idea we turn to next.

COMMUNICATION OF POSITIVE EXPECTATIONS

To explain how positive expectations are communicated, Rosenthal[17] proposed a "four-factor theory" of the influences that are likely to encourage students to do well. As Rosenthal sees it, when teachers have positive expectations they tend to

1. Give more positive feedback to those students about their performance (feedback factor).
2. Give their special students more opportunities to respond to questions (output factor).
3. Create a warmer social-emotional mood for their "special students" (climate factor).
4. Teach more material and more difficult material to their special students (input factor).

You may find it useful to think of the acronym *FOCI* as an aid to remembering how you can channel your efforts for positive expectations.

F—eedback: give more positive feedback
O—utput: give more opportunities for student output
C—limate: create a warm, invitational climate
I—nput: give students more input

The actual mechanics by which expectations are communicated are complex. The words spoken are important, to be sure. But so, too, are the subtle nuances built into the interactions that go on between teacher and student—for example, tone of voice, facial expression, posture, and other kinds of body English. Chaiken and his associates[18] studied nonverbal cues of that sort to learn how teachers' expectations are actually transmitted. They found that teachers anticipating superior performance from their students engaged in more positive nonverbal behaviors—among them smiling, leaning toward the student, making eye contact, and nodding affirmatively—than teachers with either no expectations or with low expectations. These results strongly suggest that even when teachers do not tell students outright what the world anticipates from them, the message is still there in subtle but potent ways.

COMMUNICATION OF NEGATIVE EXPECTATIONS

The transmission of low expectations is a subtle packaging of words, gestures, and interactions, which, when received by certain students on a daily basis, has the cumulative effect of influencing their work in a downward direction. Most teachers are sincerely unaware of the things they do and say that may detrimentally affect their students. Hence, it is important to develop an awareness of those behaviors that are most often associated with low expectations.

Good and Brophy[19] received a large body of research related to teachers' expectations and found an almost endless list of ways that, directly or indirectly, communicate to students the idea that they are not very capable. For example, consider the following twelve things that teachers may do unwittingly that communicate negative expectations to low achievers:

1. Seating the lows farther away from the teacher, making it difficult to monitor these students or treat them as individuals
2. Paying less attention to lows, by smiling and making eye contact less often
3. Calling on lows less frequently (thereby giving them fewer opportunities to be successful)
4. Waiting less time for lows to answer questions (thereby increasing their chances for not doing well)
5. Failing to help lows in problem situations
6. Criticizing lows more frequently for incorrect answers
7. Giving lows less feedback about their work (thereby reducing their opportunities for correcting mistakes)
8. Demanding less effort and less work from lows (thereby subtly communicating the idea that they are not capable of it)
9. Interrupting the performance of lows more frequently (thereby short-circuiting their opportunities to give correct answers)
10. Praising lows less often for correct or marginal responses
11. Interacting with lows more privately than publicly and monitoring and structuring their activities more closely (thereby communicating the idea that they *really* need special help)
12. Giving briefer and less informative feedback to the questions of lows (thereby communicating the idea that they are not important and/or not able to understand detailed answers)

As a result of daily dosages of such cues, slower students become less willing to risk volunteering answers or seeking the teachers' help. They devote more of their time to trying to please the teacher than in learning subject matter. (Being accepted and cared about is a more basic need than learning math or English.) Without sufficient feedback, slow students are unable to evaluate how they are doing, and without sufficient contact with the students, teachers are less able to be helpful. It is a vicious circle.

A NOTE OF CAUTION ABOUT EXPECTATIONS

There is nothing mystical about how a teacher's expectations work and the influence these expectations can have on students' behavior and performance. If students strive to live up to their teachers' expectations, it will be not only because the expectations are reasonable but also because of the existence of an interpersonal relationship in which teachers are viewed as basically trustworthy, friendly, warm, and sure of themselves. Students, particularly at the elementary level, are anxious to please and will work hard to meet expectations when they like the teacher and are sure the teacher likes them.

Expectations are powerful, self-perpetuating attitudes for students as well as teachers because expectations guide both perceptions and behavior. When we expect to find something, we are far more likely to see it than when we are not looking for it. For example, if Steven hates going to cocktail parties because they are "always boring" and Susan loves cocktail parties because they are "exciting and fun," is it difficult to predict which of the two will have a good time or an awful time at the next cocktail party?

If, at the beginning of a new school year, one of Michael's ninth-grade teachers is told that he is "difficult to manage" because he is "so restless," and another teacher is told that he will "be a challenge" because he is "so intellectually curious," is it difficult to predict which teacher will see a problem and which teacher will see potential? Thus, expectations also affect the way we *interpret* what we notice, something we need to be conscious of in our interactions with others.

It is entirely possible that one teacher's reasonable expectations can become another teacher's unfair demands. If a teacher is viewed as harsh, authoritarian, and unfair, it may become a matter of face-saving principle and personal strength not to do what the teacher expects. We do not easily live up to the expectations of a dictator whose primary aim is to control or hurt us. We do, however, strive harder to cooperate with a person we see as having our best interests at heart.

REFERENCES

1. J. E. R. Luginbuhl, "Role of Choice and Outcome on Feelings of Success and Estimates of Ability," *Journal of Personality and Social Psychology,* 1972, 22:121–27.
2. R. Rosenthal and L. Jacobson, *Pygmalion in the Classroom: Teacher Expectation and Pupil's Intellectual Development* (New York: Holt, Rinehart and Winston, 1968).
3. J. D. Keshock, "An Investigation of the Effects of the Expectancy Phenomenon Upon the Intelligence, Achievement, and Motivation of Inner City Elementary School Children," (doctoral dissertation, Cleveland, Case Western University, 1970).
4. E. Y. Babad, J. Inbar, and R. Rosenthal, "Teachers' Judgment of Stu-

dents' Potential as a Function of Teachers' Susceptibility to Biasing Information," *Journal of Personality and Social Psychology,* 1982, 42: 541–47.
5. J. Guttman and C. Bar-tel, "Stereotypic Perceptions of Teachers," *American Educational Research Journal,* 1982, 19:519–28.
6. W. B. Seaver, "Effects of Naturally Induced Teacher Expectancies," *Journal of Abnormal and Social Psychology,* 1973, 28:333–42.
7. M. J. Palardy, "What Teachers Believe, What Children Achieve," *Elementary School Journal,* 1969, 69:370–74.
8. W. G. Doyle, G. Hancock, and E. Kifer, "Teacher Perceptions: Do They Make a Difference?" (paper presented at the annual meeting of the American Educational Research Association, Chicago, 1971).
9. W. J. Gephart, "Will the Real Pygmalion Please Stand Up?" *American Educational Research Journal,* 1970, 7:473–75.
10. R. Snow, "Unfinished Pygmalion," *Contemporary Psychology,* 1969, 14: 197–99.
11. R. L. Thorndike, "Review of Pygmalion in the Classroom," *American Educational Research Journal,* 1968, 5:708–11.
12. R. Rosenthal, "The Pygmalion Effect Lives," *Psychology Today,* September, 1973, pp. 56–60.
13. C. Braun, "Teacher Expectations: Sociopsychological Dynamics," *Review of Educational Research,* 1976, 46:185–212.
14. H. Cooper and T. Good, *Pygmalion Grows Up: Studies in the Expectation Communication Process* (New York: Longman, 1983).
15. R. Weinstein, "Expectations in the Classroom: The Student Perspective" (paper presented at the annual meeting of the American Educational Research Association, New York, April, 1982).
16. J. Brophy and T. Good, *Teacher-Student Relationships: Causes and Consequences* (New York: Holt, Rinehart and Winston, 1974).
17. R. Rosenthal, *On the Social Psychology of the Self-fulfilling Prophecy: Further Evidence of Pygmalion Effects and Their Mediating Mechanisms* (New York: MSS Modular Publications, 1973).
18. A. Chaiken, E. Sigler, and V. Derlega, "Non-Verbal Mediators of Teacher Expectancy Efforts," *Journal of Personality and Social Psychology,* 1974, 30:144–49.
19. T. L. Good and J. E. Brophy, *Looking in Classrooms,* 3rd ed. (New York: Harper & Row, 1984), pp. 94–121.

READING 31   MARK MEDOFF
In Praise of Teachers

I find myself lamenting that the more I write, the less time I have for my students. Though I am in my 21st year as a professor, I wonder: have I stopped thinking of myself as a teacher?

This crisis of faith has me remembering in turn *my* teachers, hoping that two decades after I was last officially a student I can learn from them once again. It is not the actual teaching of a subject I recall, but surprisingly one thing—a moment, some words hurled forth, a single seminal idea.

I forget the name of my first-grade teacher in Grayville, Ill. I must have begun to learn from her to read and write, to add and subtract—starting a lifetime of joy in language and misery in numbers.

That's not my primary memory, though: she teaches me left from right. I am left-handed. "Many first-grade teachers," she whispers into my six-year-old ear, "force left-handed children to become right-handed, so they can be like everybody else." She isn't going to do that to me. This teacher will always live in my memory for that one remarkable gesture.

In 1948 we move to a small island east of Miami, which festoons upward in stucco and rococo glory out of a stretch of seashore and sand. It's called Miami Beach.

There Mrs. Rosen awaits me, raven-haired and beautiful, reminiscent somehow of Esther in the Bible. Her husband shows up one day, and she tells us he is going to teach us to draw a star. It has never occurred to me that she has a husband. (I imagine her waiting for me to grow up to have her for my own.) And why should he teach us to draw a star? Everybody knows how to draw stars. (Is that how we'll decide who gets her—who can draw the best star?)

But Mrs. Rosen's husband doesn't teach us to draw just any star. He teaches us to draw a four-pointed, three-dimensional star that appears to rise out of a flat piece of paper. This is something called an *optical illusion.* Magic!

Into Mrs. Rosen's class one day slouches a lanky lady with ray-gun eyes and skin like polished glass. Miss Barnette is director of the Marching Unit, a group of 20 boys

From Mark Medoff, "In Praise of Teachers," *New York Times Magazine* (November 9, 1986). Copyright © 1986 by The New York Times Company. Reprinted by permission.

in white ducks and white shirts who do close-order drill for fancy school occasions. Miss Barnette also heads the Safety Patrol, made up of select students who wear the most extraordinary white bandoliers across their chests and are charged with managing the safe conduct of children from one side of the busy street in front of the school to the other. To a boy's mind these are the two most prestigious enterprises in Biscayne Elementary School.

Mrs. Rosen announces that Miss Barnette is about to do something she has never done before: choose a fourth-grader for the Marching Unit, an organization heretofore made up solely of fifth- and sixth-graders—Big Kids. *Unbelievable!* More unbelievable is that—while I'm glancing around enviously at the likely candidates—she picks me.

In the fifth and sixth grades, I am a Patrolboy and the leader of the Marching Unit. Miss Barnette repeatedly preaches with religious fervor an idea I still embrace obsessively: "If you're going to do something, do it as well as you can and with all your heart, and if you're going to lead, stand forward, be proud." My own variation on her preachment is that you can't ever fully succeed unless you're willing to risk catastrophic failure.

In the sixth grade, Mrs. Ruth Waller, auburn-haired and freckled, so tough and so fair, makes me feel, for the first time, that I not only can be a member of the Marching Units and Safety Patrols of the world, but also a *good student.*

She and Miss Barnette are wise, stern, loving. And I am loath now, a middle-aged man, to think what I might be if fate had not conspired to place them in my life so they could see in me what I did not.

At Miami Beach High School, my English teachers torment me to read, to consume vocabulary and to write constantly. "Pat" Samuelson, tenth grade, handsome guy, has one of the top ten pompadours in the history of hair. I deeply covet most of the girls who deeply covet him. He makes us write a short story.

To my astonishment (because I still can't imagine I *really, seriously, no-kidding-around* have any particular worth whatsoever), he tells the class that he's giving me the first "A+" he's ever given, and he asks me if I'd read my story aloud.

I'm terrified! Part of my terror is simple stage fright; part, fear of having my secret self publicly judged. But Mr. Samuelson beckons me forward and his entire demeanor says: don't be afraid of *anything.* So I take my story from him and, in the space of 20 minutes of glory and befuddlement, write a sentence across my life: Mark Medoff, you are hereby condemned, for the rest of your days, to expose your secret self publicly.

In the first semester of my freshman year at the University of Miami, there is Dr. Robert Hively, who has given up a prospering career in optometry to teach literature. He conveys no regrets that he's making a third of the money he made before. He seems utterly delighted to be in a classroom with us, charged with salvaging and enhancing another kind of vision.

He has let his curly hair grow somewhat eccentrically for 1958, and he drives a small sports car I crave, which, given his good size, he appears to wear around his waist. He teaches me to think beyond generalities. This is not easy—especially when, at 18, I am armed with too little knowledge and intellectual dexterity to give specifics. But it is with Dr. Hively that I see for the first time how thoughtlessly one can label someone or something unfairly, incompletely, disastrously.

Dr. Helen Garlinghouse-King looks and sounds as if she came to us directly from her specialty, the Victorian Era. In the second semester of my freshman year, this seemingly remote and formal scholar with the bun and the ankle-length rayon dresses is my advanced-composition teacher. She's a stickler for grammar. She considers my use of the dash—which I hold to be "creative"—to be absolutely barbaric.

I ambush her boldly after class one day and ask if I can write a short story for next week instead of the assigned paper. Her eyes bore into me, reading *what* inside I can't imagine: "I don't know if you *can*," she says, "but you may try." And she smiles. At me.

At one o'clock in the morning the day after I turn in my story, I am awakened by the telephone. I wonder instinctively who has died. Instead of death, there is at the other end of the line the sepulchral voice of Dr. King, bearing life: "There's nothing more I can teach you about writing. I'm passing you on."

Extraordinary: to be passed on! To William Fred Shaw, teacher of a legendary course in creative writing. For 3½ years of college and for years of frustrating young adulthood beyond, Fred Shaw taunts me, cajoles, devastates and encourages me. And he teaches me most of what little I know about writing, the chief things being: there are only two ways to learn to write—read, write. And if you don't *have* to write, by all means go into other work; the frustration and rejection are not worth enduring unless one is unequivocally committed.

This slightly stooped man with ferret eyes and a laugh like volleying bazookas seems able to make each student feel he's Fred Shaw's *only* student and that Fred Shaw has little more to do in life than foster that individual's growth. He is still, aside from my parents, the single strongest influence in my life.

As a young man, Fred Shaw taught at a cow college called New Mexico State University in Las Cruces. When I'm ready to leave Stanford

University graduate school in 1966, Fred arranges for me to follow in his footsteps.

In Las Cruces, I am an instructor of English. I write prose and announce that I'll publish a novel soon. I convince several people of this, though deep in me where the truth resides I think I'm writing one of the worst novels since the advent of the alphabet.

I am also confused on another front. I don't see how, just because I've finished graduate school, I'm suddenly supposed to be a "grown-up." I'm a kid, unformed and un*in*formed, the antithesis in my mind of what I have been hired to be: a teacher. What do I know to *teach*?

There are teachers at New Mexico State University who teach me. In my first semester, I become friendly with a professor of English named John Hadsell, who is deeply involved in something called the Las Cruces Community Theater. One day he says to me, "Why don't you write a play and we'll put it on?" I do and that first play, then a one-acter, opens eight years later in New York, this time as a three-act play. The teaching gift John gives me is as great as the putting-on of my first play: a teacher has to be totally unafraid of what he might find out as he teaches what he thinks he already fully comprehends.

Arline Belkin and Tom Erhard, colleagues now in the university's theater-arts department, are role models of 20 years' standing. Through all the semesters I watch Tom teach, I never see any lessening in him of the love of what he's teaching or the love of classroom exchange—the teaching of the students *and* the students' continual teaching of the teacher. His commitment is a way of living a life.

Arline Belkin, a kitty cat disguised as a panther, takes me back to Miss Barnette and Mrs. Waller. It is she who admonishes me constantly to push myself, to go boldly, even recklessly, wherever I dare—that complacency makes for atrophy, and atrophy precedes death.

In 1972, I return to Miami Beach High School to speak to the drama class. Afterward I ask the drama teacher if any of my English teachers are still there. Irene Roberts, he tells me, is in class just down the hall.

I was no one special in Miss Roberts's class—just another jock who did okay work. I don't recall any one special bit of wisdom she passed on. Yet I cannot forget her respect for language, for ideas and for her students. I realize now, many years later, that she is the quintessential selfless teacher. I'd like to say something to her, I say, but I don't want to pull her from a class. Nonsense, he says, she'll be delighted to see me.

The drama teacher brings Miss Roberts into the hallway where stands this 32-year-old man she last saw at 18. "I'm Mark Medoff," I tell her. "You were my 12th-grade English teacher in 1958." She cocks her head at me, as if this angle might conjure me in her memory. And then, though armed with a message I want to deliver in some perfect torrent of words, I can't think up anything more memorable than this: "I want you to know," I say, "you were important to me."

And there in the hallway, this slight and lovely woman, now nearing retirement age, this teacher who doesn't remember me, begins to weep; and she encircles me in her arms.

Remembering this moment, I begin to sense that everything I will ever know, everything I will ever pass on to my students, to my children, is an inseparable part of an ongoing legacy of our shared wonder and eternal hope that we can, *must*, make ourselves better.

Irene Roberts holds me briefly in her arms and through her tears whispers against my cheek, "Thank you." And then, with the briefest of looks into my forgotten face, she disappears back into her classroom, returns to what she has done thousands of days through all the years of my absence.

On reflection, maybe those were, after all, just the right words to say to Irene Roberts. Maybe they are the very words I would like to speak to all those teachers I carry through my life as part of me, the very words I would like spoken to me one day by some returning student: *"I want you to know you were important to me."*

CHAPTER ELEVEN

Motivational Strategies for Encouraging Student Achievement

READING 32 JERE BROPHY
Synthesis of Research on Strategies for Motivating Students to Learn

This article synthesizes the conclusions drawn from a review of the literature on motivation conducted to identify principles suitable for use by teachers, especially principles for motivating students to learn during academic activities. To begin with, student *motivation to learn* can be conceptualized either as a general trait or as a situation-specific state. The *trait* of motivation to learn is an enduring disposition to strive for content knowledge and skill mastery in learning situations. The *state* of motivation to learn exists when student engagement in a particular activity is guided by the intention of acquiring the knowledge or mastering the skill that the activity is designed to teach.

From Jere Brophy. "Synthesis of Research on Strategies for Motivating Students to Learn," *Educational Leadership* (October 1987):40–48. Reprinted with permission of the Association for Supervision and Curriculum Development. Copyright © 1987 by ASCD. All rights reserved.

Several conceptual distinctions implied by these definitions of student motivation to learn guided my review of the literature. Student motivation to learn is an acquired competence developed through general experience but stimulated most directly through modeling, communication of expectations, and direct instruction or socialization by significant others (especially parents and teachers). If activated in particular learning situations, motivation to learn functions as a scheme or script that includes not only affective elements but also cognitive elements such as goals and associated strategies for accomplishing the intended learning. According to this view, teachers are not merely reactors to whatever motivational patterns their students had developed before entering their classrooms but rather are *active socialization agents* capable of stimulating the general development of student motivation to learn and its activation in particular situations.

However, teachers work within certain restrictions. Schools are formal institutions that students are required to attend in order to learn a prescribed curriculum, and classrooms are public settings where performance is monitored by peers and graded by teachers. If teachers were recreation program directors, they could solve motivation problems merely by finding out what their clients like to do and arranging for them to do it. Instead, like supervisors in work settings, teachers must find ways to motivate their students voluntarily to try to do well what is required of them.

Schools are not ordinary work settings, however; they are settings for learning. With a few exceptions (penmanship, zoology dissection skills), school learning is covert and conceptual, not overt and behavioral. We need a clear distinction between learning and performance: *learning* refers to the information-processing, sense-making, and comprehension or mastery advances that occur during the acquisition of knowledge or skill; *performance* refers to the demonstration of such knowledge or skill after it has been acquired. The term *motivation to learn* refers not just to the motivation that drives later performance but also to the motivation underlying the covert processes that occur during learning. Therefore, strategies for motivating students to learn apply not only to performance on tests or assignments, but also to information-processing activities (paying attention to lessons, reading for understanding, paraphrasing ideas) initially involved in learning the content or skills. The emphasis is not merely on offering students incentives for good performance later but on stimulating them to use thoughtful learning. Thus, strategies for stimulating motivation to learn differ from strategies for supplying extrinsic motivation for performance.

They also differ from strategies for capitalizing on students' intrinsic motivation, because intrinsic motivation is not the same as motivation to learn. *Intrinsic motivation* usually refers to the affective aspects of motivation—liking for or enjoyment of an activity. Intrinsic motivation, even for academic activities, does not necessarily imply motivation to learn. For example, students may enjoy participating in an educational game without trying to derive any academic benefit from it. Similarly, students can try to learn the knowledge or skills that an activity is designed to teach without enjoying the activity.

Guided by these distinctions concerning the nature of schooling and of student motivation, I have searched the literature for theory and research that suggest principles suitable for application by teachers in classrooms. This review and synthesis work has yielded the strategies summarized in the "Highlights" box (Ames and Ames 1984, 1985, Brophy 1983, Corno and Rohrkemper 1985, Deci and Ryan 1985, Keller 1983, Kolesnik 1978, Lepper and Greene 1978, Maehr 1984, Malone and Lepper in press, McCombs 1984, Nicholls 1984, and Wlodkowski 1978). For additional discussion and examples beyond this brief listing, see Brophy (1986a, b) or Good and Brophy (1986, 1987).

Development and organization of the list of strategies has been guided by *expectancy x value* theory (Feather 1982), which posits that the effort people will expend on a task is a product of: (1) the degree to which they *expect* to be able to perform the task successfully if they apply themselves; and (2) the degree to which they *value* participation in the task itself or the benefits or rewards that successful task completion will bring to them. This theory assumes that no effort will be invested in a task if either factor is missing entirely, no matter how much of the other factor may be present. People do not invest effort on tasks that do not lead to valued outcomes even if they know they can perform the tasks successfully, and they do not invest effort on even highly valued tasks if they are convinced that they cannot succeed no matter how hard they try.

The *expectancy x value* theory of motivation implies that, in order to motivate their students to learn, teachers must both help them to appreciate the value of academic activities and make sure that they can achieve success on these activities if they apply reasonable effort. The "Highlights" box is organized according to these *expectancy x value* theory ideas. First, it lists the preconditions necessary if teachers are to motivate their students. Second, it enumerates strategies that involve establishing and maintaining success expectations in the students. Third, it offers strategies that enhance the subjective value students place on school tasks. The latter strategies are subdivided into those that involve offering extrinsic incentives, taking advantage of intrin-

> **T**he simplest way to ensure that students expect success is to make sure they achieve it consistently.

sic motivation, or stimulating student motivation to learn.

ESSENTIAL PRECONDITIONS

No motivational strategies can succeed with students if the following preconditions are not in effect.

1. *Supportive environment.* If the classroom is chaotic or if the students are anxious or alienated, then students are unlikely to be motivated to learn academic content. Thus, in order to motivate students to learn, the teacher must organize and manage the classroom as an effective learning environment. This includes encouraging students, patiently supporting their learning efforts, and allowing them to feel comfortable taking intellectual risks without fear of being criticized for making mistakes.

2. *Appropriate level of challenge/ difficulty.* Students will be bored if tasks are too easy and frustrated if tasks are too difficult. They will be optimally motivated by tasks that allow them to achieve high levels of success when they apply reasonable effort.

3. *Meaningful learning objectives.* Teachers should select academic activities that teach some knowledge or skill that is worth learning, either in its own right or as a step toward a higher objective. It is not reasonable to expect students to be motivated to learn if they are continually expected to practice skills already thoroughly mastered,

memorize lists for no good reason, copy definitions of terms that are never used in readings or assignments, or read material that is not meaningful to them because it is too vague, abstract, or foreign to their experience.

4. *Moderation/optimal use.* Motivational attempts can be overdone, and any particular strategy can lose its effectiveness if it is used too often or too routinely.

> If teachers were recreation program directors, they could solve motivation problems merely by finding out what their clients like to do and arranging for them to do it.

MOTIVATING BY MAINTAINING SUCCESS EXPECTATIONS

Much of the best-known research on motivation is focused on the role of success expectations in determining performance. Research on *achievement motivation* (Dweck and Elliott 1983) has shown that effort and persistence are greater in individuals who set goals of moderate difficulty level, who seriously commit themselves to pursuing these goals, and who concentrate not on avoiding failure but on achieving success. Research on *efficacy perceptions* (Bandura and Schunk 1981) has shown that effort and persistence are greater in individuals who believe that they have the efficacy (competence) needed to succeed on a task than in individuals who lack it. Research on *causal attributions* for performance suggests that effort and persistence are greater in individuals who attribute their performance to internal or controllable causes rather than to external or uncontrollable ones (Weiner 1984). In particular, better performance is associated with a tendency to attribute success to a combination of sufficient ability with reasonable effort and a tendency to attribute failure either to insufficient effort (if this has been the case) or to confusion about what to do or reliance on an inappropriate strategy for doing it. The literature on motivation suggests that the following strategies (nos. 5–8) will help students maintain success expectations and associated goal setting behaviors, efficacy perceptions, and causal attributions.

5. *Program for success.* The simplest way to ensure that students expect success is to make sure they achieve it consistently. Teachers can accomplish this by beginning instruction at their level, moving in small steps, and preparing students sufficiently for each new step so that they can adjust to it without much confusion or frustration. Note that students' success levels will depend not only on task difficulty, but on the degree to which the teacher prepares the students for the task through advance instruction and assists their learning efforts through guidance and feedback.

6. *Teach goal setting, performance appraisal, and self-reinforcement skills.* Help students learn to set and commit themselves to goals that are: (1) near rather than far (they refer to tasks to be attempted here and now rather than to ultimate goals in the distant future); (2) specific (complete a page of math problems with no more than one error) rather than global (work carefully and do a good job); and (3) challenging rather than too easy or too hard. Provide specific, detailed feedback and help students use appropriate standards for judging their performance (i.e., to compare it with absolute standards or with their own previous progress rather than with the performance of peers), so that they can recognize their successes and reinforce themselves for their efforts.

7. *Help students to recognize linkages between effort and outcome.* Use modeling, socialization, and feedback to make students aware that the amount and quality of effort that they put into an activity determines what they get out of it. Portray effort as an investment, which will produce knowledge or skill development and thus empower students, rather than as a risk of failure or embarrassment. Portray skill development as incremental (open to improvement in small steps rather than fixed) and domain specific (students possess a great many different kinds of skills rather than a single IQ that determines performance in everything). Last, focus on mastery of instructional objectives rather than comparisons with the achievement of peers.

8. *Provide remedial socialization.* With discouraged students, use per-

> People do not invest effort on tasks that do not lead to valued outcomes even if they know they can perform the tasks successfully, and they do not invest effort on even highly valued tasks if they are convinced that they cannot succeed no matter how hard they try.

formance contracts, Mastery Learning Principles (additional instruction, practice opportunities, and make-up exams to allow struggling students to overcome initial failures through persistent efforts), and attribution retaining (teach students to concentrate on doing the task at hand rather than to become distracted by fears of failure; to cope with frustration by retracing their steps to find their mistake or analyzing the problem to find a better way to approach it; and to attribute failures to insufficient effort, lack of information, or reliance on ineffective strategies rather than to lack of ability).

Teachers can shape the ways students view their performance—what they see as achievable with reasonable effort, whether they define this achievement as successful, and whether they attribute their performance to their own efforts. Empty reassurances or a few words of encouragement will not do the job. Rather, a combination of appropriately challenging demands with systematic socialization designed to make students see that success can be achieved with reasonable effort should be effective.

The strategies described in this section have addressed the *expectancy* term of the *expectancy x value* formulation. The strategies explained in the next three sections address the *value* term.

MOTIVATING BY SUPPLYING EXTRINSIC INCENTIVES

Strategies for supplying extrinsic motivation do not attempt to increase the value that students place on the task itself but rather to link successful task performance with access to valued rewards.

9. *Offer rewards for good (or improved) performance*. In addition to grades, these may include: (1) material rewards (prizes, consumables); (2) activity rewards and special privileges (play games, use special equipment, engage in self-selected activities); (3) symbolic rewards (honor rolls, displays of good work); (4) praise and social rewards (teacher or peer attention); and (5) teacher rewards (opportunities to go places or do things with the teacher). Teachers should offer and deliver rewards in ways that call attention to developing knowledge and skills rather than in ways that encourage students to focus just on the rewards.

10. *Structure appropriate competition*. The opportunity to compete for prizes or recognition either as an individual or as a member of a team can add incentive to classroom activities. In addition to structuring competition based on test scores or other performance measures, teachers can build competitive elements into instruction by including activities such as argumentative essays, debates, or simulation games that involve competition (Keller 1983). Use handicapping systems such as those devised by Slavin (1983) to ensure that everyone has a good (or at least an equal) chance to win. It is also helpful to depersonalize their competition and emphasize the content being learned rather than who wins and who loses.

Extrinsic incentives and competition are more effective for stimulating intensity of effort than for inducing thoughtfulness or quality of performance. Thus, rewards and competition are best used with practice tasks designed to produce mastery of specific skills rather than with incidental learning or discovery tasks, and with tasks where speed of performance or quantity of output is of more concern than creativity, artistry, or craftsmanship.

11. *Call attention to the instrumental value of academic activities.* Where possible, note that the knowledge or skills developed by an academic task will enable students to meet their own current needs, provide them with a "ticket" to social advancement, or prepare them for success in an occupation or in life generally. Help students to see academic activities not as imposed demands to be resisted but rather as enabling opportunities to be valued.

Extrinsic motivational strategies are effective under certain circumstances, but teachers should not rely on them. When students are preoccupied with rewards or competition, they may not attend to or appreciate the value of what they are learning.

MOTIVATING BY CAPITALIZING ON STUDENTS' INTRINSIC MOTIVATION

Teachers can capitalize on intrinsic motivation by planning academic activities that students will engage in willingly because they are interested in the content or enjoy the task. Opportunities to do this are limited by several features inherent in the nature of schooling—compulsory attendance, externally prescribed curriculum, public monitoring, and grading of performance. Further, students differ in what they find interesting or enjoyable. Even so, teachers can schedule activities that incorporate elements that most students will find rewarding.

12. *Adapt tasks to students' interests*. Whenever curriculum objectives can be accomplished using a variety of examples or activities, incorporate content that students find interesting or activities that they find enjoyable. When giving examples or applications of concepts being learned, include people, fads, or events prominent in the news or in the youth culture.

13. *Include novelty/variety elements*. Make sure that something about each activity (its form or content, the media involved, or the nature of the responses it demands) is new to the students or at least different from what they have been doing recently. Do not allow a

> Extrinsic incentives and competition are more effective for stimulating intensity of effort than for inducing thoughtfulness or quality of performance.

steady diet of routine lessons followed by routine assignments to become "the daily grind."

14. *Allow choices or autonomous decisions.* Within the constraints imposed by the instructional objectives, offer students alternative ways to meet requirements and opportunities to exercise autonomous decision making and creativity in determining how to organize their time and efforts. If children make poor decisions when left completely on their own, provide them with a menu of choices or require them to get their choices approved before going ahead.

15. *Provide opportunities for students to respond actively.* Most students prefer activities that allow them to respond actively by interacting with the teacher or with one another, by manipulating materials, or by doing something other than just listening or reading. Provide students with opportunities to participate, for example, in projects, experiments, role-playing, simulations, educational games, and creative applications of what is being learned.

16. *Provide immediate feedback to student responses.* Students especially enjoy tasks that allow them not only to respond actively but to get immediate feedback they can use to guide subsequent responses. Automatic feedback features are built into programmed learning and other "self-correcting" materials as well as into computerized learning programs. Teachers can incorporate feedback features into typical activities by leading the group through an activity and then circulating to supervise students' progress during seatwork. Teachers can arrange for alternative sources of feedback when they cannot be available themselves by providing answer keys or instructions about how to check work, designating student helpers, or having students review their work in pairs or small groups.

17. *Allow students to create finished products.* Students prefer tasks that have meaning or integrity in their own right over tasks that are mere subparts of some larger entity. They are likely to experience a satisfying sense of accomplishment when they finish such tasks. Ideally, task completion will yield a finished product that students can use or display such as a map, an essay, a scale model, or something other than just another ditto or workbook page.

18. *Include fantasy or simulation elements.* Where more direct applications of what is being learned are not feasible, introduce fantasy or imagination elements that will engage students' emotions or allow them to experience events vicariously. In addition to full-scale drama, role-play, simulation games, and other "major productions," incorporate more modest simulation

> Students prefer tasks that have meaning or integrity in their own right over tasks that are mere subparts of some larger entity.

activities into everyday instruction. For example, stimulate students to think about the motives of a literary author or scientific discoverer or to imagine themselves living in the historical time or geographical place under study.

19. *Incorporate game-like features into exercise.* Transform ordinary assignments into "test yourself" challenges, puzzles, or brain teasers that:

- require students to solve problems, avoid traps, or overcome obstacles to reach goals.
- call for students to explore and discover in order to identify the goal itself in addition to developing a method for reaching it;
- involve elements of suspense or hidden information that emerges as the activity is completed (puzzles that convey a message or provide the answer to a question once they are filled in); or
- involve a degree of randomness or uncertainty about what the outcome of performance is likely to be on any given trial (e.g., knowledge games that cover assorted topics at a variety of difficulty levels and that are assigned according to some random method, such as in Trivial Pursuit).

Although many teachers associate "games" with team competitions, the term "game-like feature" has a much broader meaning; most of these features involve presenting intellectual challenges appropriate for use by individuals or by groups working cooperatively.

20. *Include higher-level objectives and divergent questions.* Most students soon become bored by a steady diet of knowledge- and comprehension-level questions. Therefore, include questions that address higher cognitive levels (application, analysis, synthesis, or evaluation) and encourage students to make sense of what they are learning by

Highlights of Research on Strategies for Motivating Students to Learn

Research on student motivation to learn indicates promising principles suitable for application in classrooms, summarized here for quick reference.

Essential Preconditions

1. Supportive environment
2. Appropriate level of challenge/difficulty
3. Meaningful learning objectives
4. Moderation/optimal use

Motivating by Maintaining Success Expectations

5. Program for success
6. Teach goal setting, performance appraisal, and self-reinforcement
7. Help students to recognize linkages between effort and outcome
8. Provide remedial socialization

Motivating by Supplying Extrinsic Incentives

9. Offer rewards for good (or improved) performance
10. Structure appropriate competition
11. Call attention to the instrumental value of academic activities

Motivating by Capitalizing on Students' Intrinsic Motivation

12. Adapt tasks to students' interests
13. Include novelty/variety elements
14. Allow opportunities to make choices or autonomous decisions
15. Provide opportunities for students to respond actively
16. Provide immediate feedback to student responses
17. Allow students to create finished products
18. Include fantasy or simulation elements
19. Incorporate game-like features
20. Include higher-level objectives and divergent questions
21. Provide opportunities to interact with peers

Stimulating Student Motivation to Learn

22. Model interest in learning and motivation to learn
23. Communicate desirable expectations and attributions about students' motivation to learn
24. Minimize students' performance anxiety during learning activities
25. Project intensity
26. Project enthusiasm
27. Induce task interest or appreciation
28. Induce curiosity or suspense
29. Induce dissonance or cognitive conflict
30. Make abstract content more personal, concrete, or familiar
31. Induce students to generate their own motivation to learn
32. State learning objectives and provide advance organizers
33. Model task-related thinking and problem solving

—Jere Brophy

> When the topic is familiar, counter students' tendency to think they already know everything there is to know about it by pointing out unexpected, incongruous, or paradoxical aspects....

processing it actively, paraphrasing it, and relating it to their prior knowledge and experience. Also, ask questions that elicit divergent thinking (opinions, predictions, suggested courses of action, or solutions to problems) in order to generate student responses that are more personal and creative.

21. *Provide opportunities to interact with peers.* Students enjoy activities that allow interaction with their peers. Build such opportunities into whole-class activities by scheduling discussion, debate, roleplay, or simulation. In addition, plan follow-up activities that permit students to work together in pairs or small groups to tutor one another, discuss issues, or develop suggested solutions to problems, or to work as a team preparing for a competition, participating in a simulation game, or producing some group product. Peer interactive activities are likely to be most effective if teachers: (1) make them worthwhile learning experiences rather than merely occasions for socializing by structuring them around curriculum objectives; and (2) arrange conditions so that every student has a substantive role to play and must participate actively (Slavin 1983).

STRATEGIES FOR STIMULATING STUDENT MOTIVATION TO LEARN

The strategies just described for capitalizing on intrinsic motivation should increase students' enjoyment of classroom activities; however, these strategies will not directly increase students' motivation to learn the content or skills being taught. The literature on motivation suggests that the following strategies will stimulate students to take academic activities seriously and to acquire the knowledge or skills that they were designed to develop. The first three strategies are general ones describing pervasive features of the learning environment that should be established in the classroom.

22. *Model interest in learning and motivation to learn.* Routinely model interest in learning by showing students that you value learning as a rewarding, self-actualizing activity that produces personal satisfaction and enriches your life. Share with students your interests in books, articles, TV programs, or movies on the subjects you teach. Mention applications of the subjects to everyday living, the local environment, or current events.

23. *Communicate desirable expectations and attributions about students' motivation to learn.* Routinely project attitudes, beliefs, expectations, and attributions concerning reasons for students' behavior which imply that you expect them to be curious, to want to understand concepts and master skills, and to see what they are learning as meaningful and applicable to their lives.

24. *Minimize students' performance anxiety during learning activities.* Protect students from premature concern about performance adequacy by structuring most activities to promote learning rather than to evaluate performance. When activities do include test-like items, treat these as opportunities for students to apply the material rather than as a chance for you to see who does or doesn't know the material. Combat test anxiety by minimizing time pressures, by portraying tests as opportunities to assess progress rather than as measures of ability, by giving pretests to accustom students to "failure" and provide a basis for marking progress, and by teaching stress management and test-taking skills (Hill and Wigfield 1984).

In addition to fostering a supportive learning environment through these general strategies, use the following strategies to stimulate student motivation to learn during specific activities.

25. *Project intensity.* Project a level of intensity that tells students that the material deserves close attention either by saying so or by using rhetorical devices (slow pacing, step-by-step presentation with emphasis on key words, unusual voice modulations or exaggerated gestures, scanning the group intensely at each step to look for signs of understanding or confusion). Projecting intensity is especially useful when introducing new content, demonstrating skills, or giving instructions for assignments.

26. *Project enthusiasm.* Present topics or assignments in ways that

> [Teachers can] portray effort as an investment, which will produce knowledge or skill development and thus empower students, rather than as a risk of failure or embarrassment.

suggest they are interesting or worthwhile by identifying your own reasons for finding the topic meaningful, and then communicate these reasons when teaching it.

27. *Induce task interest or appreciation.* Where relevant, elicit student appreciation for an activity by noting its connections with things that students already recognize as interesting or important, by mentioning applications of the knowledge or skills to be learned, or by specifying challenging or exotic aspects that the students can anticipate.

28. *Induce curiosity or suspense.* Put students into an active information-processing or problem-solving mode by posing questions or doing "set-ups" that introduce curiosity or suspense elements and motivate students to engage in the activity in order to answer some question, resolve an ambiguity, or fill in gaps in their knowledge.

29. *Induce dissonance or cognitive conflict.* When the topic is familiar, counter students' tendency to think that they already know everything there is to know about it by pointing out unexpected, incongruous, or paradoxical aspects; calling attention to unusual or exotic elements; noting exceptions to general rules; or challenging students to solve the "mystery" that underlies a paradox.

30. *Make abstract content more personal, concrete, or familiar.* Promote personal identification with content by relating experiences or telling anecdotes illustrating how the content applies to the lives of individuals (especially persons whom the students are interested in and likely to identify with). Make abstractions concrete by showing objects or pictures or by conducting demonstrations. Help students relate new or strange content to their existing knowledge by using examples or analogies referring to familiar concepts, objects, or events. Where a text is too abstract or sketchy, elaborate by filling in sufficient detail to enable students to visualize what is being described and explain it in their own words.

31. *Induce students to generate their own motivation to learn.* Do this by asking them to list their own interests in particular topics or activities, to identify questions that they would like to have answered, or to note things that they find surprising as they read.

32. *State learning objectives and provide advance organizers.* Stimulate motivation to learn when introducing activities by stating their objectives and by providing advance organizers. Prepare students to get more out of lectures, films, or reading assignments by clarifying what you want them to concentrate on as they process the information; distributing outlines or study guides; making suggestions about notetaking; or calling attention to structural features of the presentation that can help students to remember it in an organized way.

33. *Model task-related thinking and problem solving.* The information-processing and problem-solving strategies used when responding to academic tasks will be invisible to students unless teachers make them overt by showing students what to do and thinking out loud as they demonstrate. Such *cognitive modeling* is an important instructional advice. It is also an effective way to stimulate student motivation to learn because, through modeling, teachers expose students to the beliefs and attitudes associated with such motivation (e.g., patience, confidence, persistence in seeking solutions through information processing and rational decision making, benefiting from the information supplied by mistakes rather than giving up in frustration).

A STARTER SET

Although student motivation to learn cannot be taught as directly as a concept or skill, it can be developed in children by teachers who systematically socialize their students using the strategies listed here as part of a larger package of appropriate curriculum and instruction. Further research will undoubtedly identify additional strategies and qualifications on the use of ones described here. Nevertheless, the list provides a "starter set" of strategies to select from in planning motivational elements to include in instruction. In particular, these strategies remind us that students need not only incentives for applying themselves and activities they will enjoy but also motivation to learn the knowledge and skills being taught.

REFERENCES

Ames, C., and R. Ames, eds. *Research on Motivation in Education, Vol. II: The Classroom Milieu.* Orlando: Academic Press, 1985.

Ames, R., and C. Ames, eds. *Research on Motivation in Education, Vol. I: Student Motivation.* New York: Academic Press, 1984.

Bandura, A., and D. Schunk. "Cultivating Competence, Self-Efficacy, and Intrinsic Interest Through Proximal Self-Motivation." *Journal of Personality and Social Psychology* 41 (1981): 586–598.

Brophy, J. "Conceptualizing Student Motivation." *Educational Psychologist* 18 (1983): 200–215.

Brophy, J. "On Motivating Students." Occasional Paper No. 101, Institute for Research on Teaching. East Lansing: Michigan State University, 1986a.

Brophy, J. "Socializing Student Motivation to Learn." In *Advances in Motivation and Achievement,* vol. 5, edited by M. L. Maehr and D. A. Kleiber. Greenwich, CT: JAI Press, 1986b.

Corno, L., and M. Rohrkemper. "The Intrinsic Motivation to Learn in Classrooms." In *Research on Motivation in Education, Vol. II: The Classroom Milieu,* edited by C. Ames and R. Ames. Orlando: Academic Press, 1985.

Deci, E., and R. Ryan. *Intrinsic Motivation and Self-Determination in Human Behavior.* New York: Plenum, 1985.

Dweck, C., and E. Elliott. "Achievement Motivation." In *Handbook of Child Psychology,* edited by P. Mussen. New York: Wiley, 1983.

Feather, N., ed. *Expectations and Actions.* Hillsdale, N.J.: Erlbaum, 1982.

Good, T., and J. Brophy. *Educational Psychology: A Realistic Approach.* 3d ed. New York: Longman, 1986.

Good, T., and J. Brophy. *Looking in Classroom.* 4th ed. New York: Harper and Row, 1987.

Hill, K. T., and A. Wigfield. "Test Anxiety: A Major Educational Problem and What Can Be Done About It." *Elementary School Journal* 85 (1984): 105–216.

Keller, J. "Motivational Design of Instruction." In *Instructional-Design Theories and Models: An Overview of Their Current Status,* edited by C. Reigeluth. Hillsdale, N.J.: Erlbaum, 1983.

Kolesnik, W. *Motivation: Understanding and Influencing Human Behavior.* Boston: Allyn and Bacon, 1978.

Lepper, M., and D. Greene, eds. *The Hidden Costs of Reward: New Perspectives on the Psychology of Human Motivation.* Hillsdale, N.J.: Erlbaum, 1978.

Maehr, M. "Meaning and Motivation: Toward a Theory of Personal Investment." In *Research on Motivation in Education, Vol. I: Student Motivation,* edited by R. Ames and C. Ames. Orlando: Academic Press, 1984.

Malone, T., and M. Lepper. "Making Learning Fun: A Taxonomy of Intrinsic Motivation for Learning." In *Aptitude, Learning, and Instruction, Vol. III: Conative and Affective Process Analysis,* edited by R. Snow and M. Farr. Hillsdale, N.J.: Erlbaum, in press.

McCombs, B. "Processes and Skills Underlying Continuing Intrinsic Motivation to Learn: Toward a Definition of Motivational Skills Training and Interventions." *Educational Psychologist* 19 (1984): 199–218.

Nicholls, J. "Conceptions of Ability and Achievement Motivation." In *Research on Motivation in Education, Vol. I: Student Motivation,* edited by R. Ames and C. Ames. Orlando: Academic Press, 1984.

Slavin, R. *Cooperative Learning.* New York: Longman, 1983.

Weiner, B. "Principles for a Theory of Student Motivation and Their Application Within an Attributional Framework." In *Research on Motivation Education, Vol. I: Student Motivation.* Orlando: Academic Press, 1984.

Wlodkowski, R. J. *Motivation and Teaching: A Practical Guide.* Washington, D.C.: National Education Association, 1978.

READING 33   MADELINE HUNTER AND GEORGE BARKER
"If at First . . .": Attribution Theory in the Classroom

To gain predictability and control, humans seek to understand why things happen. If we find out why we were successful, we may be able to repeat that success. More important, perhaps, if we determine what caused our failure, we may avoid it in the future (Heider 1958, Kelley 1967, Weiner 1980).

Arising from social psychology, attribution theory is concerned with our constant search for the causes of our successes and failures. To what cause do we attribute what happens to us? Our *perceptions* of causality, rather than reality, are critical

From Madeline Hunter and George Barker, "'If at First . . .'": Attribution Theory in the Classroom," *Educational Leadership* (October 1987):50–53. Reprinted with permission of the Association for Supervision and Curriculum Development. Copyright © 1987 by ASCD. All rights reserved.

because they influence self-concept, expectations for future situations, feelings of potency, and subsequent motivation to put forth effort. While other factors may affect a person's intent to put forth effort, perceptions of causality constitute an important stimulant to motivate.

THREE CONTINUUMS OF CAUSALITY

In our culture (othr cultures differ) we attribute success and failure to four factors: native ability, effort, task difficulty, and luck (Frieze 1976). Native ability and effort have been found to be the most dominant factors. These four attributions exist on three continuums: locus, stability, and controllability (Weiner 1979).

1. *Locus.* Feelings of self-esteem, shame, or guilt are based on one's perception of the location of the cause. Locus can be internal or external: "me" or "not me."

Internal—"me"   *External—"not me"*
Native Ability
Effort   Task difficulty
                        Luck

If we attribute success or failure to internal locus, we are the originators of what happens rather than pawns controlled by outside forces. As an originator, a person feels proactive rather than reactive to the environment. Attribution of success to internal locus (ability, effort) results in increased self-esteem. Attribution of failure to internal locus results in shame (lack of ability) or guilt (lack of effort) (Wong and Weiner 1981).

People often explain success in terms of "I" and failure by "they" (Weiner 1979). In athletic contests, the winners explain their victory by "our skill," and the losers justify their defeat because of "poor officiating" or "luck." Parents explain their child's success by "our parenting and sacrifices" and their child's failures by "poor schools" and "bad companions." Teachers explain success by "our efforts" and failure by "that class." Clearly, these attributions help us maintain our self-esteem.

On the other hand, attributions to the "not me" can be valid if causation *is* beyond our control. Sometimes the ceiling does cave in on us regardless of our ability and effort. Careful drivers do get rear-ended.

2. *Stability.* Expectations for the future are based on whether the cause is perceived as stable or subject to change.

Unstable	*Stable*
Effort	Native ability
Luck	Task difficulty

The only attribution that offers no possibility for change in the eyes of the perceiver is native or genetic ability. "My legs are short and I'm stocky; no matter how hard I try, I'll never be a sprinter." "I have no artistic ability; there's no point in my studying art (music, drama, dance)." "I've always been a dud in math; I'll never understand it." If the person believes that failure is inevitable, there's no point in trying. Because of a person's perception of his or her ability, task difficulty can be seen as a stable cause (i.e., "Math/sprinting/music will always be easy/difficult for me").

On the other hand, a realistic appraisal of one's abilities helps us avoid frustration from expending effort when there is no possibility of success. Clearly, a deep-voiced person should not try to become a soprano. The short, stocky person's effort would be better spent on wrestling than on sprinting. The person with little tolerance for stress had best stay out of teaching.

It is the *invalid* attribution of failure to native ability that is dangerous. We are a math phobic nation, not because of native ability, but because of mechanically manipulating numbers with little or no meaning ("Yours is not to reason why, just invert and multiply"). That many people do not believe they have ability in the arts is a result of instructional experience, *not* basic ability. Moreover, recent investigations (Lane and Walberg 1987) of poverty cultures reveal that much of the problem lies in lack of language development as a result of the environment, not in the genes.

When students attribute success or failure to stable causes, they expect the same from the future as from the past. When they attribute success or failure to unstable causes, their expectations can change.

3. *Controllability.* A third aspect of causality is related to an individual's feeling of potency to affect the outcome by controlling the cause.

Controllable	*Not Controllable*
Effort	Ability
	Task difficulty
	Luck

Of all the causal attributions, the only one completely under our control is effort: we can determine how much effort we will expend. People do not exercise control over ability, task difficulty, or luck. Consequently, we put forth effort *if* we believe that the effort will influence the outcome. If I believe studying will influence my grade, I'm more apt to study. If I believe my grade is the result of the teacher's compassion, the kind of test, or just luck, there's no point in studying.

Research on high achievers, whether in mathematics, athletics, the arts, science, or business, reveals that successful people exert enormous effort (Gardner 1983, Bloom 1985). Consequently, if students are to succeed, they must believe that when they expend effort—something they completely control—they will experience success. But note that if students believe success or failure is the result of ability, task difficulty, or luck, then there's no point in putting forth a lot of effort. Also remember, it is their *perceptions* of causality, not reality, that matter in these events.

Attributions of causality often vary between the perceptions of actor and observer, between students and teachers (Jones and Nisbett 1972). Actors tend to ascribe failures to the "not me" cause. The tennis player, missing the ball, glares at his racquet as if there were a hole in it. The observer more frequently attributes the miss to a stable factor. "He always swings too fast." The student as well can attribute failure to "not me" causes: "She gave an impossible assignment." The teacher attributes poor performance to stable characteristics ("They never really work at it") or to situational characteristics ("Those kids were sure rowdy today"). The administrator's attribution may be that "she never has an orderly classroom."

When actors and observers communicate, it is important to take into account the characteristic bias of each in attributing causality.

IMPLICATIONS FOR STUDENTS

Why are some students almost always successful while others seem doomed to fail? Part of the explanation lies in their beliefs about the causes of success and failure. Educators can use attribution theory to help more students succeed.

1. *Locus* of causality determines academic self-esteem. If I believe I have ability and can achieve success with effort, I have a positive self-concept as a student. If I believe that no matter how hard I try, I will not be successful, my impres-

sion of my ability and my self-concept suffers. If I believe my A was the result of teacher indulgence or luck, my self-esteem is not enhanced. Pride results from accomplishment only when we attribute that accomplishment to ability or effort. Everyone enjoys an excellent meal, but only the cook can take pride in it.

2. *Stability* of causality prompts a student to believe either that the future is predetermined or that it can be changed by effort. If I succeeded because I "tried hard," then, if I continue to try hard, I'll succeed again. If my achievement was due to natural ability, I don't have to work hard. If my success or failure was due to external elements, there's no point in trying. It is essential that students believe they have the ability to achieve success if they expend effort and that they anticipate less success if they don't try. Note, however, that if students try hard and fail, one obvious conclusion is that they lack ability. As a result, their self-esteem is diminished, and future effort seems pointless.

3. *Controllability* of causality creates the feeling of being commander of one's fate and is a powerful determiner of emotional health. To be buffeted by one's environment produces a feeling of helplessness. When my success depends on me, it may be scary, but I'm in charge. When I cannot affect what happens to me, I become a pawn of others (deCharms 1968). Consequently, I must either become resigned to my fate or despair.

Students must accept the fact that much of what happens to them is a result of what they do. By changing actions, they frequently can alter outcomes. This association builds a feeling of potency in the individual. "If I think I can, I might; if I think I can't, I'm right." The placebo effect in medicine is testimony to the powerful effect of a person's beliefs of causality and controllability rather than reality. The same effect can be found in education.

In summary, let us examine the significance of students' attributing success and failure to the two most dominant attributions—ability and effort—on each of the continuums. If a student thinks she succeeded on an assignment because of her ability, her self-esteem will most certainly be enhanced, she will expect success in the future, and she may be motivated to attempt similar tasks. If, however, a student thinks his failure was because of a lack of ability, his self-esteem will be lower, he will expect failure, and he may not attempt a similar task in the future.

Different effects result, however, when success and failure are attributed to effort. When students attribute success to effort, they perceive that they can do the assignment and can expect success in the future if they continue to try. They may fail, but the outcome presumably is within their influence (internal, unstable, and controllable). Perceiving failure as caused by lack of effort allows students the possibility of future success with additional effort.

This latter attributional pattern, then, optimizes the likelihood of future success and subsequent motivation: success perceived as the result of ability plus effort and failure perceived as the outcome of lack of effort.

IMPLICATIONS FOR TEACHERS

Attribution theory, therefore, has meaning for the ways teachers respond to their students' performance.

1. *Locus.* It is essential that teachers diagnose where students' learning leaves off and new learning needs to begin. If the learning to be accomplished is too easy or impossibly difficult, effort is irrelevant. With a teacher's accurate diagnosis and effective teaching, students' efforts should bring success. When students find the locus of causality is within themselves, they realize they can control success.

A teacher's delighted praise or impatient criticism can convey an unintended message about that student's ability (Barker and Graham in press). Praise for success resulting from little effort teaches the learner not to work hard. Criticism for failure on a task that could have been accomplished with effort communicates to a student that he or she has the ability to succeed and should have put forth effort.

2. *Stability.* Students need to believe that their ability to be successful is stable and that they control the effort necessary for success. By emphasizing that "you can do it if you try" (and making sure they can), teachers convey to students that ability plus effort equals success.

3. *Controllability.* The way a teacher responds to a student's success or failure can signal the teacher's belief as to whether the student is in control of success or failure. Imagine your dinner guests' arriving two hours late because they hated to leave their house before a TV show ended. You would feel angry and indignant, no doubt, because they could have prevented their lateness. Suppose your guests were late because they had a flat tire, no phone was available, and the repair truck was forever in arriving. Now how would you feel? Forgiving and sympathetic, for the problem was beyond their control.

Similarly, teachers' behaviors convey unintended messages to students. For example, annoyance can say to a student that he had the ability to perform successfully and was responsible for the less-than-satis-

> Students must accept the fact that much of what happens to them is a result of what they do.

factory performance. Sympathy and understanding can communicate that no matter how much effort a student expended, he could not have accomplished the task. For a teacher to accept less from a student than she is capable of doing can convince the student of your belief that, even with effort, she doesn't have the ability to meet the expectations. Criticism of performance when the student could have done better communicates, "You have the ability."

Developmental differences figure prominently in the way students perceive the causal potential of ability and effort. Young children four to five years of age do not see an inverse relationship between ability and effort. If asked, "Who are the smart kids in your room?" they will respond. "The ones who try hard or practice a lot" (Nicholls 1978). However, a junior high or high school student who sees a fellow student is putting forth great effort may respond, "If the student has to try that hard, it may mean he is not very smart." Rather than equating ability and effort as young children do, older students distinguish these as discrete constructs: the more able a person is, the less effort may need to be put forth.

Because of these developmental differences, teachers may observe a devaluation of effort as students get older. That is, if high school or college students wish to be considered smart, they may put forth a great deal of effort to convince others they are not putting forth effort. In order to preserve their egos, they try hard to show they're not trying hard. Should they fail, they can convince others they could have succeeded had they tried. If they succeed without apparently trying, they're "smart" (Nicholls 1976). Ability and effort represent an inverse relationship.

COMMON SENSE ABOUT EFFORT

While much of attribution theory is common sense, educators should stay alert to its far-reaching implications for improving student learning. Indeed, the implications carry directly into principal-teacher and superintendent-principal interactions. For example, when a principal says "Your teaching makes that class look easy," the message is very different from the one we hear in "You're lucky to have such an easy class." Expending effort enhances everyone's chances for excellence in performance, and feeling in charge is essential to a healthy self-concept. We must downplay ability as the asset of ultimate worth and emphasize effort as the controllable variable with the highest probability of producing success. Students, teachers, and administrators must not be allowed to plateau with acceptable current performance but should expend effort to make "good better and better best."

REFERENCES

Barker, G. P., and S. Graham. "A Developmental Study of Praise and Blame as Attributional Cues. *Journal of Educational Psychology* (in press).

Bloom, Benjamin S., ed. *Developing Talent in Young People.* New York: Ballatine Books, 1985.

deCharms, R. *Personal Causation.* New York: Academic Press, 1968.

Frieze, I. H. "Causal Attributions and Information Seeking to Explain Success and Failure." *Journal of Research in Personality* 10 (1976): 293–305.

Gardner, Howard. *Frames of Mind: The Theory of Multiple Intelligences.* New York: Basic Books, Inc., 1983.

Heider, F. *The Psychology of Interpersonal Relations.* New York: Wiley, 1958.

Jones, E. E., and R. E. Nisbett. "The Actor and the Observer: Divergent Perceptions of the Causes of Behavior." In *Attribution: Perceiving the Causes of Behavior,* edited by E. E. Jones, D. E. Kanouse, H. H. Kelley, R. E. Nisbett, S. Valins, and B. Weiner. Morristown, N.J.: General Learning Press, 1972.

Kelley, H. H. "Attribution Theory in Social Psychology." In *Nebraska Symposium on Motivation,* edited by D. Lenine. Lincoln: University of Nebraska Press, 1967.

Lane, John, and Herbert Walberg. *Effective School Leadership.* Berkeley, Calif.: McCutchan Publishing Corp., 1987.

Nicholls, J. G. "Effort is Virtuous, But It's Better to Have Ability: Evaluation Responses to Perceptions of Effort and Ability." *Journal of Research in Personality* 10 (1976): 306–315.

Nicholls, J. G. "The Development of Concepts of Effort and Ability, Perception of Academic Attainment, and the Understanding that Difficult Tasks Require More Ability." *Child Development* 49 (1978): 800–814.

Weiner, B. "A Theory of Motivation for Some Classroom Experiences." *Journal of Educational Psychology* 71 (1979): 3–25.

Weiner, B. *Human Motivations.* New York: Holt, Rinehart, and Winston, 1980.

Wong, P. T., and B. Weiner. "When People Ask 'Why' Questions and the Heuristics of Attributional Search." *Journal of Personality and Social Psychology* 40 (1981): 650–663.

READING 34 SYLVIA B. RIMM
How to Reach the Underachiever

At school Paul slouches at his desk, yawns, daydreams, and slowly meanders through math. He raises his hand to ask questions but rarely to answer them. His assignments are seldom completed, his desk is messy, and his homework often lost. He may be a likable kid but he's frustrating to teach, and he's terribly frustrated himself.

At home Paul's parents are concerned. Paul tells them that he's doing better, yet he never brings home a book. His grades continue to fall. After school Paul withdraws in front of the television set, oblivious to calls to do his homework. Finally he responds that he has no homework to do. Everyone's frustration mounts, and no one looks forward to the next report card conference.

Rebecca, a fifth grader, is another child frustrating to teachers and parents. She once got good grades consistently but now vacillates between A's and F's. If there's a teacher she likes she works hard; if not, it is the teacher's fault that her work isn't correct or finished. And each year it seems she likes fewer and fewer teachers. When her teachers lose patience, she pouts and mutters under her breath.

At home and at school Rebecca loves to chatter, send notes, and talk on the phone, but such activity masks her socialization problems. Frequently her telephone conversations concentrate on negative descriptions of the very girls she considered friends yesterday. Yet her peer group determines how she spends her time.

From Sylvia B. Rimm, "How to Reach the Underachiever," *Instructor* (September 1985):73–74, 76. Copyright by Sylvia B. Rimm. Reprinted by permission.

At home Rebecca plays one parent against the other. When her mother and father set limits together, she slams her bedroom door, asserting her power. Although she defines herself in terms of what she's against, she frequently labels adults as narrow and hypocritical.

PORTRAIT OF AN UNDERACHIEVER

Paul and Rebecca are two different types of underachievers with some characteristics in common. They are both children with good intellectual abilities who do not perform well in the classroom. Most underachievers begin school with high achievement and IQ test scores. Each year, however, scores fall slightly and grades tend to get worse. Teachers often describe these children in the following terms (in any combination): inconsistent work, poor study habits, lack of concentration, hyperactivity, daydreaming, perfectionism, and disorganization. Their peer relations vary. While some show extraordinarily fine peer leadership skills, more typically they exhibit problematic aggressive behavior and sometimes have no friends at all.

Underachieving children often hide behind defenses. They sometimes make remarks like "I'm not as smart as the tests say." "I guess I just must have a learning disability." "If I did well in school, my friends wouldn't like me." They don't believe they can achieve even if they make the appropriate efforts. All their energy is spent manipulating their home and school environments to hide their low self-concepts.

LEARNING TO UNDERACHIEVE

There is no neurological or biological explanation for poor school performance by capable children. But children can be reinforced and rewarded for their underachievement years before they enter school. Loving parents concerned about providing the best educational opportunity often unwittingly initiate these patterns. Sometimes all the children in the family are affected; other times only one child. Patterns of interaction that foster underachievement emerge as a way of dealing with problematic situations such as: extreme cases of sibling rivalry, poor coordination, a particularly difficult school year, an unusual ability left unchallenged, a very competitive environment, an early illness, parents' marital problems, or a parent away from home for an extended period of time.

These patterns generally take one of two directions. Underachievers either tend to be very dependent on others, or they feel a strong need to dominate their world.

Paul, a dependent underachiever, has grown up with an overabundance of parental help. His patterns of dependency are now disabling. With few opportunities to work out problems on his own, he lacks the kinds of experience that build self-confidence. In school a typical Paul excuse might be "I did my homework; I just can't find it," or "I really meant to finish this assignment but when I got home I didn't have the book." Thus far in life he hasn't learned to take responsibility or to organize himself. Most probably he's never really needed to; at home and at school there was always someone to do it for him.

Paul might appear to have a learning disability, but his real problem is that he just can't share attention with a whole classroom of students. His constant lack of organization and poor study skills contribute to his low self-esteem. His constant need for attention makes him feel even worse about himself. And the symptoms of Paul's problems (quiet tears, forlorn daydreaming) invite teachers and parents to treat him in ways that maintain his nonproductive behavior.

IS THERE HELP FOR THE PAULS OF THE WORLD?

Dependent underachievers need more than a vote of confidence. The first step is to identify which children in your class fit this particular pattern. Next, request a parent conference to discuss the child's behavior at home and patterns that you both see.

> Children will continue to achieve if they see the relationship between their efforts and the outcomes.

Dependent underachievers will require much effort while being weaned from their "attention addiction." Cold turkey is simply not a very effective method. They need adults around them to positively insist on their independent activity and to give positive attention to the finished product. Don't make the mistake that many good, kind teachers make. Giving sympathy won't help and neither will one-to-one instruction. Fostering these well-developed dependencies continues to rob children of their self-confidence.

At school set up situations that require hard work, but ensure the possibility of success. Encourage parents to do the same at home. Children will require a lot of help in learning strategies to persevere. In many situations it will be tempting to give just a little extra help, but this is really a vote of no confidence. If tests say that children are capable and you sense that they are, insist that they make the effort. Target work completion as your goal first and then emphasize quality.

Use stickers, stars, sincere smiles, and privileges to recognize completed work. Send a note home that work has been completed. Together with parents set up rewards like 15 minutes of one-to-one time with a parent or being allowed to go to the movies or bake cookies with someone important. Ask children what they would like as rewards.

You may need to remind parents to leave children alone to do work at home and to watch closely for attention manipulation. Often parents are so used to being manipulated that it will take their conscious effort to wean themselves. Work should be reviewed only after it is completed and errors noted for the child's correction. Also remind parents to express pride and pleasure at each independent accomplishment. Adults can bestow self-confidence, but by standing back and permitting a child to struggle through, we can help children gain internal well-being.

A note of caution. Sometimes children truly do need help. Overly difficult tasks may lead to frustrations and discouragement. Determining when help creates destructive dependence is a key to helping children achieve. Children will continue to achieve if they see the relationship between their efforts and the outcomes.

"WHY SHOULD I DO THE WORK?"

Rebecca, a dominant underachiever, fits the second pattern. She has always been given too much power and so has learned to expect it. These underachievers are the children who seek continued control even in situations where they are clearly too young to feel comfortable making decisions. This pattern, once initiated, continues through inertia. Rebecca's "attention addiction" causes her to seek more "winning" than is available or emotionally healthy in any family or classroom. She has learned to manipulate parents and teachers to maintain a constant flow of too much and inappropriate attention.

Dominant underachievers, like Rebecca, are independent to a fault. They don't seem to be able to accept "no" from adults, put high priority on their social life, and are expert manipulators of everyone, including their peers. These children expect to be the center of attention and in tight control of school, home, and friends. Subjected to even reasonable discipline, they become angry and unreasonable.

In school, they are the children who get out of their seats, talk out in class, and push rules and deadlines. They feel victorious when they have caused a teacher to lose class control; although they like to argue, they insist on winning. Dominant underachievers may be belligerent and disruptive but often are merely annoyingly and persuasively manipulative. Though dominant underachievers may appear tough, theirs is a very precarious position fraught with the fear of being exposed as vulnerable and imperfect.

HELP IS ON THE WAY

Dominant underachievers need specific strategies. To temper children's controlling attitudes, teachers need to respond in ways that avoid useless power struggles. These children believe that school and family must be run on their terms. It's tempting to use "teacher power" (status and grades) to put them down or to gain control. For some younger children, outpowering will be effective, but for most children this determined and rigid approach will just challenge them to fight back. It may look like you are more powerful, but children will continue to underachieve because you have fallen into their manipulations.

Dominant underachievers need an ally, not an enemy—a teacher who sees how bright and creative they are, one who gives them recognition for their special qualities.

Most important, they need to sense that you will permit them control but within clear and defined limits. To do that, negotiate the limits and write them down together. Change the limits only if children are willing to invest more of themselves and prove their accomplishments. Use fairness as the criterion—fairness to them and to you—and point out specifics as you form your plan. Be firm and positive. The difference between firmness and rigidity is not in what you expect but in how you present your expectations and how well you listen to the child's. Firmness and fairness established, these children also need your kind persuasion and support.

Because dominant children only feel comfortable when they are in control, they are frequently on the edge of anger and depression. They need to know that you want to see their point of view but that they must also learn to examine the perspectives of others who care about them. You can help by assisting them to live within the rules. Show children that rules can be bent slightly when they are willing to invest effort. They can be in control within understood limits. Therefore, their personal control *can* coexist with the reasonable control needs of school and family.

Parents may need to be reminded that these children have never learned to accept "no." Previously "no" has only meant "who or how hard do I need to push to get what I want?" All children need clear "yeses" and "nos," but most of all they need consistency. When faced with the feeling of losing control, adults often act inconsistently. Dominant underachievers have learned this and, especially during adolescence, they will use their highly refined manipulation skills to confound adults.

As a teacher you can be supportive, but you cannot be a substitute for professional counseling. Running away, eating disorders, alcohol and drug abuse, even suicide attempts indicate these children have gone beyond the underachievement problem. Don't hesitate to recommend getting outside help.

COPING AND CURING

The main characteristic that distinguishes achievers from underachievers is the way in which they cope with competition. Subtle and not-so-subtle comparisons of children that are made at home and school may communicate to a child that he or she is either a winner or a loser. Students who have not learned to handle losing often view school as a game in which there is little hope for success. While learning to deal with winning is easy, these children need classroom situations and family experiences that will help them cope with success *and* defeat. They also need to learn to continue to try when work becomes difficult. Underachievers often avoid involvement unless they feel certain of triumph.

Millions of children who are very capable of learning with average, above average, and even gifted abilities are simply not performing up to their capability. These children direct most of their energy toward discovering ways to avoid learning in either dependent or dominant ways. They can try the patience of the best teachers. Working with parents, though, you can help these children gain confidence and a sense of real control. By helping children compete in the school game called learning, you'll contribute to their success in the competitive game of life.

> **W**hile children find it easy to deal with winning, underachievers need classroom situations and family experiences that will help them cope with success and defeat.

CHAPTER TWELVE

Strategies Useful for the Practice of Positive Classroom Discipline

READING 35   THOMAS R. McDANIEL
A Primer on Classroom Discipline: Principles Old and New

Fifty years ago, the topic of classroom control was virtually ignored in teacher education programs. Prospective teachers in those days were merely told to make good lesson plans, to be firm but gentle, and not to smile until Christmas. Not so long ago, the behaviorists came up with some interesting insights into the principles of reinforcement. They told teachers to catch the child being good—and to ignore bad behavior. Then the humanists came along and told us that good discipline is related to self-concept and communication. They reminded us to talk to our students as we would address visitors in our homes. Today we are told to be assertive, to negotiate, to analyze transactions, and to rely on logical consequences, reality therapy, and Teacher Effectiveness Training in our dealings with students. When it comes to disciplinary techniques for the classroom, the contemporary teacher suffers from sensory overload.

Meanwhile, everyone—from burned-out teachers and Gallup Poll respondents to a never-ending stream of commissions and task forces—has been telling teachers that discipline must improve, if U.S. education is ever to rise above mediocrity. At the same time, researchers have been generating volumes of data on effective schools and effective teachers. Their studies indicate that certain teaching techniques lead to better learning *and* better behavior. Teachers must master these techniques, the researchers say, if they hope to have well-managed and effective classrooms.

Although all the attention paid to discipline by theorists, the public, and the research community is a bit confusing, the beleaguered teacher has reason for hope. Ten principles—an eclectic combination of traditional and modern, practical and theoretical, pedagogical and psychological—provide some general guidelines for teachers who wish to modify their own behaviors in ways that will yield effective group management and control.

1. The focusing principle. Widely supported by experienced teachers, this principle says, in effect, "Get everyone's attention before giving instructions or presenting material." Beginning teachers often make the mistake of trying to teach over the chatter of inattentive students. They assume that, if they begin the lesson (and there are *many* beginning points within each lesson), students will notice and quiet down. This approach may work occasionally. What the students really learn, however, is that the teacher is willing to compete with them, to speak loudly enough to be heard over the undercurrent, to tolerate inattention, and to condone chatter during instruction.

The focusing principle reminds

From Thomas R. McDaniel, "A Primer on Classroom Discipline: Principles Old and New," *Phi Delta Kappan* (September 1986):63–67. Reprinted by permission.

teachers that, during group instruction, they must request, demand, expect, and wait for attention before they begin to teach. A teacher can say, "I am ready to begin"; "I am ready to begin, boys in the back"; "I am ready to begin, Lillian, and I am waiting for you." The teacher may need to speak loudly, to flip the light switch, to stand with hand raised, to ring a bell—but he or she should insist on, work for, and secure attention *before* starting to teach. Then the teacher can begin the actual instruction in a calm and quiet voice. An in-charge beginning is not repressive authoritarianism; it is the essential first ingredient in a well-mannered classroom.

2. The principle of direct instruction. The point is to get students on-task quickly and to keep them on-task consistently, so that they stay out of trouble. One of the most effective techniques for accomplishing this goal is to clearly state the assignment, the directions, and the time constraints. A teacher might say, for example: "Your task is here on the board, class. You need to use your textbook and the data-bank forms to collect information. You have only 10 minutes to work, so start right away." Some classes respond well when the teacher sets explicit goals: "We took five minutes yesterday just to distribute the construction paper. Let's see if we can distribute the paper in *three* minutes today." To keep students on-task, the teacher should make certain that the tasks are interesting, relevant, and varied and that students are motivated to engage in them. The next three principles also help to keep students on-task.

3. The monitoring principle. "Monitoring" means keeping a constant check on student performance and behavior. Teachers should make personal contact with each student during a lesson, and they should circulate frequently among their students. When students know that the teacher will evaluate their work and behavior from close range and hold them accountable, they are more likely to stay on-task. Monitoring encourages a teacher to move about the classroom and to engage in brief conferences with individual youngsters. These personal encounters enable the teacher to provide individualized instruction or feedback. The focus may be on the academic task at hand ("Freddy, your triangles look fine, but remember to label your angles") or on a student's behavior ("Mabel, put your comb away and begin your math problems, please"). In either case, such quiet conversations between teacher and student can have a significant positive effect on the classroom atmosphere.

4. The modeling principle. Long before the behavioral psychologists told us that students' behavior could be influenced by "models," good teachers recognized the importance of setting an example for their students. (As the adage goes, "Values are caught, not taught.") Teachers who are courteous, prompt, well-organized, enthusiastic, self-controlled, and patient tend to produce students who exhibit similar characteristics, at least to some degree. With sensitivity and tact, teachers can also employ students as models for the other youngsters to emulate.

One especially important modeling technique that teachers should practice is the use of a soft, low-pitched voice. Students find such a voice calming. "Soft reprimands" are also effective because they are not the norm and because, being private, they tend not to invite loud protests, denials, or retorts. It is especially important for teachers to model quiet voice levels when they are circulating among students and monitoring individual work.

5. The cuing principle. Behavioral psychology has given us new insights into the nature and effectiveness of cues (generally, nonverbal reminders about behavioral expectations) in improving classroom discipline. Of course, good teachers have always known that cues improve discipline. The teacher who raises a hand for silence, flips the light switch to get attention, or points to a group of gigglers and then presses an index finger to the lips is reminding students of certain rules, procedures, or expectations.

Some students seem oblivious to classroom cues. In these instances, teachers should 1) examine the cues they are using, 2) establish stronger and more explicit variations of these cues, 3) teach the cues to the students directly, and 4) pair the use of each new cue with a verbal explanation of the cue. A brief example may clarify this approach for the reader. Mrs. Jones always stands with her hands on her hips when she is waiting for attention. If members of the class fail to attend to her in this pose, she may decide to strengthen the cue by combining it with a movement toward the class and a clearing of the throat. Next, she may explain to the students that these cues are designed to let them know that she is waiting for attention. At the next opportunity, she will use the nonverbal cues while saying, "As you can see, class, I am waiting for your attention."

To keep behavioral expectations flowing from teacher to student, a creative teacher can develop a host of novel cues that employ proximity, facial expressions, gestures, and objects (e.g., bells, lights, "clickers") to supplement verbal cues ("Okay, boys and girls, in 10 seconds you will need your protractors"). I know of one teacher who teaches his students new ways to cue *him*, as well. Instead of asking them to raise their hands when they know the answer to a question, he asks them to put their heads on their desks (when they are restless), or to stand up (when they need to stretch), or to pull on their right ear lobes (when they need to be amused). Such experimentation helps students become more sensitive to nonverbal cues as methods of communication.

Effective communication is essential to effective discipline.

6. The principle of environmental control. There are many things in a student's life that a teacher cannot control, such as handicaps, the child-rearing practices of parents, and even whether or not the child eats breakfast each morning. But a wise teacher manipulates the classroom environment to improve both learning and behavior. A teacher can enrich, impoverish, restrict, enlarge, simplify, or systematize the classroom environment. Let us look more closely at a couple of these alternatives for improving discipline.

Often, classroom management is a problem because the students are bored, apathetic, uninterested, or unmotivated. In such situations, a teacher needs to *enrich* the classroom environment in order to improve students' motivation, attention, and involvement. A teacher might use learning centers, bulletin boards, music, or audiovisual aids to provide a variety of stimuli. He or she could open lessons with exercises requiring inductive reasoning: "Here is a replica of a kitchen implement used by the ancient Egyptians, class. What might they have used it for? What uses might we have for it today?" Enrichment involves consciously adding to or varying the classroom environment for an educational purpose. Done well, enrichment motivates students—and motivated students engage in learning rather than in misbehavior.

However, classroom management can just as frequently be a problem when students are overstimulated by the classroom environment. Overstimulated students have short attention spans, are easily distracted, and tend to be hyperactive. In such situations, a teacher needs to *impoverish* the classroom environment. If the teacher tries instead to be enthusiastic and to motivate students, the result is often disastrous; much like turning up the flame under a bubbling cauldron, the additional stimuli only raise the kinetic energy level in the classroom. Instead, the teacher should darken the room, install carpets, remove distracting materials and diversions, schedule quiet times, create quiet corners, and use such focused teaching approaches as filmstrips and lessons involving directed study. The teacher should also be a model of controlled activity, concentration, and subdued behavior—especially with regard to voice, dress, and movement.

7. The principle of low-profile intervention. This principle is derived from some of the pioneering research on group management by Jacob Kounin, but it is enjoying renewed attention from contemporary researchers. According to this principle, the teacher should manage student behavior as discreetly, unobtrusively, and smoothly as possible—avoiding direct confrontations and public encounters with disruptive students. Without delivering constant orders and commands (i.e., high-profile interventions), the teacher needs to anticipate behavioral problems and to nip them in the bud. A particularly effective approach during large-group instruction is to drop the name of an inattentive student into the middle of an instructional statement: "We need to remember, Clarence, that Columbus was one of several discoverers of America." A teacher can "drop" the names of several students during a presentation, but the name-dropping should be casual, with no hint of reprisal and no pause for reply.

Another low-profile technique is to move close to students who are starting to wander off-task. The teacher's proximity often curtails misbehavior or inattention. Such "overlapping" of teacher behaviors (e.g., moving to a trouble spot in the classroom while continuing to conduct a lesson) becomes almost automatic with practice and can be enhanced by nonverbal cues, such as touching an inattentive student on the shoulder or quietly opening his or her book to the proper page.

8. The principle of assertive discipline. This principle, made popular by Lee Canter, calls for higher-profile but nonhostile interventions that effectively communicate a teacher's wants and needs for better discipline. Actually, assertive discipline is only a commonsense combination of behavioral psychology (praise) and traditional authoritarianism (limit setting).

A teacher should begin by identifying specific roadblocks to discipline; these are usually consequences of the teacher's low expectations regarding students' behavior. All teachers should proceed from the position that no child has the right to prevent classmates from learning or teachers from teaching. Teachers should also believe that their students are able to behave appropriately.

An assertive teacher communicates these expectations to students through clearly stated and carefully explained rules. When the rules are broken, the teacher consistently follows through with systematic consequences. Meanwhile, the teacher sets limits verbally through requests, hints, and demands, and he or she uses nonverbal communication (eye contact, proximity, touch, gestures) to communicate exactly what is required of whom. Finally, the teacher engages in "broken record" confrontation—repeating requests for compliance until students recognize that the teacher cannot be diverted or ignored. These techniques, coupled with positive consequences for following rules and heeding the teacher's requests, convince students that the teacher knows what he or she wants and needs by way of student behavior. Students also come to realize that their responses will generate positive or negative consequences for *them*.

9. The I-message principle. Both the assertive discipline of Lee

A Checklist on Discipline for Classroom Teachers

Analyze your classroom disciplinary practices, and place a check in the appropriate column after each item. Then add your points (allowing four points for each "usually," two points for each "sometimes," and zero points for each "never"). Rate yourself as follows: 90–100 = excellent; 80–90 = good; 70–80 = fair; below 70 = poor.

	Usually	Sometimes	Never
1. I get students' attention before giving instruction(s).	☐	☐	☐
2. I wait for students to attend rather than talk over chatter.	☐	☐	☐
3. I quickly get students on-task.	☐	☐	☐
4. I give clear and specific directions.	☐	☐	☐
5. I set explicit time limits for task completion.	☐	☐	☐
6. I circulate among students at work.	☐	☐	☐
7. I hold private conferences/conversations during class.	☐	☐	☐
8. I model courtesy and politeness.	☐	☐	☐
9. I use a quiet voice in the classroom.	☐	☐	☐
10. I use the "soft reprimand" rather than raise my voice.	☐	☐	☐
11. I use a variety of cues to remind students of expected behavior.	☐	☐	☐
12. I teach students my cues.	☐	☐	☐
13. I enrich my classroom to improve students' motivation.	☐	☐	☐
14. I impoverish my classroom to improve attention.	☐	☐	☐
15. I am aware of the effects of my dress, voice, and movements on student behavior.	☐	☐	☐
16. I use students' names as low-profile correctors of inattention.	☐	☐	☐
17. I use proximity to improve classroom control.	☐	☐	☐
18. I communicate positive expectations of good behavior to my class.	☐	☐	☐
19. I have clear and specific rules that I teach my students.	☐	☐	☐
20. I refuse to threaten or plead with students.	☐	☐	☐
21. I consistently follow through with consequences to enforce rules.	☐	☐	☐
22. I use I-messages assertively to tell students what I want them to do.	☐	☐	☐
23. I use I-messages humanistically to communicate my feelings.	☐	☐	☐
24. I respond to behaviors I like with specific, personal praise.	☐	☐	☐
25. I use nonverbal, social, and activity reinforcers.	☐	☐	☐

Canter and the humanistic discipline of Haim Ginott and Thomas Gordon rely on clear communication between teacher and students. Both approaches to discipline advocate the use of I-messages by teachers. Because assertive discipline and humanistic discipline operate on entirely different premises, however, the I-message takes two forms.

A teacher practicing assertive discipline and the broken-record technique may communicate a demand, wish, or need in order to refocus a group or an individual student. The teacher prefaces his or her specific request with the words "I want you to . . ." or "I need you to. . . ." Such I-message assertions are more effective than "You stop . . ." messages, which focus on confrontations ("you") and on past infractions ("stop"). An assertive I-message tells students exactly what the teacher wants and expects them to *do*.

A teacher practicing humanistic discipline, by contrast, uses I-messages to communicate his or her *feelings*, so that students can understand more clearly how their behavior affects the teacher. According to Gordon, an I-message has three elements: 1) the description of students' behavior ("When you leave our classroom in a mess . . ."); 2) the effect of that behavior on the teacher ("I have to use instructional time for cleaning up . . ."); and 3) the feeling this creates in the teacher ("which frustrates me"). Such messages encourage students to change their behavior voluntarily. Both forms of the I-message have their proper places in the repertoire of the effective classroom manager.

10. The principle of positive reinforcement. One of the best-known methods of classroom management derived from the work of the behaviorists is the "catch 'em being good" principle of positive reinforcement. Punishment does not change students' behavior (except temporarily), but it can increase the incidence of negative behaviors by calling attention to them. A teacher would do better to ignore minor misbehavior, while identifying and praising good behavior. In practice, however, this is easier said than done. Teachers understand the principle of positive reinforcement, but they are not very skillful in applying it. The techniques that follow may help.

One practice that a teacher can employ is to establish *positive* rules and expectations. Once students know that the rule is "Raise your hand for permission to talk," rather than "Do not call out if you have not been recognized," the teacher can praise students for doing the right thing instead of punishing students for doing the wrong thing: "Thank you for raising your hand, George; you have certainly followed our rule to the letter."

Praise is a major technique of positive reinforcement, but it should be sincere, personalized, descriptive, and focused on students' *actions*, not on their characters or personalities. Teachers can set up a positive expectation (e.g., "Let's see how quickly we can distribute the art supplies") and then follow with praise directed at individuals or groups who conform to the expectation (e.g., "The group in the back has set up all the paints and is ready to begin"). A teacher has to *look* for good behavior and then practice describing it in a complimentary fashion.

A teacher can reward good behavior with nonverbal reinforcers (nods, smiles, pats on the back); activity reinforcers (games, field trips, free time); and concrete or token reinforcers (food, stickers, check marks). For example, a teacher might write on the chalkboard each afternoon the names of "super citizens"—students who have made some special contribution that day to the welfare of the class. These students could be the first to go to lunch on the following day. When a class is restless, the teacher might set a timer for a short interval (one to three minutes) and direct students to work quietly until the timer goes off. If they are quiet when the timer goes off (catching them being good), the students should receive a reward—perhaps some free time at the end of the period. Initially, the teacher should set the timer for a short interval, so that the class is almost bound to be on-task when the timer goes off. As the students' study habits and concentration improve, the time should be lengthened. The length of time should not be predictable, however.

Establishing good discipline involves much more than most teachers realize. The 10 principles I have presented here, and the "tricks of the trade" that they generate, are but one aspect of the art of classroom control. In the final analysis, teachers must deal with such dysfunctional behavioral manifestations as hostility, frustration, discouragement, and apathy. Ultimately, then, the quality of a teacher's discipline rests on the quality of his or her instructional practices and long-term relationships with children and on his or her ability to convince young people that school is important. School becomes important to children when teachers reach them with meaningful lessons and a professional attitude that says, "I care about you; I know that you can behave; I want to help you to be a *better* you."

READING 36   JERE BROPHY
Classroom Management as Instruction: Socializing Self-Guidance in Students

The title of this article touches on three basic themes that underlie its approach to the topic, teaching self-discipline. First, it refers to self-guidance rather than self-control. This subtle but important difference reflects basic assumptions about what students are like and what they need from their teachers. Students are seen as generally willing and potentially cooperative rather than alienated or predisposed to misbehavior. Thus, classroom management is seen as primarily a matter of telling and showing willing but ignorant students what to do, rather than enforcing compliance from students who know what to do but tend not to do it on their own.

Second, the title refers to "socializing" self-guidance in students. This is a reminder that although students have the potential to develop self-guidance, such development does not occur automatically. Instead, it must be stimulated through socialization by parents, teachers, and significant others. Third, the title is a reminder that classroom management may be thought of as a form of instruction, instead of a form of discipline or control. In particular, most of the things teachers do to develop self-guidance in their students involve modeling and instruction rather than, or at least in addition to, propounding and enforcing rules.

This article shows how these themes keep appearing in research on child rearing in the home and classroom management at school, and draws upon research and related theory to suggest approaches teachers can use to socialize self-guidance in their students.

SOCIALIZATION IN THE HOME

Mature forms of self-guidance do not suddenly appear full blown in children. Instead, they develop gradually (if at all) following passage through a series of less mature forms determined in part by children's levels of cognitive development and in part by the nature of the socialization they receive (especially in the home). This development occurs within a context of dependency on adults, not only for basic survival necessities, but also for concepts with which to understand the meanings of experience and guidance about how to respond to it.

In infancy, the connections between language, thought, and behavior are loose and the child's potential for achieving cognitive control over behavior is very limited. Over the next several years, during what Piaget calls the preoperational period, cognitive abilities become both more differentiated and more integrated with one another and with behavior. Gradually, the child becomes able to use thought, particularly thought mediated by speech and expressed as inner speech or self-talk (Vygotsky, 1962), to plan and regulate behavior. Such cognitive regulation begins with a child's physical responses to the immediate environment but gradually extends to include social interactions as well. Cognitive mediation is perhaps especially crucial in the social sphere where relatively little of what occurs can be understood merely by observing people's physical movements. In order to understand and participate in human social interaction, one must understand the language and associated concepts and referents that form the core of such activities and provide the context for meaning.

Even as their cognitive and linguistic abilities develop throughout the preoperational years (ages 2 through 6 or 7) and into the concrete operational years (ages 6 or 7 through adolescence), children remain heavily dependent on adult guidance in learning to interpret and respond to their social environments. Preschool and early elementary school students tend to identify with and seek to please their parents and teachers, developing what Kohlberg (1969) has called a "good boy" or "good girl" level of moral thinking. They tend to accept (even if they do not always follow) the conduct norms propounded by these adult authority figures because they want to please them by "being good," and being good means following these conduct norms.

Because they are so dependent on adults for information and predisposed to accept what adults tell them (at least if what adults tell them is consistent), young children tend to accept what they are told about behavioral norms without much reflection or attempt at evaluation. In Freud's terms, they "introject" moral concepts and behavioral norms—acquire them directly from statements by adults, retain them in the concrete form in which they were originally learned, and re-

From Jere Brophy, "Classroom Management as Instruction: Socializing Self-Guidance in Students," *Theory Into Practice*, 24(4), Autumn 1985. Copyright © 1985 College of Education, The Ohio State University. Reprinted with permission.

produce them in similar contexts in the future. Typically, children come to think of these norms as their own (that is, as something they always knew or they figured out for themselves), losing sight of the fact that the norms were originally taught to them by adult authority figures.

Introjected moral norms do not contribute much to effective self-regulation of behavior because they tend to be isolated verbal responses —conditioned reactions to particular situations—rather than "words to live by" that have been consciously adopted and function as part of a general philosophy that provides guidance to one's behavior (Brophy, 1977). Typically, children do not begin to actively question the moral norms to which they have been exposed and seek to develop a moral philosophy of their own until they reach adolescence and enter Piaget's stage of formal operational thinking. Even then, great individual differences exist in the degree to which previously introjected norms are consciously examined and a more mature and functional set of norms is adopted, internalized, and developed into a consistent system. These individual differences are closely related to the degree and nature of moral socialization to which the individuals have been exposed.

CHARACTERISTICS OF SUCCESSFUL SOCIALIZATION

Research on child rearing suggests that successful socialization has two noteworthy characteristics. First, such socialization is extensive in volume and rich in cognitive content. Effective parents spend a great deal of time interacting with their children in ways that stimulate the children's cognitive development (Hess, 1970). In particular, such parents socialize the children's beliefs, attitudes, and expectations about morality, social interaction, politics, and related social realities. They supply their children not merely with norms, but with concepts, labels, principles, rationales, and related cognitive input that provide a basis for understanding cognitive realities and a context of meaning within which to interpret norms and prescriptions. In short, such parents provide their children with a great deal of instruction, and not merely with a brief list of do's and don'ts.

Second, effective socialization is what Baumrind (1971) calls "authoritative" rather than "authoritarian" or "laissez-faire." Authoritative parents accept their rules as authority figures responsible for socializing their children and therefore place demands and limits on the children. However, they routinely explain the rationales underlying these demands and help the children appreciate that demands are appropriate and motivated by a concern for people's (including the children's) rights and best interests.

Contrasting patterns of parenting lack the balance and effectiveness of this authoritative pattern. Laissez-faire parents make few demands on their children. They tend to ignore them and let them do as they please, so long as they do not become destructive or annoying. This pattern is often a form of apathy or rejection, and may lead to feelings of insecurity and low self-esteem in the children. In any case, it involves requiring the children to make decisions about how to behave without first having equipped them with the principles and concepts needed for making such decisions. At best, this leads to a great deal of unnecessary and sometimes painful trial and error learning, and it also is likely to lead to traits such as insecurity, anxiety, or fear of failure.

Authoritarian parents make constant demands on their children with little attempt to explain these demands or help the children understand the reasons for them. Instead, they "boss the children around" with a "you'll do it because I said so" attitude and a readiness to punish failure to comply. This sets up the issue of regulation of behavior as a contest of wills and a matter of power exertion rather than as a self-regulation based on concepts of rights and responsibilities.

The authoritative approach is the most likely to give children both the cognitive tools and the emotional freedom to think about and evaluate behavioral norms, to consciously adopt the norms that make sense and use them to guide behavior, and to integrate them into a systematic and internally consistent moral philosophy (Brophy, 1977). In contrast to laissez-faire parents, authoritative parents provide their children with a well-articulated model of such a systematic moral philosophy, which the children can learn and use as a base from which to develop their own moral thinking. It is easier to first master and then work from such a base than to try to develop an integrated system of moral principles by working from scratch.

Authoritative parents provide their children not only with the cognitive tools for evaluating behavioral norms but also with the modeling and emotional freedom that will encourage them to do so. They consistently present behavioral norms as means toward ends rather than as ends in themselves. Ultimately, the justification for rules and demands lies in the golden rule or associated concepts of justice, fairness, or morality, rather than in the authority of the parent over the child. The children are encouraged to think about why they behave as they do and to evaluate their behavior in terms of its effectiveness in attaining the goals toward which it is ostensibly directed.

In contrast, authoritarian parents discourage such thinking by demanding conformity and submission to their authority and focusing on threat of punishment rather than moral justification in presenting their demands. If they succeed in breaking the child's will, the result will be a docile individual who rigidly follows prescribed norms and is essentially externally controlled rather than self-guided. If they fail, the result will be an individual who resents and resists authority and is prone to delinquency and crime. The docile, intimidated child lacks the emotional freedom to evaluate behavioral prescriptions because he or she has learned to equate this with rebellion against powerful authority figures; the oppositional child lacks the motivation to do so because he or she has learned to equate behavioral prescriptions with arbitrary and oppressive exertion of power by authority figures.

CLASSROOM MANAGEMENT

Theory and research on classroom management have concentrated mostly on how teachers can control student behavior rather than on how teachers can develop self-guidance in their students. This is largely understandable because of the bureaucratic nature of schools, the unfavorable student/teacher ratio, the competition for grades, the public nature of classroom instruction, and all of the other factors that make it difficult to establish the classroom as an effective learning environment. Even so, appropriate student self-guidance is an implicit ideal. The teachers who are most admired as classroom managers are those whose classes run smoothly without a great deal of cueing or direction giving, whose students are actively engaged in academic activities, and who can leave the room or turn the class over to a substitute without fear of disruption or inappropriate behavior.

Prior to the seminal work of Kounin (1970), little systematic research had been done on effective classroom management. Advice to teachers was of the "Don't smile until Christmas" variety, in which the emphasis was on control or discipline and the advice consisted of an ill-assorted "bag of tricks" based on experience rather than an integrated set of principles developed from systematic research.

Kounin (1970) approached this problem by comparing the behaviors of effective and ineffective classroom managers. He videotaped activities in ideal classrooms such as those described above and also in poorly managed classrooms in which the teachers were fighting to keep the lid on and the students were regularly inattentive and frequently disruptive. His initial approach, following the "discipline" orientation dominant at the time, was to compare the two groups of teachers' handling of disruptive incidents. Surprisingly, in view of the clear differences in effectiveness between these two groups of teachers, the analyses failed to produce consistent results. Effective classroom managers did not differ in systematic ways from ineffective classroom managers when they were responding to student misbehavior.

However, Kounin and his colleagues noticed that effective managers differed from ineffective managers in other ways that they eventually were able to define and measure systematically through reanalyses. Some of the key behaviors shown by the effective managers were the following:

- *Withitness.* Remaining "with it" (aware of what is happening in all parts of the classroom at all times) by continuously scanning the classroom, even when working with small groups or individuals; demonstrating this withitness to the students by intervening promptly and accurately when inappropriate behavior threatens to become disruptive, thus avoiding both timing errors (failing to notice and intervene until an incident has already become disruptive) and target errors (confusion or mistakes concerning which students were responsible for the problem).
- *Overlapping.* Doing more than one thing at a time. In particular, responding to the needs of individuals while sustaining group activity (using eye contact or physical proximity to restore inattentive students' attention to a lesson while continuing the lesson itself without interruption).
- *Signal continuity and momentum during lessons.* Teaching well-prepared and briskly paced lessons that focus students' attention by providing them with a continuous academic signal which is more compelling than the noise of competing distractions in the classroom, and by sustaining the momentum of this academic signal throughout the duration of the lesson.
- *Challenge and variety in assignments.* Encouraging student engagement in seatwork by providing assignments pitched at the right level of difficulty (easy enough to insure success with reasonable effort but new or difficult enough to provide challenge) and varied enough to sustain interest.

These and other principles discovered by Kounin indicate that effective classroom managers succeed not so much because they are good at handling disruption when it occurs, but because they are good at maximizing the time students spend attending to lessons and engaging in assignments. They are good at preventing disruption from occurring in the first place. Their focus is not on prevention of disruption as such but on establishing the classroom as an effective learning environment, preparing and teaching good lessons, and selecting and monitoring student performance on good follow-up assignments.

Evertson and Emmer (1982) and

their colleagues have replicated and extended Kounin's findings in a series of studies of how teachers establish effective classroom management at the beginning of the year and sustain it thereafter. These studies have replicated and reinforced Kounin's findings and have demonstrated the importance of showing and telling students what to do. Teacher clarity about rules and routines is crucial, as is the ability to explain and, if necessary, demonstrate the desired behavior to the students.

Especially in the lower grades, effective classroom managers spend a great deal of time in the early weeks of school explaining expectations and conducting lessons not only in the formal curriculum but in the routines and procedures to be used in the classroom. Their students are given detailed explanations and modeling (and, if necessary, opportunities to practice and receive feedback) concerning such matters as when and how to use the pencil sharpener or how to manage the transitions between reading groups.

In the upper grades it is less important for teachers to model or provide formal lessons in desired routines (the students are already familiar with most of these routines or can understand them sufficiently from verbal explanation) but it is just as important for them to be clear and detailed in describing what behavior they expect. At all grade levels, teachers need to insure that the students follow the desired procedures, providing additional reminders or feedback as needed.

Effective managers consistently monitor compliance with rules and demands, enforce accountability procedures and associated penalties for late or unacceptable work, and are prepared to punish students for repeated misconduct if necessary. But their emphasis is positive and prescriptive rather than threatening or punitive. This and other work on classroom management (reviewed by Brophy, 1983, and Doyle, in press) shows clearly that effective classroom management goes hand in hand with effective instruction and that it primarily involves teaching willing students what to do before the fact rather than applying "discipline" following misconduct.

STRATEGIES FOR PROBLEM STUDENTS

No comparable set of research findings exists regarding strategies teachers should use with students who present chronic personality or behavior problems and require something more than what is effective with the group, and few teachers have had training in such techniques (Brophy & Rohrkemper, 1981). However, writers interested in applications by teachers of techniques developed in psychotherapy and mental health settings have begun to suggest principles that complement those known to be effective for group management. Gordon (1974), Glasser (1977), and Good and Brophy (1984) are representative of these contemporary sources of advice to teachers about counseling problem students. Gordon's approach begins with analysis of problem ownership. A problem is owned by the teacher if the teacher's needs are being frustrated (as when a student persistently disrupts the class by socializing with friends). The student owns the problem when the student's needs are being frustrated (such as when the student is being rejected by the peer group). The teacher and the student share a problem when each is frustrating the needs of the other (the teacher gives the student work that is too difficult and the student responds by giving up and becoming disruptive).

For student-owned problems Gordon recommends "active listening," in which the teacher not only listens to the student's point of view, but attempts to reflect it back accurately to the student, with attention to the student's feelings and personal reactions in addition to behaviors and events. For teacher-owned problems he recommends "I" messages in which the teacher states explicitly the linkages between the student's objectionable behavior, the problem that this behavior causes the teacher (how it frustrates the teacher's needs), and the effects of these events on the teacher's feelings (discouragement, frustration). Shared problems would call for combinations of active listening and "I" messages.

Such communications should help teachers and students achieve shared rational views of problems and assume cooperative, problem-solving attitudes. Together they can work to resolve conflicts using what Gordon calls the "no lose" method of finding the solution that will work best for all concerned. The process involves six steps: Define the problem; generate possible solutions; evaluate those solutions; decide which is best; determine how to implement this decision; and assess how well the solution is working (a new solution will have to be negotiated if the first one does not work satisfactorily).

Glasser stresses the need to develop appropriate classroom rules (preferably in collaboration with the students) and to enforce those rules and refer to them when correcting student misbehavior. His "ten steps to good discipline" (Glasser, 1977) are designed to focus students' attention on their behavior in order to make sure that they realize and accept responsibility for what they are doing (often this alone is sufficient to change the behavior). In some cases he suggests requiring the student to develop a plan that includes a commitment to changing problem behavior and a description of steps to be taken to insure that such change occurs.

Good and Brophy (1984) suggest ways that teachers can observe and interview problem students in order to develop an understanding of why they behave as they do, as well as strategies for developing productive personal relationships with such students and counseling them individually. They stress the importance of supporting the positive elements of the student's self-concept, projecting positive expectations about the student's willingness and ability to change behavior, setting realistic goals and monitoring progress toward attaining them, and emphasizing the teacher's role as a helper rather than as an authority figure (while still exerting that authority and making demands on the student).

BEYOND MANAGEMENT: PROMOTING SELF-GUIDANCE

In combination, the approaches to classroom management reviewed above will allow teachers to establish their classrooms as effective learning environments and themselves as effective leaders for the group and counselors for individuals. In order to develop self-guidance in students, however, additional strategies are needed.

In setting limits and prescribing procedures, teachers should use an informational rather than a controlling style (Koestner, Ryan, Bernieri, & Holt, in press). They should stress the reasons for the limits and procedures, implying that these are reasonable and useful guidelines students will want to follow because they help insure the attainment of important academic or social goals. Even though acting as an authority figure, the teacher uses a tone and manner that suggests soliciting students' cooperation rather than issuing orders. The emphasis is on what to do and how this will yield desirable benefits rather than on the consequences for failure to comply. The idea is to induce students to consciously adopt the desired procedures for themselves and thus begin to use them as internal guides to behavior, minimizing the degree to which they see the guidelines as externally imposed and enforced.

As a way to insure student commitment to the guidelines, some teachers prefer to develop them in collaboration with students during classroom meetings held for this purpose. This method can be effective, but it takes time and the teacher needs to set a positive tone and provide guidance and structure to the meetings. If left on their own, students will tend to make up large numbers of overly specific rules rather than smaller numbers of general ones, to stress "don'ts" rather than "do's," and to focus on prescribing punishment for violators. Furthermore, even with this level of student involvement in rule making, the teacher remains the ultimate authority figure in the classroom. As Baumrind (1971) has shown, the form of socialization of children and youth that best fosters the development of self-guidance abilities is "authoritative," not "democratic."

The degree to which a guideline becomes functional in regulating student behavior will be determined not so much by whether the students participate in establishing the guideline as by whether they see it as reasonable and choose to adopt it for themselves. Presenting guidelines in an informative rather than a controlling style encourages students to make this choice. The following are aspects of an informational style of presenting guidelines.

First, teachers should always give the reasons for the guideline in addition to the guideline itself. If it is not easy to show that the guideline is intended as a means toward a desirable end, something is probably wrong with the guideline.

Second, guidelines should be presented with positive expectations and attributions. Teachers should assume that students will want to follow reasonable guidelines because the students themselves are reasonable and prosocially oriented individuals who want to cooperate and pursue the common good.

Third, when it becomes necessary to correct misbehavior, such corrections should emphasize the desired positive behavior ("Talk quietly so as not to disturb those who are still working."). As much as possible, such corrections should be phrased as friendly reminders rather than as power assertive direct orders, and should encourage students to see themselves as regulating their own behavior rather than being controlled externally ("You only have a few more minutes to finish your assignment" is better than "If you don't get back to work and finish that assignment before the bell, you will have to stay in during recess").

Fourth, if it becomes necessary to punish students who have not responded to more positive approaches, the punishment should be announced with a tone of sadness and disappointment rather than vengefulness or righteous indignation. The student should understand that the teacher does not want to have to punish but feels it necessary to do so because of the student's own repeated misbehavior and failure to respond to more positive approaches. The punishment is not an arbitrary exertion of power by the teacher; rather, it is an unfortunate but necessary and appropriate consequence of the student's repeated misbehavior, and one the student can avoid in the future if he or she chooses to do so.

Underlying this is the implication that students can and are expected to behave appropriately, and it is primarily their own responsibility to regulate their behavior rather than the teacher's responsibility to control them externally. The teacher is a facilitator, not a prison warden, and the student is a well-intentioned, reasonable human being, not a wild animal in need of training or a weak individual dominated by emotions or compulsions that he or she cannot control.

Finally, some students will need

individualized counseling and assistance in developing effective self-regulation. Often this can be accomplished simply through conversations designed to develop personal relationships with such students, establish the teacher as a helper and resource person, and develop the students' insights into their own behavior. The suggestions of Glasser (1977), Gordon (1974), and Good and Brophy (1984) are useful in this regard. Some students, however, may need not only general guidance but explicit instruction in methods of self-regulation of behavior. Recent developments in theory and research provide teachers interested in self-guidance with some exciting new approaches in this regard.

One set of sources has been developed through an approach called cognitive behavior modification (Meichenbaum, 1977). In this approach teachers go beyond merely telling students what to do in a general way. Instead they model the process by verbalizing aloud the self-talk that is generated and used to regulate behavior while carrying out the activity (generation of goal statements, review of strategies to be used in pursuing the goals, self-instructions produced at each step, monitoring and evaluation of performance, methods of responding effectively to failure or unexpected events, self-reinforcement for progress and success). Such modeling shows students how to regulate their own behavior by making visible the perceptions, thoughts, and other self-talk that regulate effective coping behavior but usually remain invisible to the observer.

The cognitive behavior modification approach has been used to teach students to respond reflectively rather than impulsively to multiple choice tasks (Meichenbaum & Goodman, 1971), to "innoculate" aggression-prone individuals against overreaction to provocation and help them to control their anger (Novaco, 1975), and to help hyperactive and disruptive students learn to control their behavior more effectively (Kendall & Braswell, 1982). More recently, this approach has been adapted for use in helping students cope with academic tasks and manage their learning more effectively, in addition to applications to control of classroom conduct and social interaction (Meichenbaum & Asarnow, 1979).

Other approaches to what is becoming known as "strategy training" have been developed by theorists working outside the cognitive behavior modification tradition, although their approaches are similar to and compatible with cognitive behavior modification approaches. One such approach involves modeling couples with role playing or other simulation exercises (Good & Brophy, 1984; Sarason & Sarason, 1981). Other strategy training approaches have been developed by individuals interested in teaching students strategies for reading with comprehension or for learning and problem solving with clarity of purpose and metacognitive awareness of the strategies being applied (Brown, Bransford, Ferrara, & Campione, 1983; Palincsar & Brown, 1984).

CONCLUSION

Even though schooling is compulsory and teachers must prescribe and control student behavior in order to establish the classroom as an effective learning environment, teachers can still stimulate self-guidance, and not merely compliance, in their students. This is done by deemphasizing the authority figure aspects of the teacher's role and emphasizing the rationales that justify the demands made on students, projecting positive expectations concerning students' ability to foster the common good, and encouraging students to view behavioral guidelines as reasonable and adopt them as their own.

Most students develop effective self-guidance mechanisms on their own, even though the self-talk involved in such self-guidance ordinarily is covert and cannot be observed directly. Students who have not developed effective self-guidance procedures will need direct assistance in doing so, however, and recently developed procedures for strategy training and cognitive behavior modification are suggested for this purpose.

Note: This work is sponsored in part by the Institute for Research on Teaching, College of Education, Michigan State University. The Institute for Research on Teaching is funded primarily by the Program for Teaching and Instruction of the National Institute of Education, United States Department of Education. The opinions expressed in this article do not necessarily reflect the position, policy, or endorsement of the National Institute of Education. (Contract No. 400-81-0014)

REFERENCES

Baumrind, D. (1971). Current patterns of parental authority. *Developmental Psychology Monograph, 4*(1), part 2.

Brophy, J. (1977). *Child development and socialization.* Chicago: Science Research Associates.

Brophy, J. (1983). Classroom organization and management. *Elementary School Journal, 83,* 265–285.

Brophy, J., & Rohrkemper, M. (1981). The influence of problem ownership on teachers' perceptions of and strategies for coping with problem students. *Journal of Educational Psychology, 73,* 295–311.

Brown, A., Bransford, J., Ferrara, R., & Campione, J. (1983). Learning, remembering, and understanding. In J. Flavell and E. Markman (Eds.), *Handbook of child psychology* (4th ed.)—*Cognitive development* (Vol. 3) (pp. 77–166). New York: Wiley.

Doyle, W. (in press). Classroom organization and management. In M. Wittrock (Ed.), *Handbook of research on teaching* (3rd ed.). New York: Macmillan.

Evertson, C., & Emmer, E. (1982). Preventive classroom management. In D. Duke (Ed.), *Helping teachers manage classrooms.* Alexandria, VA: Association for Supervision and Curriculum Development.

Glasser, W. (1977, November–December). Ten steps to good discipline. *Today's Education, 66*(4), 61–63.

Good, T., & Brophy, J. (1984). *Looking in classrooms* (3rd ed.). New York: Harper & Row.

Gordon, T. (1974). *T.E.T. teacher effectiveness training.* New York: David McKay.

Hess, R. (1970). Social class and ethnic influences upon socialization. In P. Mussen (Ed.), *Carmichael's manual of child psychology,* (Vol. 2, 3rd ed.) (pp. 457–557). New York: Wiley.

Kendall, P., & Braswell, L. (1982). Cognitive-behavioral self-control therapy for children: A components analysis. *Journal of Consulting and Clinical Psychology, 50,* 672–689.

Koestner, R., Ryan, R., Bernieri, F., & Holt, K. (in press). Setting limits on children's behavior: The differential effects of controlling versus informational styles on intrinsic motivation and creativity. *Journal of Personality.*

Kohlberg, L. (1969). Stage and sequence: The cognitive-developmental approach to socialization. In D. Goslin (Ed.), *Handbook of socialization theory and research* (pp. 347–480). Chicago: Rand McNally.

Kounin, J. (1970). *Discipline and group management in classrooms.* New York: Holt, Rinehart & Winston.

Meichenbaum, D. (1977). *Cognitive-behavior modification.* New York: Plenum.

Meichenbaum, D., & Asarnow, J. (1979). Cognitive-behavioral modification and metacognitive development: Implications for the classroom. In P. Kendall & S. Hollon (Eds.), *Cognitive-behavioral interventions: Theory, research, and procedures* (pp. 11–35). New York: Academic Press.

Meichenbaum, D., & Goodman, J. (1971). Training impulsive children to talk to themselves. *Journal of Abnormal Psychology, 77,* 115–126.

Novaco, R. (1975). *Anger control: A development and evaluation of an experimental treatment.* Lexington, MA: Heath.

Palincsar, A., & Brown, A. (1984). Reciprocal teaching of comprehension-fostering and comprehension-monitoring activities. *Cognition and Instruction, 1,* 117–175.

Sarason, I., & Sarason, B. (1981). Teaching cognitive and social skills to high school students. *Journal of Consulting and Clinical Psychology, 49,* 908–918.

Vygotsky, L. (1962). *Thought and language.* Cambridge, MA: MIT Press.

CHAPTER THIRTEEN

Basic Understandings About Testing and Educational Research

READING 37 LORRIE SHEPARD
Norm-Referenced vs. Criterion-Referenced Tests

Criterion-referenced testing is a significant methodological reform in the field of educational measurement. These new tests, however, should not always or automatically be chosen rather than norm-referenced tests. Normative interpretations still are essential for certain uses and, in practice, most criterion-referenced tests do not have the ideal characteristics originally intended.

To consider which kind of test is better, and for which purposes, it is important to acknowledge not only the distinctions contained in the accepted definitions but also the characteristics usually imputed to the two types of tests. Some scholars try to cool the controversy by pointing out that a single test can be both norm referenced and criterion referenced. While the ideal solution is

From Lorrie Shepard, "Norm-Referenced vs. Criterion-Referenced Tests," *Educational Horizons* (Fall 1979):26–35. Reprinted with permission of *Educational Horizons* quarterly journal published by Pi Lambda Theta national honor and professional association, Bloomington, IN 47407-6626.

to obtain appropriate normative data to interpret tests with carefully delineated content (Popham, 1976), the author believes it is also helpful to discuss proper and improper uses of the two kinds of tests as they typically are found.

DEFINITION OF NORM AND CRITERION REFERENTS

Criterion referencing was introduced by Glaser (1963). It was intended to increase the content validity of tests and, hence, their usefulness in day-to-day instructional decisions by more directly linking test questions to a carefully described criterion set of behaviors. A test is criterion referenced if criterion levels are well enough specified so that a pupil's performance will locate him accurately on a performance continuum. The statement one hears most often is that "Criterion-referenced tests tell what a child knows and can do." The criterion is the knowledge or behavioral domain against which the test is carefully mapped. Note that, by this definition, criterion-referenced tests are equivalent to what other authors call domain-referenced tests (Hively et al., 1973; Millman, 1974).

Norm referenced refers to the interpretation of test performance in terms of a norm. It indicates an individual's relative standing in a group; for example, a child's score may be at the thirtieth percentile nationally, or equal to that earned by the average second grader. Norms are obtained by administering the test to a large representative sample; most commercially available tests have national norms, but norms also can be developed for states or for local districts. Additionally, just as a child's performance can be interpreted in relation to that of other children, school scores can be compared to school norms.

210

CAREFULNESS OF CONTENT SPECIFICATION

The essential characteristic of criterion-referenced tests is the precision with which the content domain is specified and items are developed to reflect that content. Unfortunately, many tests currently called criterion referenced are not criterion referenced in this sense and do not necessarily have superior content validity. In a comprehensive review of criterion-referenced testing, Hambleton, Swaminathan, Algina, and Coulson (1978) noted that most of the criterion-referenced tests on the market are only "objectives-referenced" (p. 3). By this they mean that items are keyed to objectives but a behavioral domain has not been specified and items cannot be considered to be a representative sample from a domain. Hambleton and Eignor (1978) reviewed eleven of the most popular criterion-referenced tests and concluded that they were all objectives referenced rather than criterion referenced.

Norm-referenced tests often are characterized as being poorly developed with no logical or systematic rules for determining test content. Popham (1978b) believes that test publishers are purposely vague so that test content will appear to be appealing to diverse audiences. Although many norm-referenced tests currently available have not been developed with the precision recommended by Glaser, they are built following fairly elaborate tables of specifications and compare favorably with many objectives-referenced tests where items have been written to measure behavioral objectives. Millman (1974) has acknowledged that items in a norm-referenced test could be matched to objectives to yield criterion-referenced interpretations. The problem is not with the quality of the items themselves, then, but with their representativeness of a larger domain and with their *number* (too few for certain purposes).

It is the author's conclusion that there presently are only a few exemplary domain-referenced tests that deserve the obeisance and special praise given to criterion-referenced tests (see Hively et al., 1973). These were developed by highly qualified measurement specialists for large-scale, well-funded research or evaluation efforts. Typical norm-referenced and objectives-referenced tests are not as distinguishable by the carefulness of their content specification as they are by the *number* of items used to assess a particular topic.

DIAGNOSTIC VS. SURVEY TESTS

Somewhere in the heat of controversy over norm referencing and in the zealous overuse of norm-referenced tests by their advocates, an important characteristic of these tests has been forgotten. They are *survey* tests of achievement (Stanley and Hopkins, 1972). As the term "survey" connotes, typical norm-referenced tests were meant to provide a broad overview of attainments in a subject area. In practical terms, this means that if a subject as broad as reading is to be assessed, items will be sampled from several narrower domains, such as phonetic analysis, reading comprehension, vocabulary, study/locational skills, and so on. At the more microscopic level, it means that there may be only one or two items that measure a subskill such as consonant blends.

This is why *survey* tests are not good *diagnostic* tests. Even if the items are selected to be representative of specified domains, there are too few items to assess mastery of small instructional bits. For diagnostic purposes, there must be enough items for every subpart of the test so that achievement can be measured dependably and accurately. To cover an area as broad as reading, with diagnostic validity for every subpart, would require hundreds of test items.

The question should not be whether diagnostic tests are better than survey tests (or roughly whether so-called criterion-referenced tests are better than norm-referenced tests). Rather, it should be how to use each type of test well for its intended purpose. Norm-referenced tests should be administered relatively infrequently to monitor pupil and program progress. Properly developed criterion-referenced tests should be used for instructional diagnoses. In this case, students should be given reasonably short tests focused on the particular instructional objectives of interest.[1] With adequate focus, there still will be enough items to ensure dependable interpretation of each subskill measured. Since, for diagnostic purposes, several items are necessary for every tiny domain subpart, criterion-referenced tests of broad subject areas will be very lengthy. This feature has created some new problems for testing practice.

It is not practical to give pupils criterion-referenced tests that are hundreds of items long, covering a broad area like reading. It wastes their time and does not serve the diagnostic purpose claimed. It is the author's contention that, if a classroom teacher were given a list of the criterion behaviors these hundreds of items measure, he or she could accurately report how the child would do on many more than half of the items. *For day-to-day classroom purposes, testing should be focused only on those things the teacher does not know about a child.* It is a mistake to combine many small, criterion-referenced tests into lengthy test batteries and administer them to all children in extended

---

[1] Many practitioners ask, "How many items are necessary?" The answer depends on how specific and how homogeneous each subpart of the test is. Some suggest that five items is a good minimum number. This is a bit simplistic, since the level of specificity of domains or objectives will very much affect the number needed. If recognizing letters of the alphabet is the domain, at least 26 items are required. It would be hard to defend fewer than five items for each interpretable score; but often more items will be needed.

testing sessions. There will be a great overkill of diagnostic information, because the teacher already knows those things that are well above or well below the child's performance levels, and because the child's strengths and weaknesses will change by the time the teacher gets to the end of the test-identified list of deficiencies.

STATISTICAL VS. LOGICAL TEST CONSTRUCTION

Detractors of norm-referenced tests say that, because they are designed to rank individuals, statistical criteria used to select items will bias the content domain represented by the test (Millman, 1974). More damaging still, they say, is that such bias will cause omission of the most important topics taught in school because 100 percent items (those that everyone answers correctly) show no variance in pupils (Popham, 1978c). This change is grossly overstated; nevertheless, the author believes that the critics have identified a real danger if ever statistical criteria were used to the exclusion of logical content specification.[2] Therefore, their warning should not be dismissed lightly.

Ordinarily, publishers of norm-referenced tests do not blindly apply statistical rules to increase variance. Evidence that they do not can be found in the tables of specifications used to construct the tests and in the item statistics published with the tests. Critics would have us believe that most test items hover in the 50 percent difficulty range to maximize discrimination. In fact, most tests have many items in the 80 percent correct range, especially when data are for the highest grade in a test battery. Most experts in criterion-referenced testing acknowledge that empirical item analysis techniques can be used profitably so long as faulty items are

[2]Buros first identified this problem in 1935; see Buros (1978).

improved or replaced (see Hambleton et al., 1978). The only danger to criterion referencing from item analysis is if "bad" items are omitted, thus leaving holes in the representation of the domain.

Omitting 100 percent items does not distort the content of the tests, but rather makes them insensitive to the progress of slow groups. The critics would not really expect high school math tests to include items for elementary arithmetic. Usually it *is* safe to omit the 100 percent items. The problem they identify is only serious when the level of the entire test is too difficult for the students tested. In most cases with remedial students, for example, performance may be too low to be within the range of the test. Therefore, even great progress made in a year still may not bring the student to a point that "registers" on the scale. This problem is recognized in the increasing body of literature on out-of-level testing (Ayrer and McNamara, 1973; Yoshida, 1976).

Norm-referenced tests are not insensitive to instruction in the long run or they would not consistently show gains from grade to grade. It should be kept in mind that they are survey tests, useful for monitoring progress across years, not across months, and they must be centered at the appropriate level for the pupils tested. Perhaps it is because the critics *believe* that norm-referenced tests will so often be administered at the wrong levels that the tests are attacked so harshly. However, the attack cannot be justified on purely logical grounds. There are eminent measurement specialists who *believe* that norm-referenced tests can still serve important purposes (Ebel, 1972; Ebel, 1978; Mehrens and Lehmann, 1978; Stanley and Hopkins, 1972).

STANDARDS AND CUTOFF SCORES

Glass (1978b) and Popham (1975) both provide histories of criterion-referenced testing terminology.

They explain how cutoff scores came to be mistaken for the "criterion" rather than the desired domain of behaviors. Glass accuses Popham and Husek (1969) and the behavioral objectives movement (Mager, 1962) of defining criterion-referenced tests as those with absolute standards for determining passing and failing. Although Popham (1975, 1978c) now affirms the original meaning for the term, some experts (Hambleton et al., 1978) and most practitioners believe that a key feature of criterion-referenced tests is that they separate examinees into black and white categories of mastery and nonmastery.

The standards problem is the biggest liability of the criterion-referenced testing movement. Although some may argue that cutoff scores can be set wisely (Block, 1978; Popham, 1978a; Zieky and Livingston, 1977), all agree that they rely on human judgment and thus are fallible. Glass (1978b) is the harshest critic of arbitrarily set standards. He has reviewed the various methods for setting standards and demonstrated how each rests on human judgment and will, therefore, result in very different standards (and very different pass rates), depending on who decides. Although his attack is aimed primarily at uses of standards in minimum competency testing programs, his criticisms apply in all instances where absolute interpretations of performance are attempted.

Although misplaced cutoff scores may not be serious in the classroom setting where teachers can easily redress errors, error-laden standards will be more risky when crucial decisions about individuals are made, and they may lead to bad evaluations of programs at the state or local level. Because the standards are arbitrary, apparent strengths and weaknesses in pupil or program performance can easily be nothing more than differences in the stringency of the standards. This is very likely what happened in the Florida minimum competency testing program, where a greater percentage of students failed the math test than the communications test; and, as a result, the larger share of state appropriations was allocated to mathematics programs. But the Florida situation could easily have been due to the greater difficulty of the mathematics items relative to the arbitrarily set standard rather than to a real deficiency in math knowledge (Glass, 1978a).

Blind adherence to arbitrarily set standards, for example, 80 percent passing or four out of five items correct on every objective, will lead to instructional emphasis on the objectives with the hardest items, even though often "criterion levels" are set without looking at the items. This also means that important content will be slighted just because cutoff scores were set too low! (Where are Millman and Popham when we need them? Isn't this very like the problem of omitting 100 percent items from norm-referenced tests?)

APPROPRIATE NORMS

Because cutoff scores on criterion-referenced tests are arbitrary and lack intrinsic meaning, it is not possible to tell from them whether performance is good or bad. A school district could have an elegantly developed set of domain specifications and test items; they might even know that all students were achieving at prespecified levels; but they would not know whether their expectations had been set too high or too low (more probably the latter). Normative data are essential to evaluate test performance.

Popham (1976) has acknowledged that criterion-referenced tests cannot tell how well students *should do* without some external basis of comparison. He describes some informal comparisons with the district next door and goes on to recommend that ". . . proponents of criterion-referenced tests should encourage developers of such measures to assemble data regarding how well-described groups perform on the tests" (p. 594). In the best of all possible worlds, we should have carefully developed criterion-referenced tests accompanied by normative data. Presently, however, such tests are not available. The only things close to them are the objectives-referenced tests with norms developed by the National Assessment of Educational Progress (NAEP), which have national norms for every item, and by several state assessment programs. In the absence of norms for criterion-referenced tests, districts must use both criterion-referenced tests and norm-referenced tests. The latter may be either the traditional, commercially available standardized achievement tests or norm-referenced, objective-referenced items from NAEP or the state department of education.

Normative data or norm-referenced tests provide an external basis of comparison. They, therefore, allow more accurate statements about relative strengths and weaknesses. Since norms take relative difficulty into account, profiles of scores in comparison to norms show where pupils or schools are not functioning up to their usual level of accomplishment. For example, in the Florida case mentioned above, legislators could have been more certain that mathematics achievement was worse than language arts achievement if this discrepancy had shown up in relation to the respective national norms. Pupil strengths and weaknesses also can be seen if scores are profiled using normative data.

This advocacy of norms does not mean that norms should be interpreted as the "standards." Such a position leads to mindless statements such as "Everyone should be above the national norm." (This is not possible since, by definition, half will always be above and half below the national median or norm.) Moreover, the national average is not necessarily the best norm to use. The NAEP reports results for nine different categories of size and type of district so that, for example, suburban middle-class schools can compare their performance to that of other similar districts. In California, assessment results are reported for schools and districts in relation to aggregate background characteristics, such an average socioeconomic status and average performance on an entry test given when children start school (*California State Testing Program,* 1973). This means that urban schools with high percentages of non-English speaking children are compared to other schools with similar populations. At the individual pupil level, many test publishers provide jointly normed ability and achievement tests so that a child's strengths and weaknesses can be evaluated in comparison to averages for other children of comparable ability.

MATCH TO LOCAL CURRICULUM

Popham (1978b) has complained that another major drawback of norm-referenced tests is that they are not well matched to local curricula. Certainly, if criterion-referenced tests are locally developed or selected from commercially available item pools, they will match a local curriculum better than traditional norm-referenced tests. It is still possible, however, to select norm-referenced tests that match local curricula accurately enough to accomplish survey testing purposes and provide the external comparison described above.[3] It is the author's opinion that advocates of criterion-referenced testing tend to exaggerate the diversity in school 3R curricula, just as they believe norm-referenced testers exaggerate the uniformity. As evidence in sup-

---
[3]If extraneous objectives are covered by the test, item level normative data can be used to recompute the appropriate norms using only the relevant subsets of items; see Hopkins et al. (1978).

port of this opinion, the author offers her experience in reading the K-3 reading objectives for more than 200 school districts; they were found to be remarkably similar. Of course, this may be the subject area and level where one would expect the greatest homogeneity. Nevertheless, skeptics should remember that claiming similarity in instructional goals is not the same as saying that things are taught in the same way. In support of the diversity of programs, Popham (1978b) cited DeVault, Harnischfeger, and Wiley (1977), who found very different amounts of time spent on basic subjects in different schools. Differences in emphasis among the subjects, however, does not necessarily mean that the content varies when a particular subject is being taught.

Careful review of test materials and test items will allow teachers and curriculum experts to decide whether or not a norm-referenced test fairly reflects local curriculum. A Colorado district recently selected a test by determining not only which test had a good content match but also which had the best correlation with teacher judgments of objectives mastered (Hopkins et al., 1978).

Of course, any good evaluator should deplore the use of a single measure (norm referenced or otherwise) as the sole indicator of the quality of schooling. It is an old precept in social science research that multiple measurement is the only protection against the fallibility of each measure (Webb, 1966). Therefore, this defense of norm-referenced tests is not to sell them ever as the exclusive measure for program evaluation, but to suggest that they do provide an important and external perspective. If performance were ever to fall short of expectations because of curricular differences, parents and other interested constituencies might well wish to discuss the choices involved in selecting the local rather than the test-relevant curriculum. This does not mean that the content represented by the test is automatically preferred, but it does mean that there will be better opportunity to evaluate the goals themselves as well as goal-attainment if a wider net is cast in data collection. In the educational evaluation literature, the difference between using measures that exactly match program goals or less exactly match a broader set of goals is the key distinction between the tailored vs. medical models of evaluation (Cook, 1974) or goal-free vs. goal-based evaluation (Scriven, 1974). In each case, the latter approaches are more likely to detect side effects and long-term consequences of a program because they do not look only at the intended effects.

PROGRAM EVALUATION VS. PUPIL DIAGNOSIS AND EVALUATION

Criterion-referenced (or diagnostic) tests provide much greater accuracy and depth for the assessment of minute instructional topics. Therefore, they are the only tests appropriate when one wishes to find out things like which consonant blends or punctuation rules a child has learned. Norm-referenced tests will only infrequently be useful for making specific instructional decisions about individual pupils. Because the norms are an empirical and non-arbitrary basis for comparison, they can be used to identify a pupil's relative strengths and weaknesses, for example, better in mathematics computation than in math concepts. When combined with co-normed ability tests, norm-referenced tests can be used to diagnose learning disabilities (Erickson, 1975)[4] and to identify "under-

---
[4]There are numerous conceptual and statistical problems involved in the identification of learning disabilities (see Shepard, 1979).

achievers" for counseling purposes (see Thorndike, 1963).

For program evaluation purposes, the ideal situation would be to have the greater content relevance of criterion-referenced tests combined with normative data for making evaluative interpretations. However, appropriate norms usually are not available for locally developed tests. A first-choice alternative, if test content and form are acceptable, may be items from the NAEP (with national norms) or state developed objectives-referenced tests (with state norms). Another alternative is for evaluators to integrate the findings from both criterion-referenced and traditional norm-referenced tests. When criterion-referenced tests are used alone, the only basis for interpretation is improvement or decrement compared to previous years.

In the program evaluation context, criterion-referenced tests provide greater diagnostic information (about what *kinds of items* need remediation), just as they do at the individual level. For this purpose, criterion-referenced item pools can be administered using matrix sampling. Norm-referenced tests add an external basis of comparison for judging whether achievement is at the level it should be (considering socioeconomic factors). Norms also allow interpretations about program strengths and weaknesses; for example, a district may be well above the national norm in reading and language but below in mathematics.

The conclusion must be that both kinds of tests are needed for making decisions at both the individual and institutional levels. If one were forced to choose, it would be preferable to have only criterion-referenced tests for individual instructional purposes. Norm-referenced tests are more for program evaluation and quality control purposes but should not be the sole criterion for judging program worth.

SUMMARY

By definition, criterion-referenced and norm-referenced tests are distinguished by the referent used for score interpretation. Criterion-referenced scores reflect a well-articulated domain of behaviors; norms provide a comparison of a pupil's performance in relation to others taking the test.

Ideally, one would have tests with the greater content validity assured by criterion referencing combined with representative norms to allow interpretation of the quality of performance. In practice, however, this combination is not available (due largely to the great number of items required), and one usually has to select among tests that have other attributes in addition to those implied by the definitions. The great majority of criterion-referenced tests are not, in fact, referenced to a carefully specified domain; most are actually objectives-referenced tests. Therefore, any given criterion-referenced test may or may not have greater content validity than a particular norm-referenced test.

Usually, traditional norm-referenced tests are best distinguished from criterion-referenced tests because they have many fewer items covering the same range of content. They are *survey* tests of achievement and are only good for monitoring pupil and program progress over the long run. Appropriately selected norms for comparable ability groups or equivalent socioeconomic status (in the case of districts) provide a basis for deciding if performance is as good as can be expected. Nationally developed tests will not match local curriculum precisely; but adequate correspondence can be assured by teachers and curriculum specialists. Moreover, principles of good evaluation recommend not only comparative judgments of performance but also consideration of attainment on more than the narrowest set of intended goals.

For day-to-day decisions in the classroom, criterion-referenced tests are preferred because more items, keyed to instructional objectives, are necessary for diagnostic and prescriptive purposes. A final caution is needed, however, because of recent exhaustive testing with batteries of criterion-referenced tests. Diagnostic testing should be very focused, covering only those topics for which a child's knowledge is in question. If many criterion-referenced tests are strung together for program evaluation purposes, they should be administered using matrix sampling procedures so that students will not have to spend hours taking tests with little instructional benefit.

Note: Special thanks are extended to Evelyn Brzezinski and Kenneth Hopkins for review of the manuscript; any errors remaining, however, are the fault of the author.

REFERENCES

Ayrer, J. E., & McNamara, T. C. Survey testing on an out-of-level basis. *Journal of Educational Measurement*, 1973, *10*, 79–84.

Block, J. H. Standards and criteria: A response. *Journal of Educational Measurement*, 1978, *15*, 291–295.

Buros, O. K. Fifty years in testing. In O. K. Buros (Ed.), *The Eighth Mental Measurements Yearbook* (Vol. II). Highland Park, New Jersey: The Gryphon Press, 1978.

California State Testing Program 1970–1971: Technical supplement. Sacramento: California State Department of Education, 1973.

Cook, T. D. The medical and tailored models of evaluation research. In J. G. Albert & M. Kamarass, *Proceedings of the Washington Operations Research Council.* Cambridge, Massachusetts: Ballinger, 1974.

DeVault, M. L., Harnischfeger, A., & Wiley, D. E. Curricula, personnel resources, resources, and grouping strategies. M. L. Group for Policy Studies in Education, CEMREL, Chicago, March, 1977.

Ebel, R. L. *Essentials of educational measurement.* Englewood Cliffs, New Jersey: Prentice-Hall, 1972.

Ebel, R. L. The case for norm-referenced measurements. *Educational Researcher*, 1978, *7*, 3–5.

Erickson, M. T. The Z-score discrepancy method for identifying reading disabled children. *Journal of Learning Disabilities*, 1975, *8*, 308–312.

Glaser, R. Instructional technology and the measurement of learning, outcomes: Some questions. *American Psychologist*, 1963, *18*, 519–521.

Glass, G. V. Minimal competency and incompetence in Florida. *Phi Delta Kappan*, 1978, *59*, 602–605. (a)

Glass, G. V. Standards and criteria. *Journal of Educational Measurement*, 1978, *15*, 237–261. (b)

Hambleton, R. K., & Eignor, D. R. Guidelines for evaluating criterion-referenced tests and test manuals. *Journal of Educational Measurement*, 1978, *15*, 321–327.

Hambleton, R. K., Swaminathan, H., Algina, J., & Coulson, D. B. Criterion-referenced testing and measurement: A review of technical issues and developments. *Review of Educational Research*, 1978, *48*, 1–48.

Hively, E., Maxwell, G., Rabehl, G., Sension, D., & Lunden, S. *Domain-referenced curriculum evaluation: A technical handbook and a case study from the Minnemast Project.* CSE monograph series in evaluation, No. 1, Los Angeles: Center for the Study of Evaluation, University of California, 1973.

Hopkins, K. D., Kretke, G., Martin L. & Averill, M. *District testing report, 1977–1978.* Boulder, Colorado: Boulder Valley School District, 1978.

Mager, R. F. *Preparing instructional objectives.* Palo Alto, California: Feardon Publishers, 1962.

Mehrens, W. A., & Lehmann, I. J. *Measurement and evaluation in education and psychology* (2nd ed.). New York: Holt, Rinehart & Winston, 1978.

Millman, J. Criterion-referenced measurement. In W. J. Popham (Ed.), *Evaluation in education: Current applications.* Berkeley: McCutchan Publishing Co., 1974.

Popham, W. J. *Educational evaluation.* Englewood Cliffs, New Jersey: Prentice-Hall, 1975.

Popham, W. J. Normative data for criterion-referenced tests? *Phi Delta Kappan*, 1976, *57*, 593–594.

Popham, W. J. As always provocative. *Journal of Educational Measurement*, 1978, *15*, 297–300. (a)

Popham, W. J. The case for criterion-referenced tests. *Educational Researcher*, 1987, *7*, 6–10. (b)

Popham, W. J. *Criterion-referenced measurement.* Englewood Cliffs, New Jersey: Prentice-Hall, 1978. (c)

Popham, W. J., & Husek, T. R. Implications of criterion-referenced measurement. *Journal of Educational Measurement*, 1969, *6*, 1–9.

Scriven, M. Evaluation perspectives and procedures. In W. J. Popham (Ed.),

Evaluation in education: Current applications. Berkeley: McCutchan Publishing Co., 1974.

Shepard, L. A. An evaluation of the discrepancy method for identifying children with perceptual and communicative disorders. Boulder, Colorado Laboratory of Educational Research, *University of Colorado,* 1979.

Stanley, J. C., & Hopkins, K. D. *Educational and psychological measurement and evaluation.* Englewood Cliffs, New Jersey: Prentice-Hall, 1972.

Thorndike, R. L. *The concepts of over- and under-achievement.* New York: Colombia University, Teachers College, 1963.

Webb, E. J., Campbell, D. T., Schwartz, R. D. & Sechrest, L. *Unobstructive measures: Nonreactive research in the social sciences.* Chicago: Rand McNally, 1966.

Yoshida, R. K. Out-of-level testing of special education students with a standardized achievement battery. *Journal of Educational Measurement,* 1976, *13,* 215–221.

Zieky, M. J., & Livingston, S. A. *Manual for setting standards on basic skills assessment tests.* Princeton, New Jersey: Educational Testing Service, 1977.

READING 38 — ROBERT GABLE AND VINCENT ROGERS
Taking the Terror Out of Research

Carol Bennett walked into Vincent Rogers' office for a 4 p.m. appointment just prior to the start of spring semester in 1986. Carol, a middle school social studies teacher, is intelligent, perceptive, articulate, sensitive, and thoroughly professional. As head of the social studies curriculum revision team at Tolland (Connecticut) Middle School, she shared with Rogers her concerns about the effectiveness of the newly revised social studies curriculum. Specifically, she was concerned about the program's strengths and weaknesses, as perceived by teachers, parents, administrators, and students.

Rogers invited Carol to discuss her concerns with the 21 students (themselves, mostly classroom teachers) enrolled in his course on curriculum theory, which was just getting under way. As a result of that discussion, the class agreed to help Carol develop and carry out an informal assessment of the new social studies curriculum. When the assessment was completed, members of the class had interviewed the superintendent of schools, the building principal, the department chairperson, 20 students, seven teachers, and 21 parents.

Carol and the members of the curriculum theory class were conducting research. They had some questions worth asking, and they arrived at ways of getting answers. They had no illusions about the generalizability of their findings; the results were important only for Tolland Middle School. They did not develop an elaborate theoretical framework for the study, nor did they apply for a Carnegie or Ford Foundation grant. The validity of their data would be revealed as these data were used in the continuing dialogue among the teachers, parents, administrators, and students who had provided these data in the first place.

Meanwhile, at the Gideon Welles School in Glastonbury, Connecticut, teachers and students in grades 6 through 12 are actively involved in quantitative research projects. For example, Marianne Cavanaugh's seventh- and eighth-grade students surveyed 768 middle-schoolers to help set priorities for the After School Speakers' Forum. The students learned how to develop and distribute surveys, how to enter and analyze data, and how to graph frequencies and percentages. The four topics receiving the highest number of votes—nuclear war, friends, growing up, and drugs—were presented during the fall 1986 speakers' series.

Carol Bennett's project emphasized qualitative or naturalistic methods; Marianne Cavanaugh's project was a quantitative study. Both featured simple, straightforward, uncomplicated designs; and both yielded results that were of

---

The authors wish to thank Carol Bennett for sharing her work on curriculum evaluation; Mary Yakimowski and Steven Melnick for their help in running the microcomputer software programs; Christine Murphy, Marian Wolf, and Robert Garber for their thoughtful critiques of earlier drafts of this article; and Marianne Cavanaugh, Deborah Mulcahy, Francine Lynch, and their students in the Glastonbury (Conn.) schools for allowing this discussion of their research projects.

From Robert Gable and Vincent Rogers, "Taking the Terror out of Research," *Phi Delta Kappan* (May 1987):690–695. Reprinted by permission.

immediate and practical use to classroom teachers and the local school district. Most important, *teachers* played the dominant role in the conception and development of both studies—an event that occurs far too rarely, in our view.

We teach courses in educational research at the University of Connecticut. (Robert Gable emphasizes quantitative methods; Vincent Rogers emphasizes qualitative methods.) Both of us have directed dozens of doctoral dissertations, and we have worked together on many doctoral committees. We've been involved (sometimes collaboratively) in state, regional, and national studies, often generously funded by outside agencies. We want our research to be as good as it can be: thorough, careful, detailed, accurate. And we are convinced that classroom teachers have a significant role to play in the educational scene.

Of course, teachers have enormous demands on their time. But they are *professionals*, not clerks. Teaching is a creative, inventive endeavor; unpredictability is part of every teacher's daily professional life. Problems arise that must be solved. Sometimes the solutions are obvious and immediate. But other problems require more information, more time, more probing, more reflection. The genuine professional recognizes that, to teach well, one must know "what's really going on" in one's classroom. Sometimes, despite crowded and demanding teaching schedules, a more systematic attempt to find answers is necessary.

Each fall, dozens of teachers show up in our courses on research methods. Most of them look apprehensive. They have their notebooks open and their pens ready. They *choose* to sit at the front of the room. They give our lectures and the other class activities rapt attention, and they gather in small knots for anxious conversation when class is over.

Our students are often the victims of "research mystique"—the notion that research is beyond the ken of ordinary people. Research, in this view, is on a par with quantum physics, space technology, brain surgery.

How can we take the terror out of research for classroom teachers and other practitioners? Perhaps we should begin by stating what is, for us, a workable definition. Educational research is a *systematic* attempt to find answers to questions that puzzle or confuse us.

What kinds of questions puzzle or confuse? Most fall into four basic categories.

1. *Descriptions.* Example: What do third-graders do when they are given "free choice" time during class?
2. *Relationships between factors.* Example: What is the relationship between academic achievement in certain content areas and reading ability?
3. *Searches for the causes of given phenomena.* Example: Why do seventh-graders rate social studies as their least-liked and least-important subject?
4. *Searches for consequences.* Example: What happens to the writing production of 10th-graders when word processors are used?

QUALITATIVE RESEARCH

Perhaps the best way to demystify the methodology of qualitative or naturalistic research is to present a simple case study. The research we will describe took place in a suburban fifth-grade classroom and involved 23 heterogeneously grouped students. As part of their social studies curriculum, they were studying the Bill of Rights, the Constitution, and the branches of the U.S. government. Ordinarily, the teacher would have assessed the students' understanding of this content by means of conventional tests (multiple choice, true/false, sentence completion).

Concerned that such tests measure only superficial dimensions of students' learning, however, the teacher embarked on a more ambitious assessment process. He wanted a better understanding of what John Goodlad has called the "experienced" curriculum"—the ideas, concepts, and understandings that remain in students' minds after the teaching is completed. To gain this understanding, the teacher had to identify or create open-ended assessment methods that allowed for in-depth responses. Ultimately, he settled on five such methods.

1. *Small-group interviews.* In groups of four or five, the students took part in loosely structured interviews in which the teacher asked them to talk about such fundamental rights as freedom of the press and freedom of religion. All responses were considered acceptable, but the teacher probed for clarification and elaboration: "Can you tell me what you mean by that? Can you give me an example?" He encouraged the students to engage in dialogue among themselves, as well. All interviews were taped and later transcribed.

2. *Situational pictures.* To generate discussion, the teacher used simple sketches of a number of situations involving basic civil rights. For example, he showed the students a sketch of a nativity scene on public property that was being dismantled two weeks before Christmas, and he asked them to explain why this was happening and whether or not they thought the action was justified. He showed them a sketch of two police officers and a suspect, in which one officer was saying to the other. "Give me 10 minutes alone with him, and I'll make him talk." The teacher then

asked the students whether the second police officer should consent or object to the grilling of a suspect. All such discussions were taped and transcribed.

3. *Card sorts.* Students were given packs of 3 × 5 cards, each card containing the name and title of a key figure in one of the branches of the federal government. Each child was asked to sort the cards into two piles: "most important" and "least important." Then the child was asked to explain why he or she sorted the cards in this way. Again, the discussions were taped and transcribed.

4. *Learning logs.* Each student received a blank notebook at the beginning of the unit. Each day, at the end of the lesson, the teacher gave the students a few minutes to write responses to three questions: What do you think was the most important thing you learned today? Why do you think so? What, in today's lesson, are you still confused or uncertain about?

5. *An open-ended version of the conventional teacher-made test.* The conventional test on the Bill of Rights consisted of 10 statements with which students were asked to agree or disagree, such as, "The police may sometimes be right in grilling a person to make him or her give them information." The open-ended version added two parts to each question: 1) "If you agree with this statement, list examples of situations in which the police would be justified in grilling a suspect," and 2) "If you disagree or are uncertain, explain why you chose the answer."

The teacher used these data-gathering techniques over an eight-week period, since he was more interested in tapping students' *enduring* understandings than in tapping their immediate recall. At the end of that time, he read the transcriptions of discussions and the students' own written responses, underlining words and phrases that illustrated the students' thinking. The teacher recorded these comments on 3 × 5 cards and then grouped them by theme to see what patterns might emerge from this simple form of data analysis.

> **M**uch of the terror that research provokes in practitioners is centered on statistical techniques.

Students' comments in small-group discussions on freedom of the press included the following:

People like to know what's going on. If there was a tiger on the loose and you would be walking on the street, you wouldn't know.

Because there would be nothing to tell you what's going on. Russia could send over one of their nuclear missiles and blow this whole school away.

In all, 12 children made similar comments. The theme that emerges from this cluster of responses is, "Without freedom of the press, we wouldn't get any warning about the possible occurrence of dangerous events." The concept of freedom of the press as intellectual freedom (i.e., freedom to express ideas, thoughts, and opinions) rarely occurred for the class as a whole and did not occur at all for these particular children. Clearly, responses that cluster in this fashion reveal trends or themes that dominate the thinking of groups of children in the class.

In other cases, by contrast, only one child came up with a particular response. The interchange on cruel and unusual punishment that follows is a good example.

Chuck: Well, robbing the bank or something, you'd usually get about 20 years in prison. But if you raped somebody and they had an abortion and all of that and you kept doing it for nine months or so and they catch you, then you're going to have to get the death punishment because you're going along raping all these ladies.

Interviewer: What are you saying? Is that cruel and unusual punishment?

Chuck: Yeah, it is. Because all they're doing is having their fun in their way and they're not hurting anybody. They're just doing what they feel they should do. They didn't kill anybody. They're just having their fun.

Such personal and idiosyncratic responses defy quantification. Yet they are vitally important in assessing the learning of the students who make them. Let us review the steps involved in carrying out this research:

- The study began (as does all research) with a hunch or a question—in this case, something on the order of, "What are my students *really* learning about the Bill of Rights and the Constitution?"
- The teacher-researcher identified or developed data-gathering methods (situational pictures, card sorts, and so on).
- He gathered data and identified basic ideas, concepts, values, or beliefs.
- He clustered students' responses, in a search for similarities.
- He identified a number of themes that seemed to reflect the thinking of groups of children in the class.
- He also identified significant or unusual responses of *individual* children.

- Using these data, the teacher then reviewed the unit to identify elements requiring elaboration, clarification, or reteaching.

In qualitative studies, researchers rely on many other data-gathering techniques not used in this simple study. They observe, videotape, collect personal and official documents (letters, paintings, stories, compositions, school memos, announcements, and so on), gather photographs, examine textbooks and other teaching materials, collaborate with other teachers, and develop questionnaires. They sometimes use sampling techniques or compare one group with another, and they often combine the methods of qualitative and quantitative research. But their goal is always to observe and study human activity in its natural setting.

QUANTITATIVE RESEARCH

In conducting quantitative research, we tend to gather data in the form of numbers. These numbers can function merely as categorical labels that have no real meaning on a continuum (e.g., numbers on football jerseys), or they can represent intervals that allow us to make "less than" or "more than" distinctions (e.g., test scores). To simplify things, we will focus here on such interval data as test scores.

Using the methods of quantitative research, we can employ various statistics to answer *research questions* exploring the relationships between selected variables.[1] For example, we might ask, "What is the relationship between the number of books read by students last month and their reading test scores?" Or we might ask, "Will the math scores of students participating in special review sessions differ from the scores of those who do not participate?" Each of these research questions contains at least two variables that can be quantified or categorized. In the first instance, the number of books read by each student can be recorded, and reading achievement can be measured by a test. In the second instance, students can be categorized as participants or nonparticipants in the review sessions, and the math achievement of both groups can be tested.

We now turn these research questions into *hypotheses*, i.e., statements that contain at least two variables and thus can be tested statistically. Our first testable hypothesis becomes, "There will be no significant relationship between the number of books read last month and reading test scores"; our second becomes, "There will be no significant difference in math scores between those students participating and those students not participating in the review sessions."

Hypotheses are the keys to conducting quantitative research. Simply put, researchers gather data on one or more samples of students and then use appropriate statistical procedures to "test" a hypothesis. On completion of the statistical test, the researcher "rejects" the hypothesis, if the relationship is strong enough, or "fails to reject" the hypothesis, if the relationship is too weak.

Statistical techniques are the vehicles by which researchers test their hypotheses. Much of the terror that research provokes in school practitioners is centered on these techniques—widely perceived as formulas to be avoided because they cannot be understood, as procedures for data analysis that appear impossible to perform.

But the outlook is becoming brighter, thanks to readily available statistical software packages for microcomputers.[2] These packages will generate *all* the statistics we will describe here, as well as perform the appropriate tests of statistical significance. Researchers have only to identify the research question and the statistic needed, enter the data into the microcomputer, and interpret the results; no complicated manipulation of formulas is necessary.

Let us illustrate by first describing the popular statistical techniques for analyzing data and then demonstrating how they were used in four classroom research projects. In every case, the data were entered into a microcomputer by middle school teachers and students, and the calculations were performed using readily available software packages.

Descriptive Statistics

There are two broad categories of statistical techniques: descriptive statistics and inferential statistics. Descriptive statistics are a basic part of all quantitative research, because they allow the researcher to understand the nature of the data. Frequency distributions and graphic representations of the data, such as histograms or line graphs, depict the *distribution* of the variable in question. These depictions—in conjunction with a measure of central tendency, such as the *mean* (i.e., the average), and a measure of variability, such as the *range* (i.e., the difference between the highest and lowest points in the distribution)—quickly convey a lot of information.

Consider, for example, a research

---

[1] See Susan M. Baum, Robert K. Gable, and Karen List, *Chi-Square, Histograms, and You: A Guide for Teaching Research and Statistics to Students* (New York: Trillium, 1987).

[2] With the caveat that software is continually changing, we encourage teachers to examine such packages as the following: *Stats Plus* (Apple) and PC Statistician (IBM-PC), from Human Systems Dynamics, 9010 Reseda Blvd., Suite 222, Northridge, CA 91324; *Advanced Statistical Analysis* (TRS-80), from any Radio Shack store; *STAT-MASTER* (IBM-PC or Apple), from Little, Brown and Co., College Division, 34 Beacon St., Boston, MA 02134; *EPISTAT—Statistical Package for the IBM Personal Computer*, from T. Gustafson, 1705 Gattis School Rd., Round Rock, TX 78664; and *Statpro: The Statistics and Graphics Database Workstation*, from Wadsworth Professional Software, Boston, MA 02116.

project in which a sixth-grade student interviewed 25 peers to discover how much allowance per week each student thought was an appropriate amount. The students' responses (listed in Table 1) were entered into an Apple microcomputer, and the *Stats Plus* descriptive statistics/frequencies program was run. Table 1 shows both the original data and the computer-generated results.

For each dollar amount listed in the column labeled "Score," the frequency (i.e., the number of sixth-graders who gave that response) is listed in the column labeled "F," and the proportion (i.e., the percentage of sixth-graders who gave that response) is listed in the column labeled "P." (The column labeled "CF" lists cumulative frequencies; the column labeled "CP" lists cumulative proportions.) The computer printout also includes the mean (or average) response, $5.68;

> The desire and ability to seek answers to puzzling questions is an essential attribute of the professional.

a measure of the variability of the data, the standard deviation (labeled "S.D."); and the minimum ("min") and maximum ("max") amounts, from which the range can be calculated.

Inferential Statistics

Having gathered data on a *sample* of people and having calculated some descriptive statistics, we next *test our hypothesis* to see if it is reasonable, in light of the way in which our sample's mean and standard deviation compare to those of various other *populations* (which have been described in the appendices of those formidable statistics books). That is, we attempt to make *inferences* from our sample of people to some larger population. If the statistics we generate indicate that our hypothesis is *not* reasonable, we reject it; if the hypothesis appears to be reasonable, we fail to reject it for our sample. The inferential statistics we use to test hypotheses can be classified into two general groups: those that test *relationships* and those that test *differences*.[3]

Correlation (or *r*) quantifies the extent of the *relationship* between two variables (e.g., number of books read last month and grade on a reading test). The value of *r* can range from −1 to +1, with negative

---

TABLE 1 *Stats Plus* Descriptive Statistics/Frequencies

Data List

2.50	5.00	6.00	10.00
2.50	5.00	7.00	
3.00	5.00	7.00	
3.00	5.00	7.00	
3.00	6.00	7.00	
5.00	6.00	7.00	
5.00	6.00	8.00	
5.00	6.00	10.00	

SAMPLE	N	SUM	MEAN	S.D.	MIN	MAX
ALLOW	25	142.000	5.680	2.010	2.500	10.000

Frequencies

Sample Allowa

Score	F	CF	P	CP
2*	2	2	.08	.08
3	3	5	.12	.20
4	0	5	0.00	.20
5	7	12	.28	.48
6	5	17	.20	.68
7	5	22	.20	.88
8	1	23	.04	.92
9	0	23	0.00	.92
10	2	25	.08	1.00

N = 25

Mean = 5.68

S.D. = 2.01

*This program does not print out the digits to the right of the decimal (i.e., the score of 2 should be 2.50).

---

[3]*All* these statistical tests actually deal with relationships between variables. For instructional purposes, however, we separate the test for "relationships" from those for "differences."

values indicating inverse relationships (i.e., high scores on one variable are associated with low scores on the other variable). A value of r near zero would indicate the absence of a relationship between the two variables; a positive value would indicate that high scores on one variable tend to be associated with high scores on the other variable.

Let us suppose, for example, that a teacher recorded the number of books read last month by each of 10 students, along with those youngsters' scores on a reading test. The teacher then entered these data (see Table 2) into an IBM-PC microcomputer, for analysis by means of the *EPISTAT* program for computing Pearson correlation coefficients. (The output from the program is shown at the bottom of Table 2.) The teacher-researcher concluded that there was a positive correlation of .82 between the number of books read and reading test scores and that this relationship was statistically significant at the .05 level. If we square the value of r (the correlation coefficient), we obtain an indication of how much variation the two variables have in common: 67%.

The *t*-test is the primary statistic used to test for differences between two means. A large (i.e., significant) t value indicates that the means are statistically different, causing us to reject the hypothesis (which states that the two means do *not* differ).

For example, a sixth-grade teacher set out to discover whether review sessions would yield higher scores on a mathematics test. During the week before the test, half of the 30 students in the class (selected randomly) attended two 60-minute review sessions; these students made up the experimental group. The rest of the class (the control group) attended special music classes during the two review sessions and promised not to review for the test on their own. Both groups were told that the test was part of a research project and would not count toward students' final grades.

Table 3 contains the students' test scores and the computer printout from the *Stats Plus* program for computing *t*-tests, run on an Apple. The teacher found that the mean score of the group attending review sessions (85.0) was significantly higher than the mean score of the control group (76.3). She attributed that difference to the review sessions.

The final statistic we will present is the χ^2 (chi-square), which is used for analyzing differences between two groups when the data are presented as frequencies. A large (i.e., significant) value of χ^2 would indicate that the two groups differ and that the hypothesis of no difference between the groups should be rejected.

For example, an eighth-grade teacher and her students polled 40 students and 32 teachers, asking them, "Do you think that students should be required to attend scheduled study halls?" The computer printout from the *Statpro* chi-square program (Table 4) shows that the opinions of the two groups differed significantly; thus the researchers rejected the hypothesis of no difference.

TABLE 3 *Stats Plus t-test*

Experimental	Control
100	85
95	85
95	80
90	75
90	75
100	90
70	85
60	75
85	50
100	80
75	80
75	85
85	60
80	70
75	40

SAMPLE	N	MEAN	S.D.
EXPERI	15	85.000	12.247
CONTRO	15	76.333	10.601

HYPOTHESIZED DIFFERENCE: 0
OBTAINED DIFFERENCE: 8.667

This difference is significant at the .05 level.

TABLE 2 *EPISTAT* Correlation

	Datafile	
	# Books	Grade
1:	7	100
2:	2	75
3:	1	70
4:	8	85
5:	5	80
6:	3	70
7:	4	72
8:	4	90
9:	0	60
10:	6	92
NO.	10	10
MEAN	4.000000	79.40000
MED	4.000000	77.50000
SDEV	2.581989	12.26738

Correlation coefficient = .82

This correlation coefficient is significantly different than 0 at the .05 level.

TABLE 4 *Statpro* Chi-Square

	Yes	No	
Students	8	32	N = 40
Teachers	24	8	N = 30

Total Chi-Square 22.40

This value is significant at the .05 level.

As we write this, the winds of change are blowing—at gale force, some would maintain. Dynamic new solutions to the problems of education are being debated from Maine to California. Our vision of the ideal teacher is simultaneously undergoing significant change. With increasing frequency, we hear such adjectives used to describe the ideal practitioner as autonomous, inquiring, reflective, responsible, resourceful, and (in a word) *professional.* Surely, the desire and ability to seek answers to puzzling questions—i.e., the desire and ability to do research—is an essential attribute of the professional teacher in the Eighties and beyond.

PART FIVE
Study and Discussion Questions

CHAPTER TEN   The Many Faces of Good Teaching

Reading 28   Research on Teacher Effects: Uses and Abuses

1. Someone asks you, "Is teaching basically a science or an art?" How do you respond? *Why* do you respond the way you do?

2. How would you describe the two types of teachers who are relatively unsuccessful in eliciting achievement gains among their students?

3. What is the danger of making too much of a single study associated with teacher effectiveness?

4. Based on the research synthesized in this article, what four or five basic recommendations would you make to teachers for improving their teaching?

Reading 29   Teaching Students to Examine Their Lives

1. Can you identify the two basic steps the author suggests for teaching students to examine their lives?

2. The author says that teaching Socratically means that the teacher must allow him- or herself "to be questioned by the text." What does this mean? How would you advise someone to do this?

Reading 30   Psychodynamics of Teachers' Expectations

1. What does it mean to say that "expectations may become self-fulfilling prophecies"?

2. Can you identify and explain each of the four factors necessary for the communication of positive feedback?

3. Can you think of a time in your schooling when your own school performance was affected for the worse by a "self-fulfilling prophecy"?

Reading 31   In Praise of Teachers

1. Mark Medoff goes back in time and remembers the teachers who made a positive difference in his life. How would you describe the two or three (maybe more) teachers who made a difference in your life? What did they do that made them special?

CHAPTER ELEVEN Motivational Strategies for Encouraging Student Achievement

Reading 32 Synthesis of Research on Strategies for Motivating Students to Learn

1. What is the distinction between learning and performance?

2. How does extrinsic motivation differ from intrinsic motivation?

3. What can teachers do to take advantage of the power of extrinsic incentives and intrinsic motivation?

4. How about your own motivation—is it generally intrinsic or extrinsic? How can you tell?

Reading 33 "If at First . . .": Attribution Theory in the Classroom

1. What is the central purpose or concern of attribution theory?

2. Can you explain how one's internal or external locus and one's perception of stability and controllability are associated with one's idea of causality—that is, the causes of things in one's life?

3. How can teachers use the ideas of locus, stability, and controllability to help students work hard to do their best? Or, to put it another way, how do these three factors influence your own motivation for better or worse?

Reading 34 How to Reach the Underachiever

1. How can you tell the difference between a dependent underachiever and a dominant one?

2. What advice would you give teachers about ways to approach each of these types?

3. What is the main characteristic that distinguishes underachievers from achievers?

CHAPTER TWELVE Strategies Useful for the Practice of Positive Classroom Discipline

Reading 35 A Primer on Classroom Discipline: Principles Old and New

1. Can you identify and describe at least six of the ten principles of classroom management discussed in this Reading?

2. Which three or four of these ten principles seems most usable to you, in terms of what you know about yourself as a person?

Reading 36 Classroom Management as Instruction: Socializing Self-Guidance in Students

1. How does "self-guidance" differ from "self-control"?

2. Can you explain why effective socialization is more likely to grow out of authoritative rather than authoritarian or laissez-faire practices?

3. The author suggests that teachers are more apt to encourage self-guidance when they use an informational rather than a controlling style. What is the reasoning behind this suggestion?

CHAPTER THIRTEEN Basic Understandings About Testing and Educational Research

Reading 37 Norm-Referenced vs. Criterion-Referenced Tests

1. What is the difference between a norm-referenced and a criterion-referenced test?

2. Why aren't survey tests good diagnostic tests?

3. Can you explain why criterion-referenced tests are more useful for making specific instructional decisions about individual students than norm-referenced tests?

Reading 38 Taking the Terror Out of Research

1. Can you explain some of the basic differences between qualitative and quantitative research?

2. How do descriptive statistics and inferential statistics differ from each other?

PART SIX

Exceptional Students: Problems and Challenges

Exceptional students can be found on both ends of the learning continuum. On the one side we find students who either don't care about schooling or have trouble learning (or perhaps a bit of both), whereas on the other side we have students who are quite talented and academically able. This final section is devoted to an overview of the issues and problems frequently associated with those students we have come to see as "exceptional" because of their particular problems and academic status.

Each of the three Readings in Chapter Fourteen is concerned with students who have particular kinds of learning difficulties. In Reading 39, Melvin Levine defines the meaning of a learning disability, gives examples of the common kinds of disability that show up as difficulties in school, and suggests diagnostic approaches and treatment strategies. In Reading 40, John Langone zeros in on a problem that afflicts perhaps 10 percent of boys and 3 percent of girls—dyslexia, the outgrowth of what is thought to be a brain malfunction that affects reading ability. Langone discusses the scope of the problem, its possible causes, and the options available for helping those afflicted by it.

The dropout problem remains a national tragedy. More than 4 million young people drop out of school each year, and in some cities the number who fail to complete high school is as high as 50 percent. Who are these dropouts, and what can be done to help this problem? In Reading 41, Andrew Hahn addresses these questions in a comprehensive review of the dropout problem and possible solutions.

Some students are exceptional for a different reason: They are gifted or talented in special ways, and this is the focus of Chapter Fifteen. In Reading 42, A. Harry Passon directs our attention to the various behaviors commonly seen in the gifted and talented, and he suggests criteria by which such students can be identified. It is one thing to identify such students, but it is quite another to design and make available curriculums that allow them to express their special talents. In Reading 43, Byron Barrington argues for a curriculum-based model incorporated into existing academic curriculums but designed and taught in such a way as to accommodate the special needs of talented and gifted youngsters.

Why do so many students drop out of school? What can we do to reduce the scope of this problem? What is a learning disability? How can we recognize a learning disability when we see it? What can we do to help students with learning disabilities? What are the psychodynamics of underachievement? What behaviors should we look for when trying to identify the gifted and talented? How can we make schooling meaningful for the wide range of "exceptional" students who sit in our classrooms?

These are a few of the questions that will occupy our attention in this last section of this volume. Although there are no *simple* answers to most of the questions raised in this book, there *are* answers—some complex, some tentative, and some still to come. We know a great, great amount right now about how to improve teaching and learning. The challenge is to take what we know and apply it at the level of individual classrooms and individual teacher–student interactions in order to make schooling a more positive experience for both students and teachers in all grades. This is, after all, what the search for knowledge in educational psychology is all about in the first place.

CHAPTER FOURTEEN

Toward Understanding Students Who Have Trouble Learning

READING 39   MELVIN LEVINE
Learning: Abilities and Disabilities

WHAT IS A LEARNING DISABILITY?

"Learning disability" is the term currently used to describe a handicap that interferes with someone's ability to store, process, or produce information. Such disabilities affect both children and adults. The impairment can be quite subtle and may go undetected throughout life. But learning disabilities create a gap between a person's true capacity and his day-to-day productivity and performance.

In the past, there has been a tendency to use a single, poorly defined, term for these problems. Recently, "dyslexia," "minimal brain dysfunction" and "hyperactivity" have been some of the more familiar ones. But the kinds of disability we see are exceedingly variable, and in reality no two people with learning disorders are ever alike. It turns out (not surprisingly) that there are more ways to be different than to be the same. So a more useful approach is to describe in detail the strengths and deficits of a child (or adult), rather than to paste some kind of broad diagnostic label on him. Nevertheless, the types of handicap that we encounter do fit into certain general categories, which influence the way the problem should be treated. Here's a partial list. Although I'll talk about children, all of the same conditions can also affect adults.

Attention. By far the most common kind of learning disorder is difficulty in keeping attention focused. One 14-year-old boy described his problem this way: "Doc, I'll tell you just what my head is like. It's like a television set. Only one thing: it's got no channel selector. You see, all the programs keep coming over my screen at the same time." Because these children keep tuning in and out, their performance is unbelievably and confusingly inconsistent. They might do well one minute and poorly the next, or have one good week in school followed by another that is disastrous. They might be able to do a math problem on Thursday but fail to solve it on Friday. Because they've been caught doing something well once in a while, people keep accusing them of not really trying the rest of the time. These children may be overactive, but some have perfectly normal activity levels, and some are even lethargic. They are likely to be impulsive, to do things too quickly, and get into trouble because they haven't thought through the risks they take. They are often described as emotionally disturbed, and the parents may be blamed, whereas everyone is really an innocent victim of a subtle handicap affecting the way the child's brain organizes his ability to concentrate.

As these children get older, they may be great at grasping the big picture and understanding overall conceptions. They often have rich

Excerpted from Melvin Levine, "Learning: Abilities and Disabilities," from the September 1984 issue of *The Harvard Medical School Health Letter,* © 1984 President and Fellows of Harvard College.

imaginations and are extremely creative—even as they fail all their subjects in school because they can't easily focus on other people's details. If they are not damaged by too much criticism early in life, these children may blossom into incredible adults. But they tend to accumulate a negative self-image as "losers." They're accused of various forms of moral turpitude: laziness, poor motivation, and so on. But we know they're not lazy from observation and testing. We find that they have real trouble focusing and may fatigue very rapidly when they try to concentrate.

Attention deficits are not only the most common sort of disability, they also frequently are associated with other types of learning disorder.

Language. Some people are very good at understanding things that they see but have real difficulty interpreting complicated verbal instructions, remembering things they've heard, or expressing themselves in language. They have trouble with reading comprehension and may not be able to grasp and follow spoken directions. Sometimes they develop behavior problems because they're so embarrassed about their disorientation. When they can't keep up with other children on a verbal level, some develop terrible social problems including delinquency.

Spatial Orientation. Other children are just the opposite—terrific within language but hard-put to process information visually. They may be confused about where things are around them. This handicap sometimes shows up as poor reading or spelling, because the affected child has trouble remembering how words look and tends to reverse similar script letters, such as *p* and *g* or *b* and *d*.

Memory. Another group of children has real difficulty with retrieving information from memory—not all information, but certain specific kinds. This problem becomes more noticeable as the child gets older, because the upper grades increasingly require rapid recall of stored information. If you can't find what you need, and quickly, you're in trouble.

Fine Motor Control. A whole series of problems can interfere with the coordination of fine muscular movement, and thus with handwriting. Affected children can't quite remember how to form letters quickly and easily enough, or they have trouble controlling the pencil. The child may be extremely bright and have excellent ideas, but there's a complete breakdown between his head and the paper. Somehow the good material gets lost in the process of writing, and he becomes ashamed of what he has produced.

Sequencing. A great deal of schooling depends on a child's ability to understand or perform a series of items in correct order. Children who get mixed up about the sequence may be able to keep only two or three things straight before the task unravels. They have difficulty following instruction; they may have trouble with math; they can't organize their time. Often, when they're young, they are slow to learn the days of the week and the months of the year. Later on, telling time may be difficult for them. When they get into secondary school, they are disorganized and may find it difficult to remember the order of their classes.

These are some examples of the common kinds of disability that show up as difficulties in school (and continue to affect performance throughout life). I have focused on the ways in which they are seen as impairments, but we have to remember that the same children could be described in terms of their strengths. Their brains are likely to be more highly specialized than the average. Thus, the child with difficulty handling spatial information may be excellent with language—and can use that ability to more than compensate for his weaknesses.

HOW CAN LEARNING DISABILITIES BE IDENTIFIED?

It's not always immediately obvious that a child has a learning disability. In the first place, the main indications are quite variable from child to child. Most straightforward is academic failure or underachievement by a child who seems capable of more. A lot of visible effort may produce inadequate results. The child may appear depressed or overwhelmed and may have difficulty making or keeping friends. He then may lose motivation and stop trying. Children with attention deficits may do a lot of "bad" things impulsively—even though they are obviously not "bad" kids—just as a result of doing things too quickly.

When parents or teachers see these traits, they should not rush to make the diagnosis of a "lazy kid" (I'm not sure there is such a creature). No one should be casual about declaring that a child is emotionally disturbed or generally backward. Very often, some kind of discrete learning problem is at the heart of all this disappointing behavior.

There are definite tests that can be used to diagnose learning disabilities. At the Children's Hospital we have developed a collection of questionnaires and examination procedures that are used to pinpoint specific deficits (and strengths). It is very important, however, that the testing be done by somebody who really understands learning disabilities. Some professionals who give the tests really don't have much knowledge of the subject and may brush over, or misinterpret, important findings.

Parents who suspect a learning disability should start with the school and with their own family doctor or pediatrician. They should ask in so many words whether it's possible that their child has a learning disability and should ask what kind of testing can be done locally. A typical response to this kind of questioning is: "Oh, it couldn't be a learning disability." I don't think parents should accept such hasty reassurance; they should require hard evidence one way or the other. Children with learning problems need strong advocates, because their rights are often violated. Half of the treatment is advocacy.

Sometimes the learning disability is not nearly so bad as the things that we do to children with such disabilities. Imagine what it's like to have a problem with your memory and to grow up hearing all the time, "You can do better." The person saying this happens to be wrong, but you believe him. What does this do to your mental health? Having a memory problem may not be nearly as bad as growing up thinking you are immoral because you are not doing what everyone says you can do. Parents who have a child that is struggling have to be careful about saying, "You can do better," because that phrase can be very damaging.

CAN LEARNING DISORDERS BE TREATED?

Yes. There is a whole list of things that help. Behind all these strategies, though, there must be one guiding principle. From the moment a child gets out of bed in the morning until he or she is safely tucked into bed at night, you avoid humiliating him or her at all costs. All of the interventions you try have to come with a protective shield of some sort so that these youngsters don't have to endure more humiliation than any adult would ever tolerate. Remember, when you're an adult, if you can't dance you don't go to dances. All too often, when you're a child, they'll push you into the middle of a dance floor.

Description and Demystification

After an adequate battery of tests has been administered and analyzed by a component tester, someone must give the child, his parents, and teachers a good understanding, *in terminology that makes sense to them*, of what's going on.

Then a system must be worked out for giving the child empathy and understanding without creating a cripple. The child must remain accountable for making progress, but that accountability has to be tempered by compassion for the struggles the child is going through. An overnight revolution in his nervous system is unlikely, but we can expect an incremental, gradual improvement in performance. The atmosphere must not be accusatory or moralistic. The child must understand that he's not dumb, not crazy or lazy, but that he's struggling. Adults must show that they understand his struggle—but that they still expect him to win, ultimately, even though it won't be easy. Most youngsters can respond to that.

Professionals need to help parents see that it's not their fault and to help schools understand that some cases really are difficult. Schools often don't have the mentality that we do, say in hospitals: namely, that there can be genuinely *hard* cases. So if a child doesn't come around right away, the staff may start accusing the child and his family of not trying (once again) or of having a bad "home situation."

Bypass Strategies. The next step is to figure out what a child can do to circumvent weak areas. For example, if a child has difficulty with what we call "motor memory"—is not able to recall how letters are formed—he might be encouraged to use a typewriter or word processor. Word processors have been a real boon for children with various memory problems, as well, because everything goes right up on the screen. You always get a second chance to look at it and change things without creating a mess. That doesn't help the memory problem, but it helps to bypass it.

If a child has a sequencing problem, the teacher may be able to give fewer instructions at one time. Instead of explaining the procedure for solving a math problem, the teacher might give a couple of correctly solved examples. By looking at the whole problem, the child may be able to find a strategy that doesn't depend on following a sequence of statements.

These strategies might only work with some children, however. Everything has to be custom-fitted to the child's learning style, to a particular profile of strengths and weaknesses. This process can be fun for the teacher, pediatrician, and parents, because it's an opportunity to use one's imagination. Children, as they begin to understand what's going on, spontaneously come up with circumvention plans, and they can be quite proud of their discoveries. But there is no way that a child can be a therapeutic ally if he doesn't know what's wrong and what's right with himself.

Remediation or Rehabilitation. An effort can be made to strengthen the areas of weakness with special help given outside the regular classroom. Speech and language therapists, for example, may give the child exercises to improve his fluency and comprehension. This type of intervention is controversial. We don't have hard evidence to show that it really works, and the extreme diversity of children makes it difficult to construct valid research programs.

Home Management. Parents need advice on things they can do at home to help their child organize homework and develop normally outside the context of schooling.

Psychological Counseling. It's easy for children with learning disabilities to become depressed or otherwise emotionally disturbed. Therapy may be needed to deal with this aspect of the situation.

Medication. Youngsters with attention deficits benefit from low doses of stimulant medications. The evidence for this effect in appropriately selected children is so strong that it's virtually unethical not to use the drugs (and using them may be little different, in spirit, from an adult's taking an extra cup of coffee to get through a difficult task). Children appear not to become addicted to these drugs, and they have a low rate of adverse side effects from the small doses that are used. But if stimulant drugs are given to children with other types of learning problems, they can make matters worse. This is another reason for insisting on accurate, careful diagnosis.

Advocacy. These children need a professional advocate, preferably someone outside the school system, to give them support, follow them, and help their parents monitor progress. My bias is that the family's physician is ideal for this role.

Avoiding Unsubstantiated Treatments. At present the field of learning disabilities seems to be breaking all records for the number of "miracle" cures being offered. Special diets, one of which is popularly known as the Feingold diet, are always being touted, but the evidence in favor of them is meager indeed. A lot of parents spend a lot of money on "visual training" offered by some optometrists; this routine is not supported by good scientific studies and it can delay getting the right kind of help. Inappropriate drugs, such as antihistamines and megavitamins, are often pushed. Hypnosis is another questionable approach. Elaborate and pointless "patterning exercises" have also been promoted; I think cello lessons, or something of the sort, would be more useful.

Public Law 94-142. This federal statute guarantees that every child is entitled to a multidisciplinary evaluation and proper help for a learning disability. School systems that cannot provide appropriate services are required to pay tuition to a private school for children with learning disabilities. Parents should familiarize themselves with this law.

Is all this effort, in the long run, worthwhile? I think it is. As I said, many of these children will become remarkable adults. If they can survive schooling without becoming demoralized, they can go on to exploit their special talents in ways that are both personally satisfying and socially invaluable. After all, people with learning disabilities are simply extreme examples of our natural human diversity. Nobody has a "perfect" brain.

READING 40   JOHN LANGONE
Deciphering Dyslexia

When Mary Ferguson's teacher asked her to stand up before her eighth grade class and spell "cellar," Mary froze and said nothing. She could not associate sounds with letters. At first the teacher prodded gently, but finally, in exasperation, she asked what letter the word began with. "P," Mary blurted out. It was only one of a thousand childhood humiliations she suffered, but to this day Mary, who now runs a nursing agency in New York City, has never been able to forget the anguish and shame of that moment years ago when she was "made to feel like an idiot."

Although she was unaware of it until she was an adult, Mary Ferguson has dyslexia, a learning disorder that sorely hampers a person's ability to read, write, spell, and even speak correctly. Dyslexics confuse letters, particularly those with similar shapes, like *b* and *d*, or *p* and *q*. They twist words and sentences into briar patches where they thrash about, helpless and embarrassed. Some cannot follow or remember even simple instructions; others cannot tell left from right. A few write backwards, from right to

From John Langone, "Deciphering Dyslexia," *Discover* (August 1983):34, 38–39, 42. John Langone/© 1983, Discover Publications, Inc. Reprinted with

left—a phenomenon known as mirror-writing.

Only recently have Americans come to recognize that dyslexia is widespread. Perhaps ten per cent of boys and three per cent of girls suffer from it in one form or another. Its cause has long eluded researchers, who have attributed the disorder variously to genetic, environmental, or psychological factors. But now, by peering deep into the brain, neurologists have uncovered convincing evidence of its true cause: the brains of dyslexics are physically different from those of other people. "Virtually all modern studies point to that," said Boston University neurologist Thomas Kemper at an April conference on cerebral dominance.

To pinpoint those crucial—though at times subtle—differences, researchers have now performed autopsies on dyslexics who have died in accidents and studied brain wave patterns of children who suffer from the affliction. A sophisticated technique that permits postmortem examination of layers of brain cells reveals dyslexic abnormalities never before seen in such minute detail. New equipment that combines a computer with an electroencephalograph has enabled scientists to identify the distinctive brain-wave patterns of dyslexics—which should lead to better diagnosis at an earlier age.

Even as medical specialists get closer to the neurological causes of dyslexia, educators and child psychologists continue to emphasize the fact that with special training, patience, and hard work, dyslexics can have successful and productive careers sometimes in demanding professions.

This was demonstrated recently when researchers at Johns Hopkins University traced the adult progress of some 600 graduates of the nation's oldest preparatory school for dyslexic boys, the Gow School in South Wales, New York, near Buffalo. Most attended colleges rated "competitive" or better; more than half earned bachelor's degrees; nearly ten per cent won advanced degrees; about half of the college graduates went on to jobs at the managerial level; almost 20 per cent chose professional or technical careers in fields such as architecture, engineering, and teaching; 15 per cent became salesmen.

More surprising, better than half now read for pleasure, and only twelve per cent still consider reading a chore. Says David Gow, headmaster of the school that his father founded in 1926, "Most of our alumni have gone into disciplines that require reading. They have not all become forest rangers and hermits."

Prevented by their ailment from mentally processing words as others do, taunted by their peers, misunderstood and scolded by teachers, dyslexic children often undergo painful and demeaning ordeals, as Mary Ferguson did. Bruised self-esteem is common among dyslexics, both young and old. Says Richard Brisbin, a junior at Denison University in Ohio, who has a particularly hard time with foreign languages, "It's very difficult to explain, but there are just some things you don't understand—and you don't understand why you don't understand them."

Many parents and teachers, and even some behavior specialists, still treat dyslexics as slow and unmotivated, sometimes mentally retarded. They subject them to batteries of psychological tests and endless rounds of counseling. But most dyslexics have normal or above normal IQs. Moreover, while dyslexia is a learning disability, it is infinitely more complex than merely having trouble comprehending words. What makes it such a nightmare to diagnose and correct is that hearing, seeing, and language may all be involved. The resulting confusion takes endless variations. A dyslexic may read words incorrectly in one place and then read the same words correctly a paragraph later. Some misunderstand oral directions, or do not hear differences between words: "ten" may sound like "tin," or "loom" like "loam." What they write down is often not what was said.

The most obvious manifestation of dyslexia is dreadful spelling. Another peculiarity, reversal of digits, can make basic arithmetic a chore. Some dyslexics have difficulty speaking: they pronounce words poorly, or persistently use baby talk. Others are tone deaf. Many also lack coordination, and are unable to tie shoelaces, cut along a dotted line, or stay within the lines when coloring a picture. To orient themselves, those who cannot tell their right hand from their left often rely on a wedding ring or a wristwatch. The wife of one dyslexic never gives him specific directions: "She just points and says 'Go that way.'"

This odd collection of disabilities can all be traced to the brain, which governs the voluntary muscles and the various speech and language centers on both sides of the body. Today, neurologists know that a dyslexic's eyes and ears function normally, picking up letters and sounds in the usual way. But his *perception* of what he hears and sees is flawed, because the brain scrambles the information it receives. The brain of a dyslexic may simply be unable to process and interpret audio-visual material correctly.

Until the 1920s, medical specialists were apt to blame the problem on some unspecified congenital defect in the brain's visual center. This theory was supplanted by the pioneering studies of Dr. Samuel Torrey Orton, a University of Iowa neuropsychiatrist who maintained that dyslexia could result when one side of the brain failed to acquire dominance over the other. Orton noticed that an unusually large number of his "word blind" patients were left-handed or ambidextrous, or had "mixed dominance"

—favoring the right hand, say, but the left foot or the left eye. The lack of dominance, he concluded, sets up competition between the brain's left and right hemispheres and causes dyslexia.

Orton never had the advantage of examining a dissected dyslexic brain. It was only in 1979 that Kemper and Dr. Albert Galaburda, of Boston's Beth Israel Hospital, made the first highly detailed study —on a man diagnosed as dyslexic at age six, who was killed in an accident when he was 20. His brain looked normal during routine autopsy studies. But when thin slices of it were examined under a microscope—by a special technique known as cytoarchitectonics —abnormalities showed up in the left hemisphere. Layers of cells normally arranged in precise patterns were in disarray; bits of grey matter appeared in sections ordinarily made up of white matter; and one part of the left hemisphere was considerably smaller than normal.

Some of these same anomalies have been found in fetal brain cells, indicating that dyslexia originates with a breakdown in the brain's normal process of development. "The disorder has been thought to be a psychological one," concludes Galaburda, "but it is really neurological. And this is clearly traceable to fetal development, perhaps in the sixteenth to twenty-fourth week of the gestation period."

Galaburda bolstered his findings a few months ago in another dyslexic brain autopsy. That brain also showed cellular disturbances in the language areas of the left side. He is now processing two more brains— each one takes eight months to prepare—and hopes to confirm his conclusions soon. Says he, "Even though it's based, at the moment, on only two brains, we may be seeking something typical in dyslexia."

A large proportion of dyslexics come from families with a history of the problem. So heredity appears to be involved, although just how is unclear. Researchers know more about why most dyslexics are boys. For one thing, males are more vulnerable to a range of disorders at birth; also, the left sides of their brains tend to develop more slowly than those of girls. The male hormone testosterone may play a role. Dr. Norman Geschwind, a colleague of Galaburda's, believes that an abnormally high level of testosterone in a fetus during the formation of the brain delays the migration of nerve cells to the left hemisphere, causing left-handedness, as well as learning disabilities and other disorders.

But the left hemisphere may not be the only source of a dyslexic's troubles. Dr. Frank Duffy of Children's Hospital Medical Center in Boston has found abnormalities in still other areas of dyslexic children's brains. He uses a remarkable instrument called BEAM, an acronym for Brain Electrical Activity Mapping, that records and displays the brain's electrical activity, both as it processes information and while it is at rest (*Discover*, December 1981). The device converts data from an electroencephalograph (EEG) into a 14-color topographic map of the head, and projects it onto a video screen. Duffy has studied the brain patterns of more than a hundred dyslexic children, most of them between the ages of ten and thirteen. When he compared the patterns with those of non-dyslexics, he found differences in electrical activity throughout the brain.

Because dyslexia is harder to spot in a kindergartner than in a child between ten and thirteen, Duffy is now concentrating on younger children. Detecting dyslexia in advance of school failure would obviously make it possible to start remedial training sooner.

Spotting the disorder remains a lot easier than treating it. There is still no cure, though some medical specialists think that certain drugs may help—stimulants, tranquilizers, medication for motion sick-

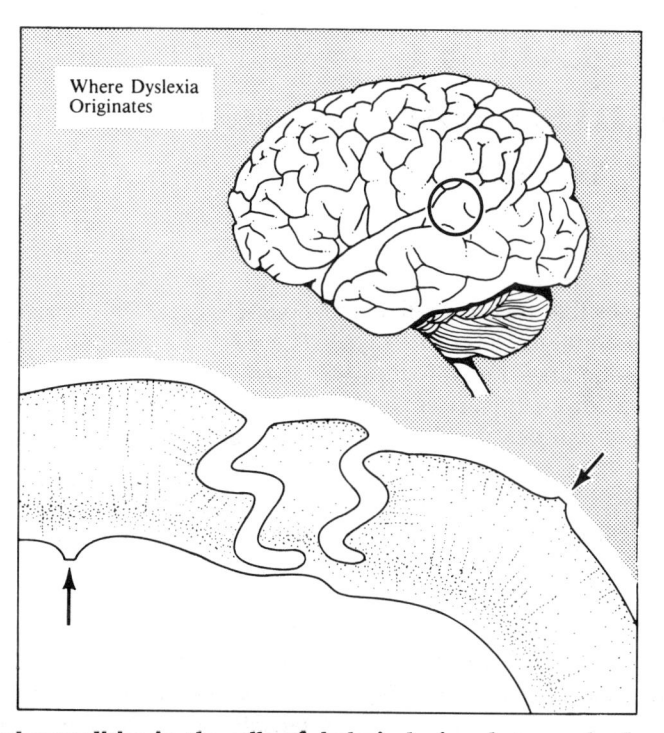

Distinct abnormalities in the cells of dyslexic brains show up clearly under the microscope. Detailed drawing shows a portion of a major language center in the left hemisphere (circled at top). Neurons (arrows) normally found in the grey matter of the cerebral cortex are misplaced, while abnormal folding has occurred at center.

ness, even synthetic brain chemicals that improve the function of defective areas. For now, the most effective way to treat a young dyslexic is through special education techniques and retraining. These children often require tutoring two or three times a week by a remedial reading specialist. But for those who reach seventh grade and still need help, residential schools like Gow may be the best bet. Gow, which enrolls boys in grades seven through twelve, uses the Orton-Gillingham method of retraining, named for Orton and Anna Gillingham, a child psychologist and teacher. It places heavy emphasis on phonetic training—on the sounds of letters and groups of letters—reinforced by unrelenting word-recognition drills that use an imaginative array of sensory techniques.

When the boys are reading Shakespeare, for example, the teacher puts on a record of the play, enabling them to read along silently with the actors. Speeches are videotaped so the students can see and hear how they deliver certain phrases. So they can feel the shapes of letters, teachers outline them on the backs of their hands. The students also "draw" huge letters in the air, stretching and bending their bodies. The boys are encouraged to follow with a finger as they read, making them aware of word sequences as well as the left to right direction of the English language. Computers and calculators are allowed in class, but their use is carefully restricted and students are taught not to rely on them.

Although most dyslexics who go through remedial programs like Gow's make measurable progress, it can be painfully slow; moreover, the older the child, the longer it takes. Even after years of rigorous drill, most dyslexics find ways to avoid writing whenever possible. Admits George Wislocki, who contributes columns on the environment to the *Berkshire Eagle,* a Massachusetts newspaper, "I can hardly spell a word, but I'm excellent at dictating."

Wislocki's candor is typical of most dyslexics who have learned to cope with the disorder. Some, like Dr. Frank di Traglia, a resident at a New Jersey hospital, can even poke fun at themselves. At the moment, di Traglia is researching a chronic form of arthritis called systemic lupus erythematosus. "But," he says with a grin, "I don't think I can spell it."

READING 41   ANDREW HAHN
Reaching Out to America's Dropouts: What to Do?

In the pages that follow, I will attempt to synthesize a broad array of research findings and program practices in dropout service and prevention. I will deal briefly with the causes and consequences of dropping out and then outline what we have learned about designing successful programs, some of which are in schools, but most of which are not.

Jacqueline Danzberger, Bernard Lefkowitz, and I titled our new book *Dropouts in America: Enough Is Known for Action* because we believed that systematic research into the causes of the dropout problem—research that often disguises itself as programs—was unlikely to generate many fresh and practical insights. After reviewing the literature relating to dropouts, we were impressed by the amount that had been written on the subject and by the number of positive steps that local schoolpeople were planning to take to assist dropouts.[1] More research, we believed, was not necessary to launch important initiatives.

Our review of the dropout phenomenon showed it to be a multifaceted problem. It starts early, has many causes, and grows incrementally worse with each successive year. Moreover, it is a problem that has both supply-side causes (schoolchildren suffering from a host of messy problems) and institutional aspects (encompassing the schools, the school boards, and state and federal policies). We were skeptical about the ability of researchers to design a rigorous social experiment that would effectively capture the

From Andrew Hahn, "Reaching Out to America's Dropouts: What to Do?" *Phi Delta Kappan* (December 1987):256–263. Reprinted by permission.

[1]Our research is reported in *Dropouts in America: Enough Is Known for Action* (Washington, D.C.: Institute for Educational Leadership, 1987).

true complexity of the problem. Finally, our research led us to conclude that the story-behind-the-story in effective dropout programs lies in implementation, casework, and long-term follow-up activities. The studies that we reviewed only occasionally addressed these essential program practices.

CITIES THAT DON'T COUNT

Most social initiatives build on a foundation of accurate, verifiable data. When we attempt to address the problems and needs of potential and actual dropouts, much of the essential data are lacking. We have informed estimates of how many students nationally are dropping out, of how many are poor or members of minority groups, and of how many are doing well or poorly in school. But on the level that really counts—in local districts and in individual schools—we simply don't know.

Among the thousands of school districts in the U.S., it sometimes seems that no two count dropouts in the same way. School administrators say that they follow local or state procedures to calculate the annual number of dropouts. But, in fact, their statistics are not always accurate, and their methods of calculating the dropout rate vary from year to year and from school to school. In part, this is because, in many localities, no central authority at either the state or the city level rigorously scrutinizes the dropout count.

Statistical manipulations have the effect of trivializing a significant social and educational problem. In Chicago, for example, students who leave school before graduation are grouped in 19 separate categories called "leave codes." Only one of these categories is labeled "drop out." Among the other categories are "lost—not coming to school," "needed at home," "married," and "cannot adjust." As a result, only a small number of school-leavers in Chicago are officially listed as dropouts.

In addition, dropout rates in nearly all large U.S. cities are tabulated annually, rather than according to how many starting freshmen actually receive diplomas four years later. Thus, if 15% of a high school freshman class drops out in a given year, the official dropout rate is put at 15%. Yet, four years later when the students gather in the school auditorium to receive their diplomas, only half of the original class may still be in school.

Using a multiyear tracking system based on graduation statistics, the Chicago Board of Education found that the city's dropout rate was 50.7%. Even more surprising was the consistently high rate among *all* students: 38% for whites, 56% for blacks, and 57% for Hispanics. The clear conclusion of this and most other reports is that dropping out is a problem not confined to a handful of minority students who couldn't learn. It is a systemic failure.

There are other questionable practices in counting students and dropouts. Some administrators maintain "ghost students" on the rolls to increase their share of average daily attendance funds. They "forget" to discharge students who have been truant beyond the legal maximum number of days (usually 20).

> **D**ropping out is a problem not confined to a handful of minority students who couldn't learn.

The underestimation of dropout rates on the local level raises serious issues of public accountability. Until a uniform and accurate system of calculating the dropout rate is developed by local school systems, dropout-prevention efforts will continue to be directed toward a smaller number of "troubled teens," rather than toward the majority of students in some inner-city schools who will leave before commencement day.

THE NATIONAL COUNT

To count dropouts, the U.S. General Accounting Office (GAO) uses the all-inclusive definition adopted by the Current Population Survey (CPS), which polls a national sample of households representative of the working-age civilian population. The CPS defines dropouts as "persons neither enrolled in schools nor high school graduates." It does not exclude from this definition such categories as "pregnant teenagers" or "needed at home." If you aren't in school and you haven't graduated, you're a dropout.

Using this source, we can answer some of the central questions about the dropout problem. Do more males than females drop out? Is the dropout rate increasing? Are the poor and minorities at greater risk of dropping out? Is the dropout rate higher for older adolescents? Which regions of the country have the highest incidence of dropouts? Is the dropout rate highest in schools with the least resources?

Who drops out? The GAO reports that, in 1985, 4.3 million young people between the ages of 16 and 24 dropped out of school—13% of the age group. Of these, 3.5 million were white, 700,000 were black, and 100,000 were from other groups. Moreover, male dropouts outnumbered female dropouts: approximately 16% of males between the ages of 18 and 19 were dropouts, while only 12% of females in the same age group had dropped out.

Are dropout rates growing worse? Dropout rates for the country as a whole are not growing worse. The public has been led to believe proclamations of "record" high dropout figures. Actually, in the 1960s the proportion of dropouts in the 16- to 24-year-old age group stood at about 20%. Since then, the rate has declined and remained steady somewhere between 13% and 14%. Among black youths, the rate fell from 21% in 1974 to 15% in October 1985.

Since there are no reliable, year-to-year analyses of age groups at the local level, we have no way of knowing for certain whether dropout rates have worsened in the nation's largest cities. However, every indication is that they have. Dropout rates ranging from 40% to 60% in Boston, Chicago, Los Angeles, Detroit, and other major cities point to a situation of crisis proportions. Yet, because the problem remains concentrated in a few places, it is open to thoughtful solutions.

Are disadvantaged students at greater risk of dropping out? Yes, they are. Although other data sources are less reliable than the CPS for tracking changes over time, they nevertheless shed light on some additional dimensions of the dropout problem. The High School and Beyond study found that about 14% of the sophomores surveyed in 1980 did not complete high school by their expected graduation date in 1982. On every reasonable indicator of hardship—from low income to limited educational background—the disadvantaged respondents (17%) were three times more likely to drop out than the advantaged (5%).

In our own survey we found that school-leaving rates tended to increase with the proportion of the student body classified as poor. For instance, city schools in which less than 20% of the student body were poor had a dropout rate of 13%. In schools in which more than 50% of the students lived in poverty, the dropout rate was 30%. Other studies have concluded that dropout rates are highest in schools where the minority population of a generally low-income student body is large.

Are students in certain parts of the country at greater risk? Yes. Our study found notable self-reported differences, both by region and by size of city. The states in the Southwest suffered the highest dropout rate (21%), while the rate stood at 18% in the Northeast, at 11% in the Southeast, and at 9% in the Northwest. Dropout rates were lowest in the Midwest, where student bodies are more homogeneous and where the suburban character of many of the schools often means smaller classes. As might have been expected, dropout rates were twice as high in the larger cities as in the smaller cities (25% as opposed to 13%).

Is the dropout problem reversible? Yes and no. The High School and Beyond survey showed that, within four years, about half of the sophomores who left school ultimately returned or were enrolled in General Equivalency Diploma (GED) classes. For these youths, dropping out was an interruption rather than a permanent condition. In California, a government study found that 39% of the 1983 dropouts had furthered their education one year later by receiving a GED or by entering a trade school or community college program.

Among those who do drop out, white students are most likely to return to high school. The surveys also show that the rates at which students return to school are consistently associated with test scores. Economist Andrew Sum reports that dropouts with ability test scores ranging from the middle to the top of the score distribution are two to three times more likely to return to school than those who score at the lower end of the scale. This association is particularly strong for ethnic minorities; the majority of high-scoring black and Hispanic dropouts return to school, while less than 23% of the low-scoring minority dropouts return to high school. In fact, there is some evidence that minority youths with high test scores may be more likely to return and complete high school than their white counterparts.

Is scarcity of resources related to a higher dropout rate? The answer to this question is a qualified yes. Bernard Lefkowitz, in *Tough Change*,[2] his book on young people growing up on their own, describes how more than 20 years ago Harvard University President James Conant wrote that the difference in spending for suburban schools and inner-city schools "challenges the concept of equality of opportunity in American public education." That inequality in spending persists today. In Texas and Massachusetts, affluent districts spend as much as $4,000 more per child than do poor districts. In Kentucky, $30,000 more per classroom is spent in wealthy districts than in poor ones.

Some researchers contend that, where dropout rates are concerned, expenditures are less important than a school's organization, the quality of its teaching and administration, and its innovations in curriculum. Harold Hodgkinson examined retention rates nationwide in 1985 and found that teacher salary and per-pupil expenditure were not related to dropout rates, while student/teacher ratios did correlate with the incidence of dropping out. He found that dropout rates among schools with the most favorable ratios were less than two-thirds as high as those among schools with the worst ratios.

I should emphasize, however, that improving the student/teacher ratio may require employing additional teachers, and that takes money. Preventing students from dropping out may also involve retraining and increasing the number of counselors, implementing a com-

[2]Bernard Lefkowitz, *Tough Change: Growing Up on Your Own in America* (New York: Free Press, 1987).

prehensive health and family planning program, providing infant care facilities for teenage mothers, developing a cooperative work/education project, offering remedial instruction, and establishing connections between the school and social services agencies in the community. All of this takes money, too.

WHAT STUDENTS SAY

A review of the principal reasons why youngsters drop out of school may provide a rough blueprint for how additional resources could be allocated most effectively. Students report many reasons for dropping out: poor grades, dislike for school, alienation from peers, marriage or pregnancy, and employment. The "good" son or daughter may leave school to help parents and siblings through a financial crisis.

But the most common reason for leaving school is poor academic performance; 42% of the dropouts in the High School and Beyond study reported grades of mostly D's in school. Male dropouts cite school and employment factors more often than females, who cite marriage more often than their male counterparts. However, some 13% of males and only 8% of females cite "had to support family" as their reason for dropping out.

Many respondents who cite "poor grades" may really mean "school wasn't for me." When disadvantaged youths in New York City were asked why they had difficulty in school, a little more than one-third blamed themselves, another third pegged the problem to their home life or other factors beyond their control, and the remaining third faulted the schools. Dropouts themselves are divided in their explanations of their problems with school, but this much is clear: there is no single essential factor.

We do know that young people at risk of dropping out resist the social control, competition, and order that characterize classrooms. In the High School and Beyond survey, one in five male dropouts indicated they couldn't get along with their teachers; more than one in 10 had been expelled or suspended.

> **S**tudents who have been held back a grade are up to four times more likely to drop out than those who have never been held back.

WHAT SOCIAL SCIENTISTS SAY

A variety of studies have identified the following 10 conditions as major risk factors indicating that a student might be in danger of dropping out.

1. *Behind in grade level and older than classmates.* Approximately one-third of all high school students are behind the modal grade by one year, and another 5% are at least two years behind. The *Harvard Education Letter* published a synthesis of studies that clearly shows that students held back actually score worse on achievement tests than similar youngsters who are passed along to the next grade.[3] Many of the students retained have low opinions of themselves, and they also appear to have fewer friends than students who have been promoted.

A 1986 study conducted by the Chicago Panel on Public School Finances found that overage students, even if they were reading at higher levels than their normal-aged peers, are 7% to 10% more likely to drop out of school. In other words, the blow to student self-esteem caused by school retention policies appears to be so severe as to cancel the positive effects of good reading skills. Put differently, the good reader who is overage is more likely to drop out than the poor reader who is the proper age for his or her class.

Flunking a grade in school has multiple effects. Students who have been held back a grade are up to four times more likely to drop out than those who have never been held back. The reason is simple: students hate being "too old" for the class. In surveys conducted between 1981 and 1984, "overage" was the reason cited by 41% of Los Angeles dropouts.

Furthermore, the students themselves aren't the only ones who don't like overage students. School administrators begin to discharge these youths as soon as they pass the legal age limit. This can be a sensible means of ridding the school of troublemakers, but it can also prompt a wholesale housecleaning of the school roster. For instance, all students over age 17 with more than 20 days of truancy might be summoned to the school and instructed to bring a parent or guardian. If students or parents do not show up, the students may be discharged or counseled to take their learning elsewhere. In both cases, the dropout rate increases. Alternative practices, such as counseling students that they have the right to stay in school until the age of 21, are hardly known and rarely implemented.

2. *Poor academic performance.* In 1983 the National Commission on Excellence in Education reported that, nationwide, the average performance of high school students on most standardized tests was lower than in 1960, when the federal government dramatically increased its support for public education. In 1986 the National Assessment of Educational Progress revealed that only 23% of young adults with less than eight years of education could write a letter de-

---
[3]Helen Featherstone, "Repeating a Grade: Does It Help?," *Harvard Education Letter,* March 1986.

scribing an error in a bill. Such skill deficits have been linked to the dropout rate and to youth unemployment.

Studies of school dropouts in Boston and elsewhere show that dropouts are more likely than other students to have scored low on, failed, or not taken proficiency examinations. In California, 41,000 out of 98,000 students left 12th grade because they failed graduation examinations or courses that they needed in order to graduate.

A number of studies have argued that dropouts have the same abilities as high school graduates who decide not to go on to college. These studies make the case that abilities, as measured by I.Q. and standardized tests of achievement, are of secondary importance to poor grades and grade promotion in predicting whether or not students will drop out.

However, Sum concludes that abilities in the basic skills are the single best predictors of dropping out. He bases this conclusion on analyses of the Armed Forces Qualifying Test scores, which show that for males and females, whites, blacks, and Hispanics, and for youth in every age group between 15 and 18, low test scores coincide with being behind in grade. He also reports findings that show that in 1979, among 16- and 17-year-olds in the National Longitudinal Survey (NLS), a majority of all dropouts (50.3%) had basic skills in the bottom 20% of the score distribution. Finally, Sum finds that 16- to 17-year-olds "with basic skills test scores in the bottom 20% of the test score distribution were 14 times more likely than those in the upper 20% to have dropped out at the time of the 1979 NLS interview."

3. *Dislike school.* This vague explanation cuts across nearly all others. Just over one-third of the dropouts surveyed in the High School and Beyond study cited this reason, males more often than females.

One reason students dislike school so much is fear. Some students are too scared to attend school regularly, and many potential dropouts feel tremendous insecurity when they enter the school building each day. Studies in the Chicago area have found that young people list fear of gang members (whose numbers are estimated to exceed 10,000 in Chicago) in and around schools as the primary reason for leaving school.

4. *Detention and suspension.* One concrete reason that so many potential dropouts dislike school is that they are frequently suspended or placed in detention. The Children's Defense Fund has found that at least 25% of all dropouts had been suspended before they dropped out and that another 20% had been designated as "behavior problems" by their teachers.

5. *Pregnancy.* Four out of five girls who become pregnant in high school drop out, while less than 10% of those who do not become pregnant do so. Pregnancy is the most common reason that females leave school. According to the Institute for Educational Leadership, 1,540 adolescent girls give birth each day in the U.S. Each year, 1.2 million American teens become pregnant. (Of these young women, nearly as many abort their babies as give birth.) The social costs of teenage pregnancy are enormous. The Center for Population Statistics estimates that, over the next 20 years, society will have to pay $16 billion to support the first-born infants of teenagers.

6. *Welfare recipients and members of single-parent households.* Youngsters in households that receive Aid to Families with Dependent Children (AFDC), in households in which a single parent juggles many roles, and in households in which the family has little income must often scramble to attain the emotional and material support they need to continue their studies. Although some of these youths succeed, far too many fail.

Dropouts are three times more likely than high school graduates to come from families that receive welfare. Robert Lerman of Brandeis University found that about 18% of all dropouts between the ages of 14 and 21 live in families that receive AFDC payments, while only 5% of high school graduates come from families that rely on this aid.

7. *The attractiveness of work.* The world of work often seems like the only alternative for youngsters who are having trouble in school. The sad fact is that the hopes and expectations of most of them will not be fulfilled. Many leave school to take entry-level jobs that offer only limited employment potential.

Stated bluntly, the *long-term* employment prospects of dropouts are dismal. In 1985 half of all unemployed youths (aged 16–24) were not in school. In part, this was because many dropouts have unrealistic wage expectations or lack information concerning job-search skills and the requirements of entry-level employment. But it is also the case that median wage levels in jobs in the service sector have deteriorated terribly from the levels of the 1970s.

It is very important to recognize that most studies show that, regardless of how badly youngsters have fared in school, they are strongly motivated to succeed in the workplace. The studies show that these youngsters want to work and *do work* when opportunities are available. If anything, the problem is that their motivation to work is too strong for the schools to hold them. For example, more than one-quarter of the male dropouts in the High School and Beyond study had been offered jobs and chose to work rather than continue their education.

8. *The attraction of military service.* For many dropouts in the later years of adolescence, the military is a "safety net" of last resort. In recent years, up to one-third of new enlistees in the armed services have not completed high school. Unfortunately, nearly half of those who entered the Army without high

school diplomas in 1981 were not thought capable of completing their first tour of duty. What school-leavers don't understand—or discover only when it's too late—is that only the better-qualified recruits find temporary or permanent careers in the military.

9. *Undiagnosed learning disabilities and emotional problems.* We found little research that specifically links dropping out to learning disabilities and emotional problems. Estimates of the learning-disabled population range from 5% to 10% of secondary school students. Yet some studies have found that less than 3% of this group are diagnosed by schools. On the other hand, advocacy organizations contend that disadvantaged minority students, who have a hard time coping with family distress and crumbling communities, are conveniently dumped into classes for the learning disabled. These groups estimate that black students are more than three times as likely to be in a class for the educable mentally retarded as are white students, but only half as likely to be in a class for the gifted and talented.

> Alternative schools work well for highly motivated former dropouts; they do not always work so well for others.

Either way, such experiences reinforce a student's growing sense of dislocation and frustration. Youngsters who are misdiagnosed as learning disabled accept the school's judgment that they are misfits. Those whose disabilities are not identified and treated blame themselves for their inability to function.

10. *Language difficulties.* Some school districts today confront populations that include students from more than 100 different linguistic backgrounds. For years, the debate has raged between proponents of English as a Second Language (ESL) and proponents of bilingual education. Should new arrivals in our schools be "immersed" immediately in classes taught only in English and have to learn rudimentary English quickly in order to follow their other subjects? Or should students learn academic skills in their native languages until their English is good enough for them to enter mainstream classes?

In 1971 Massachusetts passed an innovative bilingual education law motivated by a discouraging report that Hispanic children were not enrolling in school and that truancy laws were being selectively enforced. Ironically, today's research generally shows higher dropout rates among students enrolled in bilingual programs, though it remains difficult to disentangle cause and effect.

Are language barriers the main problem, or is it our confusion over educational policy? Is the evidence sufficient to reject bilingual education in favor of ESL instruction, or is the problem that many youngsters with language barriers do not participate in either one? How much of the dropout problem can be attributed to language problems and how much to poverty or other factors? Nobody knows for certain, but language is clearly a critical element in achieving success in school and in society.

From poor academic performance to repeated suspensions and detentions, from language barriers to emotional stress, the list of risk factors is disheartening. However, we can now identify the critical elements that foreshadow the decision to drop out, and this should give us some reason for optimism. If schools can begin to respond to these difficulties early enough, the dropout rate may be diminished significantly.

IN-SCHOOL REFORMS

Our review of the research leads to one major conclusion. An effective dropout prevention program at the high school level cannot be based on one single element, such as remedial instruction or the provision of social services. To succeed, dropout prevention for older youths requires a cohesive, integrated effort that combines the following components and perhaps others:

- mentorships and intensive, sustained counseling for troubled youngsters;
- an array of social services, including health care, family planning education, and infant care facilities for adolescent mothers;
- concentrated remediation using individualized instruction and competency-based curricula;
- an effective school/business collaboration that provides ongoing access to the mainstream economy;
- improved incentives, including financial rewards, for completing high school;
- year-round schools and alternative schools;
- heightened accountability for dropout rates at all levels of the system of public education; and
- involvement of parents and community organizations in dropout prevention.

REFORMS OUTSIDE SCHOOL

Although much can be said for each of the preceding school-based strategies, it would be a grave oversight to limit discussion of the dropout problem to strategies for students who are still in school. Millions of school-age people are now out of school, without jobs or diplomas, and we must consider their prospects. To forget these young people because their names no longer appear on a school's attendance roster would be an act of monumental indifference. And yet this is precisely how most cities deal with the dropout problem. They provide some prevention strategies tied to the schools, but they offer few services for young people outside the schools. Even the network of "second-chance" programs, such as the Job Training Partnership Act, favors school reform over programs for young people outside the school gates.

DIPLOMA VERSUS GED

Does enrolling in a program leading to an alternative degree, such as the General Equivalency Diploma (GED), serve dropouts well? The proportion of 17- and 18-year-olds taking the GED test has increased over the past decade, showing that the test has become better known and that a GED has become more widely accepted as an alternative to a high school diploma.

In 1981, 711,000 people took the GED; 72% passed. Slightly less than one-third of the GED test-takers were 19 years old or younger. These young people tended to be the most employable of the school-leavers, since the major reason they cited for pursuing the GED was "job-related."

Yet this trend has some disturbing implications. A recent Wisconsin study found that many of those who take the GED pass the test with only a sixth-grade reading level and that only about 8% of those who earn a GED and go on to college ever complete two years of study.

In the coming decade, the education reform movement must address tough questions about the proliferation of these alternative degrees. In some states, enthusiasm for the low-cost GED has led to mandates for its use in statewide welfare reform. Researchers will need to consider whether GED recipients will be at a major disadvantage in the increasingly competitive job market. Will they be the last hired and the first fired? Does the GED mask serious deficiencies in reading, writing, and computing? Are minority and female dropouts pressured to pursue the GED, while white male dropouts are offered incentives to return to conventional schools that confer traditional diplomas? Here is a topic that cries out for research.

ALTERNATIVE SCHOOL PROGRAMS

Hundreds of alternative secondary schools throughout the U.S. offer dropouts and potential dropouts a last opportunity to continue to resume their education. Eileen Foley found that, in New York City's alternative school system, truant youths and/or students with poor academic or behavioral records improved their attendance by almost 40% when they enrolled in an alternative school; they also earned 60% more school credits than they had in their former schools.

These gains held up over time, but only for some participants. Sadly, one in four of the young people in New York City's alternative schools dropped out of these "last chance" institutions, and an additional 20% were so overage for the grade they were in that it was unlikely that they could graduate by age 21. Alternative schools work well for highly motivated former dropouts; they do not always work so well for others. Foley's most important finding was that alternative schools that attract the most dropout-prone youths also had the highest rates of school-leaving among alternative schools.

Foley's finding that despite improved attendance and academic performance, many former dropouts and truants in alternative schools are still unlikely to graduate by the age of 21 raises an important question: How can the schools be more responsive to that half of the dropout population that is most difficult to reach?

Foley identified two critical elements, which she believed could enable alternative schools to retain more students: the intensity of the learning environment and the concern accorded the social and emotional needs of the students. The most successful alternative schools were those that challenged students academically and that provided personal counseling and were staffed by caring adults. Such alternative schools share some of the characteristics documented in the effective schools literature: highly targeted services for a relatively homogeneous school population, strong principals, small school size, teachers who actively participate in counseling students, student involvement in school governance and classroom activity, opportunities for learning by doing, and clear standards, rules, and regulations.

Too few school systems have alternative schools of any kind. An analysis of high school students placed in private alternative programs in Oregon showed that only one-third of the school districts offered alternative education programs. In addition, placements in these programs accounted for less than 2% of high school enrollment.

Alternative schools are often the best available option for both potential and actual dropouts, especially if the programs employ reasonable criteria for eligibility, teach real skills, and accommodate working students. Once again, however, alternative schools in and of themselves are no guarantee of success for all dropouts.

LURING DROPOUTS BACK TO SCHOOL

A casework system. As with youngsters who have not yet dropped out, my colleagues and I favor a casework system to identify and assist dropouts. In *Dropouts in America,* we propose an Educational Services Corporation to voluntarily register *all* at-risk youngsters, including those who have dropped out. The Educational Services Corporation would provide the extended outreach and individual casework necessary to mend the cracks in the system for delivering services to dropouts.

Left to their own devices, only as many as half of all dropouts will join high school completion or nondegree programs. Caseworkers, aided by a massive outreach campaign, might be able to match many more high-risk youth with available programs and services. Caseworkers would be paid by a formula that would guarantee long-term tracking of their clients until they achieved self-sufficiency. Caseworkers are not now being trained for this kind of effort, so special training programs, run in partnership with graduate schools of social work and/or education, would be necessary.

Part-time jobs. For many years, researchers have discussed whether the inducement of a part-time job would bring dropouts back to school and encourage them to continue until they graduate. The research findings on this idea are not promising.

A $218 million experiment, serving 76,000 disadvantaged youths in 17 cities between 1977 and 1981, found that by age 19 only half of the participants had graduated from high school, while almost 40% had dropped out. These disappointing results were achieved in projects that *guaranteed* minimum-wage, part-time jobs to students who agreed to stay in school.

These youths, some of whom were parents, obviously required stronger incentives than after-school jobs in order to stay in school. Many were several grade levels behind in reading and math and did not wish to return to traditional learning environments. In fact, almost 80% of the small number of dropouts who did return chose alternative education programs or GED classes rather than regular classrooms. Among those who went back to traditional classrooms, about 40% left school again, becoming in effect "double dropouts."

Jobs alone or jobs plus training. We must also consider the important question of whether jobs alone or jobs in conjunction with classroom training might work better. It is much easier just to place dropouts in jobs and let employers assume the costs of training than it is to set up special education and training programs. Moreover, during periods of high unemployment, when jobs are scarce, such training has little value.

Research findings from the National Supported Work Demonstration, a series of social experiments that ran from 1976 to 1980, offer some answers. This program provided dropouts with peer support and structural job assignments. The idea was simple. On the job, dropouts need close supervision from skilled supervisors. The organizations that took part in this program placed skilled supervisors at job sites where dropouts were employed. As each dropout progressed on the job, he or she was gradually given more responsibility.

Unfortunately, this combination of elements proved unsuccessful. The evaluation of the Supported Work project showed that young dropouts stayed in their jobs longer than they would have otherwise. However, there were no significant long-term impacts on their earnings, employment, criminal activity, or drug use.

Some experts believe that the Supported Work project failed because the connection between classroom training and work experience was weak. When remediation and real skills training were added to the original model, the findings were more positive. Perhaps the program designers were onto something: connect work experience to classroom training, and you will get dropouts to stay at least to the end of the program.

> **W**hat will work is a comprehensive, integrated approach in which each element is strengthened and reinforced by the other components.

Numerous social experiments have been funded to test this very theory. The evaluation of the Alternative Youth Employment Strategies Project, which enrolled significant numbers of dropouts with criminal records, provided evidence that classroom training, combined with work experience, was of more help to dropouts than pure work experience.

EMPLOYABILITY OF DROPOUTS

There is solid evidence that the Job Corps, the nation's largest training program for dropouts, does help participants find employment. Those who took part in the Job Corps earned an average of 15% more per year than did a similar group of nonparticipants. A higher share of participants also completed high school, entered the military, and stayed off welfare programs. Although studies reveal that the cost per participant in the Job Corps has been high (currently about $9,500), the benefits of the program exceed the costs.

Certainly, the intensity of services, the mix of remedial education and skills training, and the direct federal oversight with contracts given to private management combine to produce an effective program. In addition, the participants live away from home, which frees staff members and participants from distracting influences and allows them to take seriously the challenge of upgrading skills. Another contributing factor is the experience in program planning and design gained by the Job Corps during its nearly 25-year history. Throughout this period, the program has experimented with learning methods suitable for disadvantaged dropouts, including its own approach to competency-based, individualized instruction. The approach is now used in many centers and has, in fact, become something of a model for regular school and training systems. This process of experimentation and standardization could only bear fruit in a program that is allowed to operate for several years.

Project ReDirection offered disadvantaged teenage mothers a variety of individualized services, including day care, work experience, skills training, basic education, personal counseling, referrals to other agencies, and the guidance of an adult mentor. The first-year evaluation demonstrated that, at the end of one year, twice as many program participants had returned to school as had members of a comparison group of teenage mothers. Subsequent evaluations, however, were far less positive.

The evaluators believe that the reasons for the failure lie not so much with the program model but with its implementation. All the right pieces were present, but they were not delivered with enough intensity nor in the correct fashion. A new effort, Project New Chance, will test whether a vigorously implemented, comprehensive model can work for teenage parents.

Two out-of-school, pre-employment projects—Jobs for Youth and 70,001 LTD—attempted to find jobs for disadvantaged high school dropouts. Both programs offered career counseling, job readiness training, and some remedial education to 16- to 21-year-olds. Job development specialists tried to convince private firms to hire program participants, and, in return, members of the program staff screened prospective workers for the employer. Over 90% of the evaluation sample were high school dropouts, and two-thirds were racial minorities. The average participant read at only the sixth-grade level.

The evaluations found that participants in both programs had significantly higher levels of employment and higher wage rates than comparison groups. But these initially positive outcomes generally declined after about 14 months. The program did succeed in placing disadvantaged youth into jobs quickly and in combining job placement with training in work maturity, pre-employment skills, and limited remedial education. But the success of these programs proved less enduring than that of the Job Corps, with its intensive services and residential setting. The Jobs for Youth and 70,001 LTD programs were low-cost, short-term interventions that led to short-term results.

WHAT HAVE WE LEARNED?

The most vital lesson educators and trainers can derive from this review of "second chance" programs is the importance of integrating and relating the critical components of a comprehensive effort. Conventional education and remediation are not by themselves effective for the at-risk population. Isolated work experience will not reclaim impoverished and troubled youths. What will work is a comprehensive, integrated approach in which each element is strengthened and reinforced by the other components of the program. The following are among the important lessons to be learned about designing programs to prevent students from dropping out and to help those who already have dropped out.

- Isolated work experience programs have little value in increasing the employability of dropouts. Dropouts should work, but the experience from the work sites should be used as pedagogical reinforcement in a classroom component that is clearly connected to the job.
- Dropouts should learn, but the curriculum should relate to the "functional" skills needed in the workplace.
- Dropouts should acquire vocational skills, but first they need to learn to read.
- Dropouts should learn to read, but the learning environment should not resemble a traditional classroom.
- Dropouts should be taught by caring teachers, but the individuality of each student should be reflected in the teaching technology used.
- Dropouts should be prepared for the labor market through pre-employment / work-maturity services—but not until they are genuinely ready to conduct a job search. Writing résumés and practicing job interview skills should be "exit" services—not the centerpiece of dropout prevention or remediation.
- Above all, program services must to some degree be intensive; in the jargon of professional educators, there must be sufficient "time-on-task."

These are not revolutionary recommendations; indeed, they are part of the web of school reform described by many analysts. School administrators may argue that they do these things already. And most school districts have programs, such as cooperative education, in which students both work and study. But our visits to schools reveal that these programs have not focused on disaffected youth—that half of the dropout-prone group that is least likely to return to alternative schools or to enroll in a GED program after leaving school. Moreover, the programs usually do not interrelate work experience and classroom training.

When "second chance" efforts are fragmented, compartmentalized, and imperfectly developed and when long delays and gaps occur in the delivery of the training, the programs reinforce the youngsters' underlying sense of incompetence. Rather than offering a second chance, such programs deliver a death blow to youngsters' already fragile hopes.

Meeting these challenges will not require more research. But it will require dedicated managers and institutions willing to take on the essential task of training these young people. That's a large order, but this is a very large problem. And we know enough to begin.

CHAPTER FIFTEEN
Toward Identifying and Reaching Exceptionally Able Students

READING 42   A. HARRY PASSOW
The Nature of Giftedness and Talent

Any discussion of the nature of giftedness and talent will depend on how one defines those terms. Who is gifted? Who is talented? How are giftedness and talent manifested?

Perhaps the widest used definition these days—"used" in the sense that a good deal of the literature alludes to it and a great many school systems assert that it is the definition which guides their planning—is the so-called U.S. Office of Education definition. This definition suggested by an advisory panel to the then-Commissioner of Education, Sidney Marland, Jr., and presented in the Marland Report as follows:

> Gifted and talented children are those identified by professionally qualified persons who, by virtue of outstanding abilities, are capable of high performance. These are children who require differentiated educational programs and/or services beyond those normally provided by the regular school program in order to realize their contribution to self and society. (p. IX).
>
> Children capable of high performance include those with demonstrated achievement and/or potential ability in any of the following areas, singly or in combination:
>
> 1. general intellectual ability;
> 2. specific academic aptitude;
> 3. creative or productive thinking;
> 4. leadership ability;
> 5. visual and performing arts;
> 6. psychomotor ability.

It should be noted that "psychomotor ability" was deleted from the areas suggested by the Marland Report by PL 95-561, leaving only five areas in the OE definition.

For the most part, the OE definition has been accepted quite uncritically and, as Renzulli (1978) has pointed out, "has served the very useful purpose of calling attention to a wider variety of abilities that should be included in a definition of giftedness. . . ." However, he adds, "at the same time it has presented some major problems" (p. 181).

From 1868 on, when William T. Harris instituted flexible promotion as a way of providing for abler pupils in the St. Louis schools, various school systems instituted programs to meet the needs of the "pupils of more than average capability," "brilliant children," "pupils of supernormal mentality," "gifted" and a variety of other terms—all of which referred to individuals with high intelligence quotients and/or high scholastic attainments. "Rapid advancement classes" were started in New York City in 1900. These were classes for exceptionally bright children. By 1915, what eventually became known as the "SP" classes were designed to hasten the progress of bright children by enabling them to complete seventh, eighth, and ninth grades in two years (Henry, 1920, p. 31).

From A. Harry Passow, "The Nature of Giftedness and Talent," *Gifted Childhood Quarterly* (Winter 1981):5–10. Copyright © 1981 by the National Association for Gifted Children. Reprinted by permission.

The reviews of programs and provisions for gifted in the early years which appeared in the National Society for the Study of Education, 19th and 23rd yearbooks (Henry, 1920 & Whipple, 1924), clearly indicate that it was the highly intelligent and high academic achiever who were considered gifted, and it was the traits and characteristics of such individuals which determined the nature of giftedness. It was Guy M. Whipple who was credited with having established the "term 'gifted' as the standard designation of children of supernormal ability," having used it in Monroe's *Cyclopedia of Education* (Henry, 1920, p. 9).

Although there was a good deal of activity and some research prior to the start of Terman's so-called *Genetic Studies of Genius* in 1922—the bibliography in the 19th NSSE Yearbook contains 163 items and the 23rd NSSE Yearbook includes an annotated bibliography of 453 items—represented the first large-scale longitudinal study of the nature of the gifted. The Stanford Study "was designed to discover what physical, mental, and personality traits are characteristic of gifted children as a class, and what sort of adult the typical gifted child becomes" (Terman & Oden, 1951, p. 21). Increasing the knowledge about the origin and the physical and mental traits of gifted children was not viewed by Terman as an end unto itself. Rather, as he pointed out, in the first report:

When the sources of our intellectual talent have been determined, it is conceivable that means may be found which would increase the supply. When the physical, mental, and character traits of gifted children are better understood it will be possible to set about their education with better hope of success. . . . In the gifted child, nature has moved far back the usual limits of educability, but the realms thus thrown open to the educator are still *terra incognita*. It is time to move forward, explore, and consolidate. (Terman, 1925 & 1926, pp. 16–17).

Terman's search for subjects was aimed at locating "subjects with a degree of brightness that would rate them well within the top one percent of the school population" (Terman, 1925 & 1926, p. 19). A 140 IQ on the Stanford-Binet test and, for high school subjects, a 135 IQ on the Terman Group Intelligence Test was, as Terman pointed out, the arbitrary standard set for inclusion in the study.

The initial Terman study and the subsequent follow-up studies (which still continue although Terman died in 1956) have lent support to the hypothesis that early promise of intellectually gifted students in the elementary school is likely to culminate in relative outstanding achievement during adulthood. Among the many findings was the fact that, contrary to popular belief, mentally gifted youngsters were far superior to their less highly endowed age peers in general health and physique, mental health and adjustment, adult intelligence, occupational status and earned income, publications and patents, and even "contentment."

One of Terman's co-workers, Catherine Cox (1926), took a reverse path by studying biographical and historical records of some 301 eminent persons in order to estimate their IQ's as accurately as possible. Two IQ estimates were made—one, an average rating on records of development to age 17 (AI), and the other an average for the development from age 17 to 26 (AII). The range of the estimated IQ's was from 100 to 190. Thirteen cases were rated between 100–110 while another 30 cases were estimated to be between 110–120. After various corrections were made, Cox concluded that *"the true IQ's of the subjects of this study average above 160. It further indicates that many of the true IQ's are above 180, while but few of them are below 140"* (p. 85). [Italics in original.]

Cox (1926) drew three major conclusions from her study. She observed that, in general, those youths who achieve eminence in later life:

1. Have above-average heredity and superior advantages in their early environment.
2. Display childhood behaviors which indicate an unusually high IQ.
3. *"Are characterized not only by high intellectual traits, but also by persistence of motive and effort, confidence in their abilities, and great strength of force of character"* (p. 218). [Italics in original.]

Increasingly, superior intelligence, defined in various ways such as a percentage of the population (e.g., highest 1 or 2 percent in general intelligence) or a particular cut-off score on a test of intelligence (e.g., 125 IQ or 135 IQ) was considered as gifted and programs and provisions were made in schools for nurturing the intellectually superior child. Lists of the mental, emotional, social, and physical characteristics of children who scored high on individual or group tests of intelligence and/or high scholastic achievers have been prepared by a number of writers (see, for example, Durr, 1964, pp. 33–51; Clark, 1979, pp. 20–34; and Tuttle & Becker, 1980, pp. 11–38).

Leta S. Hollingworth was actively involved with studying the nature and needs of the gifted in New York City at the same time that Terman was conducting his longitudinal studies in California. Hollingworth defined gifted children as those "who are in the top 1 percent of the juvenile population in *general intelligence*" which, in her view, was the "power to achieve literacy and to deal with its abstract knowledge and symbols" (Pritchard, 1951, p. 49). Nevertheless, in 1931 she wrote:

By a gifted child, we mean one who is far more educable than the generality of children are. This greater educability may lie along the lines of one of the arts, as in music or drawing; it may lie in the sphere of mechanical aptitude; or it may consist in surpassing power to achieve literacy and abstract intelligence. It is the business of education *to consider all forms of giftedness in pupils in reference to how unusual individuals may be trained for their own welfare and that of society at large.* (Pritchard, 1951, p. 49; italics added)

As early as the 1940's, writers were pointing to the limitations of intelligence tests in defining and identifying the gifted. Witty, for instance, wrote:

If by gifted we mean those youngsters who give promise of creativity of a high order, it is doubtful if the typical intelligence test is suitable for use in identifying them. For creativity points to originality, and originality implies successful management, control, and organization of new materials or experiences. Intelligence tests contain overlearned materials. . . . The content of the intelligence is patently lacking in situations which disclose originality or creativity. (Pritchard, 1951, p. 81).

Writing in the American Association for Gifted Children's 1951 publication, Lally and La Brant pointed out that since schools had been traditionally concerned with academic subjects, "the search for gifted children has usually discovered the brilliant student in such areas" and that identification procedures tended to parallel the school emphasis—excluding those students talented in the arts (Lally and La Brant, 1951, p. 243). They noted that far less was known about special gifts than about the mentally gifted:

How far talents are related; to what degree general high quality behavior may be channeled early in life; to what degree certain children are especially acute in various sensory perceptions of sound, space, or color, we are not able to state definitely. Nor do we know too much about the effects of various stimuli provided during the earliest years. (p. 244).

Since the AAGC publication, definitions of gifted and talented have become more inclusive or, as Renzulli puts it, "more liberal" (Renzulli, 1978). Passow et al. (1955) defined talent as the capacity for superior achievement in any socially valuable area of human endeavor, but limiting the areas to "such academic fields as languages, social sciences, natural sciences, and mathematics; such art fields as music, graphic and plastic arts, performing arts and mechanic arts; and the field of human relations" (p. 6).

The Ford Foundation–sponsored program for the gifted in the Portland (Oregon) Public School (1959) took the position "that a definition of giftedness limited to academic aptitude was much too narrow and that there was a variety of socially useful abilities which should be identified and developed (p. 13). Portland's definition of giftedness "included approximately the upper ten percent of the most intellectually talented pupils and also the same proportion of the most talented in each of seven special aptitudes . . . art, music, creative writing, creative dramatics, creative dance, mechanical talent, and social leadership" (p. 13). Portland was one of the few school systems which defined giftedness broadly and attempted to identify and nurture a broad array of gifts and talents.

For the 1957 yearbook of the National Society for the Study Education, Witty (1958) "recommended that the definition of giftedness be expanded and that we consider any child gifted whose performance, in a potentially valuable line of human activity, is consistently remarkable" (p. 62). Witty's definition advocated a broad conception of the nature of giftedness. Phrases such as "potentially valuable line of human activity" and "consistently remarkable" raised a good many problems in terms of specificity and meaning.

Getzels and Jackson's (1958) studies of highly creative and highly intelligent youth led them to speculate that if a precedent be set by "allowing an exception to the practice of labelling only high IQ as 'gifted,' the possibility of expanding the concept to include other potentially productive groups become a genuine challenge to both educators and research workers" (p. 277).

The work of such researchers as Torrance, Taylor, Barron, and others helped revise perceptions of the nature of giftedness and to include creativity—variously defined —as either a component of giftedness and talent or as a kind of giftedness and talent to be identified and nurtured. Creativity research has focused on at least seven areas, according to Taylor (1975): "(1) the creative personality; (2) creative problem formulation; (3) the creative process; (4) creative products; (5) creative climates; (6) creativity and mental health; and (7) creativity and intelligence" (p. 12).

Creativity—defined in a number of ways—has been viewed as a necessary ingredient of intellectual giftedness and as a kind of giftedness. Gallagher and Weiss (1979) have pointed out:

There have been numerous attempts to sort out the special characteristics of the creative child—that child who possesses superior ability to generate, visualize, dramatize, or illustrate a new idea, concept, or product. While there is a close relationship between high mental ability and creativity, it has become clear that there are particular intellectual skills and personality traits that predispose certain children and adults to creative activity. (pp. 6–7).

Researchers during the past two decades have come to the conclusion that creativity can be nurtured. Parnes (1962) for example, asserts that: "the evidence of the current research does point to a definite contradiction of the age-old notion that creativity cannot be developed." I. Taylor (1975), for instance, initiated a creative development program which focuses on: "(1) transposing one's ideas into the environment; (2) formulating basic or generic problems; (3) transforming ideas through reversals and analogies; (4) generating outcomes with creative characteristics; and (5) facilitating these processes through exposure to direct sensory stimulation" (p. 26).

Calvin Taylor asserts that research indicates "that we have talents of many different types, not just 'general intelligence'." Taylor has proposed a Multiple Talent Teaching Approach—the talents identified include academic, creative, planning, communicating, forecasting, and decision making. Taylor asserts that the Multiple Talent Totum Pole Approach helps move us "toward the goal of developing fully functioning, effectively talented people. It enriches and enlivens the students and their teachers and administrators, and thereby humanizes the entire educational process" (Taylor & Ellison, 1975, p. 213).

Some researchers have focused on gifted performance of adults rather than on the potential for outstanding achievement by students. The Goertzels (Goertzel & Goertzel, 1962; Goertzel, et al., 1978), for instances, have conducted two studies of some seven hundred "eminent personalities," individuals who have achieved success in various areas—sciences, business, literature and drama, etc. The Goertzels have studied the family background in which eminent personalities were formed; the personal lives of the eminent individuals, particularly as adults; and the work which brought them the fame which represents their impact on society. The Goertzels (1978) have built composite portraits of the eminent or the gifted and talented which provide some insights into the nature of gifted. Some of the observations that they make include the following:

The eminent man or woman is likely to be the firstborn or only child in a middle-class family where the father is a businessman or professional man and the mother is a housewife. In these families there are rows of books on shelves, and parental expectations are high for all children. . . .

Children who become eminent love learning but dislike school and school teachers who try to confine them to a curriculum not designed for individual needs. They respond well to being tutored or to being left alone, and they like to go to special schools such as those that train actors, dancers, musicians, and artists. . . .

. . . , they are more self-directed, less motivated in wanting to please than are their peers or siblings. They need and manage to find periods of isolation when they have freedom to think, to read, to write, to experiment, to paint, to play an instrument, or to explore the countryside. Sometimes this freedom can be obtained only by real or feigned illnesses; a sympathetic parent may respond to the child's need to have long free periods of concentrated effort.

. . . They treasure their uniqueness and find it hard to be conforming, in dress, behavior, and other ways. . . . (pp. 336–338)

Brandwein (1955) has hypothesized that three factors are related to academic success in the sciences. These include: (a) genetic factors—high-level verbal and mathematical ability; (b) predisposing factors—persistence (willingness to spend extra time on the subject, ability to withstand discomfort, and ability to face failure and continue working) and questing, dissatisfaction with the present explanation and aspects of reality; and (c) activating factors—opportunities for advanced training and contact with an inspirational teacher.

Tannenbaum has argued that one of the characteristics of giftedness is that the individual is a *producer*, not simply a *consumer* of culture. It is not sufficient, he maintains, that a student get good grades, absorb information rapidly, and excel in convergent thinking activities. Giftedness involves new conceptualizations, divergent approaches, creative problem solutions and unusual problem solutions. In his view, students who simply consume information, no matter how rapidly, represent only one kind of giftedness and not the most significant.

Getzels and Csikszentmihalyi (1975) have turned around the focus of study from *problem-solving*, on which there is a rich body of literature and an abundance of conceptual and empirical studies, to *problem finding* on which there is relatively little systematic study. As they put it, "the world is . . . teeming with dilemmas. But problematic situations do not present themselves automatically as *problems* capable of solutions, to say nothing of creative solutions" (p. 90). Studying adult fine artists, Getzels suggested altering the paradigm of the human as "not only a *stimulus-reducing* or *problem-solving* organism but also a *stimulus-seeking* or *problem finding* organism" (Getzels & Csikszentmihalyi, 1975, p. 93). They hypothesize that problem finding seems to be a crucial component of creativity—one which has been relatively unstudied in understanding the nature of giftedness.

Asking the question, "What Makes Giftedness?" Renzulli (1978) analyzed definitions of giftedness, reviewed studies of the characteristics of gifted individuals, and proposed a new definition of giftedness which he believes is useful to school practitioners and defensible in terms of research findings. Renzulli's conception of the ingredients of giftedness include three elements. One component is *above-average ability*. A second cluster of traits "consistently found in creative/productive persons constitutes a refined or focused form of motivation known as *task commitment*" which represents energy brought to bear on a particular problem (task) or specific performance area." The third component or cluster of traits "consists of factors that have usually been lumped together under the general heading of '*creativity*'" (pp. 192–184).

Renzulli (1978) concludes with an operational definition of giftedness as follows:

> Giftedness consists of an interaction among three basic clusters of human traits—these clusters being above-average general abilities, high levels of task commitment, and high levels of creativity. Gifted and talented children are those possessing or capable of developing this composite set of traits and applying them to any potentially valuable area of human performance. Children who manifest or are capable of developing an interaction among the three clusters require a wide variety of educational opportunities and services that are not ordinarily provided through regular instructional programs. (p. 261).

What, then, can be said about the nature of giftedness and what are some of the issues raised by the fact that giftedness is usually defined operationally with some concept of its nature implicit in such definitions? Clearly, there is no widespread accepted theory of giftedness although there is a considerable body of knowledge about individual differences and their nurture. In a recent article titled, "What We Don't Know About Programming for the Gifted and Talented," Renzulli (1980) observed:

> In spite of vast amounts of research on every conceivable aspect of the learning process, we still have difficulty pinpointing the reasons for the remarkable differences in learning efficiency and creativity among persons with similar genetic backgrounds and environmental experiences. We simply don't know what factors cause only a miniscule number of Thomas Edisons or Langston Hugheses or Isadora Duncans to emerge while millions with equal "equipment" and educational advantages (or disadvantages) never rise above mediocrity. Why do some people who have not enjoyed the advantages of special educational opportunities achieve eminence while others who have gone through programs for the gifted fade into obscurity? The answer is, we simply do not know! (p. 601).

There are, of course some things we do know. The gifted and the talented come in a tremendous variety of shapes, forms, and sizes. Some gifted youngsters are only slightly above average with respect to the criteria applied while others are so unusual as to be extremely rare; some individuals are gifted/talented in a single area, while others seem to be unusually able in practically any area. Some individuals who seem to have outstanding ability have relatively little motivation or interest in developing that potential while others are both highly talented and highly motivated. Some are high achievers and quick absorbers of information while others utilize knowledge in new and different ways. Some are basically consumers of knowledge while others are potentially outstanding producers as well as consumers. Some are especially precocious, manifesting unusual potential at early ages while others are "late bloomers" and do not show unusual potential or performance until much later. There are cultural differences with respect to which talent areas are more likely to be rewarded and, consequently, which will be nurtured. Riessman (1962) has even written about "slow gifted children," individuals who may "take a long time to learn basic concepts, but when they finally do so . . . use these ideas in thoughtful, penetrating fashion" (p. 64). The gifted are clearly not a homogeneous group. As Clark (1979) put it, "the more gifted a person becomes, the more unique that person may appear" (p. 20).

There is, then, an issue as to *what* is giftedness and *who* is gifted. There are numerous lists of characteristics of gifted individuals—most of them lengthy and detailed. Obviously, not all individuals who are identified as being "gifted" possess all of the cognitive, affective, physical, or intuitive characteristics which are ascribed to gifted and talented individuals. In fact, a single characteristic in one child may actually indicate a very special gift or talent. Compilations of characteristics of gifted and talented individuals are useful only if it is remembered that individuals may not possess all of the traits and behaviors ascribed to a group of gifted/talented persons.

There are also a number of issues related to *how* such individuals should be identified. How does potential for outstanding performance manifest itself if it is indeed still only potential? There appears to be consensus that identification procedures cannot be limited to tests of intelligence, even when those tests are individual tests. A variety of techniques, procedures, and instruments must be used to identify gifted and talented students, to differentiate their educational experiences. Various kinds of rating and screening scales have been developed and used. Some identification approaches rely heavily on the performance, the products, the behaviors of individuals which are judged to be unusual, creative, or imaginative as evidence of giftedness.

Passow and Tannenbaum (1978) have pointed out that the definition of gifted and talented provides the direction for the selection and use of identification procedures and for the design of educational opportunities and differentiated curricula. In fact, the procedures and techniques used for identification affect the kinds of differentiated experiences to be provided and vice versa: identification is viewed as an integral part of differentiation (p. 14). Rather than viewing identification and educational differentiation as a two-step diagnostic-prescriptive model, Passow and Tannenbaum suggest that prescribed enrichment becomes a vehicle for identification as much as identification facilitates enrichment. For instance, standardized tests of language and cognition do not help identify a potential poet in the elementary school. Rather, a program of instruction and practice in creative poetic expression indifferent structural forms enables children with poetic talent to reveal themselves. It is the creation of pupil products which contributes to self-identification and since product development is a continuous one, identification is also seen as a continuous process, rather than a single-event test administration (p. 15). Identification of the gifted and talented is related not only to systematic observation and intelligent interpretation of test and observation and intelligent interpretation of test and observation data, but to the creation of the right kinds of educational opportunities which facilitate self-identification — identification by performance and product which results in the manifestation of gifted or talented behaviors.

Some other questions which might be raised follow: Is precocity necessarily a manifestation of giftedness? Is giftedness potential alone or must it be made visible through actual performance? Are "underachievers" indeed gifted or should only achievers be considered gifted? Can an individual be outstanding in some very narrow area, only mediocre or even below average in most other areas, and still be considered gifted? Is creative or productive behavior a component of all giftedness or is it a kind of giftedness in and of itself? Does an individual need to attain affective maturity to match his/her cognitive maturity to be considered gifted? Are there levels of affective maturity — personal, social, emotional maturity — which should be expected before identifying an individual as gifted?

All aspects of identification and nurturance of the gifted and talented depend on the underlying conception of the nature of giftedness and there are a good many operational conceptions extant. Program planners must be sensitive to the critical importance of clarification of an operational conception of the nature of giftedness and the many issues raised with respect to identification, curriculum differentiation, resource allocation, and other aspects of education and development of gifted and talented children and youth. The conception of the nature of giftedness and talent is at the heart of all planning efforts.

REFERENCES

Brandwein, P. F. *The gifted child as future scientist.* NYC: Harcourt, Brace, 1955.

Clark, B. *Growing up gifted.* Columbus, OH: Charles E. Merrill, 1979.

Cox, C. M. *The early mental traits of three hundred geniuses.* Volume II: Genetic studies of genius. Stanford, CA: Stanford Univesity Press, 1926.

Durr, W. K. *The gifted student.* NYC: Oxford Univesity Press, 1964.

Gallagher, J. J., & Weiss, P. *The education of gifted and talented studies.* Washington, DC: Council for Basic Education, 1979.

Getzels, J. W., & Csikszentmihalyi, M. From problem solving to problem finding. In I. A. Taylor, & J. W. Getzels. (Eds.), *Perspective in creativity.* Chicago: Aldine, 1975, 90–116.

Getzels, J. W., & Jackson, P. W. The meaning of 'giftedness'—an examination of an expanding concept. *Phi Delta Kappan,* November 1958, *40,* 275–277.

Goertzel, V., & Goertzel, M. G. *Cradles of eminence.* Boston: Little, Brown, 1962.

Goertzel, M. G., Goertzel, V., & Goertzel, T. G. *300 eminent personalities.* San Francisco: Jossey-Bass, 1978.

Henry, T. S. *Classroom problems in the education of gifted children.* 19th Yearbook, Part II. National Society for the Study of Education. Chicago: University of Chicago Press, 1920.

Lally, A., & LaBrant, L. Experiences with children talented in the arts. In P. Witty (Ed.), *The gifted child.* NYC: D. C. Heath, 1951, 243–256.

Marland, S. P., Jr. *Education of the gifted and talented.* Volume I: Report to the Congress of the United States by the U.S. Commissioner of Education. Washington, DC: U.S. Government Printing Office, 1971.

Parnes, S. J., & Harding, F. (Eds.). *A source book for creative thinking.* NYC: Scribners, 1962.

Passow, A. H., Goldberg, M. L., Tannenbaum, A. J., & French, W. *Planning for talented youth.* NYC: Teachers College Press, 1955.

Passow, A. H. & Tannenbaum, A. J. *Differentiated curriculum for the gifted and talented: A conceptual model.* A paper prepared for the Office of Projects for the gifted and talented, Montgomery County (Maryland) Public Schools. NYC: Teachers College, Columbia University, 1978.

Portland Public Schools. *The gifted child in Portland.* Portland, OR: Portland Public Schools, 1959.

Pritchard, M. C. The contribution of Leta S. Hollingworth to the study of gifted children. In P. Witty (Ed.), *The gifted child.* NYC: D. C. Heath, 1951, 47–85.

Renzulli, J. S. What makes giftedness? Reexamining a definition. *Phi Delta Kappan,* November 1978, *60,* 180–184, 261.

Renzulli, J. S. What we don't know about programming for the gifted and talented. *Phi Delta Kapan,* May 1980, *61,* 601–602.

Riessman, F. *The culturally deprived child.* NYC: Harper, 1962.

Taylor, C. W., & Ellison, R. L. Moving toward working models in creativity: Utah creativity experience and insights. In I. A. Taylor, & J. W. Getzels (Eds.), *Perspectives in Creativity.* Chicago: Aldine, 1975, 1-36.

Taylor, I. A. A retrospective view of creativity investigation. In I. A. Taylor & J. W. Getzels (Eds.), *Perspectives in creativity.* Chicago, Aldine, 1975, 1-36.

Terman, L. M. *Mental and physical traits of a thousand gifted children.* Volume I: Genetic studies of genius. Stanford, CA: Stanford University Press, 1925 and 1926.

Terman, L. M. & Oden, M. H. The Stanford studies of the gifted. In P. Witty (Ed.), *The gifted child.* NYC: D. C. Heath, 1951, 20-46.

Tuttle, F. B., Jr., & Becker, L.A. *Characteristics and identification of gifted and talented students.* Washington, DC: National Education Association, 1980.

Whipple, G. M. (Ed.). *The education of gifted children.* 23rd Yearbook, Part I. National Society for the Study of Education. Chicago: University of Chicago Press, 1924.

Witty, P. Who are the gifted? In N. B. Henry, *Education for the gifted.* 57th Yearbook, Part II. National Society for the Study of Education. Chicago: University of Chicago Press, 1958, 41-63.

READING 43   BYRON L. BARRINGTON
Curriculum-Based Programs for the Gifted

To be more than a passing fad, gifted and talented (G/T) programs must be designed to minimize political opposition and to address four issues: the inadequate challenge, repetition, and boredom that highly able students frequently experience in the regular classroom; insufficient opportunity for high-ability students to interact socially with "real peers" (agemates with similar abilities and interests); lack of K-12 continuity in whatever special opportunities are provided for gifted students; and inadequate information given to gifted students regarding their abilities, combined with inadequate recognition for their accomplishments. On these criteria many, perhaps most, gifted education programs are educationally ineffective and politically vulnerable.

Many program deficiencies and associated political and academic problems can be reduced by relating the gifted program to existing curriculum areas. Special services for gifted students would follow from an examination of the current educational opportunities offered to students having high ability in one or more curricular areas.

A curriculum-based model relies heavily on the expertise of those teaching subject areas. Their involvement in program development garners support from the staff, and facilitates K-12 coordination. However, a district gifted program coordinator, or at least a district gifted education committee, is still needed to provide information on the special needs and learning styles of high-ability students, to furnish administrative support for recommended programs, and to monitor the overall effectiveness and continuity of the special services as they develop.

The following steps are recommended to implement a curriculum approach to G/T program development:

1. For each curricular area, a committee shall be formed to develop improved educational opportunities for K-12 students having high potential in that subject. Each committee shall include the gifted program coordinator or representatives from the district gifted education committee and several teachers interested in improving instruction for high-ability students. Each committee shall establish a procedure to identify significantly advanced students in each grade level who would benefit from instruction more academically challenging than that appropriate for the typical student.

2. Using these recommendations, and in cooperation with the subject-area committees, the district G/T committee shall work with the administration in implementing the identification procedures in each subject area and grade level.

3. Concurrently with (2), the subject-area committee shall develop several alternative ways to provide a sufficiently challenging program for the identified students, such as subject acceleration, ability grouping,

From Byron L. Barrington, "Curriculum-Based Programs for the Gifted," *The Educational Digest* (January 1987):48-51. Condensed from *Education* 106 (Spring 1986): 345-351. Reprinted by permission of the author and *The Educational Digest.*

"clustering" by subject area, cross-grade grouping, or other academic structures. After consultation with other teachers on instructional techniques and goals, the committee shall select an approach to provide a coordinated K-12 instructional program for high-ability students. Within general guidelines needed for coordination, various schools in the district may employ different arrangements as appropriate.

4. The G/T coordinator or district committee will assist the area subcommittee with the administrative arrangements required to place the identified students in appropriate programs.

5. The G/T coordinator or committee shall monitor the services for effectiveness and to insure continuity in educational experiences.

The curriculum-based approach to gifted programming has several advantages:

1. *Meeting the primary educational deficiency for the gifted students—lack of challenge.* The primary problem in most schools is not that we fail to offer instruction for gifted students in some specific talent area, but the destruction of the gifted child's interest in the existing curriculum, and sometimes in learning in general, by forcing learning to proceed at a pace and style inappropriate to the child of high ability.

2. *Recognition of differential rates of academic development in various subject areas.* Gifted programs based on broad definitions, unrelated to curriculum, are often criticized for including students who are at (or even below) grade level in one or more instructional areas. A curriculum-based program turns the "problem" of student variability in achievement in different subjects into an asset.

3. *Staff acceptance.* A special G/T program not related to basic curriculum areas is often viewed by teachers as one more excessive demand on their time or the time of their students. Teacher resentment is often unconsciously communicated to students, tending to create problems in relationships between the identified students and their nongifted classmates. In contrast, the curriculum-based model starts with the existing program, and attempts to provide special services for the student whose academic needs would otherwise place special demands on the teacher. Staff acceptance is therefore less likely to be a problem, especially if classroom teachers have served on the subject-area committees that developed the program.

4. *Coordination of special services with the regular curriculum.* Regardless of whether acceleration, ability-grouped sections, or other instructional patterns are used, there can be a natural transition from the students' activities in the regular academic program to advanced instruction in the subject area. A focus on providing instruction appropriate to the student's development in each subject can minimize situations where students are required to complete all assignments in their regular instruction program, even though the gifted program requires an understanding of much more complex material in the same curriculum area.

5. *Ease of identification.* It is typically easier to reach agreement on appropriate identification instruments with the curriculum-based model; reasonably good measures are more easily developed if the focus is on achievement or potential in a given curriculum area. Standardized achievement tests are often appropriate. In areas where they are not available (e.g., art or music), judgment by professionals from outside the classroom, or by the student's teacher, can be used.

6. *Facilitating interaction with peers having similar interests and abilities.* This social interaction stimulates intellectual development and facilitates emotional ties to peers needed by all children.

7. *Aiding instructional continuity.* A curriculum-based model provides an organizational base for special programs consistent with the general program. Especially when students move from elementary to middle school, or middle to high school, a structure to insure continuous development is essential to an adequate G/T program.

Two objections are frequently raised to a curriculum-based model for G/T programs:

1. *Exclusion of certain talent areas,* such as creativity and leadership. Yet arriving at a consensus on a definition for creativity is even harder than defining giftedness, and there is little agreement on the type of special program that might be useful in facilitating creativity. It is also difficult to imagine how one can adequately teach science, art, or many other subjects without including activities that would promote the kinds of skills involved in creativity. Leadership involves similar problems.

It might be argued that the most effective way to stimulate leadership and creativity in gifted children would be through providing adequate programs in the existing subject areas. In many ways, a child's potential for leadership and creative thought can be effectively stimulated, and freed, by the challenge of an appropriately complex general education program.

In addition, for many talent areas not specifically covered in the existing curriculum, there are often opportunities to develop those skills

> There is little agreement on the type of special program that might be useful to facilitate creativity.

outside the school system—children's theater groups, Explorer troops, art festivals, YMCA classes, etc. The school system should not be held responsible for all areas of child development, but it should be held responsible for adequately stimulating and challenging students in the mandatory parts of the program.

2. *The problem of the gifted underachiever.* The proposed model can be criticized for failing to pick up the high-potential child already unresponsive to the school program, or the student whose background has inhibited the development of his academic potential. Eliminating the boredom and lack of challenge in the earliest school years should greatly reduce the number of gifted underachievers. In addition, just having a special program increases staff sensitivity to gifted children, including those not currently functioning at the level they could. When recognized, the high-potential underachieving child can be included in the program on a trial basis, if the student is willing to make an initial commitment. Furthermore, when underachieving students are given an opportunity to move into more complex work if they can pass a comprehensive test on the basic skills taught, they often are motivated to demonstrate that they have the skills, or (if they fail the test) to recognize that they do not know material covered in the assignments.

A continued search for students who have been missed must be a part of the program. However, the advantages of the curriculum-based model—and the greater speed with which the program can be initiated—far outweigh the potential problem of missing some students.

To survive, gifted programs must be viewed as an integral part of the basic academic program, not as an educational "frill." Challenging students who are advanced beyond their average classmates to continue to develop their potential is politically acceptable. Programs to provide that challenge, if organized around the existing curriculum, can be included as part of the general instructional budget. In addition to its usefulness in developing an academically effective program, the curriculum-based model may be the only politically viable approach for many school districts.

> **T**o survive, gifted programs must be viewed as an integral part of the basic academic program, not as a "frill."

PART SIX
Study and Discussion Questions

CHAPTER FOURTEEN Toward Understanding Students Who Have Trouble Learning

Reading 39 *Learning: Abilities and Disabilities*

1. What are the six general categories of problem areas frequently associated with learning disabilities?

2. Keeping in mind that most people have trouble learning something at one time or another, do any of the six categories of problem areas remind you of problems you've had as far as learning is concerned? Can you explain how those problems were manifested?

3. If someone asked you how learning disabilities could be treated, what would you say?

Reading 40 *Deciphering Dyslexia*

1. If you were asked to explain what dyslexia is, what would you say?

2. Why is it that a greater percentage of boys than girls suffer from dyslexia? (Or at least what is the speculation about that?)

3. What are some of the primary symptoms of dyslexia?

Reading 41 *Reaching Out to America's Dropouts: What to Do?*

1. What explanations do social scientists give for the worsening dropout rate?

2. Describe some of the plans to lure dropouts back to school.

3. How would you describe the employment future of dropouts?

4. What important lessons have been learned about designing programs to prevent students from dropping out?

CHAPTER FIFTEEN Toward Identifying and Reaching Exceptionally Able Students

Reading 42 *The Nature of Giftedness and Talent*

1. After reading this article, how would you describe a "gifted" child?

2. How are children with "special gifts" distinguished from the "gifted"?

3. Why have we had such problems identifying those students who are gifted or in other ways imbued with special talents?

Reading 43 *Curriculum-Based Programs for the Gifted*

1. Can you describe how a curriculum-based program for the gifted differs from the traditional curriculum?

2. What are some of the major advantages of a curriculum-based program for the gifted?

3. What are the two frequently raised objections to a curriculum-based model?

Index

Ability grouping
  and cooperative learning, 148–149
  mastery learning as a form of, 148
  results of between-class, 146–147
  results of within-class, 146–148
Achievement
  effects of cooperative learning on, 113–114
  effects of grade retention on, 153–156
  effects of grouping on, 142–149
  importance of placing high priority on, 167–168
  as related to the dropout problem, 239–240
  and relation to teacher behavior, 165–166
  and relationship to teachers' expectations, 176–178
Adolescence, common problems during, 45–50
Adolescent behavior
  effects of early and late development on, 46–50
  and gender differences, 49–50
  influence of hormone changes on, 46–47
Alternative school programs, description of, 242
Attribution theory
  classroom application of, 191–194
  and implications for students, 192–193
  and implications for teachers, 193

Barker, G., 191–194
Barrington, B. L., 252–254
Behavior, influence of heredity and environment on, 60–66
Block, J., 111
Bloom, B., 108–112
Bouchard, Jr., T., 61–66
Brain
  and creativity, 85
  and critical growth periods, 79–82
  development and functions of, 135–141
  and early growth patterns, 78–80
  functions of left, 83–86
  functions of right, 83–86
  and growth late in life, 86–88
  and language development, 79–80
  neural flexibility of, 87–88
  and response to injury, 88
Brain damage and dyslexia, 88, 233–236
Brain growth
  effect of age on, 87–88
  effect of experience on, 88
  effects of testosterone on, 88
  importance of early social experiences on, 80–81
  influence of enriched environment on, 86–87
  and memory development, 82–83
Brain hemispheres
  fact and fiction about, 83–86
  research related to, 84–86
Brophy, J., 164–172, 183–191, 203–209
Bruner, J., 104

Causality, three continuums of, 191–192
Child abuse, rates of, 42
Child-rearing practices, historical changes in, 43–44
Children
  effects of academic stress on, 68–69
  effects of peer group on, 69
  effects of schooling on, 68
  effects of television on, 69–70
  need for balanced priorities for, 70–71
  resilient, 50–55
  social needs of, 67
  social pressures affecting, 67–70
  suggestions for raising healthy, 44–45
  and television, 41
Children's attitudes, changes in, 42–43
Choices, importance of being stretched beyond safety of one's own, 174
Classroom climate, effects of class size on, 152
Classroom discipline
  checklist for teachers on, 201
  and dealing with problem students, 206–207
  ten techniques for handling, 198–202
Classroom management
  and dealing with problem students, 206–207
  Kounin's suggestions for, 205–206
  and promoting self-guidance, 207–208
  socializing self-guidance for, 203–209
  use of cognitive behavior modification for, 208
Classroom managers, behaviors of effective, 206
Class size
  and achievement, 151–152
  benefits of small, 152
  positive effects of, 152
Cognitive and affective goals, importance of emphasizing both, 168
Cognitive psychology, criticisms of, 5–7
Combs, A. W., 17–22
Computers
  instructional uses of, 115–117
  rationale for using, 115
Control theory, educational uses of, 10–17
Cooke, G. C., 153–156
Cooperative learning
  and ability grouping, 148–149

Cooperative learning (cont.)
  two essential conditions for, 112–113
Correctional data, cautions about using, 169
Correlational findings, errors in using, 168–169
Creativity, nurturing of, 248
Creativity research, focus of, 247
Criterion-referenced tests
  appropriate norms for, 213
  explanation of, 210–211
  and norm-referenced tests, 210–216
  and use for diagnostic purposes, 214
Critical thinking
  criteria for, 130–131
  definition of, 129
  and intellectual empowerment, 132–134
  meta-criteria for, 129–130
  and ordinary thinking, 130
  outcome of, 129
  self-corrections of, 131–132
  and sensitivity to context, 132
  standards for, 131
Cronbach, L. E., 93
Curriculum and the gifted, 252–254

Derry, S. J., 118–123
Discipline
  and students' needs, 12
  using control theory to manage, 11–12
Discovery learning, solving problems as a way to promote, 106
Divorce, rates of, 40
Dropout problem
  and alternative school programs, 242
  causes of, 239–241
  and the General Equivalency Diploma, 242
  in-school reforms for, 241
  outside-school reforms for, 241
  and related research, 244
  and resources available to combat it, 239
  and students' views, 239
Dropout rates
  and the disadvantaged, 238
  reversibility of, 238
  trends in, 237–238
Dropouts
  employability of, 243–244
  national numbers of, 237
  strategies to lure back, 242–243
Drugs, children's use of, 42
Dyslexia
  diagnosis of, 235
  neurological problems associated with, 234–236
  possible causes of, 234–236
  symptoms of, 233–234
Dyslexics, hope for, 234–236

Effective schools
  and ineffective schools, 27–28
  new evidence for, 29–33
  questions related to, 28
  and relationship to effective teaching, 24–29
  and relationship to school climate, 32–33
  suggestions for creating, 23–29
Effort, common sense about, 194
Elementary schools
  description of effective, 29–33
  examples of effective, 24–25
Elkind, D., 67
Environment and genetics, and influence on behavior, 60–66
Expectancy research, results of, 178
Expectations
  communication of negative, 178–179
  communication of positive, 178
  development of, 175–176
  and influence on our interpretations, 176
  note of caution about, 179
  psychology of teachers', 174–180

Failure, and attribution theory, 191–194
Family life, and importance for children, 52–54
Females, vulnerabilities of, 56–57
Frost, J. L., 39–45

Gable, R., 216–222
Gardner, H., 89–92
General Equivalency Diploma, success of, 241–242
Gifted
  and curriculum issues, 251–253
  definition of, 245
Gifted children, characteristics of, 246–250
Gifted programs
  effects of, 145
  a plan for, 252–254
Giftedness
  descriptions of, 247–250
  and eminence, 248–249
Glass, G. V., 151–152
Glasser, W., 10–17
Goleman, D., 86–88
Good, T. L., 23–29
Goodlad, J. L., 26, 29
Grade retention
  alternatives to, 155–156
  central issues related to, 155–156
  harmful effects of, 154
Grouping
  effects of, 142–148
  rationale for, 142–143
  types of, 143–146
Guskey, T. R., 108–112

Hahn, A., 236–245
Hamachek, D., 174–180
High schools, description of effective, 24
Humanistic education
  the case for, 17–22
  definition of, 17–18
  necessity of, 21
Hunter, M., 191–194

Insight, teaching of, 97
Instruction, metacognitive strategies for, 125–128
Instructional principles, research findings related to, 168–171
Intelligence
  crystallized, 82
  Gardner's seven different kinds of, 91–92
  and relationship to giftedness, 247
  and relationship to insight, 96–97
  and relationship to IQ, 95–98
  Sternberg's triarchic theory of, 93–98
Intelligence tests, performance on, 93
IQ, relationship of intelligence to, 95–98
Isenberg, J., 66–72

Joplin plan, 144–145

Language difficulties, and problems of dropouts, 241
Learning
  and approaches to procedural knowledge, 120–122
  class demonstrations as a way to facilitate, 107
  class discussions as a way to promote, 104
  cooperative approaches to, 112–114
  and the creative student, 247–248
  and critical thinking, 129–134
  discovery methods of, 104–108
  dropouts' problems with, 239–241
  effects of ability grouping on, 142–149
  effects of class size on, 151–152
  expository approaches to, 104
  and the gifted, 245–254
  humanistic views about, 20–22
  importance of extrinsic/intrinsic motivation in, 186
  and learning disabilities, 230–233
  mastery approaches to, 108–112
  memory functions in, 138–141
  metacognitive strategies for, 125–128
  and motivational strategies, 183–191
  principles of self-directed, 118–119
  role of personal meaning in, 20–22

Learning (*cont.*)
  Socratic questions as a way to
    promote, 106
  teacher behaviors that promote, 165
  and underachievement, 195–197
  use of computers for, 115–117
  use of examples to promote, 105
  warm-ups as a prelude to, 104–105
Learning disabilities
  and the dropout problem, 241–242
  identification of, 231–232
Learning disability
  definition of, 230
  problems associated with, 230–231
Learning disorders, approaches to
    treatment of, 232–233
Learning strategy, explanation of, 119
Learning teams
  concept of, 12–13
  operation of, 12–14
  and similarities to athletic teams,
    13–14
Levine, M., 230–233
Levy, J., 83–86
Lipman, M., 129–134

Maccoby, E., 57
Males
  and major differences from females,
    55–59
  vulnerabilities of, 56
Mastery learning
  and effects on education, 110–111
  and effects on students, 109–110
  and effects on teachers, 110
  future directions of, 111
  ways to approach, 108–112
Math abilities, sex differences in, 58
Mathematics grouping, effects of, 144,
    148
McAuliffe, K., 78–83
McDaniel, T. R., 198–202
Medoff, M., 180–182
Metacognition
  definition of, 125–126
  poor readers' knowledge of, 126
Metacognitive knowledge
  assessment of, 126–127
  instructional implications of,
    126–128
Metacognitive strategies, instruction
    of, 125–128
Memory
  and Alzheimer's disease, 139
  biochemistry of, 137, 139
  and curriculum implications,
    138–141
  declarative, 136–140
  enhancement of, 138–141
  long-term, 136
  major discoveries about, 135–141
  mechanisms of, 135–138

and neurotransmitters, 137
  procedural, 136–140
  short-term, 136
  teaching for effective use of, 139–140
Minnesota twin studies, 61–66
Mortimore, P., 29–33
Motivation
  importance of extrinsic, 186
  importance of intrinsic, 186
  intrinsic, 184
  necessary preconditions for
    successful, 184–190
  overview of ways to enhance, 188
  strategies for stimulation of student,
    189–190
  strategies to enhance, 183–191

Nongraded plans, and achievement,
    145
Norm-referenced tests
  and criterion-referenced tests,
    210–216
  explanation of, 210–211
  use of, 214

Palincsar, A. S., 125–128
Parenting, three styles of, 204–205
Passow, A. H., 246–252
Petersen, A. C., 45–50
Power, the need for feeling personal, 11
Praise
  guidelines for optimal rate of, 169
  interpreting research correctly
    about, 169
Pregnancy, rates of teenage, 41–42
Problem-solving, using strategy-
    building to encourage, 122–123
Programmed instruction, advantages
    of, 8–9
Promotion, effects of social, 153–156

Qualitative research, procedures for
    doing, 217–219
Quantitative research, procedures for
    doing, 219–222
Questions
  use of Socratic, 172–173
  ways to improve use of classroom,
    170–171

Ransom, K., 125–128
Reading, and metacognitive teaching
    strategies, 127
Reading grouping, effects of, 144, 148
Reading instruction, guidelines for
    good, 169–170
Research
  description of qualitative, 217–219
  description of quantitative, 219–222
  descriptions of various ways for
    doing, 216–222
Resilient children, factors contributing
    to, 51–54

Rimm, S. B., 195–197
Roblyer, M. D., 115
Rogers, V., 216–222
Rosen, C. M., 60–66
Rutter, M., 24, 27, 50

Sammons, P., 29–33
Schema-building, explanation of, 120
School climate and effective schools,
    32–33
School differences and effect on
    students' achievement, 30–31
School effectiveness
  factors contributing to, 31–33
  findings from, 24–29
  integrative reviews of, 25–29
  new directions in, 27–28
School leadership and relationship to
    school effectiveness, 31
Schooling
  alternative outcomes for, 27–29
  new definitions of, 26
  Skinner's suggestions for improving,
    7–9
Secondary schools, examples of
    effective, 24
Self-directed learning, principles of,
    118–119
Self-examination, Socratic questioning
    as way to encourage, 172–173
Self-fulfilling prophecies
  development of, 175–176
  and relationship to teachers'
    expectations, 175–176
Shepard, L., 210–216
Single parents, numbers of, 40
Sizer, T., 26
Skinner, B. F., 4–9
Slavin, R. E., 112–114, 142–151
Smith, M. E., 151–152
Socialization
  characteristics of successful, 204–205
  effects of authoritarian, 204–205
  effects of authoritative, 204–205
  effects of laissez-faire, 204–205
Socratic questioning
  classroom use of, 172–173
  examples of, 173
Stammer, J., 153–156
Statistics
  explanation of descriptive, 219–220
  explanation of inferential, 220–222
Sternberg, R., 93–98
Stimulus-response psychology,
    criticisms of, 10–11
Success
  and attribution theory, 191–194
  helping students achieve, 27–28
  helping students to expect, 184–185
Suicide, children's rates of, 42
Sweers, C. J., 172–173
Sylwester, R., 135–141

Teacher, why not everyone can be a, 171
Teacher effectiveness research
   danger of developing rigid guidelines based on, 171
   possible misinterpretations of, 168–171
   principles derived from, 167–168
   ways to interpret correctly, 164–171
Teacher effects
   limitations of research on, 166–168
   research on, 164–172
Teacher expectations
   importance of clearly defined, 175
   and influence on younger students, 176–177
   note of caution about, 179
   positive effects of, 174–175
   psychology of, 174–180
   and students' achievement, 176–178
Teachers
   behaviors of effective, 164–192
   and communication of negative expectations, 178–179
   and communication of positive expectations, 178
   descriptions of, 180–182
   effect of class size on, 152
   as facilitators, 14–15
   and students with learning disabilities, 230–233
Teaching
   and approaches to asking questions, 170–171
   and developing positive student motivation, 184–190
   effect of class size on, 151–152
   and effective reading instruction, 169–170
   examples of good, 180–182
   examples of metacognitive, 127–128
   and humanistic education, 17–18
   implications of attribution theory for, 191–194
   and the importance of flexibility, 171
   and managing classroom discipline, 198–202
   optimal use of praise in, 169
   and promoting self-guidance, 207–208
   and proper use of praise, 169
   proper use of research findings to improve, 164–171
   and reaching the underachievers, 195–197
   reasons behind ineffective, 166–168
   and relationship to effective schools, 23–29
   and relationship to school effectiveness, 32
   Socratic approach to, 172–173
   and strategies for stimulating students' motivation, 189–190
   summary of effective, 165
   summary of research for ways to improve, 166–168
   and the use of ability grouping, 142–149
   and use of control theory, 15–17
   and use of extrinsic/intrinsic motivation, 186
   use of learning teams in, 12–14
   and use of metacognitive strategies, 125–128
   use of professional knowledge as a way to enhance, 165–166
Teaching machines, 5
Television, and effects on children, 41, 69–70
Test construction, statistical versus logical, 212
Test standards, and cutoff scores, 212–213
Tests
   diagnostic versus survey, 211–212
   norm-referenced versus criterion-referenced, 210–216
Trotter, R. S., 93–98
Twin studies, findings from, 60–66

Underachievers
   dependent, 196
   dominant, 196–197
   portrait of, 195
   problem of the gifted, 253
   ways to reach, 195–197

Values and education, 19–20
Verbal information, tactics for learning, 119–120

Weinstein, R. S., 23–29
Werner, E. E., 50–55
Wilcox, R. T., 104–108
Working mothers, numbers of, 41